D0906225

Making Markets in the Welfare State: The Politics of Varying Market Reforms

Over the past three decades, market reforms have transformed public services such as education, health, and care of the elderly. Whereas previous studies present markets as having similar and largely non-political effects, this book shows that political parties structure markets in diverse ways to achieve distinct political aims. Left-wing attempts to sustain the legitimacy of the welfare state are compared with right-wing wishes to limit the state and empower the private sector. Examining a broad range of countries, time periods, and policy areas, Jane R. Gingrich helps readers make sense of the complexity of market reforms in the industrialized world. The use of innovative multi-case studies and in-depth interviews with senior European policymakers enriches the debate and brings clarity to this multifaceted topic. Scholars and students working on the policymaking process in this central area will be interested in this new conceptualization of market reform.

Jane R. Gingrich is an assistant professor of Political Science at the University of Minnesota. She received her Ph.D. in 2007 from the University of California Berkeley and she was a Max Weber Fellow at the European University Institute from 2008–2009. Her research interests focus on comparative social policy, political parties, and administrative reform.

Making Markets in the Welfare State

THE POLITICS OF VARYING MARKET REFORMS

JANE R. GINGRICH

CAMBRIDGE
UNIVERSITY PRESS

CAMBRIDGE UNIVERSITY PRESS
Cambridge, New York, Melbourne, Madrid, Cape Town,
Singapore, São Paulo, Delhi, Tokyo, Mexico City

Cambridge University Press
The Edinburgh Building, Cambridge CB2 8RU, UK

Published in the United States of America by Cambridge University Press, New York

www.cambridge.org
Information on this title: www.cambridge.org/9781107004627

First published 2011

Printed in the United Kingdom at the University Press, Cambridge

A catalogue record for this publication is available from the British Library

Library of Congress Cataloguing in Publication data
Gingrich, Jane R., 1978–
Making markets in the welfare state : the politics of varying market reforms / Jane R. Gingrich.
    p.   cm. – (Cambridge studies in comparative politics)
Includes bibliographical references and index.
ISBN 978-1-107-00462-7
1. Privatization.   2. Welfare state.   I. Title.   II. Series.
HD3850.G487   2011
338.9′25–dc22

2011011259

ISBN 978-1-107-00462-7 Hardback

Contents

Figures

Tables

Acknowledgements

This book would not have been possible without the help of many people. The bulk of the research involved interviews with policymakers, politicians, stakeholders, and academics and others involved in public sector reform. I would first like to thank all my interviewees. Their willingness to take time out of their busy schedules to speak with me – often more than once – truly made this book possible.

This book grew out of my dissertation. I began graduate school studying political theory, but a series of courses with Jonah Levy raised my interest in comparative politics. Jonah was not only a great teacher, but from my first inklings of interest in the politics of market reform, to the final version of the dissertation, and ensuing revisions into a book, Jonah was a tremendous source of inspiration and advice. He has read draft after draft of this project, steering me in a number of new directions and challenging me to think about the topic of market reform in new ways. The time, thought and effort he devoted to this project have been immense, and I am extremely grateful to him. I owe Jonah a deep intellectual debt, and without his persistent help, his high expectations, and his willingness to help me work through my ideas, this project would not have been possible.

I also owe great thanks to the other members of my dissertation committee. Chris Ansell's knowledge and insights on public sector reform were invaluable. Chris has also been a wonderful collaborator on other projects, and has taught me much about how to put together and execute a research project. John Zysman pushed me to see the "big picture," providing insight into the links between service sector reform and some of the broader shifts in contemporary political economy. Robert Anderson's knowledge of economics and careful reading of the theoretical sections of the dissertation, helped sharpen the analysis and develop its implications. Finally, Nick Ziegler's help has been invaluable. Nick pushed me to consider the implications of the work for changing partisan politics, helping pull together the theoretical sections of the book. As I put the manuscript together, Nick continued to be a tremendous source of encouragement and advice, both about this project and the world of political science more generally. The generous time and effort Nick has put in have been priceless.

I also owe a great deal to my colleagues at the University of Minnesota. Since joining the faculty, they have encouraged my work in multiple ways as well as offering much friendship. I would like to give particular thanks to Teri Caraway, Lisa Hilbink and Kathleen Collins, for providing comments on earlier versions of this work. Thanks also go to Gary Cohen and the Center for Austrian Studies and Center for German and European Studies for providing opportunities to present this research and collaborate on further research on social policy reform.

In revising the dissertation into a book manuscript, I owe much thanks to the European University Institute and the Max Weber Program. My time as a postdoctoral fellow at the EUI was extremely valuable, both for the opportunities it offered me to focus on my book and the tremendous feedback I received. I would like to thank Ramon Marimon for his leadership of the Program and the support he granted me. Sven Steinmo was an exceptional mentor, providing numerous comments on this work that pushed me to develop and expand the core argument. I would also like to thank: Silja Hausermann, David Art, Simon Bornschier, Roger Schoenman, Jeppe Olsen, Peter Mair, Eleonora Pasotti, Takeshi Hieda, Isabelle Engeli, Josh Derman, Paolo Masella, Karin Tilmans, the participants in the Welfare State workshop, and many other wonderful colleagues.

A number of other people helped with the development of this project, reading and commenting on drafts at various stages of revision and providing advice on the publication process. I would like to thank: Abe Newman, Carsten Vala, Erik Baekkeskov, Dorit Rubinstein, James Harney, Julie Lynch, Katerina Linos, Mark Bevir, Mark Vail, Patrick Egan, Rosie Hsueh, Jill Greenlee, Libby Anker, Rachel Vansickle Ward, Robert Cox, Sara Watson, Shannon Stimson, Stephanie Mudge, T. F. McGee, Toby Schulze Cleven, Vanna Gonzalez, Ed Fogarty, Mike Nelson, Ben Ross Schneider, and Pepper Culpepper.

I would also like to thank those who made my field research possible. Thanks go to the Institute for International Studies at the University of California Berkeley, for providing research support through the Simpson Fellowship. I am furthermore grateful for the opportunities various people offered me. In the United Kingdom, Ed Miliband, Will Cavendish, Julian Le Grand, the Strategy Unit, the public services team at Her Majesty's Treasury and the London School of Economics Health and Social Care Department were invaluable in helping me conduct my research. In the Netherlands, I benefited from the tremendous assistance of Kieke Okma, who welcomed me into the Ministry of Health, Welfare and Sport, and also her home. Alongside Kieke, Myra Klee and Titus Livius, and the staff at the library of the Ministry of Health also provided much assistance. I would also like to thank Neil Gilbert and Sven Hort, for their help in arranging interviews in Sweden. Thanks go to Meg Gingrich, Mats Magnusson, Niels Niessen and Arnd van der Meer for their careful research assistance.

Many thanks go to my editor at Cambridge University Press, John Haslam, for his persistence and dedication in developing this manuscript. I am also grateful to Josephine Lane, Carrie Parkinson and Daniel Dunlavy for their hard work and patience in answering my many questions about the production process. Thanks also go to Sarah Turner for her careful copy-editing. Additional thanks go to Kathleen Thelen and the editors of the Cambridge Studies in Comparative Politics Series.

I owe much to my friends and family. My dear friends from Canada, Berkeley, and England, have been a wonderful source of support through the years, providing encouragement, stimulating conversation, and a break from my studies. My parents, Paul Gingrich and Alison Hayford, have been a great support, encouraging my interest in political science and graduate studies and always being willing to entertain my ideas and arguments. I thank them for their generosity, encouragement and patience. I thank my two young sons, Theo and Elias. This project predates both of them, and although not necessarily hastening its completion, they have been a great source of joy throughout.

Finally, my deepest gratitude goes to my husband Ben. It is an understatement to say that I could not have completed this project without Ben's support. Ben read draft after draft of this project, providing constructive comments, pushing me to develop ideas, and offering a constant sounding board. Beyond this intellectual support, Ben has provided the greatest moral support. He has been a truly wonderful partner and I dedicate this book to him.

I

Introduction

I.I: INTRODUCTION

In 1980, Ronald Reagan was elected President of the United States on the promise of radically reforming American government by cutting spending and welfare entitlements and improving conditions for private entrepreneurship. For Reagan, American government was akin to an alligator-infested swamp, not only stagnant but dangerous. Thousands of miles away, the Swedish Prime Minister, Olof Palme, in response to a local government's attempt to privatize a childcare center, took a different stance. Palme argued that the introduction of markets would create "Kentucky Fried Children," the market standing for things American and unhealthy, a threat to Swedish children and the Swedish welfare state.[1]

Nearly three decades later, even after the worst financial crisis of the post-war era, market proponents continue to warn of the dangers of government and to extol the power of "free markets."[2] In this view, the state, particularly the welfare state, remains something of a swamp, with rigid bureaucracies employing regulations, rules, and routines that frustrate businesses, fleece taxpayers, and alienate citizens. In order to "drain the swamp," policymakers need to introduce greater competition and private entrepreneurship, with a limited state best delivering for the taxpayer, the user, and the citizen. By contrast, for opponents of markets, the solution is a fully public sector. The public sector is an antidote to the vicissitudes, distributional inequities, and moral corruption of the market. Market-oriented reforms to the welfare state, now more than ever, are

---

[1] Reagan joked in numerous speeches that "when you're up to your armpits in alligators, it's sometimes hard to remember that your original intention was to drain the swamp" regarding reform in Washington (Reagan 1982); Palme's statement was made on the Swedish radio show "Godmorgon världen" in 1984.
[2] See for instance conservative critiques of the Obama administration's stimulus package (Moore 2009).

equivalent to importing American junk-food into the public sector, fattening business at the expense of workers, social solidarity, and the state itself.

An examination of the empirical record suggests that this debate is misplaced. Behind a common language of markets lies a diverse set of outcomes both across and within countries. Reformers have introduced market forces into public social services alongside both increases and decreases in spending, regulation, consumer choice, and the role of the state itself. To take three examples from just one country, in the early 1990s policymakers in Sweden, long considered one of the most extensive and largest welfare states, began to experiment with markets in health, education and elderly care. This move delighted market proponents and depressed market critics, both in Sweden and abroad, with both groups predicting grave consequences for the size and nature of Sweden's extensive welfare state (Clayton and Pontusson 1998; Hjertqvist 2004; Bergström and Sandström 2002).

However, the most striking outcome from these market reforms is not their beneficence or destruction, but their substantial variation. Early market reforms in the Swedish health care system extended patient choice and paid hospitals based on patient flows. These reforms empowered users and reduced waiting lists but also reduced state control over spending. By contrast, reforms to the Swedish elderly care sector expanded contracting with the private sector without dramatically increasing choice. Far from reorienting the system around elderly users, these markets were largely invisible to the public and empowered local governments and managers in controlling costs. More recent reforms in the Swedish health system operated in yet a third way. These reforms focused on creating a private health care sector, giving new private providers substantial autonomy over when and where to enter the market, whether or not to treat private patients, and how to operate. This market neither promoted explicit attention to patients nor increased state and local control over care management, but rather gave private providers a foothold in the public system. Far from producing a single set of outcomes, be they good or bad, or a single "Swedish" market, these distinct types of markets had strikingly different consequences. This book, in examining health, education, and elderly care reforms in England, Sweden, and the Netherlands, uncovers great diversity in terms of the effects of markets on the use of services, the distribution of control over service delivery, and the consequent winners and losers of market reforms.

The fact that markets vary in itself may not be surprising. Scholars are used to the "real world" being more complicated than political rhetoric would lead us to believe. Moreover, there is a long history of extensive scholarship on how markets work differently across countries, with

American capitalism being different from German or French or Swedish capitalism (Hall and Soskice 2001; Zysman 1983; Esping-Andersen 1990). The argument of this book is not merely that markets work differently, but rather that markets in public services *vary systematically* and that *policymakers can manipulate this variation strategically*. Markets in public services do not operate uniformly; all good and all bad things do not go together. Nor do markets follow idiosyncratic national patterns. Rather, markets vary in how they place costs on users and in how they distribute power among (a) the state, (b) users of services, and (c) new producers of services.

Markets in public services do have one common element. When policymakers introduce competition or private actors into the public sector, they take power away from incumbent professionals. Hospitals and the doctors who work in them, schools and the teachers who teach in them, and care homes and carers, must now compete for resources that used to be guaranteed on a non-competitive basis. Yet, different markets in public services fill this power vacuum in varying ways. Some markets give power to the state or insurers as buyers of services, encouraging attention to their preferences for efficient production and cost control. Other markets empower the pupils or patients that use services by expanding user choice and encouraging producers to pay attention to users' preferences for high-quality rapid production, often at the expense of cost control. Yet a third type of markets empowers new private producers of services, outside of state or user control, giving these new producers more scope to follow their own aims, even if they promote neither cost control nor quality. Finally, markets also vary in how they place costs on the users of services. Who the market empowers over production – the state, users, or new producers – and what costs citizens face in consuming services, create sharply different patterns of market incentives.

This book challenges the highly ideological mainstream debate over markets. The focus on the "good" or "bad" effects of markets obscures the reality of what markets do: they empower different actors and thus trade off different incentives. It also challenges much of the scholarly literature in political science and sociology that focuses on nationally specific and historically stable institutions. Variation in market structures is not a matter of chance, or of long-standing historical trajectories, but of particular reform choices politicians make in taking power away from one group of actors – incumbents – and giving it to the state, users, or new producers. Indeed, as the example above of Sweden demonstrates, there is as much variation within countries as across them.

How, then, do we explain this variation in markets? Much work on the politics of markets follows from scholars' normative assessments of the value of markets themselves. Proponents present market reforms as a functional response to the problems of declining efficiency and effectiveness in modern governance (Savas 2000). Critics, instead, see market reforms as a dysfunctional response driven by the disproportionate power of business in contemporary politics (Pollock 2004). By contrast, scholars of the welfare state or advanced political economies have tended to argue that market structures are largely stable or "path dependent" and follow existing national or program-specific trajectories (Pierson 2001; Tuohy 1999).

The existing debate leaves crucial outcomes unexplained. To take an example, explored in detail in this book, market reforms in Dutch health care took nearly twenty years to introduce. During this time period, the country's economic health waxed and waned, with little noticeable impact on reform outcomes. The Dutch employers' association and players in the health insurance field also often opposed change, and yet this opposition was not always effective at blocking change. Moreover, when the government finally introduced major market reforms in 2006, it quite radically broke with the traditional Dutch health care structure, turning social insurers into private for-profit organizations, expanding contracting with hospitals, and dramatically increasing the costs individuals pay up-front. Analyses that rely on functional pressures, business interests, or historical continuity do not explain the Dutch experience.

Existing approaches also obscure some of the most important questions about market reform. The puzzle offered by the turn to the market is not simply a question of why markets emerged, but why policymakers chose particular types of market. Why did the Right in the Netherlands support strong insurer contracting in health care and elderly care but pupil choice in education? Why did the Swedish Left support competition in health care around patient choice but resolutely reject markets that gave private hospitals substantial autonomy? Why did the British Conservative party introduce strikingly different types of markets across elderly care, health and education? And why indeed, did left-wing parties across Europe introduce markets at all, given their preferences for strong public welfare states?

In answering these questions, this book develops an argument that emphasizes the explanatory role of constrained partisan preferences. Market reforms initially arose as the political prominence of welfare services grew. Politicians across the political spectrum faced new incentives to turn "inward" and directly reform service delivery as a way of addressing public concerns about quality and costs in a fiscally constrained environment. As both left-wing parties ("the Left") and economically liberal and Christian Democratic parties ("the Right") tried to appeal to a volatile electorate concerned about services, without dramatically increasing spending, they looked to influence the way services were produced and consumed. Markets, in taking power away from professionals and creating new constituencies of winners and losers, were attractive tools. Both parties used markets as tools to empower groups who supported their particular long-term partisan goals. Because the Left and the Right's long-term goals differed, so too did their preferred markets. The Right, aiming to limit the size of the welfare state, used markets to cut public provision and build new support bases for more private financing and production. By contrast, the Left, aspiring to sustain support for public benefits, although not necessarily public production, and to safeguard its own electoral position as the guardian of welfare benefits, used markets to enhance the welfare state's legitimacy and efficiency.

In practice, however, parties face constraints on their actions. At their core, markets reshape power in the system, ending traditional bargains with those who provide and receive services and creating new winners and losers. Understanding how partisan actors approach particular markets requires looking at how existing institutional structures shape the trade-offs among these varying outcomes. This book argues that it is not national-level institutions, particular electoral systems, or the weight of history that constitute the most important constraints. Rather, it is the existing structure of the health, education, or care system that affects the ability of parties to introduce preferred markets without facing heavy electoral or ideological costs.

The Left has often turned to markets when it felt citizen frustration with low quality or low productivity in the public sector risked eroding support, particularly among the middle classes, for an extensive welfare state. Facing this pressure, it prefers to make an electoral appeal through markets that empower users by expanding choice, but only where services are already provided similarly to all citizens. Here, increasing choice promises to tie lower- and middle-class citizens to both the welfare state and to each other, by providing them with comparable benefits. However, where services are provided differently across groups of citizens, or not provided universally, empowering users through choice risks giving the middle and the lower classes different benefits and fragmenting their support for the welfare state. Because it cannot bring these groups together through choice, for these services the Left will instead use markets that build up state power over service production as a way of creating new incentives for producers to control costs. The Left will generally avoid reforms empowering new private producers, as these threaten to limit public control over the welfare system and thus contradict its core goals. Instead, the Left chooses between reforms that empower users through choice where services are uniform, but those that empower the state as a purchaser where services are fragmented.

By contrast, in an unconstrained world, the Right would like to give power to new private producers and limit the role of the state. However, giving power to private producers has electoral risks, and these risks grow where services are universal and are more salient to the public.

Consequently, right-wing parties will introduce reforms favoring new private producers only in less salient or more marginal services. Conversely, for universal, salient services, the Right will use choice-based markets if it can build on existing fragmentation in the system to target the benefits of choice to its middle- and upper-income constituents. Where services are provided uniformly however, choice promises to accomplish the Left's goals not the Right's. For these services, the Right uses markets that build up state power. Thus the Right, unlike the Left, does use markets that empower new private producers, but only where services are more limited and the electoral costs of change are low. Where services are universal, it follows the reverse calculus to the Left, empowering users where services are provided differently across citizens but building up state power where they are more uniform.

Thus, the variation in market outcomes across and within countries follows from *who* built the market and whether the existing *institutions* allow them to appeal to the electorate and their particular constituents. Existing institutions pre-structure the political opportunities parties face but they do not fully determine the outcomes. Instead, political battles over the shape of the market matter, and we see the Swedish Social Democrats, the British Labour party and the Dutch PvdA make similar calculations to each other, as do the Swedish Moderate party, the Dutch Liberal party, and the British Conservatives.

In conceptualizing and explaining variation in markets, this book provides a new approach to understanding a crucial area of welfare state transformation. The stakes of this variation in market reforms are tremendous, both substantively and analytically. Substantively, welfare services are big-ticket expenditures and sources of employment in many Organization for Economic Co-operation and Development (OECD) countries. OECD countries spend on average over 6% of GDP on health services, 6% on education, and a further 2% on social services, with these numbers running much higher in many of the wealthier member states; and employ nearly 10% of the civilian workforce in health and social services alone.[3] Moreover, these services matter greatly to citizens. Large portions of the population regularly use education, health care, and other welfare services. Different types of markets, by redistributing resources and power over these crucial sectors, are of central importance to citizens and policy-makers alike.

Analytically, the claims of this book speak to a number of debates in the study of political life in advanced industrial countries. First, contra those

---

[3] This includes public expenditure on health, family services, care for the elderly (Adema and Ladaique 2009) and public education expenditure (OECD 2006). Health and social care employment is from OECD (2008b).

who argue that markets are uniformly good or bad, this book shows the need to take market variation seriously. Markets are neither straightforward retrenchment, nor are they incremental reforms to stable state structures: different markets matter profoundly for who benefits from change and its overall impact. Second, the book speaks to debates about the importance of partisanship for political outcomes in a post-industrial era. This book shows that parties matter. New electoral and economic constraints have not ended partisan distributive battles, but brought them into the structure of the state itself. Within this new terrain, parties use markets strategically to reshape the state to achieve their long-run ideological and electoral aims. Partisan strategies are not invariant across time and place, but nor do they disappear as new fiscal, institutional or electoral constraints emerge.

The following pages develop these arguments, presenting a typology of market variation and its consequences. The following chapter provides a further development of the theory of constrained partisanship.

1.2: HOW MARKETS DIFFER

Market-oriented reforms take numerous forms. They can alter the scope of public responsibility for services by changing the level of spending, cost-sharing, benefits, or coverage. Market reforms can also involve changes to the delivery of publicly funded services, either expanding the role of private actors or shifting the incentives within the public or non-profit sector to make it mimic private production (Le Grand and Bartlett 1993). These delivery reforms include greater outsourcing, splits between public purchasers and providers, management by contract, or user choice.

Much of the literature on market-oriented reforms of public services treats this list of reforms in equivalent terms, assuming a similar logic behind a wide range of practices and resulting market structures. One line of literature presents markets as the "solution" to the problems of government, promising that a broad range of market mechanisms – from contracting to vouchers to public-private-partnerships – will improve the efficiency, quality, and responsiveness of services (Osborne and Gaebler 1992; Savas 2000; Lundsgaard 2002). A second line of literature presents markets in an opposing light, seeing markets as eroding the capacity and power of the public sector, to the detriment of citizens (Leys 2003; Pollock 2004; Suleiman 2003). However, as the brief examples above show, this polarizing debate between markets in services as "good" and markets in services as "bad" misses much of what markets in services are doing. Markets have dramatically changed the way services operate, but not in a uniform way.

The chief feature that distinguishes markets from other forms of organization is that they influence behavior by manipulating incentives for consumers and producers of services. Of course, in practice, all systems of production and allocation create incentives; and markets themselves are always embedded in bureaucracies and networks that shape how they operate. Nonetheless, we can distinguish among these modes of organization. What makes markets different from hierarchical "command and control" systems, where a central agency defines processes and outcomes, and from "network systems" of management, where users and providers operate on the basis of mutual trust, is that they use competitive mechanisms to allocate scarce resources to producers and users. In a competitive process, a service producer can lose custom, and this threat of exit, rather than a hard budget constraint or informal network sanctions, creates particular incentives over service delivery.[4] Equally, the "buyers" of services respond to price or quality signals to make their decisions, shaping the overall allocation of services.

But what are competitive incentives? Who are the buyers of services? Can they really make providers compete? Work in the field of public economics suggests that some form of market failure or imperfection besets many public services (Barr 2004). These features mean that markets in public services will never match a neoclassical model of perfect competition (or even approximate it), where resources are allocated and produced efficiently based on competition among equal participants. However, there is no single "second-best" public service market. Several structural features of public services create significant trade-offs among different modes of distribution and competition, and the concomitant incentives that they create.

In terms of the allocation of benefits, the most compelling economic rationale for the public financing of welfare services is that many such services produce "positive externalities," meaning that purely private markets tend to under-supply these services. Because the benefits of these services accrue to both the individual and society, if individuals must bear the full cost of provision there will be a less than socially optimal amount of provision and consumption (Barr 2004). Equally, in private insurance markets, the problem of "adverse selection" emerges, where only people with higher risks choose to purchase insurance, reducing coverage and raising costs. Conversely, where third-party payers cover much or all of the costs of services, many economists argue that there is a risk of "moral hazard," leading individuals to over-consume services (Barr 2004; Pauly 1974). While theoretically, economic analysis could offer a rationale for a particular amount of cost-sharing between public and private, in practice externalities are difficult to measure and the countervailing problem of moral hazard means that there is not a single perfect balance between

---

[4] See for instance Hirschman's (1970) discussion of "exit."

public and private financing. The chosen balance of public and market modes of allocation of services will create different incentives for users, and a different overall distribution of services.

Moreover, technical aspects of welfare services mean that market-like competition in their delivery – not just financing – differs from perfect competition. First, as opposed to public procurement of basic goods, which have one "principal" (the contractor) and one "agent" (the producer), in public services there are three sets of actors: payers, users, and producers of services. The presence of separate payers and users fragments demand, raising the question of who the principal is to whom the agent is supposed to respond – the payer of the service or the user (Lowery 1998). Second, the presence of information asymmetries, where the supplier of the service, such as a doctor or social worker, knows more about the cost and quality of the service than the user, make it difficult for consumers to "shop around" for producers or insurers. This situation means that unregulated competition can lead to non-competitive outcomes (Barr 2004; Arrow 1963). Quality in public services is also hard to define. What is an educational outcome? A pupil completing a year? His or her test scores? How much he or she has learned? While policymakers can specify some outcomes, it is hotly debated whether they cover all aspects of quality. Where it is difficult to specify a more amorphous concept, such as quality, and where new issues regularly arise that cannot be specified in advance, it is difficult to construct contracts that stipulate how actors should behave in unforeseen circumstances (Tirole 1999; Hart *et al.* 1997). Problems of "incomplete contracts" mean that varying contractual structures allocate control between "principals" and "agents" differently, structuring incentives, and ultimately outcomes, in divergent ways. Indeed, some forms of competition may leave the agent in a stronger position than either principal.

Each of these market "problems" – externalities, multiple principals, information asymmetries and incomplete contracts – means that without some type of public intervention in financing and regulation, the service is likely to be either over or undersupplied. Moreover, depending on how information, contracts, and demand are shaped, the incentives that producers face in the delivery of services may promote attention to the buyer, or to the user, or even give new producers the scope to follow their own interests. Policymakers, then, face sharp trade-offs in introducing markets on two dimensions: how they shape individual and collective responsibility for allocating services (the allocation dimension) and how they structure control over production (the production dimension). There is not a single free, competitive, benchmark against which to assess the introduction of market incentives in services.

The allocation dimension

The first dimension of variation in public service markets concerns whether price and selection mechanisms are used to allocate services, or whether services preserve a strong collective guarantee of access and funding. In a system where individuals either pay for part of the service or bear significant risk in procuring high-quality services, then their budget constraint partly determines what they are able to consume and the overall allocation of services follows a more market-like pattern. By contrast, competition among providers can occur within a fully publicly funded and regulated system. If producers are compensated for different individual risks and costs, and responsibility for accessing high-quality services is borne collectively, then an individual's consumption decisions will not be based on the price of the good and allocation patterns are not market-like. A system of allocation on price promises to create incentives for responsible consumption (potentially overcoming the "moral hazard" problem) but threatens to erode access to services among low-income or high-risk groups.

There are two factors that determine whether market incentives emerge on the allocation dimension. First, the system of *financing* services can place greater or fewer costs on individuals. Explicit policies of co-payments, means-testing, or incentives for private consumption are borne directly by those who use the service and, therefore, when they are sufficiently large, can make individuals more responsive to price and change incentives for individual consumption. The failure to fully fund services can have the same effect. Where the quality of public services is low, wealthier citizens are more likely to "opt-out" of the public system and purchase services privately. Second, where *regulation ensuring access* is weak, producers may have an incentive to target lower-cost users of services, recruiting more attractive or profitable clients while reducing services for riskier and poorer populations (so called "cream-skimming"). Both greater private financing and weak regulations against cream-skimming will encourage the distribution of the service based on recipients' income or risk profile.

The production dimension

The second dimension of variation concerns whether the structure of competition gives the state (or third-party payers), users, or new producers control over the incentive structure in the delivery of services. The state as the payer and regulator of services, individuals as users of services, and new private producers of services have different preferences for efficiency, quality, and profits respectively. Competition can give one set of actors more control to exert their preferences.

The state as the payer of services would like to achieve value for money in production. Where the state is an effective "principal," it will structure the costs and benefits of competition to give producers incentives to produce at the lowest cost possible for a given amount and quality of production. To control production, the state needs the capacity to clearly specify outcomes, to provide managers the autonomy to achieve these outcomes, and to monitor and discipline non-compliant producers. Although these contracts may be incomplete, the state's ability to renegotiate contracts is crucial to maintaining control over the production process.

By contrast, users of services experience them directly, taking all the benefits from high-quality production, while paying primarily indirectly, through taxation. Where users are effective principals, producers gain by appealing to their preferences for high-quality, responsive production, emphasizing the non-economic aspects of production. For users to be effective principals, a quasi-contractual set of rules must exist, which clearly specify their right to "exit," link funding to their choices, and monitor and discipline producers who fail to respond to these choices.

Finally, producers of services often seek profits (the returns to a firm's shareholders following costs and depreciation). While many producers are motivated by a public-service ethos and are genuinely dedicated to service delivery, in a market-oriented environment with little regulation they have incentives to seek profits by overcharging users and / or cutting costs. These incentives are amplified when providers are privately owned and responsive to share-holders; however, there is evidence that both non-profit providers and publicly owned providers also respond to incentives (Eggleston and Zeckhauser 2002). When the state or users are ineffective principals, new firms have the space to pursue rents or profits without necessarily responding to the desires of the state or users of services. Producers will be in this position where the market is only weakly competitive or where contracts are not clearly specified and the procedural rights of users are weakly enforced.

While the allocation dimension hinges on the system of financing and regulation, the reforms that shape the production dimension involve the structure of competition and control. First, the *logic of competition* may operate through contracts or choice, the former giving producers the incentive to appeal to the preferences of the state as a purchaser of services and the latter giving them incentives to appeal to users of services. Second, the *logic of control* determines whether the state or users as the "principal" can control producers as the "agent." Here the system of specification and monitoring and the broader regulatory environment shape outcomes. Where contracts are complete or the rights of users are clearly specified and monitored (for instance, the state controls market entry, pricing, quality regulation) and the state can re-bid contracts or users can exit if production is not satisfactory, then purchasers and users maintain control.

By contrast, where contracts or user rights are not clearly specified, there is little oversight, and it is difficult for the purchaser or user to renegotiate, then the producers have the upper hand. Varying types of competitive reforms and accompanying systems of oversight shape the nature of competition among producers of services in distinct ways.

Six types of markets

As argued above, markets vary in both how services are distributed to citizens (the allocation dimension) and how competition shapes the relative power of the different actors (the production dimension). The claim of this book is that specific types of market reforms produce six qualitatively distinct types of markets, which shape incentives over market allocation and production in different ways. Reforms that introduce more private financing of services or reduce the regulation of access move from greater collective responsibility for the allocation of services towards more individual responsibility. Reforms that empower the state, users, or producers, through different systems of competition and control create variation on the production dimension.

Table 1.1 (see below) outlines the ideal types of market competition, providing examples from the upcoming chapters. Although the

TABLE 1.1: *Variation in market types*

Presents six ideal types of markets and one example each from the upcoming empirical chapters.

		Production dimension: who has effective control?		
		State: "Efficiency aims"	Users: "Quality aims"	Producers: "Profits and rents"
Allocation Dimension: Responsibility for Access	Collective	Managed Market *Recent English contracting in education*	Consumer-Controlled Market *Swedish health care market in the early 1990s*	Pork Barrel Market *English elderly care market in the 1980s*
	Individual	Austerity Market *Dutch health care markets*	Two Tiered Market *English education market*	Private Power Market *English elderly care market since the mid-1990s*

implementation of reforms is not always seamless and the intentions of policymakers do not automatically translate into perfect exemplars of different market types, the features under the control of government actors (the systems of financing and regulation and the logic of competition and control) shape market structures in systematic ways that approximate these ideal types.

(a) State-driven markets – Managed Markets and Austerity Markets

Markets that give the state (or purchasers) greater control are based on the argument that market mechanisms can generate efficiency gains but that to achieve these gains the state must play a role in specifying and monitoring performance. State-driven markets increase the power of the state to set incentives for cost-efficiency, which changes how all producers operate. These markets work by empowering managers to be entrepreneurial through clear and direct incentives, building on market instruments such as well-specified contracting or outsourcing, increased managerial autonomy, and transparent financial rewards for efficiency. The resulting market structure gives producers the space to respond to new incentives for improved efficiency, while also clearly specifying and enforcing these incentives. *Managed Markets* use few direct or indirect price signals, punishing producers who are inefficient without allowing them to pass costs onto users. By contrast, *Austerity Markets* either directly privatize part of the service funding or give producers the space to shift some costs onto users. Thus while Managed Markets maintain a strong collective guarantee of access, Austerity Markets introduce incentives for individuals to consume fewer services by privatizing financing, or loosening regulations on access.

Increased state and managerial control over the cost structure wrests control over production from professionals and existing producers. Incumbent producers as a broad category thus lose from these reforms. Firms or producers who gain new contracts may be winners, but the state now intrudes on both "meat and potatoes" issues (for example, working time and wages) and professional autonomy (for example, clinical or pedagogical freedom) and thus these benefits are limited. By contrast, the winners in these markets are the state, taxpayers, and the new cadre of managers, regulators, and jurists, who gain greater ability to steer the system. Users of services may benefit if improved efficiency also leads to improved service delivery, but appealing to users is not the overriding goal. Finally, while Managed Markets insulate individuals from new costs, Austerity Markets do not, meaning that some individuals may "lose" in these latter markets.

At their best, state-driven markets introduce strong incentives for productive efficiency and improved basic performance, with less direct emphasis on ameliorating responsiveness or innovation. These markets work through a legalistic structure with clear standards and tight control, which maintains public accountability. While these markets risk less cost-inflation, quality erosion, or decreases in public control than other types of markets, they also risk being less effective in achieving real change.

A couple of examples, drawn from the empirical chapters, help to clarify how state-driven markets work. Chapter 5 argues that recent changes to Local Education Authorities (LEAs) in England offer an example of a Managed Market. The British government introduced reforms that out-sourced provision of school support services in those LEAs that inspectors deemed were failing to produce high-quality, efficient services. Policymakers introduced competition for the provision of these services through carefully specified and monitored contracts, with further regulation guaranteeing pupils' access to services. The emerging competition among producers has enhanced state control over service delivery, without shifting costs onto pupils.

Recent health care reforms in the Netherlands, discussed in chapter 4, moved the Dutch system towards an Austerity Market. Nearly two decades of reform has aimed at introducing greater competition in the health care system, leveling distinctions between private and social insurers, and enhancing competition among insurers for clients and among hospitals for contracts. The resulting market competition has boosted the role of the purchasers (the insurers) and the state in setting prices, quality standards, and specifying the scope of competition. However, these reforms also increased direct user charges, introducing incentives for users to consume more carefully. While both the English and Dutch reforms produced markets that enhance the role of payers in steering the system and setting incentives for efficiency, they differ in how they emphasize individual responsibility for consumption.

In general, given political parties' different preferences about whether citizens should be exposed to individual costs and risks, the Right prefers to use Austerity Markets, while the Left is drawn to Managed Markets. The Right would ideally prefer reforms that promote private producers, or benefit its own voting base, and thus Austerity Markets are not a "first-best" reform. However, where services are universal and provided uniformly across citizens, the Right finds it politically difficult to reduce state control and empower new private actors and has few opportunities to target benefits to middle-class constituents through user choice. In this inhospitable environment, still drawn to markets, the Right will use Austerity Markets as a way of introducing efficiency and building up state control over the cost structure. The Left, by contrast, is more comfortable with enhancing state power as a way of sustaining the welfare state, but as these markets offer little to users, it also sees Managed Markets as a second-best option. In contrast to the Right though, it chooses them for services that are either non-universal or differentiated across users, where consumer choice markets risk exacerbating differences across users and undermining cross-class support for the welfare state.

(b) Consumer-driven markets – Consumer-Controlled and Two Tiered markets

Consumer-driven markets empower the users of services, enhancing their choice of producer and creating incentives for producers to respond to users' preferences for high-quality production. These markets build on the conviction that giving service users an "exit" option will stimulate innovation and improvement in service delivery.

Like state-driven markets, consumer-driven markets also work by challenging the position of producers. However, they differ in that they look to stimulate competition among producers by expanding users' choice of provider and linking funding to these choices. Users have the scope to genuinely exercise choice, thus creating incentives for producers to respond to them. Because producers are competing for relatively cost-insensitive users, these markets lead to a greater emphasis on quality, but at the risk of increasing public expenditure. *Consumer-Controlled* markets match greater user choice with collective financing of services and few incentives for producers to shift costs onto users. By contrast, *Two Tiered* markets impose direct or indirect costs on users. The former markets avoid linking the final distribution of services to market forces, whereas the latter markets give users more financial responsibility and may give producers incentives to appeal to users in a stronger market position. Both types of markets are introduced through reforms that expand choice for users and pay producers based on these choices, alongside regulation that specifies the procedural rights and roles of users and makes these choices meaningful. Consumer-Controlled markets combine this competition with strong public financing, regulation, financial compensation to avoid cream-skimming, and reforms to enable choice for weaker users (for example, information provision) while Two Tiered markets use more individual cost-sharing or do not extensively compensate for differences across users.

Individual users are the core group of winners in these markets, as they gain direct, tangible benefits in terms of greater choice and responsiveness. Whereas Consumer-Controlled markets spread these benefits across all individuals, in Two Tiered markets, higher-income, lower-cost, or lower-risk individuals are at an advantage. In both markets, the "losers" are less concentrated than in state-driven markets. While incumbent producers lose some control over production and must compete for resources, the quality-enhancing and inflationary potential of these markets benefits them. The state is also in a mixed position, gaining control over setting market incentives, but losing some expenditure control. Weaker consumers may also lose in Two Tiered markets.

Two different risks accompany these reforms. First, when paired with strong cost control or low levels of system capacity, these reforms may be ineffective at spurring actual competition. In these cases, the market will strengthen the position of producers, giving them the ability to select users rather than the contrary. Second, where there is sufficient funding and capacity, but users' actual choice is only weakly developed, the market may push towards cost-inflation without accompanying quality improvements.

The Swedish health care reforms, mentioned above, offer an example of reforms that led to a Consumer-Controlled market. In 1991, the Swedish Federation of County Councils, building on local reforms, expanded patient choice for hospitals and increased financial incentives for hospitals to compete for patients. Patients previously restricted to hospitals in a tightly defined geographic area, irrespective of its quality, gained the right to receive care elsewhere. This emerging market worked through incentives for producers to be responsive to users, reduce waiting lists, and focus attention on quality, without leading to cost-shifting onto individuals.

By contrast, chapter 5 shows that the initial movement towards school choice in England demonstrates a "soft version" of the Two Tiered market approach. Here, reforms extended choice to all pupils in the state school system, but also allowed a new class of privileged schools to emerge, which were given more autonomy and latitude to select pupils, raising the specter of inequity among schools and pupils. The emerging market created competition around pupil choice and changed how schools responded to pupils; however, it also created some new forms of segregation among schools.

Once again, the Right and the Left are drawn to different forms of consumer-driven markets, with the Right preferring Two Tiered markets that encourage differences among users while the Left prefers Consumer-Controlled markets that insulate users from costs. The Right is drawn to Two Tier markets for universal services that are provided differently across citizens (for example, a streamed education system), where it can build on this differentiation to target the benefits of choice to its constituents. These markets offer the Right the chance to create a broad electoral appeal and cement new public support for markets, without risking the backlash that direct privatization might bring for a more universal service. By contrast, the Left resists choice where services are differentiated, fearing precisely the outcomes that the Right hopes choice will deliver – more differentiation among citizens. It is drawn to choice where services are universal and uniformly provided across citizens. For these services, choice promises to create a quality focus that ties large groups of users to the welfare state.

(c) *Producer-driven markets – Pork Barrel and Private Power markets*

Producer-driven markets differ substantially from the previous two, allowing new players in producing services the room to shape service delivery in line with their own preferences. *Pork Barrel* markets have their origins in a classic patronage model, where lucrative contracts and benefits are extended to preferred producers without well-developed competitive stimuli. These markets combine greater producer control with strong collective responsibility for financing. *Private Power* markets emerge where there is similar producer control, but more opportunities for cost-shifting onto individuals. Both these markets rest on the belief that producers will have more room to innovate when there is less state interference. While these markets superficially seem an odd pairing, both cede power to producers and reduce the state and user control.

Reforms that introduce competition through either expanded contracting or user choice can create producer-driven markets if the contracts and / or procedural rights of users are not clearly specified, or if new producers have a positive right to enter the market without strong public oversight. In both cases, producers compete only to receive contracts or custom, rather than on actual performance. The state has little ability to renegotiate contracts or regulate outcomes, and users are limited in their ability to exit. New producers are in a strong position, able to pursue profits in ways that conflict with the state and users' preferences. Pork Barrel markets emerge in a looser fiscal environment where producers have incentives to capture profits through rent-seeking from the state. By contrast, Private Power markets arise where tighter fiscal constraints push producers to pursue profits through user fees or reduced quality.

The new firms that receive public funding are the clear winners in these markets, with incumbent producers losing out from this shift. The implications for the state are ambiguous. On the one hand, it loses control over producers and the production process. On the other hand, in Pork Barrel markets, incumbent politicians may gain direct support from private producers (for example, campaign financing), and in Private Power markets, the state "wins" in crude terms where costs are cut. Finally, individual users stand to lose from these reforms, as the quality and performance of services may decline, and they will have little room for recourse through market or democratic means. In Private Power markets, individuals also bear direct costs, whereas in Pork Barrel markets, they stand to lose as taxpayers.

Producer-driven reforms lead to a radical change in the structure of provision and the role of the state. Hart *et al.* (1997) argue that where there are incomplete contracts and producers have more control, private providers demonstrate greater ability to pursue cost-cutting innovations, but are also more likely to do so at the expense of quality. As a result, these markets promise innovation but face the risk of rent-seeking and uncontrolled cost-cutting at the expense of efficient or high-quality production.[5]

The English elderly care market demonstrates a case of a market that initially had a Pork Barrel character and later, following several substantial reforms, developed into a Private Power market. In 1980, the government introduced reforms providing nearly unlimited public funding for lower-income senior citizens to receive care in private nursing homes. The government introduced these changes without significant oversight of the private care industry, creating a Pork Barrel market that provided substantial funding for the private sector absent real competition among nursing homes. In response, the private sector's market share increased dramatically and costs exploded as private homes raised rates and provided care to individuals with little medical need. Public expenditure buoyed a relatively inefficient private market, which benefited producers while offering little to the state or users.

In 1991, in response to this cost inflation, the British government introduced new legislation that limited funding and transferred responsibility to the local governments, while also requiring them to promote home care and contract out at least eighty percent of new services to the private sector. In cutting funding and requiring inexperienced local governments to contract with the private sector absent strong national regulations on quality, a Private Power market emerged. Private firms competed to receive contracts, rather than to satisfy the larger aims of the state or users, with firms making up for low public payment levels by lowering quality and shifting costs onto individuals. The result was a system of low-quality provision, poor safeguards for the health of the elderly, and even cases of abuse (see ch. 6).

Unlike the previous two pairs of markets, the Right largely introduces these markets. The Left resists both Pork Barrel and Private Power markets, as their very structure undercuts state control over welfare services, something the Left aims to sustain. The Right will introduce both types of markets where it can avoid the electoral costs of devolving power to new private actors. This occurs largely where services are not universal and are provided on a more residual basis to a limited group of citizens (for example, a means-tested service) or where the Right can target these reforms narrowly at the margins of the system, rather than engage in system-wide reform. The Right will choose Pork Barrel markets over

---

[5] These authors argue that the conditions of incomplete contracting are intrinsic to particular goods. The argument in this book is that for most services the contracting structure determines who controls the process. Through careful contractual specification and regulation, the state can increase its residual rights of control, whereas, without this effort, producers retain these rights.

Private Power markets where fiscal constraints are less binding or where channeling resources to producers provides electoral benefits to politicians, for example, through increased campaign contributions.

(d) Other forms of markets?

In practice, markets in public services can vary in other ways; in who provides services, how many services are outsourced, whether markets extend to core services (for example, clinical care) or ancillary services (for example, cleaning), and so on. Moreover, market elements have long existed in most public services, particularly in Continental Europe, where non-public providers play a central role in managing and delivering services. These issues raise both a theoretical and an empirical question for the above typology: does it exhaust variation in how markets *can* be structured, and does it account for the long-standing cross-national variation in how they *are* structured? The following paragraphs address these points in turn.

First, one could ask whether the typology "slices" the issue of market variation in the right way: why not focus on the balance of public, private not-for-profit and for-profit providers, the wage structure of workers and so on? Although it is clearly the case that market structures can vary in ways that extend beyond the two dimensions specified here, and that these differences are important, they do not alone define the core incentives in a market. The competitive mechanism at the heart of public service markets follows from how the "demand" side (users and purchasers) and the "supply" side (producers) interact to both deliver and distribute services. Ownership structures, labor market regulation and other factors may influence one or the other side of this equation, but they do not define its fundamental features. By contrast, the above typology maps the basic incentives over how services are both produced and allocated, defining both how the competitive stimulus works to shape what producers deliver services and to whom.

Equally, one could ask, why stop at three sets of actors? Surely, local and national governments and profit-making insurers act differently as buyers, as do different types of patients and pupils and profit and not-for-profit producers. At the margin, each of these differences matters. Nonetheless, focusing on the broad categories of actors who fund, use, or produce services – that is, dividing actors based on their relationship to the competitive process – provides the most leverage in mapping the incentives that markets create. Local and national governments may have slightly different preferences, but they do not have a fundamentally different relationship to the competitive process, likewise for other groups of consumers or producers. Moving towards a more fine-grained analysis is likely to be more descriptively accurate, but provides few additional tools for understanding the competitive mechanisms that markets create (or, as future chapters show, the political dynamics behind them).

Second, it is also true that markets in the welfare state are nothing new. Only a few countries have ever adhered to a fully publicly provided and funded model of welfare provision, and only for a brief period of time. Many Anglo-Saxon and Continental European countries have always relied on private providers to deliver services, often giving them a substantial role. Moreover, even in the fully public systems of Northern Europe, the state has long been deeply entwined in the private economy, blurring the distinctions between the state and the market. However, these pre-existing structures mostly split on the balance of public and private actors, not the degree of competition. Even in Continental Europe, where an autonomous non-profit sector played a crucial role in delivering services, few services were competitively produced or allocated. Here, too, services followed traditional bureaucratic or networked models of organization. The move to market reforms, then, represents a new form of policy and the introduction of competition in these services constitutes a real change.

The six types of markets reviewed here do not exhaust all theoretical or empirical variation in how markets can operate, but they do elucidate the core mechanisms defining competitive production and allocation of services. As such, this typology offers insight into basic market variation and its consequences.

1.3: THE STRUCTURE OF THE BOOK

The fundamental argument of this book is that markets vary – they vary in how they place costs on citizens, what incentives they offer producers, and what this means for the relative power of users, the state and producers. This variation is not a matter of chance, but follows from partisan calculations, albeit under institutional constraints. Chapter 2 develops this causal argument in more depth, contrasting the constrained partisan approach to alternative explanations of the nature and origins of market reforms.

In order to demonstrate these claims empirically, the book draws on contrasting case studies of reform to health, education, and elderly care, in England, the Netherlands, and Sweden, across both left- and right-wing partisan control of government. Each of these countries had significantly different "starting points" vis-à-vis the market. The first case, England, combines a large public sector with a less expansive welfare state. Although the political parties and some of the market reforms cover other parts of the United Kingdom, this book largely focuses on the reform experience in England. Scotland has long controlled its own education policy (with further differences in health policy), and devolution in 1999 provided

Scotland, Wales and Northern Ireland with more control over their health, elderly care, and education policies. The second case, Sweden, offers one of an expansive and primarily public welfare state, while the third, the Netherlands, combines a strong public guarantee of funding with a large non-public service sector. Each case belongs to a different welfare regime (Esping-Andersen 1990), varying more generally in how they structure relations between the state and the private market.

Equally, health, education, and long-term care fundamentally differ in both their structure and the functional pressures they face: with health being an increasingly expensive, fast-growing sector affecting all citizens, education facing fewer cost-pressures, and long-term care a newer and more limited area of public spending. The core finding in examining market reforms in each sector, across countries and across time, is one of systematic diversity in the way markets operate. There is no single English, Swedish, or Dutch market and equally there is no single health, education, or elderly care market. Instead, the cases show the value of a more nuanced typology of markets, demonstrating that policymakers built markets to promote different winners and losers among the state, users and producers.

The core research involved over 165 interviews with policymakers across the three countries from 2004 to 2006, and analysis of primary and secondary documents. In each case, I spoke with bureaucrats, politicians, and cabinet ministers integrally involved in the reform process, tracing both how existing markets worked and why policymakers constructed markets in particular ways. The combination of variation across program, country and time permits a detailed examination of both how the markets worked and the political choices behind them. When we scratch below the surface of the similarly superficial language of market reforms, we see that both market outcomes and the political debates about markets transcended questions of "more or less" markets and hinged on issues of market design.

Studies of diversity in market structures and party strategies build on a mix of research techniques. The "gold standard" for both studies of markets and partisanship tends to be quantitative work, which can show, at a broad level, that partisan action actually translates into varying outcomes, such as the level and composition of spending. In the area of services, broad cross-national studies have found fewer partisan effects (Jensen 2008). The approach in the following chapters is slightly different, using largely qualitative case studies. The more fine-grained approach developed here suits the task at hand: studying trends that are often emergent and transcend differences in spending. In systematically mapping at a theoretical and empirical level differences in markets and their relationship to parties, the analysis shows that partisan strategies do actually matter for outcomes, that parties select different markets, and that these markets, in turn, have indeed shaped the way services are produced and allocated.

Chapter 3 begins this analysis, asking two questions. First, why did markets emerge on many countries' reform agendas in the early 1980s? Second, why did the Left, an apparent opponent of markets, accept or even promote market reforms? This chapter demonstrates that both the Left and Right in England, Sweden and the Netherlands approached markets in social services as a way to create new electoral appeals in a fiscally constrained climate. However, they approached markets in distinct ways, with the Left deploying markets to sustain the long-run political viability of the welfare state, while the Right used them to create inroads into dismantling the welfare state.

Chapter 4 takes the first step in examining how these differing partisan stances developed into specific market reforms, looking at market reforms in health care. The debate over markets has been fiercest in health care, as many commentators see markets as synonymous with an erosion of the state, whether viewed positively or negatively. However, when we scratch below the surface of health care markets, we see that the market reform experience has been highly varied and has largely not led to a cutback or erosion of state power. Early market reforms in England and the Netherlands introduced contracting that increased the power of the state and / or insurers as buyers of health, while changes in Sweden and more recent reforms in England have delegated power to patients at the cost of strong budgetary control. In all three cases, the Right, facing seemingly inexhaustible growth in public health spending, looked to introduce markets as a way of challenging the legitimacy of the public health care system. However, the universal and uniform nature of these systems led parties on the Right to pursue less ideologically preferred contracting strategies. By contrast, the Left turned to markets out of growing concerns that long queues were encouraging middle-class citizens to "opt out" of the public system. In Sweden and England, the uniform nature of these health care systems allowed the Left to address these concerns through choice-based markets, whereas in the Netherlands, where health care provision was more differentiated by income, it compromised with the Right on a move towards more contracting.

Chapter 5 turns to the education sector. Markets have been a key motif of education reform, with reformers in England, Sweden, and the Netherlands all promising increased choice and options for parents. However, in England, policymakers have recently tempered expanded choice with more contracting; in Sweden, initial choice-based markets effectively delegated power to schools, not parents; and where choice has emerged in England and the Netherlands it has also placed new costs on parents. Moreover, the same actors that eschewed choice in health care have supported it in education. This chapter shows that the more fragmented structure of the education system in the Netherlands and England allowed parties on the Right to build choice-based markets as a way of targeting the benefits of competition to their upper-middle-class constituents. Left-wing politicians, who supported choice in health, have been more reticent about it in education, fearing choice will expand inequity. In Sweden, the less fragmented education system created different opportunities for parties, limiting the Right's ability to make broad appeals while giving the Left incentives to develop choice.

Chapter 6 turns to reforms in the area of care for the elderly. These services are often of a newer vintage than education and health care, with public responsibility and markets growing in tandem. Market reforms in this sector show the widest variation: from markets in England that empowered private actors and dramatically undercut state and local control; to markets in Sweden that have introduced greater managerialism and local control over providers; to markets in the Netherlands that expanded competition around user choice. Once again, we see partisan differences. The British Right, lacking the institutional constraints it faced in either the health or education sectors, pursued a strategy of directly stimulating private involvement absent regulation or oversight. By contrast, both the Right and the Left in Sweden and the Netherlands faced stronger constraints, pursuing more limited contracting and choice-based reforms.

Chapter 7 concludes, firstly by reflecting on the broader implications of the book for our understanding of markets, post-industrial welfare states, and partisan politics more generally. It then examines the broader applicability of the argument, examining health care reforms across the OECD. The chapter ends with a discussion of the implications of the work in relation to contemporary debates fuelled by the credit crisis about the changing roles of states and markets.

2

Markets and politics

This chapter looks at the major academic debates over the introduction of markets in the public sector. The first section reviews four alternative approaches to understanding markets in the welfare state, each of which presents markets in a particular way: as right-wing policy, as the "solution" to problems of governance, as a corrupt neoliberal agenda, and as variable, but largely historically determined. Despite the differences among these approaches, this chapter argues that none of them capture how markets in public services actually work, instead presenting markets as either uniformly good or bad or idiosyncratic and contingent.

The second section of the chapter argues that because these approaches do not conceptualize market variation on its own terms, none of them captures the politics of markets. Markets in welfare services are not equivalent to retrenchment, nor do they operate uniformly or in a historically determined fashion, but rather, they vary systematically. Reforms that build on these differences offer policymakers powerful mechanisms to change the way the state spends on, and produces, services. Accounting for this variation requires returning to, but also reconceptualizing, partisan battles in constrained environments.

2.1: POLITICAL PARTIES AND DISTRIBUTIVE STRUGGLES AROUND THE WELFARE STATE

Much work examining the politics of the welfare state has focused on social and economic policy as a site of distributive conflict among political parties and other actors such as unions and employers. Scholars working in this area offer convincing empirical evidence that partisanship mattered for the build-up of the welfare state and for the shape of macroeconomic policy. Power resource theorists, for instance, argue that where unions and left-wing parties were stronger, they built welfare states that not only redistributed income across classes but also modified the logic of capitalism in pro-labor and egalitarian ways (Esping-Andersen and Korpi 1984). The social democratic logic of the welfare state works against markets, with successful Left policy "decommodifying" workers and turning back the frontiers of the private market (Esping-Andersen 1990). Others have come at the question of partisanship and the welfare state from different angles, focusing on macroeconomic policy. This work too, presents markets as largely the preserve of the Right (for example, Hicks and Swank 1992; Franzese 2002).

This literature speaks to questions about the politics of market reforms, since it analyzes different partisan social and economic policies and their resulting outcomes. However, in so doing, it largely casts markets as equivalent to state retrenchment, and thus, as instruments of right-wing policy. A first premise of the partisanship approach is that macroeconomic and welfare policies have varying distributive implications in terms of income and employment. In this framework, market-oriented policies limit state spending and benefit employers or upper-income citizens through lower taxes. A second premise is that political parties select policies that promote the interests of the social groups that they represent. In general, the Left works for the interests of lower-income groups through more extensive and more redistributive spending on social transfers and through pro-employment macroeconomic policy, whereas the Right represents higher-income groups through more restrictive social transfers and pro-investor macroeconomic policy (Alt 1985; Hibbs 1977). Given the way these scholars conceive of the distributional implications of markets, it follows that they see market policies as largely the preserve of the Right, often even defining what it means to be on the Left or the Right in terms of positions vis-à-vis the division of state and market responsibilities.[1] Finally, they argue that varying political, social, and economic outcomes reflect the relative success of the Left and the Right. Market reforms, in this logic, are equivalent to welfare state retrenchment, and the move towards markets suggests the relative strength of the Right over the Left in the contemporary era.

However, in future chapters I show that the distributive implications of markets vary – not always benefiting the constituents of the Right – and that the Left has used market reforms differently to the Right. These findings raise the question as to why parties approach markets differently. The traditional partisanship literature, in focusing on the way parties use macroeconomic and spending policies to achieve their aims, does not provide clear predictions as to how parties might use markets that alter

---

[1] Quantitative studies of manifestos and expert coding of party positions often explicitly define Left and Right party preferences vis-à-vis their stances on the state and the market (for instance, Budge *et al.* 2001).

microeconomic incentives and thereby produce more complex distributive outcomes.

If market reforms are not just about the relative power of the Right in pushing its agenda, what are they about? Three alternative approaches have emerged in popular discourse and the academic literature that understand both markets and the politics of markets differently to the conventional partisanship literature, challenging its core assumptions about the role of parties in shaping outcomes. The first two approaches see markets as a replacement for politics, arguing that they work in a singular and homogenizing way. The global rise of market reforms marks the end of the traditional theories of the welfare state, because it marks the end of the welfare state itself and the distributive struggles that produced it. A third approach takes a different stance, arguing that markets, far from being homogenizing, follow from existing political structures and do not radically break with them. However, market reform is equally apolitical, reflecting the logic of pre-existing institutions, rather than ongoing distributive struggles.

The following section reviews these approaches, arguing that none of them fully captures what markets in the welfare state do, or why different actors might prefer different markets. Instead of throwing the partisan baby out with the bathwater, the second half of the chapter argues that we need to return to theories of partisanship but modify them in several ways to (a) directly conceptualize markets as distributive policies with multiple dimensions, (b) examine partisan preferences over both the allocative and productive aspects of markets, and (c) theorize partisan strategic calculations in mature welfare systems.

2.2: THE RISE OF MARKETS, THE END OF POLITICS

Both academic and popular discourses on markets often portray them in simple terms – as present or absent. The normative tone of these discussions varies substantially; market proponents celebrate the move away from a corrupt or inefficient political system even as market critics mourn the loss of a traditional public sector. Yet both approaches challenge the core assumptions of the partisan scholars, that the instruments of government vary and that distributive struggles over welfare policy matter, arguing instead that markets represent the end of politics.

Two cheers for markets

A first approach, advanced by "public choice" scholars, draws on assumptions from economic theory to argue that all elected politicians, whether on the Left or the Right, use the apparatus of government to serve their own interests (Buchanan and Tullock 1962). Because the rationally ignorant voter pays little attention to the government, public spending on services gives rent-seeking politicians resources to further their own ends and public provision creates a bureaucracy out to service its own needs and not those of users (Tullock *et al.* 2002). The crucial distinction is not who controls the instruments of government, but the size of the state itself.

Markets, in this reasoning, are the cure for a corrupt public sector. While public choice scholars recognize that private markets are subject to failures, they argue that unlike the inefficiencies in government, markets continue to expose self-interested actors to competitive pressures (Wolf 1979). The only way to counteract the tendency of politicians and bureaucrats to use public resources for their own aims is to reduce the size of the state and empower private interests (Tullock *et al.* 2002; Shleifer and Vishny 1998). Markets replace the state, and differences that emerge in markets can be aligned from better to worse, roughly equivalent to from more to less, rather than differences in kind. Although these scholars propose varying reforms in health, education and care services, from vouchers for users, to tax savings accounts, to outright spending cuts, in each case the underlying claim is that markets will limit the size and scope of the state and replace it with a superior form of allocation and production (for example, Rinehart and Lee 1991; Goodman *et al.* 2004).

In seeing markets as ending politics, public choice scholars have struggled to explain why self-interested politicians choose to disengage from a status quo built to benefit them and actually introduce markets (Derthick and Quirk 1985). In general, they claim policymakers will resist reform unless a constellation of external forces changes their interests. For instance, Shleifer and Vishny (1998) argue that while contextual factors, such as rules limiting unions or patronage, increase the likelihood of market-based reforms, dramatic privatization follows from the interests of actors outside of politics who stand to benefit from it. Explaining reforms requires focusing on these interests, rather than independently theorizing the political process.

A second pro-market approach, often labeled New Public Management (NPM), emerged in the 1980s as another way of understanding the state and the political process. There is little consensus across practitioners and scholars as to precisely what NPM is, but its proponents largely reject the claim of public choice scholars that governments are inherently predatory. However, they argue that governments are vulnerable to these critiques precisely because they do operate inefficiently and fail to satisfy citizens' demands (Hood 1991; Kettl 1993). For instance, David Osborne and Ted Gaebler (1992: 14) argue that the Weberian rule-based bureaucracy has become inflexible, hard to manage, and focused on inputs over results: "The product was government with a distinct ethos: slow, inefficient, impersonal."

Markets, for NPM proponents, are also a relatively undifferentiated solution to the problems of government. Markets restrict the role of politicians to defining broad goals, while giving civil servants (or private contractors) the incentives to execute them efficiently (Osborne and Gaebler 1992). In contrast to the public choice approach, these scholars see markets as a technocratic means for improving public services, not a replacement for them (Lundsgaard 2002). Yet like public choice scholars, they often draw on a single baseline – a well-functioning private market – to promise "all good things go together." Markets do not produce different distributional outcomes; rather, they promise to improve efficiency, save money, and offer users choice, quality, and responsiveness.

NPM proponents are generally not aiming to explain the introduction of markets, and it is important to distinguish proponents from those analyzing the NPM project. Nonetheless, many NPM scholars do offer an implicit theory of the political process. NPM analyses focus on the government as a bureaucratic organization that delivers – or fails to deliver – public goods, not as a locus of distributive conflict among actors. Markets improve the efficiency of government, and policymakers will introduce markets as growing fiscal pressures and citizens' demands increase the political costs of inefficiency (Savas 2000; Ferris and Graddy 1986). For instance, Osborne and Gaebler's (1992) examples of innovative governments in Visalia, California and St. Paul, Minnesota, are those where the tax base had eroded so significantly that policymakers were forced to reform: necessity being the mother of market invention. The result is a largely functionalist understanding of the politics of markets, where the need for improvement drives their introduction, with little analysis of the distributive struggles around markets or the process of reform.

Markets against politics?

As the market reform agenda gained steam, a line of critical scholarship emerged, rejecting the diagnosis of public sector failure and defending the public sector as a collective sphere that can and does pursue the public interest (Berliner and Biddle 1995). These scholars, in stark contrast to market proponents, see markets as rooted in conflictual economic relationships. Competition sets producer against producer and citizen against citizen, creating both inefficiencies and waste in the delivery process and leading providers to put profits ahead of the public's interest. Instead, they argue that we need a genuinely public sector in order to pursue aims like health, education, and safety (Box *et al.* 2001; Suleiman 2003).

Unlike market proponents, these critics do see markets in political terms, arguing that they elevate the needs of business above the public.

Nonetheless, in making these claims, critics often follow market proponents in understanding markets in uniform terms. For instance, Allyson Pollock (2004: 14) argues that all market reforms in the British National Health Service (NHS), from private capital funding of hospital construction to competition among public hospitals, are "selling out the NHS" and turning health into something that can be "bought and sold." Critics of markets in education further argue that vouchers, Charter schools, and private sector contracting similarly harm equity and undercut a richer and more comprehensive form of education (Molnar 1996). This blanket criticism of all forms of market activity follows from a framework that sees the market as diametrically opposed to the state.

Because the critical perspective sees markets as elevating the interests of business over those of the public, it emphasizes these same interests in explaining market reform. One line of argument predicts that market reforms will follow from the power of organized business lobbies. For instance, Pollock (2004) traces reforms in the British NHS directly back to the "revolving door" among business actors and government. Equally, Michael Apple's (2001b) analysis of education reform argues that the motives of business are clear – to transform American public education into a profitable industry. A second line of argument focuses on the more diffuse power of capital, arguing that policymakers increasingly hew to the ideological agenda of global capital for market promotion (Leys 2003). In both cases, the pressure for markets is relatively undifferentiated, following from the growing power of business over states. Markets do not just represent the politics of the bourgeoisie, but the conclusion of a political game in which the Right has won.

Uniform markets? Uniform causes?

Although the public choice, NPM, and critical approaches each understand markets differently, all present them as an alternative to the state with uniformly good or bad effects. This uniform presentation of markets leaves the variation uncovered by the empirical chapters of this book unexplained. For instance: why did contracting for elderly care in England reduce state control over the private sector, while contracting in Dutch health care increased it? Why did market reforms in the English health sector in the 2000s expand competition *and* state spending and oversight? The series of unanswered questions grows when we ask why policymakers build different types of markets. The empirical chapters of the book show that business pressures alone do not explain reforms: health care reform in the Netherlands occurred despite criticism from the core business association. Swedish policymakers introduced reforms favorable to private schools before a substantial private sector existed. Yet the move to the market was hardly just a functional response to cost pressures. For instance, in the early 1990s, local and national governments in Sweden and the UK experimented with different reform models in health care, education and elderly care, despite facing similar fiscal constraints.

These problems in characterizing and explaining change arise because neither market proponents nor critics carefully examine the distributional trade-offs across market structures. Even though the most ardent pro-market scholars admit that markets in health, education and care services do not match economic models of "perfect competition," most do not analyze how these features give policymakers distinct reform choices. Instead, they advocate particular models of competition as recipes to achieve a broad range of results (for example, efficiency, quality), sidelining the question at the heart of their analysis of the political process: whose interests does it serve? The result is a thin understanding of the way markets work. NPM analyses are even more apolitical, presenting markets as a tool in the hands of politicians that will improve government, without clearly examining the stakes of different types of market reforms.

Critical scholars take the opposite tack, equating the existence of market failures in these services with uniformly negative market performance. Although these scholars do see markets in political terms, the flow of power is always in the direction of concentrated business interests. In juxtaposing a mythical public sector past to corrupt market reforms, this stance also leaves a theoretical lacuna in articulating how markets can benefit different groups.

Each approach, in seeing markets as a replacement for politics, has little to say about the interests or processes that generate them. Public choice scholars offer a clear theory of political preferences based on self-interest, yet the focus on external actors as the agents of change allows only a limited interpretation of how these interests emerge in the public sector reform process. Equally, the critical approach, in assuming that markets uniformly benefit business to the detriment of labor, citizens, and the state, reads actors' preferences off their economic position without theorizing a broader range of goals. NPM scholars are not focused on examining preferences, but implicit in their approach is the idea that politicians want to improve services, but without specifying actual reform aims. This vagueness over what actors want grows when it comes to questions of specific reforms. Because these scholars see markets only as a matter of more or less, they largely theorize the decision-making context in terms of whether it permits market reforms – that is, whether political or labor market institutions encourage or block their introduction. None directly speaks to politicians' strategic calculations in a given institutional context. Each of these approaches leaves open questions over how to explain policy-makers' different choices over markets.

2.3: MARKETS ARE PATH DEPENDENT – PAST DISTRIBUTIVE STRUGGLES MATTER

Much of the public debate on markets follows those listed above, seeing them as "all good" or "all bad" for the welfare state. Within political science, however, scholarship on markets has often taken a different tone. A substantial body of work in the field of comparative political economy takes variation in market structures seriously, arguing that both broader capitalist markets and the organization of the state differ across contexts.

Two major research agendas speak to these questions: those examining variation in national models of capitalism and those examining programmatic continuity in the welfare state. Both conceive of markets as fundamentally variable and institutionally determined, but also as stable and relatively apolitical. Institutions may represent the cumulative effect of political decisions, a congealed partisanship effect, but these past choices constrain future options to such an extent that distributive battles no longer drive welfare state politics. The die is largely cast against convergence among countries, but towards convergence among actors within a country. The following paragraphs argue that this emphasis on historically determined markets downplays the political dynamics behind market creation in the public sector.

A first approach focuses on cross-national differences in market structures. Esping-Andersen's (1990) famous typology distinguishing among three types of "welfare capitalism" posits that social policy alters the logic of capitalism in nationally specific ways. Other work focuses on non-welfare institutions, such as labor markets, arguing that they create different types of economic coordination among firms (Hall and Soskice 2001). This work suggests that markets can and do vary, and that a constellation of national institutions shapes this variation.

While acknowledging the theoretical diversity in market structures, this emphasis on national variation encounters problems in characterizing and explaining market creation in public services. Countries with different national welfare, labor market, and financial institutions have initiated similar market reforms. For instance, "social democratic" Sweden and more recently "liberal" Britain both introduced competition around choice in health care and contracting in elderly care. Moreover, policymakers have introduced different markets in the same country. In the late 1980s in England, the Conservative government introduced markets built through strongly regulated contracting in health, weakly regulated contracting in elderly care, and individual choice in education.

This experience points to several problems in applying the "national models" approach to new forms of market creation. Those focusing on nationally specific market structures often draw on the logic of private sector markets, without independently examining how market mechanisms work in the public sector. The "Varieties of Capitalism" literature, for instance, directly theorizes the mechanisms governing different forms of product competition. Yet, the logic of variation follows from an analysis of how pre-existing national institutions shape coordination (or lack thereof) in private markets (Hall and Soskice 2001), not a model of how the competitive mechanism can operate within the state. This theorization sees markets as historically determined and stable: change within markets is largely endogenous to these existing structures and non-strategic. New markets are either continuous with existing structures or an assault on them. Partisan politics, or battles between employers and unions, may have been important at a critical juncture in the formation of the welfare state, but it is unclear what the stakes of new struggles over markets are.

A second approach focuses on the logic of programmatic, not national, institutions. This approach emerged in response to the seeming shortcomings of partisan approaches in explaining developments in the welfare states in the 1980s and 1990s. Paul Pierson (1996, 2001) maintains that many social programs demonstrate remarkable "path dependence," with diverse program structures persisting across time. He also argues that partisanship may have mattered during the build up of the welfare state, but mature welfare systems buffer themselves against change and thus minimize new patterns of contestation. For instance, Pierson uses both an "economic" and a "political" logic to argue that social programs become "locked in" in particular ways. The economic logic states that programs are often hard to change because there are increasing returns to production due to high fixed costs to change, adaptive expectations, and complementary institutions (Pierson 2000). At the same time, there are political costs to change, as policies create large groups of policy-takers who organize to block change and mobilize the electorate against reform (Pierson 1996). The prime example is a pay-as-you-go (PAYG) pension system, which funds entitlements through contributions from the current working population, rather than through returns on invested capital. The economic costs of moving away from a PAYG system are tremendous, as workers would essentially have to pay twice – funding current pensioners while also saving funds for their own retirement. These reforms are also politically difficult, as both powerful interest groups and the electorate mobilize against cuts. Although the origins of these transfer programs may vary, once enacted, they limit further reform.

This book, like other recent work on the welfare state, shows that the emphasis on continuity does not match the empirical record. Both changes to PAYG pensions, and the political coalitions behind them, are more extensive than Pierson suggested (Häusermann 2010). In services, change has been even more substantial. To continue with the above examples: early market reforms in the English NHS strengthened and recast the role of the state and radically altered the position of physicians, elderly care reforms created a substantial new private sector, and education reforms empowered parents in new ways. Moreover, in the early 1990s, policymakers reformed programs with similar structures, British and Swedish health for instance, differently.

As with the national models approaches, this experience points to analytical problems that the programmatic path-dependence approach faces in conceptualizing and explaining market variation in services. In presenting existing structures as contingent and self-reproducing, this approach does not directly theorize the more complex range of opportunities actors have in introducing reform. For instance, in services, the costs of changing from non-competitive to competitive services often fall, not increase, over time, as more information and better computing technology make it cheaper to price services and construct contracts. Moreover, the political costs vary. Services rest on a trilateral set of relationships among the state, citizens and incumbent and new producers. Citizens may resist cuts to services, but it is not clear that they have the same interests in resisting changes to the way services are delivered. Even where citizens and producers do resist change, the more complex set of players allows reformers to construct alternative coalitions to offset this opposition. Politicians do not have a fully open opportunity space, but nor do existing structures necessarily foreclose substantial reform.

This book builds on Pierson's argument that programmatic design is of central importance, yet it argues that these structures are not determinative of outcomes. If politicians can introduce more change than his approach suggests, then we need to theorize both what it can look like and what political actors actually want in introducing change. This approach speaks to a more recent literature on institutional change, which sees change as neither exogenous to political institutions nor fully path-dependent (Streeck and Thelen 2005; Thelen and Mahoney 2010). Different instruments of governance – with different distributive implications – still exist, and political battles over these instruments matter, even as they occur within institutions that shape the overall nature of change.

2.4: MARKETS AS A SITE OF DISTRIBUTIVE BATTLES – BRINGING PARTIES BACK IN

I argued in chapter 1 that market design determines both the allocation of services to individuals and whether competition is structured around the preferences of the state, users, or producers of services. This argument follows from an understanding of both public services and markets that is distinct from those advanced by the traditional partisanship, public choice, NPM, critical, or pure path-dependency approaches. Some forms of market failure beset most public services, from health to education. There is not a perfectly competitive market in these areas that operates as a benchmark for market reforms. The presence of market failures in these services means that policymakers face sharp trade-offs in restructuring services through different types of markets.

This understanding of markets suggests that policymakers have a series of choices in introducing markets; however, these choices do not necessarily mirror those that the traditional partisanship approaches emphasized. Instead, they dovetail with work on economic privatization (for example, Feigenbaum *et al.* 1998) and economic policy that suggests that parties in the contemporary era take a more nuanced approach to micro-economic reform rather than focusing only on spending and macroeconomic policy.

First, a number of studies show that where dramatically increasing or decreasing spending is limited – due to electoral or fiscal constraints on government – parties on the Left and the Right routinely reform the composition and character of spending to target benefits to their existing constituents or to create new constituents. Boix (1998) argues that, in response to the limits of Keynesianism, parties have moved to the "supply side" of the economy, with left-wing parties focusing on policies aimed at improving productivity (i.e., education spending) while the Right focuses on the conditions for investment. Parties are not fighting over fiscal policy per se, but over how to structure particular types of spending / tax breaks in order to shape the labor market in ways favorable to their constituents.

Other work looks "under the hood" of spending in particular areas. Ansell (2010) finds partisan differences in the composition of education spending, with right-wing parties targeting spending to higher education and left-wing parties spending more on primary and secondary education. These differences have important distributive implications for the constituents of the Left and Right. Häusermann (2010) looks at pension reforms that simultaneously retrench and expand benefits, effectively cutting benefits to standard male employees while creating new credits for non-typical workers, such as women who have taken time off to care for children. Her analysis traces how a broad range of actors, including parties, take diverse stances towards reshaping pension benefits. Levy's (1999) analysis of "vice into virtue" approaches to public spending also examines this phenomenon. He shows how left-wing parties in Continental Europe have reshaped health, pensions, and family policy by targeting abuses in the system in order to raise funds to pursue more redistributive aims. In each case, left- and right-wing parties have pursued new strategies for *allocating* benefits, that are both distinct from past approaches but not necessarily convergent.

Second, work on regulation, privatization and corporate governance suggests that political actors have responded to the constraints on spending or other traditional activities by reshaping the role of the state as a regulator and producer of goods and services. Majone (1994) argues that there has been a turn to a "regulatory state" in Europe. Regulation, unlike spending, is not crowded out by fiscal constraints on the state, and often not by electoral constraints. However, the effects of regulation are neither apolitical nor uniform. Particular regulatory policies can favor different actors. In some cases, as Vogel (1998) shows, deregulation can mean "more rules" that strengthen the state, while in others it can give rent-seeking firms control. Equally, corporate governance reforms may shift power to managers, shareholders, or workers in firms themselves (Gourevitch and Shinn, 2007). What is common to such reforms is that they reshape incentives in public or private *production* to empower new actors.

Scholars studying privatization, deregulation and corporate governance have come to different conclusions on the importance of political parties, but there is evidence that parties have expended considerable effort introducing such reforms. However, partisan differences are often surprising: Cioffi and Hopner's (2006) study of corporate governance reforms in Germany, for instance, finds left-wing parties often supported reforms expanding shareholder rights and the market orientation of firms, against the wishes of Christian Democrats, who supported a less competitive status quo. Understanding partisan preferences over productive issues is not as simple as arguing that the Left supports more state control and the Right less, rather it requires mapping the distributional consequences of varying reforms and the particular trade-offs partisan actors face in introducing them.

Taken together, this work suggests that parties are still relevant actors, and that they are constantly renegotiating structures of allocation and production in ways that extend beyond spending and macroeconomic policy. In order to understand the politics of markets, we need to directly theorize the character of markets, preferences over them, and policy-makers' scope for action.

A theory of constrained partisanship

The following section argues that market reforms do not spell the end of distributive struggles in mature welfare states, but rather, a shift in the terrain of partisan political conflict. This argument rests on several key claims.

First, following the typology of markets developed in chapter 1, I argue that markets vary systematically both in how they allocate services and how they shape incentives over the production of services. Second, I argue that political parties introduce different markets in order to achieve distinct goals. Finally, I argue that parties use different types of markets to respond to the constraints presented by the particular program they are reforming. Past distributive struggles shape the trade-offs parties face in introducing new market policies, but they do not determine the outcomes. Equally, parties must navigate electoral pressures and lobbying from organized interests, but these pressures are not determinative. Parties are the key actors driving market reform.

This argument builds on long-standing research showing the importance of political parties in determining social and economic outcomes. Yet, it breaks with the traditional partisanship literature in theorizing a wider set of available policy instruments, conceptualizing preferences over production, not just spending, and seeing partisan calculations as responsive to existing structures rather than constant across time.

Markets as diverse instruments of reform

Chapter 1 develops a typology of markets in public services that rests on two postulates: first, market structures can have different allocative effects, sometimes placing more risks and costs on individuals and sometimes insulating individuals from risks and costs; second, markets introduce different logics of competition in production based on whether they give control over competitive incentives to the state, users, or producers.

Some markets structure the allocation of services to more extensively reflect individual income or risk (Austerity Markets, Two Tier, and Private Power markets). Others introduce competition in production without placing costs on individuals (Managed Markets, Consumer-Controlled, and Pork Barrel markets). Markets, then, can, but do not necessarily, change how individuals access services. All markets do change the way incumbent producers deliver services, often reducing their control over production in favor of the state, users, or new producers. These differences matter because the state as a regulator or "buyer" of services, patients, and pupils as users of services, and the professionals and organizations that provide services do not necessarily have equivalent interests. Markets that introduce competition through contracting and greater managerial control (Managed Markets and Austerity Markets) empower the state to set its preferences for cost control. Reforms that expand pupil or patient choice and back this choice with financial incentives (Consumer-Controlled and Two Tier markets) empower users and their preferences for responsiveness and quality. Finally, reforms that give new private actors substantial autonomy absent strong regulation (Pork Barrel and Private Power markets) allow them scope to innovate but also to pursue their own aims.

Markets structures vary in terms of the way they allocate services to citizens and who "calls the shots" over the flow of resources and incentives in the productive process. Macroeconomic policies are not the only game in town; microeconomic changes targeting the production and allocation of services have important distributive effects.

Partisan preferences

The study of parties and the welfare state suggests that parties on the Left and the Right have strong and varying preferences over distributive outcomes, while sharing the common preference to get and stay elected. The following two sections argue that when it comes to market reforms, we need to look at how varying markets fit with parties' ideological goals in a given electoral and institutional context. Parties use markets to better align existing institutional structures with their core preferences, but they are also always operating within the constraints that these same structures pose.

While the preferences of left- and right-wing parties are not fixed across time and space, these "families" of political parties are linked by similar core ideological stances vis-à-vis the welfare state. Economically conservative right-wing parties prefer a more streamlined and smaller welfare state (particularly in the area of taxation), and a larger private sector and / or more competitive production. Christian Democratic parties have tended to support more generous state funding. But their preferences for a more limited role for the state, private providers, and more differentiated public programs, do fit with those of more economically conservative right-wing parties (van Kersbergen 1995). The Left, by contrast, prefers outcomes that secure the viability of the welfare state and promote social welfare to assist weaker members in society. While some left-wing parties support public ownership and control as an end in itself, over time, they have become less attached to defending public production than ensuring the sustainability of public programs (chapter 3 discusses this shift more extensively).

Clearly, parties have preferences over other issues that affect market design – the position of low-wage workers, support for private industry, the role of subnational units – however, the following pages argue that their core preferences over the size and scope of the state are the key drivers of their stances towards markets. The Right's support for more limited programs, lower taxes and less public provision and the Left's support for maintaining social spending and broad social programs are of central importance.

The literature on partisanship has long highlighted these distinct preferences in ideology; however, parties, when looking at potential reforms – including markets – need to combine policies favoring their ideological aims with policies acceptable to their constituents and the median voter. Many have argued that this electoral dynamic either erases partisan distinctions (for example, Downs 1957) or may trap political parties – particularly those on the Left – in advocating narrow policies benefiting their constituents (Rueda 2005). In this work, parties' actions are highly constrained.

I argue that parties do face powerful constraints but reject the idea that partisan action is always derivative of voter or constituent preferences. Instead, I argue that electoral success is partly endogenous to policy choices. Parties generally try – although they cannot always manage – to introduce policies that achieve their ideological goals while also appealing to a broad group of voters. Power resource scholars have long argued that the success of the Left in modifying capitalist structures came from their ability to homogenize risk across broad groups of citizens (Esping-Andersen and Korpi 1984). Where the Left was powerful, it created welfare programs that linked the risks middle-class workers faced to those that lower-income workers faced. In the long run, this approach helped the Left both pursue greater redistribution and win elections. By contrast, where the Right was more powerful it worked to fragment risks across groups, creating benefits that built on the different labor market risks that social classes faced. The resulting welfare state was both less redistributive and provided fewer political resources for the Left. Writing about privatization and reform of the state, Biais and Perotti (2002) have made similar claims about the Right. They argue that where the Right has been able to privatize in ways that diffuse ownership widely (through cheaper prices) they link the ownership risks of middle and upper-income groups, aligning the interests of the median voter with further privatization and the Right itself.

This work suggests that parties look to restructure welfare systems in ways that are conducive to both their long-term distributive and electoral goals. In the abstract, the Left's preference for more redistribution and upholding the welfare state should lead it to support markets that draw together lower- and higher-income citizens and ensure the fiscal and political sustainability of the welfare state. By contrast, the Right should support markets that weaken the links between lower- and higher-income citizens, and tie citizens to more limited or differentiated programs and private actors.

Often, parties (for reasons articulated below) cannot introduce policy that maximizes both electoral and ideological success. However, in contrast to those that argue that this dynamic leads parties to abandon broader distributive aims, I argue that parties look to maximize electoral success within ideological constraints. Put differently, parties will introduce policies that best achieve their electoral aims within the framework of their overall goals for the welfare state. The Left will not jettison its support for the longevity of the welfare state to win votes, or vice versa for the Right, but both parties will use different policies to respond to their particular electoral environment.

Given their distinct preferences, parties are drawn to different forms of markets. In the area of allocation, these differences are relatively straight-forward. Where possible, the Right's goals for lower taxes and more limited public services lead it to support more individual responsibility for accessing services (for example, Austerity Markets, Two Tier markets, and Private Power markets) as a way to limit spending and public support for services in the long run. By contrast, the Left's preferences for extensive public services lead it to support collective financing (for example, Managed Markets, Consumer-Controlled markets, and Pork Barrel markets) that ties citizens together and to the state.

When it comes to production, we also see a baseline preference for different markets. The Right, aiming to lower taxes and support greater private entrepreneurship, is drawn to markets that actively reduce the role of the state by increasing the power of non-state producers (for example, Pork Barrel and Private Power markets). These markets promise to both limit the state and create concentrated private interests who will support further market-oriented reform and Right policy. By contrast, consumer-driven markets (Consumer-Controlled) best meet the Left's preferences for maintaining and enhancing support for public services. These markets make services appeal to middle-class quality standards, tying these groups to the public sector and the Left itself.

Strategies in constrained environments

Political choices, though, do not occur in an unconstrained world. Parties are reforming services that are already in existence, not working from a blank slate. Existing institutions reflect past distributional battles, and while not determinative, these structures can advantage and disadvantage different core preferences. Where the Left previously built services that matched its preferences, it faces different trade-offs in later reforming them than for those that were built by and for the Right, and vice versa.

Existing institutions can create either direct electoral costs to reforming particular markets; or they can exacerbate the risks, and decrease the benefits, to particular market strategies, creating ideological costs to particular types of markets. In general, the further the programmatic status quo is from a political party's preferred end point, the more costs (either ideological or electoral) a party encounters in introducing its preferred markets. These costs do not mean parties are relegated to making incremental changes – market reforms are generally substantial – rather, they push parties to less attractive options that maximize electoral gain within their ideological framework.

Services across the OECD differ in many ways: the size of the public sector workforce, existing unionization rates, financing mechanisms, and so on. Two dimensions, however, are of particular relevance: their degree of *universality* and the degree of *uniformity*. These two features shape electoral and ideological costs and benefits to market strategies, leading to particular market strategies. The universality and uniformity of services may either drive a wedge between a party's electoral and ideological goals, forcing less attractive reform options, or bring them together, allowing preferred policies. Because parties have different preferences, the degree of universality and uniformity in programmatic structures affects the Left and the Right differently.

First, some public services are universal, offering relatively comprehensive coverage to the whole population (or a large sub-group, such as the elderly), whereas others are residual, offering less generous or less comprehensive benefits that are limited to smaller sub-groups of the population. The universality of a service establishes the particular electoral costs and benefits to change. Over time, as Paul Pierson (1996) argues, universal public services tend to foster strong electoral support and make the public resistant to cuts or eroding quality. These services limit parties' ability to introduce unpopular reforms, such as cuts, and encourage popular ones, such as quality improvements; whereas, for residual services, parties have far more leeway to cut services and see fewer gains to broad public appeals.

Second, public services vary in their degree of benefit uniformity. OECD countries differ in how services build on income and social divisions in the population. For instance, the health care systems of Scandinavia, parts of Southern Europe, and Britain offer relatively uniform health benefits to citizens – all classes of citizens access the same system, creating more homogeneity in the risks that they face. By contrast, other health care systems institutionalize income differences. The German system allows upper-income citizens to opt out into a private actuarial health insurance system, a fragmentation in benefits that holds, to a lesser extent, in other social insurance systems. OECD countries display similar dynamics in education systems. Some countries provide largely equivalent education across pupils, whereas others stream pupils based on ability (which is heavily correlated with income) at a young age. These divisions mirror, although are not identical to, differences in transfers (Esping-Andersen 1990). The uniformity in benefits affects the ideological costs and benefits of particular reforms. Where services are more uniform, improving the existing system is likely to tie citizens to the public sector; by contrast, where services are fragmented, building on the existing structure is likely to exacerbate existing fragmentation. These differences shape the opportunities for the Left and the Right to engage in particular reform strategies.

As argued above, the overriding goal of the Left is to support or enhance the long-run sustainability of the welfare state as a redistributive agent, and the Left as its political guardian. In the build-up of the welfare state, the Left supported more universal and uniform services that linked the interests of lower- and middle-income groups to the state. Given these preferences, where services are universal and uniform, the status quo favors the Left's interests – encouraging the Left to support it. Yet, the Left often faces intense pressure to change these systems, especially in the face of rising middle-class demands for more responsive services (see ch. 3). The structure of the service allows the Left to use its preferred Consumer-Controlled markets without facing a heavy electoral or ideological price. The universality of the system makes the Left's overriding preferences for maintaining, or expanding, the service, popular. At the same time, its existing uniformity means that the Left can empower users without dramatically exacerbating existing social divisions; choice applies to everybody and does not give any one group a new benefit.

By contrast, where the system is residual or fragmented, the Left is more constrained. Here, it has less to gain from reforms that promise to sustain the status quo, and Consumer-Controlled markets threaten to exacerbate existing divisions. In these systems, if drawn to markets, the Left will pursue Managed Markets that build up state control over service production without risking inequity. These low-key reforms enhance state power as a way to manage performance and costs, improving the fiscal sustainability of the welfare state without aggravating existing social divisions (for fragmented services) or incurring the electoral costs of expanding unpopular programs (for residual services). Because the Left, unlike the Right, is more ambivalent about markets, it will avoid those that fundamentally challenge its core ideological preferences for a sustained welfare state. As a result, we expect the Left to avoid producer-based markets, using Managed Markets for both universal but fragmented services and residual services.

The Right generally favors policies that will reduce state spending (and thus taxation) and support more private actors and, as a result, it faces the reverse institutional calculus to the Left. Historically, the Right supported more limited, residual services. Where universal services did emerge, the Right pushed for a more fragmented structure that offered upper-income constituents specific benefits. Christian Democrats supported more extensive services than economically liberal parties, but they also built welfare states that allowed more differentiation among citizens and greater scope for private providers in service delivery. Universal and uniform programs were less attractive and, consequently, these programs are often the hardest for the Right to reform.

For popular universal services, the public is more likely to resist producer-driven markets (Pork Barrel / Private Power). These markets reduce state control over the service and threaten lower quality. As such, the Right faces heavy electoral costs to dramatic cuts or privatization. In the abstract, Two Tiered markets (individual responsibility, consumer choice) are the next best option. These markets are popular, effective at breaking up public monopoly provision, and provide middle-class constituents with particular benefits (for example, schools that respond to their particular concerns). However, in uniform systems, consumer choice threatens to increase support for public funding and enhance middle-class support for the system – working against the Right's core preferences – indeed, supporting the Left's goals. As a result, the Right is likely to avoid the markets and support Austerity Markets in uniform systems. Austerity Markets are less a priori ideologically or electorally attractive, since they build up state control and offer few direct benefits to the Right's constituents, but they do promise to deliver cost control and increase the market-orientation in the system without the electoral or ideological costs of the alternatives.

Universal but fragmented systems give the Right more opportunities. For these services, the Right has more vested in the status quo, as it benefits its middle- and upper-income constituents and in some cases private providers (for example, schools and hospitals). The universality of these services continues to limit more radical privatization, but Two Tier markets that extend current differentiation are attractive. The Right can build on the existing fragmentation to target benefits to constituents who support its preferences for lower taxation and a smaller state, with fewer risks of across the board cost increases. For universal but fragmented services, the Right will pursue a "second-best" Two Tier market.

Finally, residual services, which most constrained the Left, offer the Right the most opportunities. The lower levels of public visibility and popularity allow the Right to achieve higher-order preferences for cutting spending and greater private involvement through producer-based reforms, by limiting the electoral costs of targeting benefits to the private sector. Here, right-wing parties can pursue Pork Barrel or Private Power markets.

To summarize, the Right, which prefers to lower taxes, support greater private provision, and limit the state, all while maintaining electoral viability and support from upper- and middle-income constituents, will find it easier to introduce preferred policies in services that are already provided more meagerly and residually. For these services, it can achieve its "first-best" preferences for Private Power or Pork Barrel markets. However, where services are universal, this move is limited, leading it to pursue lower order preferences for Two Tier markets, where services are fragmented and Austerity Markets, where services are uniform. By contrast, the Left, who would like to expand and improve publicly financed services and tie a broad group of citizens to the welfare state, all the while aiming for

TABLE 2.1: *Variation in market outcomes*

Outlines the predictions for market variation based on partisan control and the existing program structure.

Party	Residual	Universal	
		Fragmented benefit structure	**Uniform benefit structure**
Right	Producer-driven Private Power/ Pork Barrel markets	Consumer-driven Two Tiered markets	State-driven Austerity Markets
Left	State-driven Managed Markets	State-driven Managed Markets	Consumer-driven Consumer-Controlled markets

electoral viability, will find it easier to do so where services are universal and uniform than where they are fragmented or residual. In the former it can achieve its "first-best" preference for a Consumer-Controlled market, but in the latter it moves towards Managed Markets. Table 2.1 (see above) summarizes these expectations.

In examining the predicted variation in Table 2.1, three features require further explanation. First, the Right may use either type of producer-driven market. This occurs because Pork Barrel and Private Power markets each offer particular benefits. Pork Barrel markets (collective responsibility, producer orientation) promise to build highly concentrated support for markets in the long-run, creating new producer interests who may also directly support the policymakers who introduce them. By contrast, Private Power markets (individual responsibility, producer orientation) promise to cut costs and the scope of welfare state services. The Right is more likely to pick Private Power markets when fiscal conditions are extremely tight, and the gains from cost-cutting offset any potential losses in concentrated producer support.

Second, the above discussion assumed that the parties were engaged in full-scale market reforms. In practice, policymakers have other options at hand: to avoid reform, to use non-market mechanisms and to introduce more limited markets. The predictions here are for likely, but not determinative, outcomes. Indeed, the goal of the analysis is to illuminate parties' core preferences and the trade-offs they face in introducing markets. Some parties may choose different paths, preferring to tinker with markets around the edges of a service rather than fundamentally altering it. In this situation, the precise reform outcome may not match those outlined here, but the above theory nonetheless speaks to the decision-set that policymakers face. For instance, if policymakers wanted to introduce a Pork Barrel market in a universal and uniform service, the theory predicts that in order to avoid a public backlash they would need to substantially limit its scope.

Third, although policymakers often introduce markets into a non-competitive public sector, political actors are also constantly reforming and reshaping already existing markets, introducing market reforms into services that already have been reformed along market lines. Prior market reforms create a new "starting point" that shapes the strategies of future policymakers.

Extensive change on the allocation dimension can introduce fragmentation in a uniform system. This new fragmentation opens some options for the Right while requiring the Left to either adjust its preferred market strategy or reintroduce more uniformity through non-market means. Changes in the area of production also shape future reform options. Markets that cede power to producers (Pork Barrel and Private Power) are particularly difficult to change once introduced. These markets delegate power to the private sector. In order to change them, future governments need to build an infrastructure of control, rehire or retrain public sector employees, and overcome opposition from these producers. Such changes are certainly possible, but they can be difficult. By contrast, markets that increase state control (Managed Markets and Austerity Markets) are easier to alter. These markets enhance policymakers' control over the system without creating vested interests (outside the state) in the status quo. Finally, markets that cede power to consumers (Consumer-Controlled and Two Tier) are in an intermediate position. They maintain or increase the state's regulatory capacity, but reducing choice is often electorally unpopular. Parties looking to introduce novel markets into already competitive environments must respond to the existing market structure as well as the program structure.

What about unions and professional associations?

The above focus on party strategies raises the question of what role other actors play – in particular the professionals and other workers who produce public services. As chapter 1 argued, markets almost always take power away from incumbent producers, giving it to the state, users, or new producers. Why would incumbents ever agree to this power shift? How are parties able to get around unions and professionals' associations, particularly in the Continental and Northern European countries where these actors have a significant role in the system?

Political parties must always balance broad electoral aims with their economic and ideological aims. This dual pressure forces continual adjustments in strategies (Kitschelt 1999). Unions and professional organizations, by contrast, have fewer incentives to change in the short-run; they are membership organizations that represent the interests of professionals and workers who often have a deep attachment to the status quo. The empirical chapters show that these groups have rarely put structural reforms on the agenda, generally advocating instead for more resources. Indeed, the status quo bias of professional organizations is often profound. The British Medical Association (BMA), for instance, has opposed all major reforms to the British health service – from its creation as a public health system to its proposed privatization (Klein 2006).

Even as parties put markets on the agenda, they must address the concerns of these groups. Many times, unions and professional associations emerge as the most vociferous opponents of markets, lobbying governments, within parties, and engaging the electorate in protest. These protests have at times been successful: for instance, the Dutch Christian Democrats turned away from the introduction of dramatic competition in the health care system in the early 1990s in response to strong opposition from physicians, insurers and employers (see ch. 4).

In most cases, though, unions and professional associations have not been determinative in shaping the overall character of markets for three reasons. First, chapter 3 and the ensuing case studies show that political parties have become more detached from concentrated interests in the arena of public services – reducing union influence within parties. Although some left-wing parties rely on public-sector workers as a core electoral constituency, in many countries, their links to unions are weaker than in the past. Similar shifts occurred within Christian Democratic parties, who are increasingly detached from non-profit providers in the European Continent. Second, in the face of opposition from these groups, rather than alter or abandon markets, parties have pursued strategies for addressing their concerns. Sometimes, these strategies involve outright confrontation, demonstrated most obviously by the Thatcher government, which simply ignored the interests of the medical professionals and teachers in introducing reforms. More often though, they involve limited concessions that soften or compensate for market reforms, but do not alter their core logic. For instance, recent health care reform in England included major pay increases for physicians, and reformers in the Netherlands exempted some physician services from co-payments in the face of lobbying. These concessions are important, but they have ultimately not been determinative in shaping the logic of markets. Finally, in some cases, policymakers have been able to convince these groups to support change. Decades of austerity budgets, growing bureaucratic control, and markets themselves, have substantially eroded professional power, putting producers in a more defensive position. In this environment, unions and professional associations have at times been willing to accept market reform as a way to gain some additional resources. This situation is most likely where markets promise some benefits to producers or encourage more funding.

The following chapters show that while these groups are important, the core theory, which focuses on the way parties, operating in particular institutional contexts, use markets to achieve their strategic aims, remains central to explaining change.

2.5: CONCLUSION

The above theory hinges on three assertions. First, partisan actors are central to explaining the process of change (in contrast to outside interest groups, bureaucrats, or business pressure). Second, these partisan actors have distinct preferences. Third, these preferences are mediated by the universality and uniformity of the service.

Table 2.2 (see below) contrasts this approach to the others reviewed in this chapter. None of the alternative approaches are "wrong," but each is partial. In contrast to the emphasis on "efficiency" imperatives in the NPM approach or business pressure in the critical approach, the argument advanced here takes diverging elite preferences over reform seriously. While external pressures or functional imperatives may be important in motivating action, they do not alone determine its character, and this book argues that we need to examine a broader set of preferences to understand change. Second, it takes the context of decision making seriously. Unlike the NPM, public choice and critical approaches, which minimize the influence of contextual factors, the argument here builds on institutionalist insights about the impact of existing institutions in shaping the trade-offs actors face. How preferences play out is contingent on the opportunities and costs that particular choices present – "first-best" preferences in an ideal world may not be the "first best" for a particular program.

The theory presented here is, equally, not meant to explain all change towards the market in all places. Three particular limitations are worth highlighting. First, where policymakers introduce reforms under extreme duress – because of short-term time horizons or external pressures – different political logics are likely to be in play. In some cases, policymakers, desperate to enact change in a fiscally constrained environment, engage in reforms that are less strategic than those presented above (for example, see Pollit and Bouchkaert 2004). And yet other times, policymakers have far less autonomy than is presupposed here. Particularly in developing countries, or those reliant on international organizations, policymakers may introduce markets to appease sponsors rather than construct strategic appeals. In both cases, where policymakers lack the time or power to introduce preferred market reforms, partisan politics is less likely to matter.

TABLE 2.2: *Alternative approaches to explaining the political process*

Contrasts different approaches to understanding the political process, markets, and market variation.

	Theory of markets	Preference formation	Strategic calculations	Outcomes
Public choice	Markets limit the state; are beneficial; operate uniformly	Policymakers maximize personal gain	Decision-making environment is more or less conducive to market change	Reflect the power of pro-market external actors
NPM	Markets make the state more efficient; are beneficial; operate uniformly	Policymakers pursue diffuse social benefits	Policymakers are able to pursue "first-best" strategies	Reflect technical needs channeled through economic and social demands
Critical	Markets limit the state; are harmful; operate uniformly	Policymakers respond to business groups; preferences follow these groups	Relative power of business interests determines outcomes	Reflect the goals of business interests
National models	Markets operate in nationally specific ways	Preferences are derived from existing institutional structures	Context strongly determines outcomes	Reflect existing national or programmatic logic
Constrained partisanship	Markets vary in systematic ways	Parties on the Left and Right have distinct preferences	Programmatic structures shape the electoral and ideological costs / benefits to actions	Varying markets reflect partisan strategies

Second, in some policymaking contexts parties are less important than I have argued. In many local governments, for instance, political actors may be non-partisan or the partisan basis of decision-making is less pronounced. In these environments, market reforms are likely to follow a more idiosyncratic path.

Finally, market reforms often appear to diffuse across contexts. This book accepts that ideas about markets, and market reform "fads," may be important proximate causes of reforms. However, in practice, as the following cases show, partisan actors tend to adjust generic ideas about markets to fit their specific aims.

Indeed, in most OECD countries, parties remain the key actors who choose when and how to introduce markets to public services. In so doing, their aims and strategies are far more important than much of the literature on markets, and even the literature on parties, has often allowed for. While not determinative, the way that parties respond to their particular institutional environment is often the key factor behind market reform.

The following chapters develop this argument, turning first to the historical development of markets and the changing nature of the strategic environment and partisan preferences that put markets on the political agenda and second, to the analysis of multiple markets across the health, education, and care sectors.

3

The rise of markets

The previous chapter argued that political parties use markets as tools to reshape welfare structures in ways favorable to their long-run ideological and electoral interests. This claim raises a prior set of questions – why do policymakers use markets in the first place? Why have different political parties, particularly those on the Left, introduced markets? This chapter answers these questions by placing markets within the changing strategic setting for parties in the 1980s.

The rise of the market agenda in social services was by no means obvious. Through much of the post-war period there was broad political consensus that markets were inappropriate in much of the public sector (Lowery 1999). Public involvement in these areas arose because they were prone to market failure, creating uncertainty over the operation of markets. Although some argue that in some contexts citizens demanded neo-liberal policies (Prasad, 2006), when it came to the public services, citizens rarely demanded, and often resisted, markets. Yet, beginning in the 1980s, policymakers began to introduce competition into, and later privatize, public utilities and state-owned enterprises, raising nearly one trillion dollars globally by the late 1990s (Megginson and Netter 2001). Reformers in New Zealand brought this agenda to services like health and education, and by the late 1980s, it had diffused far beyond New Zealand: to the more market-oriented UK, the seemingly inhospitable terrain of Sweden's expansive public service sector, and the historically private, but not competitively managed, Dutch welfare state. Moreover, politicians across the political spectrum used markets, including the Social Democratic and Christian Democratic parties that avoided them through the post-war period.

This chapter examines this puzzling rise of markets, arguing that it emerged as part of a larger partisan response to the changing strategic environment in the 1980s. Policymakers, facing both growing fiscal pressures and constraints on traditional policy instruments – macroeconomic policy and state spending – alongside growing electoral demands to govern services, began to examine the internal structure of the state. In so doing, they questioned professional control over service delivery and turned to administrative reforms. Markets gave politicians powerful tools to challenge incumbent producers, with different types of markets offering parties new ways to achieve their ideological and electoral aims in constrained environments.

However, as chapter 2 argued, this turn to markets did not spell the end of distributive politics; parties used markets differently to achieve distinct goals. The Right, while always drawn to markets, began to advocate them extensively in the face of growing fiscal pressures. Market reforms promised to streamline the size and the scope of services, without the electoral costs of direct cuts. It used particular markets as a first step towards a broader agenda of reducing the welfare state, building public support for further change. The Left, by contrast, initially resisted new markets in services. However, as the Left moved away from their traditional support bases in trade unions and made new appeals to service users, they began to consider markets as a way of making service providers responsive to their goals. This move did not spell Left convergence with Right policy; the Left looked to sustain public support for the welfare state, not encourage its demise. Christian Democratic parties underwent a conversion similar to the Left, but with outcomes similar to the Right. While Christian Democrats had long supported private provision, they also insulated providers from competition. As these parties moved beyond confessional voters to make a mainstream appeal they began to consider markets, following the Right in using them to streamline state responsibility, albeit within limits.

This chapter traces the broad evolution of market reforms by the Left and the Right in three different contexts – the UK, Sweden, and the Netherlands. In each case, we see that underneath a common trend towards using markets to unsettle existing structures of provision, parties did so for different ends.

3.1: THE EMERGENCE OF MARKETS

Although there is considerable debate over how to characterize the "golden era" of the welfare state, in broad terms, post-war political conflicts were steady and limited. Politically, parties on the Left and the Right had secure constituencies (based on class or religious affiliation), competed for voters in the center by developing "catch-all" party structures, and largely accepted the tools of Keynesian demand management.[1] All these features pushed

---

[1] See Lipset and Rokkan's (1967) classic discussion of stable political cleavages; Kircheimer (1966) on catch-all parties; Glyn *et al.* (1990) on economic policy.

towards a stable, circumscribed, policy space. Partisan preferences over the scope of and size of the state varied, leading to important distributive battles over spending, but this conflict occurred within limits.

This conflict among political parties on issues of spending rested on a relatively stable set of cross-party bargains between the state and producers over service production. When reformers first developed public services they often faced heavy resistance from professionals, but by the 1970s, most professionals accepted public involvement in services, through either production or extensive regulation. Equally, most political actors accepted significant professional control at the delivery level. Prior to the extension of public responsibility for services, business organizations, churches, and workers' groups provided many services privately. In countries like Sweden or Britain, political actors had to strike complex bargains with these professionals to secure their acquiescence for a publicly provided system. For instance, in Britain, health reformers allowed physicians control over aspects of remuneration and clinical issues (Tuohy 1999; Klein 2006). In Continental Europe, non-state actors maintained a more direct role in providing services, such as non-profit hospitals and schools.

The economic and political challenges of the post-1970s era both weakened the efficacy of traditional policy instruments – changing the debates over spending – and reopened questions of how to organize service production. Policymakers of all political stripes began to face constraints on traditional policy instruments and new pressures to reform services.

On the one hand, the economic turmoil caused by the oil shocks of the 1970s and the collapse of the Bretton Woods system, combined with the more gradual transition towards "post-industrial" economic structures, brought rising economic volatility, lower productivity growth, and growing unemployment and budget deficits to many economies (Frieden 2006). Most countries initially turned to Keynesian policies to address these problems; yet, the second oil shock in 1979, and continuing problems in the 1980s, appeared to limit the value of such policies in stimulating growth (Scharpf 1991). By the 1980s, scholars advocating NPM and Public Choice approaches (see ch. 2) further linked the structure of the welfare state and labor market regulations to poor economic performance (Lindbeck and Snower 2001). Increasing spending was difficult and many saw it as threatening, not stimulating, the economy.

On the other hand, electoral volatility began to increase, as class, religion, and self-proclaimed party identification became less stable predictors of the vote (Dalton *et al.* 1984). This electoral volatility attenuated parties' links to their traditional support bases, providing them with reasons to become more sensitive to voters. This sensitivity pulled in a different direction to cost pressures, pushing parties to appeal to citizens demanding responsive services (Le Grand and Bartlett 1993; Rothstein 1998; Kumlin

2004). Under pressure to respond to these demands for improving the quality of schooling and health care, cutting or capping spending was electorally risky.

Scholars contest the impact of these shifts on both political parties and governments more generally; however, much research presents them as narrowing the scope of political conflict. Some argue that the combination of global economic integration and the shift to the service sector, in limiting Keynesian policy, has made governments themselves less effective, limiting distinct partisan policy instruments (Moses 1994; Strange 1995). Others argue that existing institutions mobilize actors to oppose change, making new policies politically difficult (Pierson 2001). Even where partisan differences remain, institutions may narrow the scope of conflict in practice (Iversen 2001). These claims suggest that changes in post-industrial economies or institutions have constrained the "supply" of government policy to such an extent that distinct partisan approaches have declined in importance in structuring outcomes.

Others argue that growing economic and electoral pressures have weakened the "demand" for distinctive partisan policies. Analysis of how parties, particularly on the Left, reconcile electoral and economic objectives has a long history (Przeworski and Sprague 1986). Through the post-war period, the challenge for the Left was to develop policies promoting the interests of workers – a numerical minority – with electoral success. Power resource scholars argued that the Left bridged these dual goals by supporting programs dampening the risks associated with the market for broad classes of citizens (Esping-Andersen and Korpi 1984). However, the electoral and economic pressures of the 1980s complicated this strategy. The constraints on traditional economic and welfare policies meant that the Left could offer less to its constituents, who were also shrinking in number, yet moderating and adopting centrist economic positions was likely to open it up to new electoral challenges in multiparty systems (Kitschelt 1999). In response, the Left could move away from economic issues in order to catch new values-based voters (Kitschelt 1999), towards more limited policies adhering to traditional constituents (Rueda 2005), or towards a new, but often amorphously defined, third way that appealed to the middle classes (Giddens 1998). In each case, the Left could no longer connect its distributional and electoral aims through policies that appealed across classes, reducing its distinctiveness.

While this literature pays less attention to the Right, it does suggest limits on the Right's preferred policies. Seemingly, the growing economic pressures and the declining fortunes of the Left opened the door for more conservative policies, with some arguing that the challenges of the 1980s augured a trend towards the dominance of the Right (Przeworski and Wallerstein 1984). Yet, the welfare state hardly declined in importance to voters, making it difficult for the Right to cut programs (Pierson 2001). Indeed, public support for existing social spending has pushed against significant retrenchment (Brooks and Manza 2007). In response, right-wing parties in competitive electoral environments had to limit retrenchment policies or spread the blame for cuts (Kitschelt 2001). Christian Democratic parties encountered even greater challenges. Growing secularization and electoral volatility complicated their distinct economic and religious appeals to bridge social divides (Kalyvas and van Kersbergen 2010; van Kersbergen 2008). Despite the ostensible benefits-changing political conditions provided the Right, this literature suggests that these changes also limited its capacity to combine its distributional and electoral aims.

Both arguments imply that changes emerging from the end of the "golden era" limited the scope for politics. Empirically, these claims are subject to much debate (Allan and Scruggs 2004; Garrett 1998; Korpi and Palme 2003). This chapter does not directly engage these debates about spending; instead, it argues that these growing pressures have created new forms of political activity that often substitute for partisan battles over spending.

The argument is two-fold. First, economic and electoral pressures did not end distributive politics but pushed partisan actors to consider administrative reforms, including markets, as a new terrain for policy. Second, parties maintained distinct preferences in approaching markets, seeing them as powerful tools to challenge existing practices and reshape services in ways favorable to their distinct ideological aims.

To address macroeconomic challenges while making electoral gains, absent substantial spending, policymakers on the Left and the Right began to examine the quality and costs of services. In an era where the public protested long hospital waiting lists and poor-quality schools and where health and education costs were often growing faster than overall price inflation, deferring to professionals over the financing and quality of services was less attractive. Public sector reforms, something that remained squarely under political control, allowed policymakers to encroach on these protected domains and influence the incentives on the ground. Figure 3.1 (see below) shows data from the Comparative Manifestoes Project documenting the rise in mentions of the need to improve governmental efficiency for three different types of party families from the 1940s to 2000 (Budge *et al.* 2001; Klingemann and Volkens 2006). Mentions of governmental efficiency are a crude measure of attention to administration reform, but they nonetheless give a sense of the growing importance of administrative reform. Although Conservative parties focus more on governmental efficiency than Social and Christian Democrats, mentions have more than doubled for all parties.[2]

---

[2] Figure 3.1 shows an estimate of the average mentions of governmental efficiency for a given party group in each year, smoothed using a Lowess procedure.

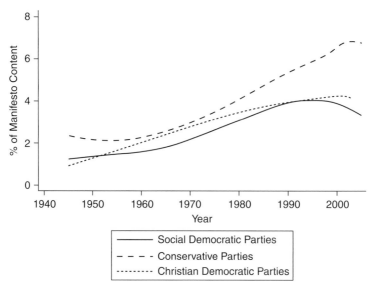

FIGURE 3.1: Mentions of governmental efficiency by party type
Mentions of improving governmental efficiency in political manifestos, for Social
Democratic, Christian Democratic and Conservative parties from 1945 to 2005.

This interest among parties was not just cheap talk, but resulted in
substantial administrative reform. Through the 1980s and 1990s, many
OECD countries decentralized power to subnational governments,
enhanced regulation, and restructured the civil service (Ansell and
Gingrich 2003; Pollit and Bouckaert 2004; Majone 1994). These reforms,
although diverse, all targeted the structure of the state itself. In public
services, they often hit at core areas of professional autonomy – control
over pay, training, and freedom of professional practices (see Friedson
1986 on professionalism).

For instance, in the area of health care, most OECD countries have
changed their hospital payment systems to make hospitals more aware of
financial resources (Gilardi *et al.* 2009) with several also introducing
performance-related payments in primary care (OECD 2010). In 2000,
forty-one of fifty European countries had introduced, or were planning to
introduce, targets on health performance (Wismar *et al.* 2008) and many
have established national and local oversight agencies. These reforms
increase government control over the content of care, often limiting professional autonomy over delivery practices. We see similar shifts in the
education sector. Across Europe, few countries explicitly pay teachers
based on performance, but most have expanded schools' financial

autonomy and responsibility as well as state testing and monitoring of pedagogical activities (Eurydice 2007, 2009). In both sectors, these shifts have substantially changed the position of professionals, users, and the state itself.

However, markets, and the broader public sector reform agenda, were not just a functional response to the pressures on mature welfare states. Instead, they emerged because parties saw them as instruments for reshaping services in distinct ways. Markets directly target the incentives for service users and producers, precisely the parts of state activity that are often hardest to control by central dictate. Yet, in doing so in varying ways, they offered different parties distinct tools to restructure the state in ways favorable to their overall aims.

Market proposals were instantly attractive for the economically liberal Right. While right-wing parties through the "golden age" accepted a relatively substantial role for the state, they maintained a preference for more restricted state responsibility and reduced taxation.[3] Both growing economic difficulties and the Left's electoral problems pushed the Right to develop these ideas through the 1980s. Across Europe, the Right began to more aggressively challenge the foundations of the public sector, first rejecting traditional Keynesian policies and then questioning extensive public financing and provision in the welfare state. Although more radical plans to cut social spending ran into electoral constraints, a number of organizations, most prominently the OECD, advocated market-like reform in the health and education sectors as a way to make services more efficient (OECD 1992; Hirsch 1994). Implicitly, these proposals promised the benefits of markets without the political fall-out of privatization (Lowery 1999). In adopting these proposals, however, the Right saw them as streamlining the state: limiting its benefits and the role of public providers. Markets offered a way to reshape services along these lines without immediately antagonizing the electorate, with the long-term aim being to create new bases of social support for further privatization of financing and service delivery.

The Left, by contrast, approached markets differently. Initially, in the face of rising economic and electoral pressures, most left-wing parties resisted (and many continue to resist) calls from market entrepreneurs. These parties had long aimed to address social inequity and the interests of public employees through both Keynesian policy and a publicly funded and non-competitive service sector (Glyn 2001). Even in Continental Europe,

---

[3] Although the literature on the center-Right parties is less developed than for Social Democrats or far-right parties, studies of manifestos (Budge *et al.* 2001), macroeconomic policy (Hicks and Swank 1992) and the welfare state (Huber and Stephens 2001) show these parties favor less taxation and redistributive spending.

where the Left accepted the involvement of non-state actors in delivering services, it supported state and local control – with little competition – as a way to promote equity and redistribution.

In the 1980s, some left-wing parties began to examine the structure of the state and bargains with producers. These parties often faced serious electoral problems and saw improving health and education services as a way of directly appealing to citizens as public service users (rather than workers). This move opened the door for public sector reform. Initially, many left-wing parties avoided markets, turning instead to decentralization or participatory reforms. However, these reforms signaled a new willingness by the Left to challenge the public sector status quo.

In looking to appeal to the electorate through public services, the Left had to deliver the promised improvements. Facing this pressure, the Left began to consider markets. Particular types of markets offered a way to unsettle incumbents and create incentives for financial or quality improvement. These parties no longer saw markets as threatening to state capacity and equity but as a set of tools that they could use to achieve their broader aims. In improving the existing system or managing costs, the Left hoped to maintain or build a political constituency for the welfare state. This stance involved a new willingness to challenge traditional structures of welfare state entitlement and the professional bargains that supported it, but it was nonetheless born from a distinct desire to improve the long-run viability and legitimacy of the social welfare system (see also Klitgaard 2007a). To use Peter Hall's (1993) language, it constituted a "second order" change for the Left, a radical re-evaluation of the relationship between means and ends, without rejecting the ends themselves.

Christian Democratic parties fell in between these two stances. The Christian Democrats faced pressures that mirrored those of the Left. These parties had long supported extensive public funding of services but also autonomy for private actors to deliver services, building Continental European welfare states around these twin goals (van Kersbergen 1995). Yet, through the 1980s, supporting these welfare structures was increasingly problematic. Many combined passive social benefits with high payroll taxes, exacerbating the problems of unemployment and weak economic growth (Esping-Andersen 1996). At the same time, the growing secularization of European society left Christian Democratic parties searching for new voters (Kalyvas and van Kersbergen 2010). Like parties on the Left, they had to make new electoral appeals at the same time as their preferred policy instruments came under fire. However, unlike the Left, Christian Democrats were far less vested in preserving a cross-class coalition for extensive state spending. These parties had long advocated more individual responsibility, differentiated benefits, and the principle of subsidiarity in delivering services (van Kersbergen 1995). Building on these goals,

Christian Democrats often moved towards more conservative economic and social policies (for example, see van Kersbergen 2008). This shift brought them closer to their right-wing colleagues on economic issues, increasing their willingness to use markets to limit the state.

3.2: MARKETS IN PRACTICE

This section provides evidence for the above claims, by examining market reforms in the UK, the Netherlands and Sweden. In all three countries, the Right put markets on the political agenda following the economic problems of the 1970s, with the Left later turning to markets in quite different ways. Chapters 4 through 6 examine how each party used *particular* markets to achieve its goals in a constrained environment.

The United Kingdom

The Conservative and Labour parties have long dominated the British political scene. Despite disagreeing on a number of fundamental issues, through the post-war era, each supported a limited welfare state and some state intervention in the economy (Beer 1965). This consensus both restricted the size and scope of the state, with the expansion of the British welfare state falling behind other European countries through the 1960s and 1970s, but also insulated it from market forces. The Conservative governments from 1979 to 1997 challenged this consensus, putting market reforms squarely on the agenda. Facing strong electoral constraints on cutting services, they used markets to limit the state in the long run. The subsequent Labour governments (1997 to 2010) continued to use markets; however, they aimed to sustain, not cut, public support for the state.

The Conservative turn to markets
The Conservative party made the first moves towards market-oriented reform to the welfare state as part of a broader shift in its economic and social policy. The Conservative party of the mid-twentieth century drew together free market and pro-business constituents and those with a strong traditionalist bent (Beer 1965). Its support for the mixed economy began to crack during Britain's severe economic recession of the 1970s. Initially, the Conservative government under Edward Heath (1970 to 1974) addressed Britain's deteriorating economy with traditional Keynesian policy and negotiation with the unions. However, Heath's failure to either halt economic decline or appeal to the electorate through these policies, pushed many in the party to consider more radical economic and social policies that directly challenged the post-war model.

In 1974, the Conservatives elected Margaret Thatcher as leader on a neoliberal platform promising to cut public spending, reduce inflation, and support the private market. Although Thatcher targeted social service expenditure as part of her larger critique of the British state, the Conservatives initially remained cautious in advocating direct cuts or market-based reforms to services (Timmins 2001: 391). When elected in 1979, the new Conservative government focused its efforts on the monetary system. The government did reform the social security system (see ch. 6) and public housing sector (so-called council housing), but it followed through on its election promise to spare the NHS from spending cuts and it shelved radical education reforms. After the Conservatives' second victory in 1983, the government emphasized privatization of the public sector (i.e., utilities, telecoms). From 1979 to 1990 the Thatcher government moved nearly fifty percent of public workers to the private sector, raising £27.5 billion in revenue (Richardson 1994). These moves continued to largely exempt public services like health, education, and to a lesser extent, care.

The size and scope of public social services, though, made them too important to ignore. Thatcher and many of her party colleagues were heavily critical of spending on public services, but they were also keenly aware of the electoral limits on reform (Timmins 2001, ch. 17). Citizens strongly backed the core principles of public services. For instance, in 1984, a majority of citizens reported supporting the universal health service, with only twenty percent favoring expanding private medical treatments (Jowell and Airey 1984). This support turned systematic public service reform into a political challenge. Conservative think tanks had been advocating market reforms in health, education and care from the 1970s, but the Cabinet vetoed these early attempts as too politically risky. In 1982, when a report from the Central Policy Review Staff (an internal government think tank) outlining options for radical cuts to the welfare spending, including abolishing the NHS, was leaked, it created much political embarrassment for the government. The Cabinet was forced to publicly reject the proposals, and Thatcher promised that the NHS was "safe" with the Conservatives (Timmins 2001).

Even as the electorate's attachment to services limited the Conservatives' ability to cut spending, it encouraged the party to focus on their structure. Increasingly, the party questioned the power of professionals in central decision-making and service delivery (Evans 2004). Outside of the public sector, the government challenged the unions and critiqued the clubby organization of the professions, for instance, elite lawyers (Brazier *et al.* 1993). The Conservatives' assessment of public service professionals was even more scathing. Thatcher saw the civil service as inefficient and bloated, and argued that the professional practices of university professors, teachers, social workers, and, to a lesser extent doctors, looked to promote a left-wing agenda (Evans 2004).

Following a third electoral victory in 1987, the Conservatives moved these critiques into action, applying a mix of market reforms to education, health care, and care services, as well as to the structure of local government and pensions. These moves did not always cut spending or public employment, but they did begin to reshape services along market lines. The government further introduced the "Next Steps" program, introducing more managerial and market incentives in the civil service (Hood 1990). Thatcher's successor, John Major, extended these reforms (Campbell and Wilson 1995).

Chapters 4 through 6 show that the precise structure of markets varied, depending on the opportunities that the Conservatives encountered. But at the core of this market project was a desire to reduce the size and role of the state. For instance, John Moore, the minister responsible for privatization and later health and social security, stated with respect to industrial privatization:

The overall performance of these [nationalized] industries was characterized by poor – in some cases negative – return on capital, low productivity, high costs, high prices, bad labor relations, inefficient use of resources, and unsatisfactory service to customers ... The nature of state ownership itself was to blame, because state ownership inescapably produces poor performance.

(Moore 1992: 117).

But Moore goes on to state that "widening the ownership of industry is an end as well as a means." Despite the Conservatives' promises to sustain public services, the party's actions suggest that a more substantial reduction in public responsibility was also at the heart of its reform project. Leaked documents from a 1983 Cabinet meeting argue for the desirability of more individual responsibility and private provision in health and education services (van Hatem 1983). These statements, combined with the party's continual degradation of public responsibility, its use of market reforms aimed at reducing public responsibility where electoral risks were low (see ch. 6), and its own statements suggesting that public services were too extensive (Timmins 2001: 317; 371–2), suggest an understanding of markets targeted at reducing the size of the welfare state vis-à-vis the private sector.

However, as Andrew Gamble (1988) argues, the Conservatives also wanted to ensure the state was strong enough to act. In accepting public choice analyses of the state bureaucracy (see ch. 2), the Thatcher government wished to extricate itself from the dominance of incumbent public producers (Evans 2004). Markets that introduced competitive incentives into areas of professional control fundamentally challenged them, both strengthening and limiting the state.

Thus, the Conservatives came to markets in public services as part of a broader response to the seeming failures of earlier welfare state policy. In focusing on the internal organization of the public sector, the Conservatives' reforms, although hardly popular, were less jarring to the electorate than direct cuts. The Conservatives used different forms of markets to achieve both a smaller and stronger state in areas where the electorate would not countenance outright cuts (for example, in health and education) and directly supporting the private sector where it would (elderly care). In reshaping the state along market lines or limiting the scope of public responsibility, markets offered a first step towards creating support for more extensive privatization in the longer run.

Labour's use of markets

Labour's understanding of markets also grew out of the new challenges it faced, but it developed rather differently. Through the 1970s, the limited success of Labour's traditional Keynesian approach to the economy led to disenchantment in the party and growing support for a more radical social-ist agenda (Jones 1996). Although in 1979, Labour elected Michael Foot as leader on the promise of bridging the radical socialist and "right" wings of the party, Foot could not navigate these divisions. In 1981, four MPs from Labour's "right" wing left the party, forming the Social Democratic Party (SDP), leaving Labour to veer further left. This move alienated the party from both its traditional economic base and the rising number of middle-class voters. Party member Gerald Kaufman described the subsequent 1983 Labour manifesto as the "longest suicide note in history," with Labour promising greater nationalization, increased public spending, increased taxation on wealth, a reduction of the working week, and radical changes in foreign and nuclear policy. In response, its support even among the working class dipped to below fifty percent (Evans *et al.* 1999).

After losing the 1983 election, the party moved back to the political center. In so doing, it faced the challenge of addressing Britain's new economic conditions in a way appealing beyond its narrow left-wing base. Initially, Labour did so by adopting a defensive posture vis-à-vis the welfare state, vehemently opposing the Conservatives' market-based reforms in health, education, and care (Jones 1996). This stance won the party support in the area of social services. Before the 1992 election, only 26% of citizens named Labour as stronger on managing the economy, compared with 38% naming the Conservatives, whereas 49% thought Labour was stronger on the NHS and 38% on education, with only 23% and 27% listing the Conservatives in these areas (MORI 2006).

However, this support failed to translate into electoral victory. In response, the party elected Tony Blair as leader in 1994, on the promise of change. Blair needed to convince voters frustrated with the Conservative government, but uncertain about Labour, that the party no longer adhered to its radical past. To do so, Blair continued to reorient the party towards the center of the political spectrum, and emphasized its ability to manage the economy and the welfare state.

In the arena of economic policy, Blair promised to maintain the Conservative party's spending targets for two years, make the Bank of England independent, and borrow only for investment over the business cycle. Blair also limited the party's links to organized labor, lowering the unions' block vote at the annual conference and abolishing Clause IV, which committed the party to nationalizing the means of production, from its constitution (Glyn and Wood 2001). This latter move was primarily symbolic; still, it signaled a shift in how the party was appealing to voters.

When it came to the welfare state, Blair made explicit pitches to citizens as taxpayers and users of public services, not as workers or union members. He pledged not only to do "what works" in public sector reform, but to put public services at the center of Labour's agenda (Blair 1998). Slogans like "Education, Education, Education" in 1997 and "Schools and Hospitals" in 2001 advocated public services as a way to promote economic growth and appeal to the middle classes. Where the Conservatives had approached public services cautiously, Labour emphasized them, promising both fiscal prudence and improved quality (Driver and Martell 2006).

In so doing, Labour too began to examine the structure of the state. In opposition, some in the party argued that the state was increasingly distant from citizens and began to advocate more democratic participation (Driver and Martell 2006). These ideas combined with more concrete questions about public service delivery itself. Increasingly, Labour derided the "postcode" lottery in health care (variation in access to services across the country) and low pedagogical standards in education. While overtly supporting professionals, these critiques targeted their activities, with Labour backing more oversight, standardization and central involvement to make services meet public standards (Powell 1999).

When Labour entered government, it felt it had to rapidly improve services in order to maintain its credibility with the public (Interview: Michael Barber, former senior Labour Political Advisor, 2004). However, its own pledge to limit spending for two years meant it had few resources to accomplish these goals. Initially, the Labour government looked to legislate its way to service improvements, introducing a mix of centrally directed performance strategies and targets, alongside increased inspection and oversight. These moves left the existing markets in health, education and care in place, expanding state control over the work of professionals.

By the end of the 1990s, this centrally directed regulatory approach began to meet its limits, as performance improvement stalled. In response, both Blair and Chancellor of the Exchequer, Gordon Brown, agreed to massively increase public spending. A growing economy and weak Tory opposition relaxed the fiscal and electoral constraints on Labour. Labour announced a planned increase in expenditure of £68 billion from 2000 to 2004, a real increase of 4.5% per annum overall (compared to an average 1.2% from 1997 to 1999) with expenditure on health, education, and transportation rising by 7%, 6.7% and 16% per annum respectively (Driver and Martell 2006).

Far from reducing the party's interest in the structure of the state, this investment further politicized incentives in service delivery. The public was supportive of increased spending; yet its magnitude raised questions. Labour needed to show the funding was producing better services. A senior political advisor to Labour stated that the government's long-term strategy required "short-term results" (Interview: Michael Barber, former senior Labour Political Advisor 2004). Labour saw service improvement as politically important in other ways. Through the 1990s, public dissatisfaction with services encouraged some wealthier citizens to "opt out" of the public system and buy private care and education. As frustration with public services again grew in the late 1990s, these trends resurfaced (see chs. 4 and 5). Like the Left elsewhere, Labour saw maintaining middle-class support for the welfare state as crucial to sustaining both the state's legitimacy and Labour as its guardian.

The pressure to ensure that service providers used the new funding effectively and that it retained middle-class support led the Labour leadership's self-proclaimed pragmatism on markets to give way to open advocacy of them. While many popular accounts emphasize a split between Blair's advocacy of markets and Brown's ambivalence, in practice, both premiers used markets (Driver 2009). Initially this move was limited to contracting in single sites or expanded choice for particular client groups, but Labour subsequently introduced more competition around user choice, increased opportunities for private providers, and introduced market-inspired financial incentives (Department of Health 2004; Department for Education and Skills 2004).

As with the Conservatives, Labour's use of markets was born in part out of a desire to gain control of the services and force producers to adhere to its political goals. However, Blair's market advocacy did not signal his transformation into Thatcher. Rather, Labour saw markets as a way of sustaining public services. Partly, it saw them as proving its fiscal responsibility. More importantly, after years of experimenting with central dictates – with mixed success – markets presented a way to control incentives on the ground, making incumbent producers responsive to the state or users. Markets offered a way of reorienting the welfare state around Labour's goals, sustaining its fiscal and public legitimacy in the long run.

Labour saw the relationship between markets as a means and its ends in a new light. For instance, Blair (2006) argued that:

The reason I am passionate about change in public services, making changes that are difficult and challenging, including learning from business and the voluntary sector, where it is sensible, is because I believe in public services ... I know that if having put in this extra money we can't show clearly and demonstrably that the service has got radically better then the consent from the public for investment is in jeopardy. That is why change is not about attacking public services but saving and inspiring them.

Thus the turn to markets in reforming British social services was, at the broadest level, born from a series of political and economic challenges. However, for the Conservatives, markets were an ideologically preferred but electorally constrained step towards reorganizing the state along market lines. Labour, by contrast, saw them as a way to maintain public support for services, and to legitimate its new spending on them.

Sweden

The left-wing Social Democratic Party (SAP) dominated the Swedish political system from the interwar years, belonging to all governments since 1932 save those from 1976 to 1982, 1991 to 1994, and since 2006. The result was the development of one of the world's most extensive welfare states, including a large publicly funded and provided social service sector. Markets, while promoted in the private economy, were resolutely rejected in the area of social services, with the Swedish public system crowding out private alternatives. Indeed, through the 1970s, public sector employment growth comprised 100% of total employment growth, and by 1980, the public sector employed 30% of all workers and few private hospitals, schools or care providers existed (Wallin 1991). This situation began to change in the 1980s, with a slow but growing use of private provision and some competition in the public sector. As in the UK, the Right made the first move along these lines, but the SAP has also used markets.

Markets and the Swedish Right

Swedish parties historically lined up along a conventional Left–Right spectrum, arrayed from the Left party and SAP on the left to the centrist Center and Liberal parties, and the Moderates on the right. Through the post-war era, though, there was much consensus over an extensive welfare state and public provision. When in 1976, for the first time since 1932, an election resulted in several non-SAP governing coalitions, these governments largely followed the SAP's expansionary Keynesian policy and

64 Making Markets in the Welfare State

actually engaged in more nationalization of major industries than the SAP had through the entire post-war period (Lane 1994).

As in Britain, growing economic and political difficulties in the 1970s both challenged this consensus and politicized public services. During this decade, the labor movement began to make demands fervently at odds with the interests of the Swedish Employers Federation (then SAF). Alongside escalating wage demands, the major trade union federation, LO, advocated worker-owned "wage earners' funds" to purchase shares in companies financed through taxes on private profits (Pontusson and Kuruvilla 1992). While the employers had long accepted extensive state involvement in the economy, they saw these proposals as going too far towards socializing the ownership of the means of production. The SAF responded by proposing an equally fundamental break with the post-war consensus around the welfare state.

The centrality of public services in Sweden, particularly education, made them major targets. The SAF challenged not only the spending on the welfare state, but also its organization, including the size of the public sector and the incentives within it. Through the 1980s, conservative think-tanks such as Timbro, MAS, Ratio, and the SAF's own internal think tank all published documents promoting neoliberal policy and private alternatives in the welfare state (Nilsson 2003: 76–7). One commentator described the SAF's annual congress in 1980 as an "orgy of neoliberalism" (Elmbrant 1993: 62).

The SAF's discontent began to galvanize an ideological shift within the Moderate party. Through the early 1980s, the party promoted the need for a "system shift" in Sweden, away from a public monopoly over welfare programs and towards more room for private entrepreneurship (Blomqvist 2004). This critique met with support among parts of society, but the associated market reforms ran into electoral limits. The Moderates lost votes in 1982 after espousing radical reforms. They gained votes in 1985, particularly among young urban voters, but this rested on a more moderate market promotion (Hancock 1998). Swedish voters were frustrated with aspects of service delivery and attracted to lower taxes but, ultimately, they also supported extensive public involvement in services (Svallfors 1991). In response, the Moderates backed away from their more radical suggestions, promoting "choice" rather than overt privatization (Blomqvist 2004).

While the core of the Moderates' critique targeted the scope of and size of the public sector, it also looked at incentives in the state itself. In particular, the party challenged the efficiency of local government monopolies – by the Counties and municipalities – in health care, care services, and education (Moderata samlingspartiet 1984; Nilsson 2003: 14). The Moderates did not view public sector workers as critically as did the British Conservatives but the party did begin to fundamentally rethink the organization of the state.

The other non-Socialist parties were far less vociferous in their challenge to the Swedish state than the Moderates, but they worked with the party. This cooperation first emerged in several municipal governments, leading to limited, but high-profile, market reforms (Olsson 1993). In 1983, the SAF helped establish a private company, Pysslingen AB, to provide private childcare services (Olsson 1993). The national SAP government limited this move, leading some municipalities to back away from contracting with Pysslingen, but the Moderate-dominated Stockholm suburb of Nacka worked around these restrictions (Mahon 2005). This move constituted a small – but ideologically important – step towards promoting a more diverse public sector.

A series of events in the early 1990s gave the Moderates new opportunities. Sweden's economic fortunes soured, putting questions of welfare reform at the fore. These macroeconomic shifts combined with the election of a national non-Socialist governing coalition of the Moderates, Liberal party, Center party, and the newly formed Christian Democrats in 1991, and non-Socialist governments in 212 of the 289 municipal governments (Montin and Elander 1995).

Nationally, the non-Socialist government put market-oriented reform high on its agenda, reversing the SAP's limits on commercial childcare providers and introducing a privatization commission to promote economic reform (Lane 1994). The government rapidly introduced market forces in the education sector (see ch. 5), and locally right-wing politicians did so in health and elderly care (see chs. 4 and 6). However, these four non-Socialist parties formed a minority government, and within the coalition, the Liberal party, and others, were more supportive of aspects of public provision (Hajighasemi 2004). This diversity limited how far the Moderates could push markets.

Local non-Socialist politicians, particularly in the Stockholm area (where a fifth of the population lives), remained committed to the "system shift" in Sweden. These governments introduced significant market reforms in health, education and elderly care in the late 1990s. In 1998, both Stockholm County and Stockholm City elected Moderate-led coalitions, who promoted an aggressive reform agenda. Stockholm County, led by Ralph Ledel, explicitly flaunted national budget rules in protest of Stockholm's high equalization payments, and privatized a public hospital (see ch. 4). Stockholm City, led by Carl Cederschiöld, introduced a new system of consumer choice in elderly care that allowed users to buy "top ups" from private providers (see ch. 6), greater school selection in upper secondary education (see ch. 5) and considered privatizing public housing. In 2001, the SAP ran its national election campaign against the non-Socialist block on the slogan "Don't let them do to Sweden what they have done to Stockholm," focusing on Stockholm as a site of right-wing

activism (Barnes 2001). In both cases these governments did not dramatically cut spending – even increasing it – but politicized service provision.
In so doing, they followed nearly twenty years of conservative policy
towards the welfare state, using the language of "choice" as a way of
introducing broader market reforms into services.

Both nationally and locally the non-Socialists, particularly the
Moderates, promoted a variety of market reforms with ostensibly
different aims. Within this movement, the Moderates have emphasized
reducing the size of the public sector, lowering taxes, and offering
more private alternatives (Nilsson 2003). These moves were aimed at
creating social support for a "system shift" – even as this language fell
out of Moderate discourse – and more private alternatives. In speaking
of local government, the locus of health education and care services,
the Moderates' 1991 program stated:

> The municipalities have virtually a monopoly and dominate politics in many areas.
> People's lives are therefore being controlled by actions taken by communal politi-
> cians. Our society today has been shaped by the idea of collectivity and that the
> public sector is the most efficient, which has allowed little room for alternatives and
> freedom of choice for the individuals
>
> (quoted in Nilsson 2003: 5).

Markets were a response to this public domination, promising to reduce
the size and scope of the welfare state.

The Left – the SAP's shift towards markets

Despite its rhetoric against markets, the SAP also used them to reshape the
organization of the public sector. Like the Moderates, the SAP began to
consider public sector reforms in the early 1980s. Unlike the Moderates,
this consideration did not emerge from an ideological attraction to markets
but, rather, from a shift in the SAP's calculations about how to promote and
sustain the welfare state – and the party itself.

During the 1970s, Sweden's economic problems combined with new
political problems for the SAP; its core union base was demanding more
radical economic change while being less able to deliver electoral support
(Bergström 1991). Initially, the SAP responded to these challenges by
moving leftwards, expanding Keynesian fiscal policy and building on the
unions' proposals for greater workplace democracy (Blyth 2001). The party
paid the price for this radicalization and in 1976 its share of the vote fell to
its lowest since 1932. The SAP faced a challenging situation. Sweden's
faltering economy and high levels of unemployment limited its macroeconomic flexibility (Benner and Vad 2000). Yet, the party also had to make
new political appeals. Its traditional support from LO was not delivering
electoral victories and middle-class voters were more volatile.

In response, the SAP moved back towards the center. In the 1982 election campaign it watered down its support for the unions in favor of a "third way" that supported private markets and the welfare state (Premfors 1991). On its return to government in 1982, the SAP's first order of business was to pursue an austerity program aimed at reducing public expenditure and restoring Sweden's economic competitiveness. This move included a devaluation of the Krona and significant cuts to public spending (Olsson 1993). The SAP followed through on LO's demands for wage earners' funds, but the program was more modest than LO had hoped for. Moreover, as part of its austerity package, the government intervened with price controls when the unions failed to deliver wage moderation (Benner and Vad 2000). The SAP also began a program of privatizing state-owned enterprises, albeit in a low-profile manner (Lane 1994). Together, these moves demonstrate a step away from the unions.

As the party moved away from LO and towards a broader electoral appeal, it became more interested in making services meet middle-class standards. What began in the 1982 elections as a subtle shift towards emphasizing the welfare state – rather than support for workers – as the party's key priority, emerged more forcefully through the decade. Indeed, the party picked up votes as it emphasized its defense of the welfare state (Bergström 1991).

In staking its appeal on the welfare state, the SAP felt under pressure to deliver. Although it publicly defended the public sector – for instance, moving quickly to introduce legislation limiting private child-care providers in response to the SAF's gambit – the party leadership was increasingly critical of its organization. The party's "left" wing expressed growing concern about the distribution of power in society, arguing that the bureaucratic structure of the welfare state perpetuated these power differentials (Olsson 1993). This group resolutely rejected markets, but claimed that the large central government was alienating citizens and stifling the goals that the welfare state aimed to achieve. At the same time, the minister of finance, Kjell Olof Feldt, and others on the "right" wing of the SAP contended the government needed to improve the fiscal performance and quality of public services or they would lose the support of the middle classes (see Feldt in Heclo and Madsen 1987: 179). Despite their differences, both critiques demonstrated a new willingness in the SAP to question the logic of the existing public organization.

In order to address these concerns, in 1982 the SAP established a new Ministry for Public Administration responsible for building a program of public sector renewal (Pierre 1993). The minister of public administration, Bo Holmberg, faced a difficult task in balancing the three-way demands of party traditionalists, who opposed change, the demands of the "left" for participatory reforms to address the uneven distribution of power in society, and the demands of the "right" for markets to increase efficiency (Premfors 1998). Holmberg initially responded by eschewing both direct privatization of services and the introduction of internal markets but he did begin to rethink the nature of public production. In so doing, he flirted with private sector models for making services more user-friendly, consulting executives from SAS airlines and other companies when designing a range of service charters to distribute to other departments (Pierre 1993). Holmberg also introduced the "Free Commune Experiment," giving a select number of municipalities more organizational control over their activities, setting the stage for substantial decentralization in the 1990s.

This move towards public sector "renewal" ostensibly involved improving the state's relationships with its employees (Gustaffson 1987). Yet, the reforms increasingly brought it into the arena of professional practices, through service charters suggesting professional approaches and greater auditing of financial practices. Even the decentralizing reforms, which seemed to remove the central government from service delivery, showed a new willingness to play with incentives in production.

These early reforms, however, did not do enough to improve the cost-effectiveness or quality of services. Through the 1980s the SAP had largely frozen (or cut) spending on services (Benner and Vad 2000), meaning its promotion of the welfare state to appeal to the middle classes was accompanied by few real resources. By the late 1980s, the SAP began to feel the consequences of this fiscal austerity, with growing queues in hospitals and care entering the public debate (see chs. 4 and 6). While the public was not necessarily receptive to the Moderates, parts of the SAP worried that its discontent could galvanize support for privatization. Indeed, by 1990, net support for increasing private health provision reached nearly forty percent of the electorate, up from only ten percent several years earlier, with support for private production in elderly care and other sectors also growing (Henrekson 2001). These concerns dovetailed with worsening economic performance. Both pressures strengthened the voice of the "right" wing of the party, particularly in the Ministry of Finance, in dictating the logic of public sector reforms (Premfors 1998). Feldt and his colleagues' reform recommendations, including "internal markets" and even for-profit providers in social services, grew in importance, and one of Feldt's colleagues replaced Holmberg in the Ministry of Public Administration. These market advocates argued that the Swedish state was adequately funding services but that it needed to introduce clearer incentives in order to ensure it spent more effectively (Premfors 1998).

This limited acceptance of markets grew in the early 1990s. In 1990, the SAP published its program for the upcoming decade, prioritizing public sector reform and opening the door for some consideration of markets. In emphasizing the importance of public sector renewal, the SAP again challenged parts of the public sector status quo, warning against services that allowed producers to serve their own interests rather than those of users (SAP 1990). Although largely advocating decentralization and non-market reforms to the public sector, the program does consider limited non-public provision in non-essential services and cooperative organization and non-profit delivery (Sainsbury 1993). The SAP turned more substantially towards market reforms in its 1991 budget proposals, where it promoted limited competition within the public sector, contracting with private actors, and user choice in public services (Sveriges Regering 1990).

Like the Moderates, as the public sector grew in political importance the SAP began to question the functionality of traditional public sector management, leading it to markets as a means of reorienting incentives. But the goals behind this reorientation varied dramatically. The SAP maintained its basic commitment to the welfare state. In conducting its early discussions of public sector reform, it did so with the presumption of maintaining welfare state quality (Gustaffson 1987). As it moved towards markets, proponents recast them as limited instruments that it could structure to promote quality and efficiency. Markets were bulwarks against the erosion of the welfare state, not a step towards it. It is worth quoting Feldt at length on this point:

We can meet this challenge [posed by the Right] only if the welfare state is witnessed to be as effective in satisfying people's needs as is the commercial sector of society. If the public sector is not in accord with people's needs and demands and moreover is full of a massive thicket of regulations, then the Right's message of freedom will break through. [. . .] I believe that we can, and should, alter a major part of the public sector, make it more effective, more service oriented, and more accountable, and I believe that input of voluntary cooperation can play a role in this. But I don't think that we can or should alter the fundamentals of the public sector.

(Quoted in Heclo and Madsen 1987)

Feldt's stance towards markets clearly demonstrates a shift in how the SAP understood markets and their role in the public sector, but it remained wedded to the core principles of social solidarity and an extensive welfare state. Markets, in this logic, were a way of addressing the economic and political challenges facing the welfare state, improving its productivity and sustaining its legitimacy (Klitgaard 2007a). They would draw citizens to the welfare state, actually preventing them from turning away from it. Indeed, the party's program and budgets of the early 1990s continually reaffirmed its commitment to extensive and universal public services and the limits to markets (SAP 1990). The party also rejected markets bringing changes on the allocation dimension (through extensive users fees) and those on the production dimensions (full scale privatization) that could undercut the universal welfare state (Sainsbury 1993).

As the economy recovered and problems with different market reforms emerged, the SAP's support for markets cooled. Following its return to office in 1994, it looked to reverse the spending cuts to services introduced during the recession and to enhance quality through regulatory and participatory reforms (Gould 2001; Lundahl 2002b; Whitehead, Gustafsson, and Diderichsen 1997). While the SAP did not directly reverse (with some exceptions) markets, it did not actively promote them in the same way.

As in England, the Swedish Right and Left came to markets differently, and used different markets to achieve their varying political goals, the Left to reorient sagging public support back to the welfare state and the Right to limit such support.

The Netherlands

In contrast to Sweden and Britain, the Dutch welfare state has always relied on a large number of non-profit providers. However, like Sweden and Britain, until the 1980s, there was little competition in public services, with the Dutch government managing them through regulation and corporatist bargaining. Despite this differing starting point, we see a similar trajectory towards markets. The center-Right coalition of the Christian Democrats (CDA) and the Liberals (VVD) put markets on the agenda in the mid-1980s, first reforming welfare transfers and then services. As elsewhere, the Left (PvdA) later used markets but did so differently. When a more ideologically cohesive center-Right CDA–VVD–D'66 coalition (2002 to 2006) emerged, it made significant inroads in introducing markets.

The move to the market on the Right
From the nineteenth century to the mid-twentieth century, the Dutch polity was divided among a number of different loyalties, primarily Catholic, Protestant, and secular liberals and socialists, affiliated to both different political parties and broader civil associations (Andeweg and Irwin 2002). The three Christian Democratic parties were dominant in the post-war political system. These parties built the Dutch welfare state around their preferences for both extensive social benefits and a central role for non-state actors (i.e., the churches and social partners) in delivering services. Historically, these parties eschewed discussions of markets in the public sector. Even in 1980, when they merged to form the Christian Democratic Appeal (CDA), they looked to protect non-profit service providers from competition (Cox 1993). The opposition parties also accepted this system, with the famed Dutch system of "accommodation" promoting support for non-state service delivery (Lijphart 1968). The Dutch Labor party (PvdA) largely looked to enhance equality and social spending within

the parameters of the existing system (Wolinetz 1993; van Praag Jr 1994). Equally, the more market-liberal VVD accepted an extensive state presence (Irwin 1998). Smaller parties sometimes advocated more change, but they generally had a limited governing role.

Dramatic economic decline and high unemployment in the 1970s led policymakers across the spectrum to question the structure of Dutch public services. The discovery of large natural gas reserves in the 1960s pushed up the value of the Dutch guilder, making Dutch manufacturing exports less competitive in the world economy. The Dutch government, responding to new pressures for building the welfare state in the 1960s, spent the increased gas revenues on social programs. When gas prices fell, the government was left with large fiscal commitments and an uncompetitive manufacturing sector, leading to a severe economic decline dubbed the "Dutch disease" (Visser and Hemerijk 1997).

Changes in the electorate coincided with these economic challenges. From the mid-1960s, the Dutch electorate was increasingly volatile and new parties emerged. Prior to 1963, no more than eighteen seats out of 150 in the *Tweede Kamer* had changed parties from one election to the next, with this number growing to thirty seats in the 1967 election and forty seats in the 1971 and 1972 elections (Irwin and van Holsteyn 1989). These shifts hit the Christian Democratic parties hard, as the secularization of Dutch society reduced the number and loyalty of confessional voters. In 1972, the Catholic party's (KVP) support fell from a post-war average of 30% of the vote to only 18%, with the number of practicing Catholics voting KVP falling from 95% in 1956 to 72% in 1968 and to 52% in 1994 (Irwin 1998).

All political parties, but particularly the Christian Democrats, faced the challenge of responding to Dutch economic decline while also competing for voters. Initially, both the PvdA-led Den Uyl (1972 to 1977) and the Christian Democratic Van Agt (1977 to 1982) cabinets responded to these challenges by extending social spending, looking to stimulate the economy and appeal to voters. However, in targeting this expenditure to passive benefits distributed through the social partners, this approach neither improved state capacity nor the economy (Cox 1993).

In response, the newly formed CDA considered a change in approach. Through the 1980s, the CDA began to support both fiscal responsibility and social solidarity as ways to attract non-sectarian voters (Lucardie 2004). Initially, it focused on economic policy, advocating limited spending cuts to social benefits in order to stimulate more individual responsibility. This approach emphasized the necessity of fiscal austerity, not a full-blown critique of the welfare state (Green-Pedersen 2001a). When it came to public services, the CDA continued to support the churches and the non-profit sector in delivering services, and more individual and familial responsibility in financing them (Lucardie and ten Napel 1994; van Kersbergen 1995).

The VVD, on the other hand, confronted these new challenges in ways similar to the Swedish Moderates or British Conservatives. The VVD did not advocate an unequivocal "system shift", but from the early 1980s, it emerged as a powerful voice for restoring Dutch economic health through fiscal restraint (Daalder and Koole 1988). Through the 1980s, it prioritized cuts in spending, putting these at the head of its agenda (see Timmerman's (2003) analysis of coalition formation).

In 1982, a new CDA–VVD coalition government, led by CDA leader Rudd Lubbers, emerged. This coalition professed a "no nonsense" commitment to fiscal austerity, promising to reduce the deficit, target inflation, and restore economic competitiveness (Cox 1993). Because of its centrality to overall spending, the government also looked to cut social spending on pensions and unemployment benefits, as well as to limit public sector wages. Indeed, it froze spending on social security and limited eligibility, which Green-Pedersen (2001a) estimates reduced real benefits by thirty-four percent between 1983 and 1995.

As the CDA and the VVD looked to cut state spending, they began to examine the structure of the state itself. Lubbers II (1986 to 1989) focused its efforts on the disability system, where the number of claimants had doubled between 1975 and 1985 (Visser and Hemerijck 1997). In so doing, evidence emerged that the employers and unions were using the disability system to offload the costs of economic restructuring rather than address the needs of those with disabilities (Cox 1993). Because the sickness and disability systems were managed and funded collectively, but benefited individual firms and employees, both groups had the opportunity and the incentives to use the system for reasons other than medical necessity (Visser and Hemerijck 1997). Increasingly, the government saw the problems in the disability system as lying in the structure of management. Lubbers II looked to solve this "crisis in governance" by targeting both the level of funding and its corporatist organization (Visser and Hemerijck 1997).

Within this examination of public spending, the Lubbers government began to consider market reforms. Lubbers I asked the Ministry of Finance to establish an inter-departmental commission to prepare proposals on privatization (de Vries and Yesikagit 1999). The consequent reforms were not politically salient and limited to the small state-owned industrial sector (de Vries and Yesilkagit 1999; Andeweg 1988). However, the Lubbers II government (1986 to 1989) increased the prominence of public sector reform, stating its intention to consider privatization for all services that did not need to be provided by the government (Van Damme 2004).

Lubbers II further considered proposals for de-bureaucratization, greater competition, for-profit alternatives, and individual fees in health and elderly care, and to a lesser extent education (chs. 4 through 6).

Both the disability reforms and this broader examination of state activity demonstrate an important shift in the CDA's position. The CDA's long-standing ties to non-state actors had long led it to protect the autonomy of the corporatist system. However, as the immediate economic crisis of the early 1980s lifted, the CDA, still seeking a new political identity in a more competitive electoral environment, began to loosen its ties with non-state actors. Although this move was initially highly limited, and much of the critique of corporatism emerged outside the CDA, in 1992 the leader of the CDA's parliamentary faction, Elco Brinkman, forcefully challenged efficacy of the Dutch corporatist model (Hendriks 2001). These criticisms, something largely unheard of in the CDA before the late 1980s, demonstrate a move that parallels those of the British or Swedish Left. As religious voters were less able to secure electoral victory, in the mid-1980s the CDA began to attract non-religious voters (Lucardie and Ten Napel 1994). It did so by emphasizing its skill at economic management alongside its support for social programs. In so doing, the CDA began to examine the internal structure of the state, including services, as a way to make new appeals, opening the door for a discussion of greater competition in public services.

Despite these shifts, the CDA still split with the VVD on the way to structure competition. It continued to worry about the effects of competition on its constituents in the private sector and lower-income individuals. This split, combined with the prioritization of fiscal austerity measures and reforms to the disability system, limited market reforms in services. Most proposals did not make it past high-level political discussions and those that did made little headway in the legislative process. Indeed, the VVD, despite supporting markets in principle, opposed certain market reforms favored by the CDA, out of concern that they could increase expenditure (chs. 4 and 6).

New elections in 1989 further limited changes. The PvdA replaced the VVD as the CDA's governing partner, again under Lubbers' leadership, creating a coalition less ideologically committed to markets. The new minister of finance, PvdA leader Wim Kok, moved away from advocating economic privatization (Van Damme 2004). Disagreements between the CDA and PvdA over how to introduce markets led Lubbers III to water down reform plans in social services. Moreover, the reform of the disability system absorbed much of its effort. Changes making benefit levels contingent on the overall level of economic activity and tightening eligibility were extremely unpopular, with over one million people protesting in Amsterdam. Ultimately, support for the PvdA and CDA fell in the 1994 election, from 31.9% to 24% and 35.3% to 22.2% respectively (Visser and Hemerijck 1997).

This experience initially chastened Wim Kok's "Purple" coalition (PvdA, VVD, D'66), elected in 1994, and it moved controversial market reforms in social services off the agenda. However, by the mid-1990s, key VVD politicians within the Kok government re-emerged as active proponents of privatization and reduced spending (Van Damme 2004). The VVD had moderated its market advocacy to join the PvdA and D'66 under Kok, but both the PvdA's own ideological moderation and the improving Dutch fiscal climate emboldened the VVD. The VVD-controlled Ministry of Finance pushed for market reforms in the public sector, and met with some success. Van Damme (2004) argues that the Kok government through this period promoted a naïve view of markets that equated competition with fewer rules.

Behind this enthusiasm about markets lay a particular set of strategic aims. The VVD saw more competition and private delivery and financing as a way to limit the welfare state – and produce lower taxes – in the long run. The VVD had long advocated separating redistributive policy from health and elderly care policy, and allowing more differentiation in the education system. Markets promoted these longer-run goals, reshaping how citizens would relate to the state:

One thing is clear. This [improvement in services] cannot be done through the State's budget mechanism. Which is why market forces and competition – and in turn consumer choice on the part of citizens as customers for these services – must be allowed free play in these areas. The state's job is to establish rules and minimum requirements, but not to determine through its budget mechanism the extent to which transport, education, care services and house construction are available to users above a basic minimum. It is the budgets of the users themselves that must determine this.

(VVD 2006)

The period from 1994 to 2002 was the first time in seventy-six years that the CDA was in opposition, prompting much internal re-evaluation (van Kersbergen 2008). Through this period, the CDA began to emphasize a socially (rather than economically) conservative agenda, reinvigorating a discussion of Christian values and community promotion (van Kersbergen 2008). Although the Dutch economic "miracle" of the late-1990s rekindled enthusiasm in the corporatist "polder" model, the CDA continued to revise its traditional support for the non-profit sector and corporatist management. Its traditional allies in societal organizations had become more distant, partly because they distanced themselves from the CDA as they sought to appeal to the Purple coalition, but also because the CDA saw them as less able to deliver it votes (Lucardie 2004). In the early 2000s, the short-lived success of the Pim Fortuyn movement, which critiqued, among other things, the clubby nature of Dutch corporatism and the poor quality of health and education services, raised further questions within the CDA about the existing system.

In questioning the Dutch state, the CDA looked to maintain a more basic welfare offer than the VVD but was more open to cuts than the PvdA. The CDA saw markets as a way of reshaping the state to be more effective and more limited. Unlike the VVD, the CDA advocated limits on the market, advocating a separate sphere for civil society (Lucardie 2004). Indeed, the CDA used more limited market advocacy to stake out space as the voice of fiscal *and* social responsibility. However, in considering markets, it moved closer to the VVD, allowing the two parties to compromise.

When the CDA and VVD re-emerged as coalition partners under Jan Peter Balkenende (2002 to 2006), this ideological overlap allowed the Dutch government to agree on the desirability of particular markets, expanding both private providers and individual responsibility. The result was the dramatic market-oriented reform in the health care system in 2006, alongside substantial reforms to elderly care, and, to a lesser extent, education. Unlike the Christian Democrats of the 1960s, 1970s or even the 1980s, under Balkenende the CDA was willing to push through these reforms over the heads of doctors and care providers' protests (see chs. 4 and 6).

The Dutch Right then, came to markets more slowly than the Swedish or British Right. The VVD initially supported markets as a form of cost-cutting, and it was willing to jettison plans for markets when they collided with cost-cutting initiatives. As Dutch fiscal conditions improved, and pressures for spending on services grew, the VVD engaged in more thorough-going market advocacy. Here, it saw markets as a way to limit the state and align the interests of the public with a more limited public offer. By contrast, the CDA's reorientation was more gradual and subtle. The party had built the Dutch welfare state, and was vested in its structure. However, as Dutch fiscal problems coincided with growing electoral problems, the CDA began to question the status quo. In response, it moved towards a more conventional center-Right position, looking to limit, but not eliminate, social programs and sustain private alternatives. This stance allowed it to appeal to secular voters concerned about the Dutch economy but not willing to countenance massive cuts. When the two parties rejoined government together in the early 2000s, these similarities allowed particular types of market reforms.

Markets on the left
The PvdA came to markets later and differently than either the CDA or the VVD. Initially, like the SAP and Labour, the PvdA moved leftwards in

response to new economic problems and electoral volatility. In the late 1960s and early 1970s, a radical "New Left" constituency gained control of the party, following an explicit policy of polarization with the Christian Democratic parties (Wolinetz 1993; van Praag Jr. 1994). This confrontational stance won the PvdA votes, but excluded it from government (Green-Pedersen 2001b).

In 1986, the party elected the moderate former trade union leader Wim Kok as leader on the promise of more centrist policy. The party also reformed its internal governance structure, reducing the power of the more radical rank and file. These changes allowed Kok to move the party towards accepting reforms to the Dutch economy and welfare state (van Praag Jr. 1994). Unlike the SAP and Labour, it was less vote-seeking than office-seeking that motivated the PvdA's initial moderation (Green-Pedersen 2001b). In order to exert influence on the policy process, the PvdA needed to compromise with the CDA, and in its manifesto it stated its willingness to govern with the CDA and reform the welfare state (van Praag Jr. 1994).

However, it was not just the need to compromise that pushed the PvdA to re-evaluate aspects of the welfare state. Traditionally, the PvdA had defended the municipalities and local public service providers but, through the 1970s, it also supported extensive central regulation of services as a way to promote access and uniform quality. This stance, when combined with the CDA's support for non-profit providers, contributed to an increasingly bureaucratic state and strong non-state providers (Cox 1993). As evidence of ongoing inequities in the health care system (see ch. 4) and the problems in the disability system emerged, the PvdA began to question the functionality of both this bureaucratization and corporatism.

Thus the combination of office-seeking, financial pressures on the welfare state, and growing concerns over its effectiveness, led the PvdA to consider reforms aimed at restructuring services. The PvdA did not lead the charge towards markets, but it was willing to negotiate with the CDA under Lubbers on market reforms to the disability system and some services. This move cost the party dearly. The PvdA had begun moving away from its base in the unions through the late 1980s but the unpopular disability reforms further alienated these supporters.

Seeking new voters and governing credibility the party began an internal discussion – and conflict – over its direction. Most obviously, this move involved ideological moderation as Kok steered the party towards the center. Yet, the PvdA also sought to increase its appeal to the middle class in other ways, a difficult balancing act in a system with constant competition from the Left (the Socialist party) and the center (from D'66 and the CDA). Initially, the party focused on labor market reform. Its rallying cry through the 1990s was "Jobs, Jobs, Jobs," shifting from promoting redistribution of income to redistribution of work (Seeleib-Kaiser *et al.* 2005). This stance contributed to the famous Dutch "flexicurity model," which paired better benefits for part-time and atypical workers with more labor market flexibility (Visser and Hemerijck 1997). However, in promoting both more flexibility and higher rates of employment, the PvdA further examined welfare state transfers and services, which were largely funded through payroll taxes and linked to job creation.

This move by the PvdA, combined with the VVD's stance, and the absence of the CDA – traditional defenders of the corporatist system – from government, encouraged the Kok governments to consider public service reform. The Kok I government committed itself to restoring the "primacy of politics" – effective political and economic decision-making – by reducing the role of advisory committees (and thus the corporatist partners) in service delivery (Hendriks 2001). This move affected the management of health and care services, eliminating a number of advisory boards. Most dramatically, Kok I "privatized" the management of the disability and sickness systems, moving it to an independent board using an actuarial, rather than social, insurance model (Visser and Hemerijck 1997). It also introduced a project to improve Dutch microeconomic performance by stimulating competition, deregulation, legislative quality, and applying European Union Competition Law (Van Damme 2004). This project first targeted the business sector, but after 1998, Kok II (1998 to 2002) extended it to parts of the public sector (i.e., water and rail).

In enacting public sector reforms, the PvdA began to consider market reforms as a way of creating incentives for quality and cost control (PvdA 1998). By the early 2000s, the Dutch government had subjected services like health and elderly care to nearly two decades of austerity budgets, and public concerns about the quality and timeliness of these services – not just their costs – had become a mass electoral issue. Workers in these sectors were also making demands; in 1998, both secondary school teachers and hospital workers conducted high-profile strikes.

Yet the PvdA turned to markets differently than the VVD and the CDA. Unlike these parties, the PvdA was not looking to reduce the size of the state or reorient social support towards the private sector. Rather, its support for income redistribution and its long-standing advocacy of the municipal sector meant that it saw improving public services as key to its political appeals. Sustaining public services on equitable terms, not reducing them, was central. Echoing Labour and the SAP, the PvdA presented markets as a way to maintain the public legitimacy of the welfare state, but also as having limits.

Public services should excel in accessibility, quality and reciprocity. Government is responsible for this; it is a matter of principle. Who supplies these services is not a matter of principle. If the market can do it better, the market should supply public services. If government can do it better, government should do so ... Public services should be of high quality and appeal to everyone. Only then are taxpayers prepared to pay for them. A society that invests in its citizens can count on reciprocity.

(Partij van de Arbeid 2005)

The PvdA had never been as invested in public ownership as many other left-wing parties (van Praag Jr. 1994) but, in moving away from defending the public sector and towards markets, the PvdA was engaging in new political appeals. However, markets were a way of sustaining public services, not cutting them. In practice, this meant that the PvdA was far less willing than the CDA or VVD to expand private financing and more favorable to building up state capacity.

These differences made cross-party negotiations difficult, and chapters 4 through 6 show that it was disagreements among the CDA, VVD and PvdA over what type of market to introduce, not whether to introduce them, that limited reforms. Even when the PvdA returned as a coalition partner with the CDA in 2007, its willingness to compromise on market reforms only extended so far. More recently, in the face of discontent from its base over market reforms, and tightening competition from the left, the PvdA has turned away from markets (Volkskrant 2010).

The evolution of markets in the Netherlands fits the same general pattern as in Britain and Sweden. Growing economic and political challenges put public sector reform on the agenda, and policymakers, seeking to address both cost and quality, turned to markets. Despite the consensual Dutch political system and its market-oriented starting point, disagreements among the CDA, VVD, and PvdA over the shape of markets long restricted change.

Conclusion

This chapter charted the rise of markets in public services in the UK, Sweden, and the Netherlands, embedding these shifts in the particular challenges the political parties faced through the 1980s and 1990s. The goal of the chapter has been to demonstrate that significant challenges for both the Left and the Right made them turn to public service reform. Yet in so doing, political parties maintained distinct stances towards markets. The ensuing chapters extend this analysis to specific areas of market creation – health, education, and elderly care – showing that these distinct partisan stances have translated into different market structures.

4

Health care markets

The debate over the role of markets in public services rages most fiercely in the health sector. Health services affect people at all points in their life, are provided by professionals with strong organized interests, and have experienced faster growth than almost all other economic sectors. Consequently, citizens using the health care sector, the large and growing health care workforce, and taxpayers who foot the bill for public expenditure, all have a major stake in health care reform. The question of what markets offer to patients, workers, and taxpayers, takes on a particular urgency, as health services can be literally a "life or death" matter.

This chapter shows that despite using a common language of markets, left- and right-wing parties have built qualitatively different markets. In England and the Netherlands, conservative reformers increased private responsibility for financing somewhat, while more dramatically expanding competition through clearly developed contracting. These Austerity Markets increased the power of the state and insurers as purchasers of services, while undercutting doctors and offering little to patients. By contrast, in recent years, Britain's Labour party modified the English health care market, increasing public financing and competition around individual choice. These reforms built on the early experience of Swedish health care reform, where policymakers on the Left also introduced competition among hospitals for patients. These Consumer-Controlled markets had dramatically different outcomes than the Austerity Markets – reorienting care around patients and reducing waiting times, albeit at the expense of financial control by the state. Finally, more recent markets introduced by the Swedish Right ceded control to private providers. In contrast to the Dutch or early English reforms, which emphasized cost efficiency and state control, these Pork Barrel markets gave funding to private actors without increasing state power.

This chapter first presents a brief review of markets in the health care field and then, for each country, looks at how market reforms produced different competitive structures and moves on to explain the political logic behind these changes.

4.1: THE DEBATE OVER MARKETS

Debates over markets in health care are highly polarized. Proponents of markets point to long queues, dirty hospital wards, and foregone medical testing in publicly funded health care systems, arguing that state involvement in health care is cutting short the lives of patients (Gratzer 1999). Public financing insulates individuals from the real costs of care while public production creates inefficiencies, waste, and limits on physicians' freedom that ultimately harm patients (Goodman *et al.* 2004). Opponents are equally grandiose in their claims, arguing that markets elevate profits above patients. Markets undercut the state, and the problems of unequal access and cost-inflation in the United States should serve as a warning that markets create both inequities and inefficiencies (Pollock 2004). Behind these arguments lies a curiously similar assessment of what markets in health do. Markets limit the state's presence in health financing and production, placing costs on patients and allowing doctors and hospitals to respond to incentives. However, while there have been substantial market reforms in health services across advanced industrial countries, their impact on the state has been far from uniform.

In terms of spending on health care, many countries have explicitly increased private financing of health care services: raising fees and co-payments, co-insurance rates, removing care from the public package and encouraging private insurance through tax breaks.[1] Table 4.1 (see below) demonstrates that in about half of the advanced industrial democracies for which cross-time data is available, there has been a shift towards more private expenditure as a percentage of total health expenditure (which includes some long-term care expenditure). However, not only is this movement towards private spending not universal, but there are complex configurations within countries. Nearly all OECD countries have increased total public spending in the past decades, with stable or expanding rates of public coverage (OECD 2008b). Moreover, many countries have explicitly extended public benefits in one area, while cutting in others. For instance, Japan both increased citizens' co-insurance rates and added

---

[1] Japan (2003) and Belgium (1993) both raised the co-insurance rates (the percentage of the cost the patient pays) for physician visits; Italy (1982), Portugal (1990) Finland (1993), Spain (1993), and Austria (1997) introduced fees for office visits or pharmaceuticals; the UK (through the 1980s), Austria (1996), Spain (1993), and Germany (1997) removed benefits from the public package; and Italy (1999), Australia (2000), and Denmark (2007) all promoted private health insurance through tax incentives.

TABLE 4.1: *Private expenditure as a percentage of total health expenditure*

The percentage of total health care expenditure that comes from private sources.

	1980	1990	2000	2006
Australia	37.4	33.8	33.0	32.3
Austria	31.2	27.2	24.2	23.8
Canada	24.4	25.5	29.6	29.6
Denmark	12.2	17.3	17.6	15.9
Finland	21.0	19.1	26.6	24.0
France	19.9	23.4	20.6	20.3
Germany	21.3	23.8	20.3	23.1
Italy	N/A	20.5	27.5	22.8
Japan	28.7	22.4	18.7	18.7
Netherlands	30.7	32.9	36.9	37.5[*]
New Zealand	12.0	17.6	22.0	21.7[*]
Norway	14.9	17.2	17.5	16.4
Spain	20.1	21.3	28.4	28.8
Sweden	7.5	10.1	15.1	18.3
Switzerland	N/A	47.6	44.4	39.7
UK	10.6	16.4	19.1	12.7
United States	58.8	60.6	56.3	54.2

*Netherlands is from 2005, NZ from 2003 (Source: OECD 2008b)

new long-term care benefits (with similar patterns in Germany and the United States and to a lesser extent Belgium and the Netherlands). Countries have also followed different patterns over time, with Germany, New Zealand, and Italy increasing and then later eliminating or decreasing charges, while the cases below demonstrate that the UK, Sweden, and the Netherlands all experienced tight budgeting, some cost-sharing, and cuts in the early 1990s, and invested public funds in health in the 2000s. Despite the aggregate trend towards private spending, the state is still very much present in health care financing.

In the area of production, OECD countries have also engaged in a slew of market reforms, both expanding private production and introducing competition among public and private actors. A number of countries with historically public provision have allowed new non-public providers into the system.[2] Moreover, the UK (2000s), Sweden (1989 to 1991),

[2] Data on private care varies across countries. In Australia, from 1992 to 2005, the number of private day facilities grew from 72 to 256 (Australian Bureau of Statistics 2007, 1994). Private care in New Zealand grew from 31% to 38% of care spending through the 1990s

Norway (1997 to 1999), Denmark (1993, 2002 to 2007), Italy (1978, 1992), and Spain (1993, 1996) all introduced reforms expanding financial incentives around patient choice, and many of these same countries, as well as the Australian states (1990s) and New Zealand (1993) also introduced "internal markets," where hospitals and doctors compete for contracts with public purchasers (OECD 2010). Other countries, with historically private non-profit provision, have also moved to promoting competition among providers. For instance, Germany (1996, 2006), the Netherlands (1990, 2006), Switzerland (1994), and to a lesser extent Belgium (1993 to 1995) all gave social insurers, the health purchasers, more autonomy and financial responsibility. Nearly all OECD countries have reformed the way they pay hospitals to make their funding more dependent on actual activity levels, sometimes with the explicit aim of creating competition among both private and public hospitals for resources (Kimberly and de Pouvourville 1993; Gilardi *et al.* 2009).

The outcomes of these changes have neither matched the claims of market proponents or detractors nor led to a straightforward erosion of state capacity. Market reforms sometimes increased and other times decreased costs; sometimes improved attention to patients and other times left them out (Freeman 1998; Ranade 1998; Freeman and Moran 2000; Docteur and Oxley 2003). Moreover, markets have not uniformly limited the state. Most OECD countries have introduced reforms that have strengthened state control over budgets, hospital and physician payment, and quality and performance regulation (Saltman *et al.* 2002; Figueras *et al.* 2005; Saltman and Figueras 1997). Indeed, in many cases, policymakers have linked reforms giving the state a stronger role in measuring quality, monitoring providers, and setting standards as a prerequisite for competition. For instance, in 2006, Germany both centralized the federal government's control over health care expenditure and introduced more competition. Broadly, there has not been a single movement towards or away from either the market or the state.

These mixed outcomes become less puzzling in light of the typology developed in chapter 1. This typology suggests that different market structures represent systematically varied strategies for reshaping health care. First, differences emerge along the allocation dimension. Many health economists argue that health insurance can create problems of "moral hazard," where patients have incentives to over-consume health

---

(French *et al.* 2001). Recent reforms in Denmark expanded the volume of private provision; in 2008 it was 71.7% higher than in 2007 (Vrangbæk 2008). In Finland, the number of private outpatient visits per 1,000 inhabitants grew from 2,561 to 3,235 between 1996 and 2005, with a flat rate of growth in the public sector (National Institute for Health and Welfare 2007). Some Spanish and Italian regions also expanded private contracting (France and Taroni 2005; Cabiedes and Guillén 2001).

care once they have insurance (Pauly 1974). Reforms to *financing* that place direct costs on individuals or loosen *regulations* on insurers, allowing them to select based on risk, target these incentives by making patients more sensitive to prices and risks. Conversely, critics point out that being under-insured or facing high costs can lead some groups to consume too little health care, producing further inequities (Nyman 2003). Thus whether market reforms occur alongside strong guarantees of public financing and regulation (Managed Markets, Consumer-Controlled, Pork Barrel markets) or increased costs and risks for individuals (Austerity Markets, Two Tier, and Private Power markets) produces differing incentives over individual consumption and the overall allocation of health.

Second, in the area of production, health policy scholars debate the value of different *logics of competition*. Some advocate strengthening health purchasers and giving more weight to their financial concerns, claiming this will force physicians to integrate clinical and financial management and improve efficiency (Enthoven 1978; Ellis and McGuire 1993). Others advocate more patient choice, arguing that competition for patients will improve quality (Saltman and von Otter 1987). However, those examining providers suggest that because health is such a complex good, it is difficult to construct perfect contracts (Eggleston and Zeckhauser 2002). For either of the above reforms to change the way doctors and hospitals act, there must be a logic *of control* in place that gives purchasers or patients the ability to enforce competition. Absent this oversight, newly empowered providers have incentives to follow their own preferences, rather than those of either the purchaser or the patient.

Markets in health then, vary substantially. Markets that give purchasers much latitude to contract (Managed Markets and Austerity Markets) will create competition to satisfy cost-conscious purchasers rather than quality-conscious patients. Where hospitals and doctors compete for relatively cost-insensitive patients (Consumer-Controlled and Two Tiered markets) they will focus on quality over cost. Finally, where producers retain much control (Pork Barrel and Private Power markets) they face fewer constraints on innovation, but also much space to follow their own interests. There is no single health care market, and the effect of marketization on the state can take multiple directions.

The politics of multiple markets

Why do markets emerge in health care? Why do policymakers choose different markets? Historically, the move towards markets grew out of common pressures on mature health care systems. Across the OECD, costs have gone up dramatically since the 1970s, straining public budgets (OECD 2008b). These cost concerns have dovetailed with growing demands among citizens for high-quality, timely, services. In many health care systems, long waiting lists have emerged as a key political issue. Figure 4.1 (see below) demonstrates the average waiting time for cataract surgery, a common surgical procedure, in eight countries deemed to have waiting problems. Here we see patients waiting months for surgery, in contrast to the United States and much of Continental Europe, where waiting times for surgery are close to zero (Siciliani and Hurst 2004).

Where waiting lists are less of a problem policymakers often face intense cost pressure; indeed, the absence of queues often signals over-capacity (too many doctors and hospitals) (Siciliani and Hurst 2004). These growing costs and other concerns about the future of the health care system have galvanized public dissatisfaction. Table 4.2 (see below) shows that across countries with considerable diversity in expenditure and waiting times, large numbers of patients are dissatisfied with the care system.

Thus, policymakers across the OECD and across the political spectrum have faced intense pressure to address both rising costs and the demands made by the public and the media over everything from waiting times to the prevalence of hospital-born infections. Under stress to avoid massive tax hikes without alienating the public, these politicians saw deferring to the doctors on the question of how much care to provide, what drugs to prescribe, and how quickly to provide care as problematic. Markets, in changing the incentives for providers, offered a solution.

These pressures did not, however, eliminate political differences. Instead, they posed both different opportunities and challenges for

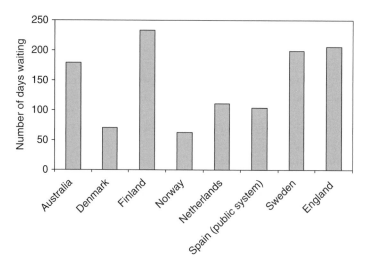

FIGURE 4.1: Waiting time for cataract surgery in 2000
The average number of days patients spent waiting for cataract surgery across eight countries.

TABLE 4.2: *Citizens' views on the health care systems in 2007*[3]

Citizens' attitudes towards the need for systematic health system reform across health systems with different levels of total spending and waiting-list problems.

			Percent reporting		
	% of GDP devoted to health	Waiting times a problem for surgery	Only minor changes needed	Fundamental changes needed	Rebuild completely
AUS	8.7	Y	24	55	18
CAN	10.0	Y	26	60	12
GER	10.6	N	20	51	27
NETH	9.5	Y	42	49	9
NZ	8.0	Y	26	56	17
UK	8.4	Y	26	57	15
US	15.3	N	16	48	34

political parties. The Right saw the mounting pressures in the health care system as an opening to introduce more substantial reform. While the European Right has rarely advocated a full move towards a market system, maintaining a skeptical stance towards "American medicine," many right-wing parties have long criticized extensive state involvement in public health care systems. As growth in the health care sector promised to both increase public expenditure and public involvement in the economy, the Right began to advocate reforms aimed at lowering taxes and shifting care out of the public or exclusively non-profit sector (see ch. 7 for more discussion of Right health policy).

The Right, then, has supported markets that allow more private financing or more private actors. However, many European health care systems, particularly those operating as national health care systems (i.e., public financing and provision) are relatively uniform. These systems have experienced the most intense waiting list pressures, providing an audience for the Right's proposals, but they are also difficult for the Right to reform. Addressing waiting lists through choice-based markets (Two Tier or Consumer-Controlled) is likely to be popular, but risks encouraging

---

[3] The data on health expenditure is for 2006, except for the Netherlands (2004) and New Zealand (2003) (OECD 2008b). The waiting-list assessments come from Siciliani and Hurst (2004). Survey responses are from the Commonwealth Fund *International Health Policy Survey* (2007).

more public activity and expenditure, and sustaining public support for the status quo. Here, more constrained right-wing parties have turned to Austerity Markets, to give the state more control over costs.

The Left's goals and subsequent trade-offs look different. Left-wing parties have traditionally supported the development of public health care systems and put a high priority on guaranteeing access to health care based on need. However, the pressures created by long waiting and rising costs hit the Left hard, as wealthy citizens unwilling to wait months or even years for operations began to opt into the private sector. Moreover, in some countries, reforms of the disability systems put more costs on employers for their employees' illnesses, giving them incentives to purchase private insurance or care (for example, see Brouwer and Hermans 1999).

As the Left found it difficult to maintain (or improve) equal access through the status quo, it was drawn to markets that expanded choice without placing large direct costs on individuals (Consumer-Controlled markets) as a way of forcing doctors to speed up and cater to publicly funded patients. In the universal and uniform health care systems of much of Northern and Southern Europe, these markets promised to tie large groups of individuals to the public system, rather than enabling them to opt out. However, where the existing system was more fragmented across social groups, as in much of Continental Europe, choice threatened to exacerbate existing divisions, and the Left was drawn to contracting (Managed Markets) as a way of enhancing state power over costs and access in the system.

The following sections provide evidence for these claims, looking at the experience of England, Sweden, and the Netherlands.

4.2: ENGLAND – FROM AUSTERITY TO CHOICE

The British National Health Service (NHS) is often taken as the archetype of a public health care system – since the government finances and provides most care.[4] Despite some reforms to the NHS in the mid-1970s, its structure in the mid-1980s had not substantially changed since its founding in 1948. Over eighty-five percent of expenditure was publicly financed, most hospitals were publicly owned, and general practitioners (GPs) largely worked for the NHS. Technically, the organization of the NHS was highly centralized, but in practice, regional units were responsible for day-to-day operations and professionals maintained a high degree of clinical, financial and managerial autonomy. Alongside this public sector, a small parallel private sector existed, staffed in large part by the same

---

[4] There are long-standing differences in health policy in England, Scotland, Wales, and Northern Ireland, which devolution in 1999 enhanced. The Scottish and Welsh regional assemblies have largely eschewed market-oriented reforms (Greer 2004).

physicians who worked in the NHS. Thus the NHS in 1980 was a universal and uniform health care system, but one with strong local centers of control and competition from the private sector.

From 1989 to 2005 the NHS underwent a double transformation, with the internal market reforms of the Thatcher government moving towards an Austerity Market (individual responsibility, state contracting), before Labour's introduction of a Consumer-Controlled market (collective responsibility, individual choice). In both cases, the Conservative and Labour parties have claimed to support patient "choice" and appeared to be using a common language of markets, but they constructed radically different markets following their distinct goals.

Towards an Austerity Market

The first move towards a market in health occurred in 1989, when the Conservative government published its blueprint for a "quasi-market" within the public sector (Le Grand and Bartlett 1993) in its white paper "Working for Patients" (WFP) (Department of Health 1989). A series of reforms created a system of hospital competition for contracts from public purchasers and new risks for individuals. These plans actually did little to "Work for Patients," instead reshaping the NHS along the lines of an Austerity Market that enhanced state and managerial control.

In its pure form, an Austerity Market not only changes how individuals consume care but also reshapes the way the state relates to hospitals and doctors. The state withdraws from traditional steering mechanisms, but re-emerges as a purchaser able to structure the goals of producers in ways that cut to the heart of what they produce. The Conservative party did not fully construct this ideal type. However, in shifting some costs onto patients and reorienting the system around the central government as a cost-conscious purchaser, it moved strongly in this direction. The result was the emergence of new inequities among citizens alongside competition among hospitals on financial performance, dramatically increasing state power over doctors and hospitals.

Two sets of reforms accomplished this shift. First, on the allocation dimension, while the government maintained the standard single payer structure, it introduced new charges and created new risks for individuals in accessing care. Between 1979 and 1997 the Conservatives reduced NHS coverage for certain procedures, and expanded tax relief for the purchase of private insurance (Webster 1998). There is continuing debate about whether the Conservatives purposely under-funded the NHS as a strategy to promote the privately financed sector (Klein 2006). The Conservatives vehemently deny this claim, pointing to expenditure growth through the 1980s (Klein 2006: 124), but in 1997, Britain still spent less than most other

European countries and patients faced long queues (Robinson and Dixon 1999). As a result, private financing grew from 10.4% to 19.6% of total health expenditure from 1979 to 1997, and the number of citizens with private insurance grew from 6% to 11% through the 1980s (Klein 2006; OECD 2004b).

The Conservatives also reshaped the system of access by creating new divisions among GPs. The reforms allowed (but did not require) GPs to form purchasing organizations (General Practitioner Fund Holders – GPFHs) that received budgets to buy diagnostic tests and care for their patients. Both the Labour Party and the British Medical Association expressed concern that these changes could create inequity among patients depending on their differential access to GPFHs. By 1997, there were 3,500 GPFH schemes, up from 294 in 1991 (Robinson and Dixon 1999). This shift did not create large inequities, but GPFHs were able to secure shorter waits for their patients without creating a positive spillover for the whole NHS (Propper *et al.* 2002).

Second, and much more importantly, the Conservatives introduced competition in the production of services. Here, the logic of competition was through contracting, rather than patient choice. The reforms created two new types of public purchasers responsible for carrying out centrally set objectives: District Health Authorities (DHAs), regional organizations responsible for purchasing hospital care for patients in their districts, and the aforementioned GPFHs. Despite WFP's claim to introduce the principle of "money following the patient," in practice the central government allocated fixed budgets to the purchasers, with only limited scope for overruns, and hospitals were funded by purchasers' contracts. Patients largely followed the referral choices of their GPs, and DHA contracting discouraged referrals to non-contracted hospitals (Ghodse 1996). Indeed, an OECD (1994) evaluation of the reforms found no real expansion of patient choice, a sentiment echoed by a key official at the Department of Health involved in drafting WFP: "I don't remember choice getting much emphasis"; instead, the focus was on contracting (Interview: former Department of Health official, 2004).

Competition was not only geared around contracts, but, in contrast to the elderly care reforms (see ch. 6), it was also accompanied by a logic of control that enabled the purchasers to enforce their preferences for cost efficiency. At first glance, the reforms appeared to empower the hospitals and doctors themselves, as purchasers had little experience and hospital supply was limited (Harrison 2004). However, the regulatory environment surrounding the "internal market" supported purchaser contracting. The central government restricted hospitals' ability to drive up prices and how they could spend excess revenues, and also required them to maintain business leaders on their non-executive boards. The reforms further created a new infrastructure of oversight, requiring the hospitals to publish financial data and increased the power of the inspectorate and the Audit Commission to examine performance.

This competition altered the production of services. Despite a slow start, by 1994, about fifteen to sixteen percent of DHAs' contracts involved providers outside of their district (Appleby *et al.* 1994). When this contracting combined with the low margins that many hospitals faced, it was sufficient to create some competition. In London, the effects of the market were most evident. London had long been "over-resourced" in terms of hospital beds, and historically GPs outside London referred patients to London hospitals (Tuohy 1999). As the market developed, purchasers outside of London limited these referrals to cut costs, and a number of London's prominent hospitals began to face financial difficulties.

Whether this competitive pressure actually increased efficiency is a matter of debate; in crude terms it did, hospital activity at a given level of expenditure increased (Le Grand *et al.* 1999; Baggott 1997; Propper and Söderlund 1998). Although this was an Austerity Market, where we expect costs to decrease, expenditure also increased. However, a planned increase of 4.5% (a concession to the medical profession) drove much of this spending, with growth slowing by the mid-1990s (Her Majesty's Treasury 2009). Moreover, management costs ate up much of this new spending (Baggott 1997).

The market dramatically redistributed power in the NHS. In forcing hospitals to compete to satisfy powerful purchasers, it created upward lines of accountability that replaced the old systems of local and professional control. This move empowered a new managerial cadre responsible for implementing the state's preferences over cost control, with the number of managers in the NHS growing by ten percent – while the number of nurses fell by twelve percent – in the first three years of the reforms (Audit Commission 1996b; Baggott 1997). The competitive structure and the ascendancy of managerial objectives gave the state power to challenge physicians' control over work and pay, and more controversially, their implicit autonomy over what to prescribe, how to treat patients, and where to refer them (Giaimo 2002). Harrison and Ahmad (2005: 134) argue that these changes "rendered unwise any medical strategy which ignored institutional interests." These pressures forced a change in hospital culture, with hospitals producing financial reports, actively marketing themselves, and even establishing private units (Rivett 1998; Baggott 1997; Ferlie 1996). Physicians' representatives did maintain an important role but the market weakened their power in steering the NHS (Giaimo 2002). Thus, physicians both individually and collectively lost power.

This shift to purchaser power not only cost physicians but also left patients out. The market did not reward competition on quality. A former senior DHA manager stated: "I cannot remember a single discussion about quality" (Interview: Stephen Thornton 2004). Equally, within the Department of Health, a senior official involved in the reforms stated: "No, I don't recall this discussion [of quality], efficiency was Mrs. Thatcher's concern" (Interview: former Department of Health official, 2004). This lack of concern in purchasing translated into a lack of results in production. While waiting lists fell in a few areas, there is little evidence that quality on a range of indicators increased, or that the market reoriented NHS care around patients (Baggott 1997). When in the early 1990s, the Major government introduced a new "Patient's Charter" aimed at creating responsiveness to patients, Martin Powell (1997: 83) argues that "while patients were armed with information, they could do nothing directly with it" as they lacked choice. GPFHs, who were more responsive to patient flows, on the other hand, did reduce waiting times for their patients (Audit Commission 1996b).

In gaining more power over the production process the state was the major "winner" in this market; however the market, in clarifying the upward lines of accountability, drew attention to the government's use of financial objectives in the care process. Consequently, when the market began to bite in ways that the public did not like, the politicians in Westminster paid the price. This outcome was most evident in the case of London's hospitals, where the near bankruptcy of some of London's most venerable hospitals was hardly politically appealing and the government was forced to roll back the market to deal with the "London problem" (Klein 2006). Equally, increased managerial control over clinical decision making exposed the implicit rationing of resources long conducted in the NHS, leading to new public demands to reduce variation and the implicit rationing of health benefits (Klein 2006; Interview: Stephen Thornton, former DHA manager 2004). While not a popular success, Conservative policy explicitly created an Austerity Market in the NHS, reshaping production around the state's preferences for cost control and placing some new costs on individuals.

Reshaping the market – towards a Consumer-Controlled market

When Labour entered government in 1997, it inherited a health service that looked very different to both the one it built in 1948 and which the Conservatives encountered in 1979. Hospitals now competed for contracts, the central government weighed in on areas long controlled by professionals, and patients continued to feel the pinch of long queues and funding lower than other countries. Initially, Labour engaged in little market-based reform, looking to limit the inequities in the Austerity Market while using increased state control to layer further regulations on providers.

Then, starting in 2000, Labour began to dramatically change the character of the market, returning to a stronger collective guarantee of allocation and introducing new competition around individual choices in production. This Consumer-Controlled market worked through hospital competition for patients, giving hospitals an incentive to appeal to patients interested in timely and high-quality services. Two key changes were made: along the allocation dimension, and along the production dimension.

First, along the allocation dimension, whereas the Conservatives had moved somewhat towards greater individual responsibility, Labour dramatically moved away from it. In the area of financing, Labour doubled real public expenditure between 2000 and 2008, dramatically increasing NHS staff, and targeting funds to deprived areas to decrease regional variation (Department of Health 2000b; Her Majesty's Treasury 2009). Alongside public spending, Labour rejected new patient charges and rescinded tax credits for the purchase of private insurance (Department of Health 2000b). Moreover, it abolished divisions among GPs, returning to a uniform system of regulation on access for all patients.[5] Socio-economic inequalities in health outcomes did not radically diminish under Labour, but the government did make some progress on meeting its targets on life expectancy and infant mortality (Department of Health 2007).

Second, as with the Conservatives, more significant reform targeted the structure of production. Although Labour introduced several seemingly different logics of competition – including greater contracting with the private sector, autonomy for hospitals, and enhanced choice – the overriding logic of the reforms has been to fund hospitals on patient flows and expand choice. In stark contrast to the Conservatives' emphasis on financial allocation following contracts, Labour introduced a new national "payment by results" (PbR) tariff that funded hospitals partly based on how much they produce rather than a fixed budget. This shift gave hospitals strong financial incentives to increase activity. Labour first combined these changes with an expansion of patient choice for planned care (for example, hip replacements, cataract surgery), later extending it to any provider meeting NHS quality and tariff requirements (Department of Health 2004). Most patients continue to select their local hospital, but hospitals nonetheless must compete, to some extent, for relatively cost-insensitive patients.

This emphasis on choice is ostensibly subject to a number of competing tendencies, including national and primary care contracting with NHS providers and private treatment centers. In practice, though, this

---

[5] Labour did reintroduce "practiced-based commissioning," where individual GPs, like GPFHs, receive budgets to purchase care. However, this move was more uniform, and largely subordinated the logic of payment based on the fixed tariff.

contracting has been largely subordinate to the logic of funding based on the national tariff, and contractors have few tools to restrict patient choice. One senior Department of Health official argued that at first there was significant tension among different competitive principles, but that this tension was resolved in favor of "free choice" (Interview: Department of Health official, 2004). Equally, the funding of private treatment centers uses the national tariff and follows the patient, effectively bringing private capacity into the broader NHS rather than offering a distinct logic. Even the most controversial of Labour's reforms, the use of private funding of NHS capital expenditure in exchange for long-term facilities management contracts (the Private Finance Initiative: PFI), and reforms allowing high-performing hospitals to convert into self-owned institutions with greater autonomy (Foundation Hospital Trusts: FHTs), are largely complementary with the expansion of choice. While critics expressed concerns that FHTs and PFI give the private sector too much autonomy (Pollock 2004), both are limited in scope and FHTs must play by largely the same competitive rules as other hospitals.

The logic of control accompanying all of these reforms ensured hospitals did compete for patients. Labour built on the existing infrastructure of central control, extending it to pricing (through the PbR tariff), quality, and clinical practices. It further provided patients with information on wait times and hospital performance. This regulation was backed up by increased monitoring, with a proliferation of centrally established performance indicators, a new oversight agency (the Healthcare Commission), and an independent agency to regulate and monitor FHTs.

This new market, alongside the dramatic increase in spending and staffing in the NHS, altered the way hospitals compete. Most obviously, it gave hospitals an incentive to focus on reducing waiting lists. In 1997, the median waiting time for hospital outpatient services was over fourteen weeks, falling to around four weeks by 2009, and the total number of people waiting halved from over 1.2 million to under 600,000 over this period (Thorbly *et al.* 2010). Waiting times in hospital emergency rooms have fallen from nearly a quarter of patients waiting more than four hours in 2003 to under two per cent in 2006 (Alberti 2007). These reductions have been more pronounced in England than in the other UK countries, which largely eschewed market incentives while also increasing spending on health (Alvarez-Rosete *et al.* 2005). As NHS waiting lists fell, so too did the use of privately funded care – in particular private insurance (Timmins 2004).

However, as hospitals have sought to respond to financial incentives, expenditures increased, often more than anticipated, leading to financial problems in some hospitals and claims of a "cash crisis" in the NHS (Timmins 2006). Increased staffing, pay rates, and activity all pushed spending up. As expected from a Consumer-Controlled market, despite extensive central performance monitoring, financing based on patient volume weakened the government's levers of cost control.

In 1987, patients were largely allocated to hospitals based on the choices of GPs, funding followed historical patterns, and hospitals faced little competition. By 1997, hospitals competed for contracts, faced strong budgetary incentives, and patients had little choice. In contrast, when Labour left office in 2010, hospitals and physicians had incentives to produce more and attract more patients in order to remain solvent, and patients, armed with new information and options increasingly had the scope to choose.

Why these changes?

Why did the Conservative party introduce an Austerity Market despite its rhetorical promises of more choice? This question is particularly relevant as it did pursue a consumer orientation in education policy (1988) and a greater producer orientation in elderly care (1989). Thus, the choice of such a market was not given. Why did Labour follow a market strategy? Why a Consumer-Controlled market? In order to unpack these questions, we need to look at what both parties wanted in each of the sectors and the strategic options they faced in the universal and uniform NHS.

Members of the Conservative party held varied stances towards the NHS, but the party's baseline preferences were for more private funding and provision. Margaret Thatcher (1993: 607), writing on the NHS, said: "If one were to recreate the National Health Service, starting from fundamentals, one would have allowed for a bigger private sector – both at the level of general practitioners and in the provision of hospitals; and one would have given much closer consideration to additional sources of financing for health, apart from general taxation." Parts of the party, particularly Thatcher, strongly supported more private financing, taking a critical stance towards the fully funded public structure (Timmins 2001: 386; Ham 2000: 9).

Despite these preferences, through the post-war period the Conservatives did little to modify the basic structure of the NHS. The party supported both the basic logic of public provision and spending and the system of professional control that underpinned it. Both Labour and Conservative governments involved the British Medical Association (BMA) and the various Royal Colleges of Physicians and Nurses in health policymaking, deferring to professionals on issues of manpower planning and pay as well as clinical management at the delivery level. A limited system of medical corporatism existed, with powerful stakeholders involved in the governing process.

Both these professionals and the electorate rallied around the status quo. The BMA opposed almost all major legislation regarding the NHS, from its creation to its reform through the 1980s and 2000s. In the 1970s, it battled against the Labour government's proposal to eliminate private beds in NHS hospitals, and by the 1980s, acting increasingly as a medical trade-union, it protested against Conservative policies (Klein 2006). Other workers, from nurses to hospital cleaners, were organized in a range of unions, which played a powerful but often fragmented role, again supporting the NHS. The public was equally strong in its defense of the NHS, with British citizens repeatedly affirming support for the principles of the NHS and rejecting an "American Style" system (Blendon *et al.* 1989). These interests limited reform.

However, beginning in the early 1980s, politicians across the political spectrum began to scrutinize the structure of the NHS, opening the door for more substantial change. Outside of government, much of this criticism targeted the Conservatives. The media, opposition Members of Parliament, and physicians themselves leveled claims of underfunding at the government (Klein 2006). As these claims increased in intensity, the number of citizens expressing dissatisfaction with the government's handling of the NHS grew from twenty-five percent in 1983 to forty-six percent in 1989 (Klein 2006).

This public pressure worked against the Conservatives' core preferences, creating demand for more spending. In response, the Conservatives began to examine the structure of the NHS more carefully, including the role of physicians. The party rejected the diagnosis of underfunding, seeing instead its organization as problematic. A 1983 review by Sir Roy Griffiths, the director of Sainsbury's supermarket chain, advanced a scathing critique of the collegial style of administration based on physician self-regulation in the NHS (Department of Health and Social Security 1983). As the government enacted Griffiths' recommendations for more management, new performance measures uncovered broad variation in resource usage, strengthening its convictions regarding the inefficiency of the service (Klein 2006). Influential Conservative think tanks criticized the lack of incentives for innovation, efficiency and responsiveness to users in the NHS.[6] The central government maintained control of overall spending but the Conservatives saw the system of decentralized management and strong professional power as creating few incentives for efficiency in production.

This emphasis on the problems of professional control at the ground level dovetailed with the Thatcher government's broader critique of interest

---

[6] For instance: Butler and Pirie (1988) from the Adam Smith Institute, Willetts and Goldsmith (1988) from the Center for Policy Studies.

groups and corporatist decision-making (see ch. 3). The party saw the involvement of medical professionals in the decision-making process as making it slow and inefficient. Kenneth Clarke, the Secretary of State for Health who introduced the 1989 reforms, critiqued the NHS as "dominated" by interest groups with little regard for patients or the long-term health of the service (Ham 2000: 50).

In response to these concerns, the Conservative government considered options for fundamental reform. Through the 1980s, various conservative think-tanks had produced reform proposals drawing on different logics of competition. Both Alain Enthoven, a key proponent of the managed care system in the United States, and the British economist Alan Maynard, advocated creating new public purchasers who would contract with providers (Ranade 1997). Others proposed voucher schemes that expanded choice, with different views on levels of government regulation (Butler *et al.* 1985; Willetts and Goldsmith 1988).

Sifting through these options, the Conservative leadership had to navigate public and professional discontent while advancing its own broader ideological preferences for reshaping the structure of the NHS. The design of the NHS, as a universal and relatively uniform service, with similar and comprehensive benefits to all citizens, offered a further constraint. As Margaret Thatcher (1993: 607) stated: "we were not faced by an empty slate." The universality of the service gave it high salience, limiting radical reform to the structure of allocation. In the early 1980s, a government plan considering privatizing parts of NHS financing was leaked to the press, and a strong negative public reaction forced the government to back-pedal (Timmins 2001: 390). The party was also constrained in reforming the supply of services, facing electoral disapproval of a producer-driven market. During the 1988 review, Thatcher and her advisors considered introducing vouchers, tax breaks for private insurance, outright privatization and radical purchaser-oriented reforms, but these suggestions did not make it past Cabinet discussions because they were seen as both politically and economically costly (Ham 2004; Klein 2006: 149–51; Tuohy 1999: 68).

Despite the language of "money following the patient," the uniformity of the service made the party ambivalent about expanding choice. The Secretary of State for Health, Kenneth Clarke stated: "If we were to introduce a true market – even insurance based – we would produce very well paid doctors and a very expensive system, but I doubt we'd produce any more quality. General practitioners and health authorities are much more informed customers of services than any patient" (Clarke 1990: 1386). Greater consumer choice was potentially inflationary and difficult to introduce, and in contrast to the education sector, it offered few direct gains. Conservative constituents were increasingly turning to the private sector – something the party supported – which decreased the gains from targeting large portions of funding to them.[7] Given these institutional constraints, the Thatcher government crafted a less optimal set of reforms, introducing market forces aimed at emphasizing efficiency within the public system.

This strategy emanated from the party itself. Thatcher organized a small group to meet and develop the NHS reforms, consulting outside groups informally, but explicitly denying them a formal role. In this process, fear of the electorate figured prominently, but largely as a passive constraint. Nearly sixty percent of the public believed the Thatcher government had a covert agenda to privatize the NHS – something it opposed (Blendon *et al.* 1989) – and the Conservatives backed off on preferred policies many times to defuse these concerns (Ham 2000: 9; Klein 2006: 112–13, 149–51; Timmins 2001: 361, 388, 459). Yet, the public was hardly clamoring for an Austerity Market; a 1989 survey found seventy-one percent of respondents disapproved of the reforms (Blendon *et al.* 1989). Public demands were for maintaining and improving the basic structure of the NHS, increasing funding, not introducing incentives for doctors or empowering managers (Blendon *et al.* 1989). The Thatcher government was able to work around this disapproval by avoiding direct cuts and privatization.

Concentrated interests formed a much more active constraint. The Thatcher government had excluded the Royal Colleges and the BMA from drafting the reforms, breaking with long-standing policy. This move infuriated the doctors, as did the content of the legislation, with the BMA arguing that the NHS needed a modest amount of additional resources, not fundamental change (Klein 2006: 147). Nonetheless, the Conservatives forged ahead, essentially ignoring the physicians' protests.

The Conservatives were able to work around the electorate and the doctors for several reasons. First, Thatcher capitalized on the electoral strength of the Conservatives vis-à-vis Labour to force the legislation through Parliament (Tuohy 1999). Second, backbenchers, who often were cautious about antagonizing the doctors, followed the party leadership. Through the 1980s, physicians and other health professionals complained bitterly about Conservative policy, particularly insufficient funding and excessive managerialism in the NHS. The Conservative government weathered these complaints, emboldening it vis-à-vis the professionals (Klein 2006). Finally, the professionals, although vocal, were disorganized. Doctors

---

[7] Margaret Thatcher insisted on increasing tax relief for those purchasing private health insurance, over the objections of the Treasury that this would be costly and simply substitute public for already existing private expenditure (Lawson 1993; Thatcher 1993; Timmins 2001: 459). That she insisted demonstrates the importance of supporting the existing private health insurance industry to those right-wing Conservatives, who preferred to target funding to this sector rather than to the NHS itself.

were split across their professional organizations and the BMA, and nurses and non-professional staff were part of a number of unions (Klein 2006). The reforms further divided doctors, giving new powers to GPs over the traditionally powerful hospital-based specialists. The growing weakness of professionals, combined with the power of governing parties in the United Kingdom, allowed the Thatcher government's approach.

The Austerity Market would not have been the Conservatives' first choice in an unconstrained world, but it nonetheless built on the party's overriding preferences. This market, in enhancing the incentives for limited private insurance and more cost-efficiency created a small private inroad into the NHS. More substantially, in an era where health care costs were exploding, the market challenged physicians' power, putting the government in a stronger position to steer the health care system. In so doing, it both defused blame for the short-term problems in the NHS and pushed the political debate away from the level of spending and towards issues of efficiency (Giaimo 2002). Together, these moves reshaped the logic of service in a way more conducive to the Conservatives' preference for a more limited but able state.

Labour's reforms

Labour's calculations looked different. Like the Conservatives, it too turned to markets in the face of growing short-term political pressure; however, because its core preferences differed, it built a different market. Through the post-war period, Labour supported the basic logic of the NHS as a fully publicly funded and largely publicly provided system. While it had an uneasy relationship with physicians, it relied on them to ration resources at the ground level, and, increasingly, as allies in defending the NHS from the Conservatives' reforms.

This stance began to shift in the 1990s. Blair's reorientation of the party towards the middle of the political spectrum constituted not only an ideological moderation but also a change in how the party understood the NHS. Klein argues that Blair's third way put "consumer politics" above "producer politics," with waiting lists, hospital cleanliness and responsive care at the center of Labour's strategy (Klein 2006: 188). In so doing, Labour increasingly spoke of the NHS as a funding mechanism "free at the point of delivery," rather than a system of public production. Nonetheless, the party's core goal was to aggressively support both this financing principle and equal access to care. Alan Milburn (2003), the former Secretary of State for Health, argued: "the principles of the NHS are right: service is free at the point of use, based on the scale of patients' need, not the size of their wallets," with Labour's goal "maintaining the NHS as a universal service."

Initially, this preference led Labour to take a highly critical attitude towards the Conservatives' Austerity Market, arguing that it was causing both inefficiencies and inequalities in access (Department of Health 1997). Instead, Labour proposed a centralizing strategy. The party introduced a plethora of performance targets, new national organizations aimed at evaluating best-practices, standardizing care, and returning to a more uniform system of allocation. Yet, despite its anti-market rhetoric, this early strategy built on aspects of the Austerity Market that enhanced the power of the state as a purchaser of services: the principle of splitting purchasers and providers and the system of managerial control within hospitals.

However, Labour faced a growing number of programmatic and political pressures that led it to re-evaluate this stance. In the 1997 election campaign, Labour promised only limited spending on the NHS as a way of gaining fiscal credibility with the electorate. This promise meant Labour's grandiose claim of tackling poor quality and waiting lists in the NHS was initially matched by limited funding. Early government policy aimed to manage public discontent, rather than eliminate it, by preventing a winter flu-season waiting crisis (Interview: Senior Labour Political Advisor, 2005). By 1999, Labour saw the continuing problems of quality, access, inter-physician variation, and, most importantly, the failure to meet its 1997 election promises on waiting-list reduction, as signs that its centrally driven plan was failing (Sherman 1999).

Labour had staked serious political credibility on improving the NHS and the limits of its initial policy had threatening political ramifications. In the 2001 general election, a candidate running solely on the platform of health policy defeated a Labour MP in Wyre Forest. This defeat combined with a trend towards more citizens purchasing care privately, rather than using the NHS (Browne 2001). Labour perceived middle-class "opt-out" into the private sector as eroding longer-term support for the NHS – one of its core political assets (Powell 1999). As a senior party official stated: "if welfare state institutions are not similar to others, then they will be ditched" and the party needed to "ensure [the public's] affections for the NHS are maintained" (Interview: Senior Labour political advisor, 2004a).

In response, Labour leadership in the Treasury agreed to increase funding, while reformers in the Prime Minister's office and the Department of Health examined organizational reforms. The first step involved a massive spending drive, with a promise to bring NHS spending up to the European average, resulting in a doubling of real expenditure between 1997 and 2009 (Thorbly and Mabin 2010). As performance improvements lagged behind spending increases, Labour again began to question the structural incentives for physicians in the NHS (Interview: Senior Labour political advisor, 2004a). Labour saw underfunding as a major cause of public discontent and middle class "opt out," yet it also viewed these problems as exacerbated by the parallel system of private care. Many NHS doctors worked part time in the private sector (often in NHS hospitals) where they earned more, meaning their lucrative private business was, to some extent, dependent on the failure of the NHS. Increasingly, Labour felt that structural changes were necessary to reduce the incentives for physicians to allow long queues in the public sector. As a senior political advisor stated: the challenge was to create a "labor market" that would "challenge the cartel market [of doctors] ... because top down could not touch the part outside the NHS [the private sector]" (Interview: Senior Labour political advisor, 2004a). Competition would help limit the ability of doctors to funnel patients to the private sector.

In light of these fundamental concerns, in 2000, the Department of Health conducted an intensive evaluation of the NHS that resulted in the *NHS Plan*: a ten-year strategy to ensure new spending would translate into actual improvements in the NHS and articulating a new willingness to use private sector capacity for the NHS (Department of Health 2000). The plan considered everything from moving to a social insurance system to delegating more control to producers, with other strands of Labour policy, such as contracting, FHTs, and PPPs, offering further reform alternatives.

Labour too, then, had a number of reform options at hand. Yet, it chose a different path to the Conservatives. To understand its choice, we need to look at how the existing institutional structure shaped its options. In contrast to the constraints the uniform and universal benefit structure posed to the Conservatives, the basic logic of the NHS reflected Labour's core aims, tying a broad swathe of citizens to a largely equitable structure. Initial Labour policy furthered this structure, countering the Conservatives' moves along the allocation dimension and returning to a more uniform system. Within this system, Labour perceived expanding choice as the ticket to improving the NHS. Consumer-Controlled markets promised to reduce waiting lists by giving hospitals incentives to treat patients rapidly, enhancing the public's support for the universal NHS, and in turn for Labour. Milburn's statements on choice are instructive: "My dread is that if the NHS doesn't improve we end up losing them [to private health coverage], and we end up with a poor service that is only for the poor" (Timmins 2002).

The new market would force providers to be more responsive to patients and treat them within the public sector, stemming patient opt-out to the private sector. Simon Stevens, the health policy adviser at Number 10 Downing Street responsible for developing many of these reforms, stated the goal was to create "constructive discomfort" among providers, to improve performance (Stevens 2004). These incentives combined with an increase in public capacity – through Labour's spending on investment in infrastructure and training – and publicly funded private treatment centers, would reduce waiting times and thus the demand for a privately financed system. Labour explicitly used one form of market to stop another, with the massive increase in spending and the Consumer-Controlled market both aimed at reducing demand for private insurance and sustaining the legitimacy of the NHS.

This strategy was born from Labour's own calculations about how to make the service meet its longer-term aims. Concentrated interests and the electorate were at best pleased with the direction of reforms, and occasionally hostile, but did not directly drive them. Labour's policy was not as threatening to physicians as the Austerity Market. It consulted widely on its early policy, gaining support from major stakeholders for its 2000 *NHS Plan*. However, as Labour experimented with contracting, hospital autonomy and centrally set performance measures, parts of the medical establishment began to question the direction of reforms. These protests combined with unease among parts of the Labour "left wing" to create internal dissent within the party. The government faced a serious backbench rebellion on legislation to extend hospital autonomy (Foundation Hospitals Trusts), one of the few reform measures that had to go through the legislative process.[8] Like the Conservatives, the party leadership pushed through, building on the power of the British executive branch. The party went farther than the Conservatives in appeasing professionals. Labour's spending muted medical protest, particularly as, from 1997 to 2007, average pay for community and health professionals grew by nearly seventy-five percent (Thorbly and Mabin 2010). Doctors, concerned about funding cuts and proposals to reduce their control over training, did join other trade unions to protest Labour's policy in 2006. This protest galvanized media and public concern, but did not fundamentally change the direction of policy, even as Gordon Brown took over the premiership.

The party also navigated electoral obstacles. Unlike the Conservatives, who saw the electorate as a constraint on preferred policy, Labour was keen to appeal to voters through the NHS reform. Despite this stance, the public was skeptical of the content of many of Labour's reforms, supporting choice but remaining unaware of much of the government's efforts here and ambivalent about the use of private capacity in the NHS (MORI 2004, 2006). The public wanted reduced waiting lists and better services, but they were hardly demanding the particular policy mix Labour introduced. As a result, Labour had to work hard to convince the electorate of its approach, underplaying competition and emphasizing results: waiting list reduction, more staff, and higher quality (for example, see Brown 2008).

---

[8] The government introduced many reforms using the power granted to the Secretary of State for Health through existing primary legislation.

Whether or not this approach worked is a matter of debate. Health economists have heavily criticized the Labour government's spending, arguing that it fell short of achieving the maximum results (Maynard and Street 2006). Politically, the market also did not garner electoral support (Alvarez-Rosete *et al.* 2005). Nonetheless, Labour policy did stem the flow of patients to the private sector, buoyed support for the NHS itself, and put the Conservatives in a defensive position – all of which are likely to matter for future health policy.

The last two decades of British health reform demonstrate that the shape of markets can differ substantially and that political parties use these differences strategically. Both the Conservatives and Labour wanted to challenge professional control over health care, creating new incentives aligned with their long-run preferences. The Conservatives, who supported more private production and financing, faced heavy constraints in achieving this goal, choosing a less optimal Austerity Market that increased state power over the NHS. Labour, by contrast, invested in supporting the basic structure of the NHS, and feeling the need to deliver, turned to a Consumer-Controlled market to create incentives for more activity and shore up public support. The next pages show that a similar logic played out in Sweden.

4.3: SWEDEN – PATIENT CHOICE AND PRIVATE CONTROL

Through the post-war period, Sweden's health care system evolved towards a fully public financed and delivered system. A series of reforms increased state involvement in medical training and limited private beds in public hospitals (1959), made care largely free at the point of use and turned physicians into salaried public employees (the "Seven Crowns" reforms of 1969), brought the remaining private physicians under the social insurance fee schedule (1975), and shifted control over private physicians to the counties in 1985 (Immergut 1992).

By 1985, the Swedish health care system was a publicly financed and delivered universal and uniform system, managed by the sub-national county councils.[9] Over 90.4 percent of total expenditure came from public sources, with only minor patient co-payments and a miniscule private insurance market (OECD 2008b). On the delivery side, in 1985, 18.8 percent of physicians had some private work, but this work was primarily part-time and less than one in ten thousand physicians was not dependent on public revenue and its accompanying regulations (Rosenthal 1986).

---

[9] There are currently twenty counties and one municipality responsible for health care services.

Today, the basic elements of this structure remain in place, yet as in Britain, a series of market reforms have changed the way that services are produced. A first set of reforms, promoted by the Social Democrats (SAP) in the late 1980s, expanded patient choice and altered hospital funding to respond to patient movement, tending towards a Consumer-Controlled market (collective responsibility, individual choice). However, as the inflationary consequences of this market emerged, politicians on the Left and the Right limited it. Politicians from the right-wing Moderate party put a second set of markets back on the agenda. These markets aimed to create a self-sustaining privately funded health care sector by increasing the autonomy of private providers at the cost of state control through Pork Barrel markets (collective responsibility, producer control).

Towards Consumer-Controlled markets

Markets first emerged in the late 1980s to early 1990s, when both SAP and non-Socialist governments introduced reforms expanding hospital competition for largely cost-insensitive patients. As with the recent NHS reforms, this Consumer-Controlled market improved quality and responsiveness by making hospitals compete for patients without creating a market-like allocation of benefits. The overall thrust of this early market was to expand choice; however, local control over the health system meant that several counties introduced more choice than others and some paired choice with more individual risk (leading to Two Tier markets).

In the early 1990s, some counties moved towards more a market-like distribution of health benefits on the allocation dimension. Tight budgeting through the 1980s reduced public spending from 9.6% of GDP in 1980 to 8.8% by 1990, with a further reduction to 8.1% by 1995 as Sweden entered a severe economic crisis in the early 1990s (Hjortsberg and Ghatnekar 2001). In response, many counties introduced patient fees, with fees rising by an average of thirty percent across Sweden from 1993 to 1998 (Bergmark *et al.* 2000). Where fees emerged, they had an impact, with a growing proportion of citizens reporting that they did not seek medical care because of fees (Bergmark *et al.* 2000). However, this trend was variable. The national government further limited its impact by removing tax breaks for the purchase of private health insurance in 1988, and, as the economy improved in the mid-1990s, giving counties additional payments to exempt children, low-income individuals, and other groups (Hjortsberg and Ghatnekar 2001). Moreover, the Health Care Act of 1982 outlined a basic regulatory structure requiring the counties to provide health based on need – not the ability to pay. Overall, private spending in Sweden remained well below the OECD average and the robust regulatory structure continued to guarantee care based on need. Thus, movement on the allocation dimension was variable and less explicitly aimed at reshaping consumption than in the Netherlands, or even the UK under the Thatcher government.

Several reforms to the production dimension did change the ways hospitals produced care. Traditionally, Swedish patients had little choice of care provider, with counties assigning citizens to a local primary care provider and hospital, restricting care across county lines. In 1985 a center-Right governing coalition in Stockholm County made the first moves towards changing this system, expanding women's choice of maternity care and giving clinics financial incentives to attract expectant mothers. It was the SAP, though, who pushed to expand competition through choice in the late 1980s. In 1988, a new SAP-led coalition in Stockholm County extended patient choice to all primary care providers and hospitals within the county. In 1991, the SAP-controlled Federation of County Councils (FCC) further expanded patient choice across county lines and encouraged counties to expand choice internally. The SAP in national government (backed heavily by the non-Socialists) cemented this approach with the 1991 "Care Guarantee," giving patients waiting for common procedures choice of provider after a fixed amount of time (Blomqvist 2002). By 1993, all twenty-six counties had extended choice for primary care, with seventeen also extending choice of hospital without a referral and the other nine allowing choice with a referral (Anell *et al.* 1997). The financial mechanisms accompanying choice varied but most counties used some patient-based funding.

Some counties, including Stockholm, ostensibly developed an alternative competitive model. Beginning in 1989, and introduced in 1991 (by the SAP and later the non-Socialists), Stockholm County developed a market model that drew on the logic of the British purchaser-provider split. The county's expressed goal was to promote efficiency and cost-containment through purchasing (Anell 1996; Bergman 1998). Dala and Bohus counties introduced similar reforms, with FCC and the Ministry of Finance promoting them, and later half of Swedish counties made similar changes (Anell *et al.* 1997). In practice, however, the purchasers were not able to restrict choice or specify production limits, and the total volume of treatment followed from patient demand. Contracts with physicians included per-patient components and most counties paid hospitals using an activity-based system related to patient volume. If production exceeded the agreed-upon contracts, hospitals simply sent the bills directly to the purchasers (Anell *et al.* 1997; Diderichsen 1995). Unlike in the early NHS market, it was individual choices, not purchasing decisions, which set the incentives for hospitals.

The logic of control accompanying the reforms looked to ensure that hospitals and clinics responded effectively to patients. The national regulatory structure outlined providers' responsibilities, limiting their ability to select or refuse patients and requiring them to prioritize patients on the basis of clinical need. In the 1990s, the national government, through the National Board of Health and Welfare and professional groups, began to oversee providers and gather information. Hospitals and doctors did not have a right to enter the market, set prices, or provide care to whom they pleased, and they had to conform to basic rules on quality and patient access.

Like the more recent changes to the NHS, the Consumer-Controlled thrust of this market gave hospitals and clinics incentives to respond to patients. Most importantly, hospitals increased their activity – between 1992 and 1993, productivity increased and waiting lists fell twenty-two percent (Harrison and Calltorp 2000). Although fewer than five percent of patients actually exercised choice (Harrison and Calltorp 2000), the financial incentives were sufficient to change production in important ways. For instance, Stockholm County funded maternity clinics based on patient choices. Consequently, less popular units experienced revenue shortfalls and a ward in one of Stockholm's smaller hospitals even closed (Saltman and von Otter 1992). In this competitive environment, wards began to change their practices to appeal to mothers, even remodeling delivery rooms to allow new birthing practices (Saltman and von Otter 1992). Rothstein (1998) finds similar results in the region outside Malmö, where a more informal movement towards choice in maternity care in the 1970s put pressure on other hospitals to appeal to patients' needs. Outside of maternity care, there is also evidence of change. Garpenby (1994, 1997) argues that during the late 1980s and early 1990s providers began to develop and use quality measures, and he finds that they did so more extensively in regions where competitive pressures were greater. Unlike the early English market, professionals in Sweden responded to the new competitive incentives by focusing on quality.

Tight budgeting kept overall costs constant during this period, but the increase in activity and emphasis on quality created new cost pressures. In contrast to the early Austerity Market in the NHS, where rising expenditure came through planned spending, cost increases in Sweden stemmed from unplanned increases in the places where competition was strongest. For instance, Diderichsen (1995) shows that despite a decreasing mortality rate for cardiovascular diseases between 1991 and 1993, hospitalization increased eighteen percent and costs per treatment increased, suggestive of "supplier induced demand." Whitehead *et al.* (1997) also find Stockholm's purchasers' budget deficits increased where competitive incentives were present (for example, cataract surgery), again suggesting the inflationary potential of competition.

The Swedish market configured the winners and losers of reform similarly to the English Consumer-Controlled market in offering direct benefits to citizens. The rapid reduction in waiting lists in urban areas neutralized much of the political discontent around the health care system (Harrison and Calltorp 2000). As choice increased and waiting lists fell, so too did support for the private sector. In 1994, a Statistics Sweden study found that only twenty-two percent believed they could receive better care there, down from forty-eight percent in 1991 (Dagens Nyheter 1994). Equally, the reforms were not as hard on physicians as in an Austerity Market: they maintained much control over clinical issues – including the measurement of quality – and benefited from increased funding in the system (Interview: former Stockholm County official, 2005a).

The choice-based character of this market meant that neither the national nor the local government gained as much power through purchasing as in an Austerity Market. In Western Sweden, where competition across county lines was most developed, it upset the counties' traditional mechanisms of budgetary allocation and planning. In response, the counties first began to scale up production to retain their own patients, and then reduced choice to regain control over costs and planning (Anell 1996).

The Consumer-Controlled market was also a success in reducing waiting times and appealing to patients – indeed, as it turned out, too much of a success. As the above example in Western Sweden demonstrates, as policymakers began to feel the financial consequences of choice, they scaled it back. In Stockholm County, politicians realized that the market was unlikely to cut costs and doing so would require political decisions to make cuts in staffing (Interview: former Stockholm County official, 2005a). The non-socialist coalition began this process, capping production and reducing "hard" competitive incentives. When the SAP returned to power in 1994, it introduced an "employment guarantee" for public employees, further limiting workforce restructuring.

Nonetheless, patients today continue to have wide choice of primary care provider, hospital, and the scope to move across county lines, something that many do exercise, albeit with hospitals facing fewer financial incentives related to this choice.

From consumers to producers

In the late-1990s, scholars were writing post-mortems on the Swedish market project (Whitehead *et al.* 1997; Harrison and Calltorp 2000). The announcement of the death of Swedish markets though, was premature. Beginning in the early 1990s and gaining steam in the late 1990s and 2000s, Sweden entered a second period of market making. During this period, parties on the Right looked to expand the size and power of the private sector absent clear public oversight, creating Pork Barrel markets. These markets work by allowing private producers access to public funding without creating genuine competition among them. Although only limited versions of this market emerged in Sweden, two sets of reforms drew on its logic.

The first move along these lines occurred in 1994, when the national level non-Socialist coalition introduced the so-called "Family Doctor" reform. Traditionally, Swedish patients did not have personal physicians, instead attending a local clinic for primary care. The Liberal party had long pressed for introducing personal physicians, like British GPs, arguing that they would promote stable relationships between physicians and their patients and thereby save money and improve quality. The non-Socialist coalition took this proposal forward, but paired it with plans to give private physicians the right to establish a practice where they pleased, irrespective of local need, and charge higher fees.

A second movement towards promoting private entrepreneurship, absent strong control, was taking hold in the counties. Local politicians had first begun contracting with private providers in the 1980s, when Stockholm contracted with City Clinic AB, a private clinic providing extended services that catered to patients who lived in the suburbs but worked in Stockholm City (Rosenthal 1986). This effort expanded in the 1990s as Stockholm's non-Socialist government required its purchasers to consider tendering out services worth more than twenty percent of their budget (Whitehead *et al.* 1997).

Originally, much of this contracting was heavily controlled (taking the form of a Managed Market) and restricted to primary care. However, in the early 1990s Stockholm's non-Socialist government began to discuss the possibility of privatizing one or two of Stockholm's smaller hospitals. Initially, the county could not find a private company willing to assume the financial risk of taking over a hospital and restricted its reforms to transforming the legal status of one medium-sized hospital, St. Göran's, into an independent publicly owned company (Interview: former official Stockholm County, 2005a). Further reform was halted, but not reversed, when the SAP returned to power in Stockholm in 1994. However, when a non-Socialist majority re-emerged in 1998, it moved quickly to privatize St. Göran's, selling the rights to provide hospital services to the company Bure AB (now Capio AB). The logic of both the Family Doctor reform and the privatization of St. Göran's demonstrate an important market strategy – stimulating private providers in single sites without strong oversight, creating Pork Barrel markets.

Neither of the reforms created new incentives on the allocation dimension. In the area of financing, early proposals for Family Doctors allowed private doctors to charge higher fees, but the final changes did so largely at a cost to the public purse, not patients. Equally, the privatization of

St. Göran's did not introduce new fees. Ongoing national and local regulation on access continued to guarantee health care based on need.

On the production dimension, ostensibly, the Family Doctor reforms and the St. Göran's reforms introduced different logics of competition. The Family Doctor reforms gave patients the choice of doctor, compensating physicians for each enrolled patient with a small fee for service element. By contrast, Stockholm County's contract with St. Göran's, not patient choice, determined its reimbursement. Despite these differences, both changes were accompanied by a logic of control that ceded much power to the producers of services. The Family Doctor reform undercut the counties' ability to plan capacity by giving private doctors the right to enter a market and the scope to set higher fees. Equally, St. Göran's was tendered hastily, without strong state controls on aspects of its behavior. For instance, although Stockholm's own auditors found aspects of the contracting process well administered, an independent review criticized the process for being too hasty, and not following Swedish public procurement laws (there was not an open competition) (Öhrlings PricewaterhouseCoopers AB 2005; Jonsson 2002). The contract also gave the private sector new sources of control, allowing Capio to treat privately funded patients, in addition to public patients, and leaving open the question of commercial expansion. Moreover, Stockholm chose to tender a hospital with a favorable market position (Jonsson 2002). St. Göran's is located in one of the wealthier parts of Stockholm, with a less severe patient mix than other similar hospitals, and prior to the reform the County had closed a nearby hospital, increasing St. Göran's volume of care. In both cases, the reforms allowed private providers into the most profitable markets without strong oversight.

In practice, the SAP altered both reforms shortly after their introduction, limiting their impact. The SAP rescinded the Family Doctor reform when it returned to power nationally in 1994, allowing existing private doctors to keep their practices but returning control over the private sector to counties. In response to the privatization of St Göran's the national SAP was even more dramatic, introducing a ban (colloquially known as the "Stop Law") on further county-led privatization of acute care hospitals and prohibiting existing private hospitals from treating non-publicly funded patients.[10]

---

[10] Following a review led by SAP parliamentarian Per Axel Sahlberg, and pressure from the Green party to restore local autonomy, the SAP revised the "stop law" to allow the sale of hospitals to for-profit companies, but not the sale of university hospitals, requiring all counties to maintain at least one public hospital. The non-Socialists, on their return to government in 2006, withdrew these limitations. Locally, Stockholm County decided to allow Capio, and other public independent hospitals, to treat privately funded patients, and re-introduced the free establishment of private physicians.

Despite these reversals, where these markets did develop the results are telling. Contracting with private physicians is now well established in parts of Sweden, for instance, in Stockholm up to fifty percent of doctors are involved in private practice (Hjortsberg and Ghatnekar 2001). Many of these physicians are heavily monitored, but some do have the scope to determine where they operate and at what cost – and have used this power to locate in more desirable areas and raise costs (Interview: former Stockholm County official 2005b; Whitehead *et al.* 1997). A study by the Swedish newspaper *Dagens Nyheter* found that 226 new private doctors entered Stockholm's market following the Family Doctor reforms, with only a marginal increase in actual usage (by 12,000 visits per year, meaning each new doctor was adding only fifty-three visits per year to the total), with costs for private doctors increasing thirty-six percent (Böe and Stenberg 1996). The contracting of St. Göran's is a more positive story, with St. Göran's using its new autonomy to innovate. St. Göran's was already highly productive prior to the contracting, and Capio has continued this trend (Hjertqvist 2004). Patients are positive towards St. Göran's, and the staff and the unions support Capio (Lofgren 2002). Indeed, Capio has used St. Göran's as a flagship institution for its international health services business.

More broadly, the introduction of powerful private producers in the care sector has started to reshape the balance of power away from state or patient control. While the SAP's policies on private doctors and limiting hospital privatization blunted this emerging market, both reforms gave new power to a number of private (for-profit) players, changing the face of Swedish health care.

Why these markets?

Why was the SAP open to Consumer-Controlled markets but not Pork Barrel markets? Why, although initially supportive of choice, did the non-Socialists move away from it and towards Pork Barrel markets? As in the UK, the answer to these questions lies in the way political parties responded to new pressures on the universal and uniform health care system.

The development of Sweden's universal and uniform health care system largely followed from the SAP's legislative action. Through the 1960s and 1970s, the party waged a number of battles with physicians, pushing through legislation bringing private doctors into the publicly run and financed sector (Immergut 1992). Conservative politicians and physicians remained skeptical of the structure. However, until the mid-1980s most actors accepted its broad contours, with the counties and many health professionals supportive of the existing structure.

Partisan support for the system began to crack in the 1980s, as the Moderates and others on the Right critiqued the fully public nature of the system. Initially, in the face of these criticisms, the SAP looked to defend the universal and uniform Swedish health care system from change, particularly market oriented reforms. The party resisted proposals from Moderate politicians for market reforms, promising to defend the public sector in both the 1982 and 1985 elections (Olsson 1993). However, by the mid-1980s, the SAP, too, was beginning to question the system.

Direct cost-control measures had halted rising expenditure in health, but many politicians and administrators saw budgetary caps as a crude instrument to address long-run productivity or quality in the health sector (Federation of County Councils 1991). At the same time, growing affluence, particularly in the larger cities, and media reports of long waiting lists fuelled citizens' expectations for – and frustration with – the system (Diderichsen 1995; Saltman and von Otter 1992). Public opinion data from the 1980s show that citizens saw the health care system as unresponsive to patients and were increasingly open to private care (Federation of County Councils 1991; Henrekson 2001). These pressures on the health system created political pressure for the SAP. Although the numbers were small (particularly by international standards), growing waiting lists were leading more citizens to take out private health insurance. Between 1986 and 1990, the number of policies provided by the two largest health insurance companies, Skandia and TryggHansa, grew from 4,500 and 1,000 to 15,000 and 5–6,000 respectively, and a new insurer, Wasa, anticipated 23,800 individual policies (Rosenthal 1992). Private insurers began to advertise in newspapers and one, TryggHansa, directly advertised its contract with a private hospital to "business class" Swedes too busy to wait for public services (Saltman and von Otter 1987; Rosenthal 1986). Moreover, the private clinics contracted by certain counties were increasingly attractive to urban professionals (Saltman and von Otter 1987).

As in England, where the Labour party was concerned that poor quality in the NHS could lead citizens to "opt out" to the private sector, the SAP had to address cost and quality problems in the public system to avoid long-run problems and citizens turning to private insurance (Interview: former SAP health advisor, 2006). Increasingly, the party leadership saw supporting the status quo as not enough to sustain an equitable and publicly financed health care sector.

Initially, the SAP attempted to address the problem of waiting lists through additional earmarked funding, but this move did not reduce waiting times and the party abandoned it (Hanning 1996). In response, some in the SAP began to consider structural reforms to the health care system, moving beyond spending policies and focusing instead on reshaping the incentives for health professionals, county managers and the central government itself (Federation of County Councils 1991).

This turn towards examining the structure of the health system led some in the party leadership to consider markets. Parts of the SAP, particularly in the Ministry of Finance, began to consider purchaser-provider splits and limited contracting (akin to Managed Markets) that promised to improve efficiency (Interview: former health advisor, SAP, 2006). Blomqvist (2002) documents the rise of professional economists in the 1980s in the Ministry of Finance, many of whom built on the logic of managed competition to promote reforms similar to those in the NHS. The Swedish Institute for Health Services Development (SPRI), a government-sponsored agency, also began to develop plans for internal markets and activity-based payments to hospitals (Hakansson *et al.* 1988).

At the same time, several Left-leaning scholars developed plans for more competition through patient choice. A series of influential articles by Richard Saltman, an American academic, and Casten von Otter, a senior trade union economist, argued that the Swedish health care system lacked mechanisms for identifying and correcting organizational failure – privileging producer over patient convenience (Saltman and von Otter 1987). Saltman and von Otter argued that the solution lay in reforms appealing to patients as users of services, rather than the needs of employees. They rejected both "neo-liberal" policies of co-payments and private financing and contracting reforms like those introduced by the Conservatives in the NHS, advocating instead for expanding patient choice within the publicly financed and provided system (Saltman and von Otter 1989). Put differently, they presented a Consumer-Controlled (collective responsibility, individual choice) market as a way of making hospitals and doctors more responsive to patients, thus sustaining patient support for the public system.

The SAP, then, had a range of market options. Its precise choice of market followed from the specific trade-offs that the existing structure offered it. Despite the attraction of improved cost-efficiency through Managed Markets, the generous uniform structure of the health care system meant that a Consumer-Controlled market promised to benefit a broad group of constituents and enhance public support for the health care system. Competition through choice offered a way of addressing the demands of frustrated middle-class citizens within the public system rather than outside it. Indeed, supporting a shift towards greater choice in 1988, Gertrude Sigurdsen, the Social Democratic minister of health, laid out precisely this logic: "People should be able to visit the doctor, the health centre, or the hospital they wish, also across county lines. Attempts with such choice have been shown to reduce the demand for private alternatives" (Weinberger 1988; Saltman and von Otter 1992: 49).

Although market proposals in Sweden emerged from a variety of local and national actors, we nonetheless see the move to the market followed from the calculations of party elites looking to reshape incentives in the health system. Neither the public nor stakeholders were demanding such change. The public was open to private alternatives, with sixty percent supporting a reduction in the size of the public sector in 1990 and even SAP voters expressing more positive views towards private alternatives (Nilsson 2009). However, the SAP did not introduce private alternatives, it expanded choice. Although choice was also popular, in rejecting private actors, the SAP was not just following the immediate preferences of the electorate.

Unlike those undertaken by the Thatcher government, these shifts did not immediately antagonize the core players in the health care system. Physicians were cautiously supportive of these early moves. The SAP's austerity budgets in health had been hard on health professionals, limiting their resources in a time of growing demand. In this light, both hospitals and physicians saw aspects of the Consumer-Controlled market, which would connect actual work to the payment system, as offering extra funding (Interview: former official at Stockholm County, 2005a). Equally, these markets emerged largely locally, and preserved County control, limiting potential opposition from the Counties. Thus, although the SAP and non-Socialists introduced market reforms that altered local and physician control, the major stakeholders in the health care system were initially supportive of the changes.

The politics of the producer-based markets looked quite different. Although the SAP was willing to accept, and even promote, greater patient choice and some contracting with private doctors and clinics, its furor towards the Family Doctor reform and St. Göran's illuminates its stance towards markets. Despite the SAP's rhetoric against profit in health care, at both the national and local levels it widely accepts the involvement of profit-making companies in the elderly and primary care sectors. Local politicians rarely reverse (even increase) private contracts in these sectors, and there is no national "stop law" banning such contracting. Thus the SAP does not oppose either competition or private actors in health outright. However, it acted quickly and emphatically against producer-based markets in healthcare – often over the heads of producer groups.

This reaction is indicative of the SAP's broader strategy with respect to markets in health. By the mid-1990s, the political situation had changed for the SAP. At this time, the SAP increasingly faced competition from the Left party on the left as well as the non-Socialists on the right (Madeley 1999). Parts of the electorate, scarred by the cutbacks from Sweden's recession of the early 1990s, took a strong line against privatization. These electoral pressures changed the SAP's calculus, pushing it – at least rhetorically – away from markets and encouraging a defensive posture vis-à-vis the health system.

Even after this electoral pressure cooled in the late-1990s, the SAP continued to oppose producer-based markets, demonstrating its broader ideological concerns about this *type* of market. Both the Family Doctor and St. Göran's reforms challenged the SAP's long-standing preferences on health care in two ways. First, in giving private actors either the right to enter the market, or reduced public control over the market, the party saw these moves as reducing state control over the health care system. The SAP's health minister, Lars Engqvist, drew comparisons between the SAP's rejection of the free establishment of physicians and its concerns over for-profit hospitals, arguing both could erode public control over the system (Olausson 1999). The SAP also initially expressed concerns about the implications of transferring physical capital to the private sector through hospital privatization (Interview: SAP health advisor, 2005). Second, the SAP worried that the Family Doctor reforms could fragment public sup-port for the public system, encourage the private insurance sector, and bankrupt the counties (Johansson 1993). With respect to St. Göran's, the SAP raised the possibility that private contractors would treat privately funded patients and open the door for a fast-lane (so-called *gräddfil*), where private patients could jump the public queue. Indeed, Engqvist argued that the sale of St. Göran's was part of a strategy to make private insurance necessary in Sweden's health care system (Dagens Medicin 1999). Both factors risked eroding public control over the health sector and overall solidarity in the system, a central SAP goal (Interview: SAP health advisor, 2005), creating a two-tier health care system. Moreover, as reform of the sickness system and long queues in the public sector had increased both employer and citizen demand for private health insurance, the party saw a real risk to opening the door to private actors able to take private patients (Sahlin and Johansson 2006).

Taken together, we see that in the late 1980s the SAP introduced Consumer-Controlled markets in an attempt to sustain the health care system, expanding choice to force physicians and other providers to reduce waiting lists and be more responsive to patients. In the universal and uniform system, choice promised to tie citizens to a system that the party supported. However, these same goals led it to oppose markets that threatened to fragment public support. This rejection of the private hospitals and doctors was popular with the public, but also followed from the party's own goals.

Moderates and markets

Unlike the SAP, the Moderate party maintained a preference for more private entrepreneurship in financing and providing care, as part of its ideological opposition to the Swedish welfare state (for example, see Moderata samlingspartiet 1984). Although many Moderates cut their teeth in local politics, the party was heavily critical of county management of the health care system (Nilsson 2003). The Moderates wanted a slimmer state at both the national and local level.

Through the 1980s, these general preferences developed into a more substantial critique of the state. As in other sectors (see ch. 3), the Moderates increasingly challenged both public financing and production, advocating both limited private production and financing, and a move towards both private and social insurance, as a way of both limiting the public sector and county management (Nilsson 2003; Pettersson 2001). Some members of the party went farther, advocating substantial privatization of funding and production by offering those that could afford it the "choice" to purchase care privately (Nilsson 2003: 58–65). Others were more cautious, proposing contracting with private physicians and internal competition in the public sector (Nilsson 2003; Blomqvist 2002).

Initially, as part of Stockholm's governing coalition in the mid-1980s, the non-Socialist coalition considered both expanding choice within the public sector for maternity care and engaging in limited private contracting. As costs increased (during a period of economic decline) and choice in the uniform health care system began to neutralize public discontent – buttressing support for the public system – choice alone was increasingly unattractive for the non-Socialist parties. The non-Socialists continued to strongly support "waiting list guarantees" which promised choice across county line for a targeted number of procedures. Nonetheless, the non-Socialists turned away from across-the-board patient choice, and in Stockholm and elsewhere they reduced the financial incentives supporting choice and reintroduced production caps.

This shift did not lead the Moderates to abandon markets in health care; instead the party turned to more limited producer-based reforms as a way of navigating these institutional constraints. The Moderates first pushed for a producer orientation in the Family Doctor reforms. The Family Doctor reforms had long been a priority of the Liberal party, but neither the Liberal party nor the Liberal minister who took the reforms forward had traditionally paired this advocacy with a demand to give private doctors the right of free establishment (Interview: former Stockholm County official, 2005a). However, the Moderates, who both supported the private sector and disliked county management, pushed hard for this policy.

These reforms ran up against heavy opposition from some health professionals and the county councils. The power of the Swedish legislative assembly meant that Swedish governments could usually enact policy against the opposition of health stakeholders. However, the non-Socialist coalition was in an unusual situation. It was a minority coalition, dependent on the support of either the Socialist block or the small right-wing "New Democracy" party in introducing legislation. This situation made it more vulnerable to protests from outside stakeholders. Although the Swedish Medical Association supported the reforms and the opportunities they offered physicians, general practitioners and other physicians – concerned that the law could benefit private physicians at the expense of county employees – and nurses, opposing the move away from the clinic model, opposed the reform (Karlsson 1992). The county councils, concerned about a loss of power, also challenged the reforms. The SAP, and increasingly New Democracy, began to echo these concerns. This opposition helped to delay the reform until relatively late in the non-Socialists' national reign and limited its coverage of specialists and fees.

However, advancing further change along these lines remained a top political priority locally. In the lead up to the 1998 election, the non-Socialists in county elections campaigned on the promise of privatization of hospitals, with Stockholm's non-Socialists vowing also to reform Stockholm's largest hospitals, Karolinska and Huddinge (Sörbring 1998). Once elected, the Moderates in Stockholm placed hospital contracting at the fore of the party's agenda, reaching an agreement with Bure AB shortly after coming to office (Interview: Stig Nyman, Christian Democrat, head of health council, Stockholm County 2004). The non-Socialist coalition combined this move with greater public spending on care (without raising taxes), and more contracting and corporatization of several other hospitals (Sörbring 1999). Non-Socialists in Skåne and Västra Götaland also made the first steps towards privatization following the 1998 election.

In so doing, these politicians promised that privatization would benefit users, taxpayers and workers in the sector (for example, see Widegren *et al.* 1999). However, in rapidly privatizing a hospital and allowing the possibility of privately funded patients – something rarely practiced in Sweden – the Moderates also elevated their long-standing goal of enhancing the private sector and limiting state control to the top of the agenda (even above cost control, as witnessed by rising costs through this time period). Put differently, the party privileged one type of market – Pork Barrel markets – over choice or state contracting.

In contrast to the Family Doctor reforms, these changes fell on more fertile ears. Earlier reforms turning St. Göran's into an autonomous hospital garnered support from the workforce. The head of one of the nurses' unions, Eva Fernnvall, argued that after decades of austerity budgets multiple employers might actually help the nurses, giving them more opportunities to focus on patients (Interview, Senior Represent Vårdförbundet 2004). Moreover, Stockholm's rapid privatization of much primary care in the late 1990s was popular with staff – with ninety-seven percent of privatized staff supporting the shift (Sörbring 2001). Health care workers, frustrated with tight budgets and increasing political interference, saw the producer orientation as favorable. Unlike the Family Doctor reforms, the County itself introduced these shifts, limiting local opposition. Much of the uproar around St. Göran's came from the national parties.

The non-Socialists were also able to navigate electoral constraints, despite introducing producer-driven markets in a uniform health care system. The public was hardly demanding change: net support for private alternatives was negative (more opposed it than supported it) and lower in the mid-1990s and 2000s than in the late 1980s (Nilsson 2009: 273). However, both shifts were possible because both changes were limited to the margins of the health system. The Family Doctor reforms expanded public funding to new doctors, and therefore did not immediately threaten existing physicians, or citizens' benefits. Equally, the Right limited the reforms in Stockholm County to a single hospital rather than the whole health care system. Where the Right did engage in more substantial reform – through more direct contracting – they largely moved towards a state-controlled strategy, eschewing rapid privatization of the whole system. The non-Socialists then, targeted their more extensive efforts at the edges of the system, rather than engaging in full-scale reform (ch. 5 demonstrates a similar strategy in education). In so doing, they traded off depth for breadth – pursuing "higher order" preferences in more limited scope.

Market reforms in Sweden involved more actors than in Britain, and occurred across different levels of government. Nonetheless, we see that in both cases markets were partisan political creations. Growing waiting lists and rising costs galvanized public discontent with the health care system. This discontent seemed to offer the Right an opportunity to introduce markets, however, broad popular appeals through choice offered little to right-wing parties in universal, uniform health systems. In response, the British Conservatives looked to manage discontent, building a less preferred Austerity Market. The Right in Sweden took a different tack, targeting markets at the margins of the system, navigating electoral constraints by limiting reforms. By contrast, in both countries the Left saw growing waiting lists as threatening its goals of sustaining a universal and uniform system, by encouraging citizens to opt out of the public system. These parties built on the existing structure to introduce broadly popular appeals through choice, while rejecting alternative forms of markets. Debates about which type of market have been just as central in Sweden and the UK as the original choice to introduce markets.

4.4: NETHERLANDS – A SLOW PATH TO AN AUSTERITY MARKET

Unlike the Swedish and British health systems, the Dutch health care system works through multiple insurance funds. Beginning under the

German occupation and extended in 1956, the government created a social health insurance system that built on the efforts of mutual societies, firms, and the medical sector (Okma and Björkman 1997). This system was compulsory for workers earning below a certain income and financed through payroll taxes. Higher-income workers were left to purchase insurance from private insurers, who although heavily regulated, were permitted to charge risk-related premiums. Next to this fragmented structure of basic insurance, the government established a universal catastrophic insurance scheme (AWBZ) in 1968, funded through payroll taxes and administered by the social and private insurers. By the mid-1980s, the care system was managed by social and private insurers, close to thirty percent of funding came from private sources, and most care in the Netherlands was provided by the private non-profit sector (OECD 2004b).

Despite this historic use of private management, provision, and funding, the reforms introduced in 2006 represent the culmination of nearly two decades of conflict over reforming the health care system along the lines of an Austerity Market (individual responsibility, state contracting). The first phase of reforms in the late-1980s moved gradually towards this market, but political conflict limited more radical changes and it was not until the early 2000s that the Austerity Market re-emerged on the agenda. Why, given the Netherlands' seemingly "market-oriented" starting point, have market reforms in health care been as controversial – perhaps even more controversial – than in Sweden and Britain? This section will argue that in order to answer this question, we need to look at how the universal but fragmented Dutch health system shaped the calculations of major political parties over the merits of different types of markets.

Towards the Austerity Market

Two packages of reforms have gradually transformed the Dutch health care system into an Austerity Market, where hospitals compete for contracts from cost-conscious purchasers while individuals also bear direct costs. As in England, the resulting market only approximates the ideal type. Nonetheless, we see that policymakers explicitly paired reforms aimed at making individual users more responsive to price signals with those making insurers and the state stronger buyers of health care.

A 1987 report drawn up by a government convened expert committee first proposed market reforms in the health care system. The "Dekker Committee," named after its chair, Wisse Dekker, drew on American models of "managed competition" to advance two major proposals (Blomqvist 2002; Greß *et al.* 2002). The first proposal was to integrate the private and social insurance systems by creating a government-defined basic care package covering about eighty-five percent of expenditure. This package would be funded through a mix of payroll taxes and a new flat-rate premium that enrollees would pay up front. Insurers could set the flat-rate premium at different levels, and offer optional insurance for services not covered in the basic package. The second proposal would give insurers the right to selectively contract with hospitals and doctors. Insurers would have to purchase carefully so as to cut costs and improve quality in order to attract enrollees.

In practice, the reforms building on this report (introduced first by the CDA-VVD governing coalition and its CDA-PvdA successor) failed to integrate the private and social insurers and only partially strengthened the insurers as purchasers. A series of reforms between 1989 and 1992 started to build and expand the basic care package, introduced a flat-rate premium for the social insurers, expanded the social insurers' scope to selectively contract with physicians and negotiate prices with hospitals, and required the social insurers to compete nationally. However, a final package of reforms that would have completed the integration of the social and private insurers and enhanced the insurers' purchasing role was scrapped due to political disagreement (Okma 1997: ch. 3).

Through the 1990s, the so-called "Purple Coalition" of the PvdA, VVD, and D'66 pursued few major reforms to the health care system, using the traditional lever of fixed government budgeting to control expenditure. In the early 2000s, this coalition revived Dekker's plans, again proposing to integrate the social and private insurers and strengthen the insurers' contracting role for basic care. When a CDA-VVD-D'66 (Balkenende II) coalition was elected in 2003, the new VVD health minister Hans Hoogervorst dramatically extended these proposals. Unlike previous proposals, Hoogervorst looked to integrate the private and social insurers by bringing the social insurers under private law (rather than bringing the private insurers under public law), which meant insurers would now face more liberal regulations on financial solvency and have the ability to turn a profit and provide voluntary insurance. Moreover, in contrast to previous plans to finance insurers largely through the tax system, Hoogervorst expanded the size of individual premiums and co-payments.

Both the early reforms and those in 2006 placed more risk on individuals and increased the power of insurers as contractors, building on the logic of an Austerity Market. First, both reforms intentionally moved towards more individual responsibility on the allocation dimension. The 1990 reforms introduced a small flat-rate premium that citizens would pay up front, moving away from fully financing health insurance through social insurance. The 2006 reforms considerably expanded this premium, with all citizens formerly covered under the social insurance system no longer paying any income-related premiums for basic care (they continue to do so for catastrophic care) and instead paying a much larger flat rate premium.[11] While many individuals receive an income-related subsidy, they nonetheless face strong price signals. The 2006 reforms further extended co-payments for care itself, introducing a "no-claims" bonus that would give citizens a reduction of 230 Euros in their premium if they did not use the health care during the year (with the exception of GP visits). The subsequent governing coalition removed the no-claims bonus, turning it into a flat deductible, but the basic thrust of the market remained: citizens had more financial incentives in purchasing insurance and using care. Indeed, Minister Hoogervorst (2004) stated: "By means of co-payments we intend to make the consumer more aware of the cost of health care and enhance his sense of responsibility for the costs of the system."

By contrast, both sets of reforms maintained relatively strong regulations on access, aiming to limit individual medical risk. The early reforms failed to integrate the social and private insurance systems, but did establish robust regulations in both sectors. Social insurers were required to accept all applicants and could not charge enrollees different rates, and further legislation later gave all individuals without a supplementary pension or with low income access to social insurance (den Exter *et al.* 2004). Through the 1980s and 1990s, the government also layered more regulation on private insurers, requiring them to offer certain categories of citizens a fixed package of care at a standard price. Early criticism from health policy scholars that the 1990 reforms failed to adequately compensate insurers for different risk pools, thereby creating incentives for insurers to "cream skim" lower-risk patients (van de Ven *et al.* 1994; Schut 1995), led the government to refine the system of risk adjustment through the 1990s.

The 2006 reforms extended this regulatory structure, creating a single insurance system and "leveling the playing field" between private and social insurers. Technically, insurers must largely charge their enrollees the same premium and cannot select enrollees based on risk. In practice, many do offer collective contracts to employers and other groups, which offer discounted prices, opening the door for some differentiation.

Together, these changes on the allocation dimension dramatically extended individual financial risk, though they continued to limit responsibility based on medical risk. The flat-rate premium rose from 70 EUR per year in the early 1990s to 239–390 EUR in 2005 and following the 2006 reforms it can top 1,200 EUR. Price signals have had an effect on consumer behavior – for instance, in the first few months of 2006, eighteen percent of

[11] These flat rate premiums amount to 45% of total expenditure, with the government contributing 5% from general taxation and employers contributing 50% through a payroll tax. The government and employers' contributions are pooled and distributed to the insurers based on a risk-adjusted capitation formula.

people switched insurers, selecting those with a collective contract, lower rates, or lower deductibles and higher rates (Smit and Mokveld 2006). However, as take-up rates among low-income individuals for assistance with premiums were lower than anticipated, there were concerns about the affordability of coverage (ZN Weekly 2006a). Although under one percent of Dutch citizens report costs prevent them from seeing a physician, out-of-pocket spending has increased and there has been a rising (albeit small overall) number of uninsured (Schäfer *et al.* 2010).

On the *production dimension*, both the 1990 and 2006 reforms introduced a logic of competition that enhanced the insurers' ability and incentives to contract with providers. The earlier reforms expanded insurers' scope to contract with hospitals, allowing them to negotiate on variable costs up to a fixed ceiling. While patients maintained much choice of physician, these reforms introduced the possibility of selective contracting of physicians (although not hospitals). Moreover, they gave the social insurers new financial incentives to purchase based on cost, extending their financial responsibility for cost overruns from three percent of expenditure in 1993 to fifty-three percent of expenditure by 2004 (den Exter *et al.* 2004). Indeed, for some services, the insurers bore a hundred percent of the responsibility for cost overruns. Although the reforms also expanded citizens' choice of social insurer, policymakers largely saw this move as a mechanism to create financial incentives for the insurers to purchase responsibly (Ministry of Welfare Health and Cultural Affairs 1988). As one senior official involved in the Dekker reforms stated: "We knew if we provided real choice, patients won't always go for cheapest solution, and this is where government gets into trouble, because it still wants to control costs" (Interview: Hugo Hurts, Ministry of Health official, 2004). Although in practice insurers were often limited – hospitals always negotiated the maximum fees and there was no real selective contracting of physicians – the early logic was aimed at enhancing their power.

The 2006 reforms dramatically extended this logic. These reforms expanded insurers' incentives to control costs by increasing the size of the flat-rate premium and their responsibility for cost overruns. Next to these incentives, the reforms expanded insurers' scope for contracting. As part of the 2006 reforms, the Dutch government introduced a new hospital financing system, which pays hospitals based on what they produce using a new product classification system called Diagnosis Treatment Combinations (DBCs). The government initially set maximum prices for over ninety percent of DBCs (and insurers can negotiate lower prices), but since 2006 has moved to allow open price and volume contracting for over thirty percent of procedures (Schäfer *et al.* 2010). The reforms maintain patients' choice of physicians, but they allow insurers to charge higher fees to patients who visit physicians outside of their contracts.

Both sets of reforms introduced a logic of control that has supported the power of the purchasers and the state itself. As in England, the market in the Netherlands initially appeared to empower the producers. Insurers lacked purchasing skills and there was little excess supply of services. However, central government regulation on maximum prices, overall expenditure, and market entry, soon limited the scope of hospitals and doctors to exploit their market position. The 2006 reforms removed some of these constraints, but insurers are increasingly developing their purchasing skills and the government retains the ability, and the willingness, to reassert price control (Interview: Ministry of Health official 2004). This regulation combined with increased monitoring of providers. In 1998 the government established an independent market regulator (NMa) for the entire economy, including health care, and in 2006 it introduced a Care Authority (NZa) dedicated to regulating the health care market. These regulators enhanced the insurers' purchasing role, for instance, by restricting physicians from contracting collectively. From the mid-1990s, the government further introduced an independent health care inspectorate (IGZ) that monitored the quality and performance of health providers.

Like the Austerity Market in the early English NHS, this market has reshaped production to emphasize cost efficiency. Although it was tight budgeting that drove the reduction of health care spending from 9% to 8.5% of GDP through the 1990s, changes in the behavior of insurers also played a role (den Exter *et al.* 2004; Helderman *et al.* 2005). Initially, insurers had limited ability to selectively contract and a 1995 study by the Sickness Fund Council found that the main effect of the early reforms was to promote consolidation in the insurance sector (Helderman *et al.* 2005). However, over time, insurers began to take a more active role in structuring contracts. For instance, the social insurers challenged the cartel power of providers of medical devices, reducing prices by up to a third (Helderman *et al.* 2005; den Exter *et al.* 2004). Today, selective contracting remains limited, but insurers are taking a stronger role in structuring contracts (Schäfer *et al.* 2010).

The more competitive climate also changed the behavior of insurers and hospitals in more subtle ways. Through the 1990s, the social insurers began investing in new tools of financial management, aiming to promote financial efficiency, protect their own financial position, and to some extent, provide customer-focused care (van de Ven and Schut 2000). Hospitals, too, invested in cost-accounting equipment and performance monitoring, looking to better define prices and products (den Exter *et al.* 2004). These hospitals also moved away from employing medical professionals in management roles and towards trained managers and rationalized employment practices (Interview: hospital manager, 2004). Traditionally, hospitals contracted with specialists rather than directly employing them. A 1993 government committee, headed by the former Dutch Prime Minister, Barend Biesheuvel, proposed bringing medical specialists under hospital control. When the government enacted these proposals in 1997, hospitals had already started contracting more extensively with specialists and some, such as pediatricians, had already agreed to become hospital employees (van de Ven and Schut 2000).

Although the evolution of competition was gradual, the emerging market created a new set of winners and losers in the health care system. Like the early NHS market, the introduction of competition through contracting strengthened the position of the insurers and the state. Following both fiscal austerity in the 1980s and the early market reforms, a number of small regional social insurers exited the market, with the number of social insurers falling from fifty-three to twenty-six between 1985 and 1993 (den Exter *et al.* 2004). The remaining insurers further consolidated their position by merging with commercially oriented private insurers. By 2005, almost all social and private insurers were linked through a common holding company – something non-existent before the reforms – with the five largest holding companies controlling seventy percent of the market (Helderman *et al.* 2005). In 1995 the umbrella organizations of the private and social insurers also merged, further aligning their interests. The 2006 reforms, in erasing the divisions between the social and private insurers, formalized this concentrated insurance system.

Equally, the state, by more actively supporting the purchasing function of insurers, began to increase its power. Until 1995, medical professionals ran the health care inspectorate as a self-regulating body. As the emerging market created a need to both manage competition and address the public's concerns about quality, the state assumed responsibility for monitoring quality and ended professional self-regulation (Interview: Ton Sonneveldt, Senior Official at Health Care Inspectorate, 2004). The 2006 reforms furthered this shift, establishing a new government regulator (NZa) to monitor the market.

These changes dovetailed with a broader shift in Dutch politics towards challenging the position of the corporatist partners (see ch. 3). Traditionally, the organizations representing major actors (for example, the physicians, or hospitals) in the health care system were intimately involved in all areas of management. This system came under fire from both the Dekker Committee and a 1993 parliamentary commission (de Jong Commission), which targeted the thirty-six advisory bodies in the health care system and internal corporatist representation in all the major parastatal organizations. In response to these concerns, the government moved to limit the decision-making power of non-state actors and reduced the overall number of advisory bodies (Okma 2001). Moreover, the state began to circumvent these actors altogether, conducting negotiations with individual firms on its own terms (Helderman *et al.* 2005). The Austerity Market enabled these shifts, both offering an alternative management logic and, as in the UK, moving the state beyond budgeting and regulating the sector to setting rules in areas traditionally guarded by the professionals.

The shifts discussed above – the rationalization of the position of medical specialists and greater state involvement in quality monitoring – have meant professionals have lost power in this market. Initially, Dutch hospitals and physicians reacted in ways that helped them maintain substantial control. A series of hospital mergers in the 1980s gave many hospitals regional monopolies and, as the market developed, hospitals continued to consolidate their position as a way to eschew competition (Lieverdink 2001). Physicians in the hospitals also remained involved in management, even as it became professionalized (den Exter *et al.* 2004). However, since 2006 the market has further weakened providers' positions. Initially, the insurers had over-funded hospitals, with costs rising in the 2006 to 2007 period. However, as insurers and the state limited this overfunding, hospitals began to face financial difficulties and reduced profitability (Schäfer *et al.* 2010).

Finally, in a similar vein to the early NHS market, the Austerity Market, in emphasizing cost efficiency, did little to reward quality or responsiveness (den Exter *et al.* 2004). Although it is difficult to separate the impact of the market from the government's tight budgetary control through the 1990s, over this period waiting lists and concerns about quality grew (den Exter *et al.* 2004). Dutch hospitals, like their counterparts in the UK, emphasized cost control, and it was the central government, not the hospitals, that put quality improvement and inspection on the agenda in the late-1990s. As waiting lists grew through the 1990s, this lack of responsiveness galvanized new patients' movements. This emphasis continues today, with patients' advocacy groups deriding the unclear position of the patient in the post-2006 system (ZN Weekly 2006b) and the government itself admitting that the market might not always put patients first (Schäfer *et al.* 2010).

As in the NHS, the Austerity Market recast the role of the state – and the insurers – away from simply controlling the overall budget in health care to setting incentives at the micro level. Far from reducing the size and scope of the state, this new market challenged the corporatist system and strengthened its position in setting incentives for efficiency through the health care system.

Why these markets?

Why did Austerity markets emerge in the Netherlands? Why has reform unfolded so slowly over the past twenty years? Dutch political parties have long held different preferences over the structure of the health care system.

The CDA historically supported public funding, within limits, and looked to defend the role of non-profit and confessional providers and insurers. The PvdA, by contrast, supported more state and municipal involvement in funding and provision, and protested the distinctions between the private and social insurers. Finally, the VVD backed a more limited public offer in terms of financing, and greater private, including for-profit, involvement in provision.

These preferences shaped the contours of debate in health care but did not lead to sharply polarized policy. The traditional style of Dutch health politics emphasized consensual and gradual policy changes, incorporating the interests of major stakeholders and the political parties. Indeed, representatives of health care insurers (public and private), providers, as well as employers and unions, were intricately involved in the policy process. This involvement of stakeholders in decision-making rested on substantial autonomy for these actors at the level of health delivery. The political parties mostly accepted the basic logic of an extensive state-financed system, with strong professional control in decision-making at all levels.

This commitment began to crack in the 1980s as Dutch economic problems grew. The government initially addressed problems of cost control and equity in the health care through "temporary" regulation and strict budgeting. However, by the mid-1980s, policymakers across the political spectrum saw the combination of statist and corporatist decision making as problematic. Nearly every decision – from how to pay physicians to whether to build a new hospital ward – went through the central government. However, the apparatus of central decision-making involved a plethora of advisory bodies and parastatal agencies with insurers, providers, and other social groups represented on their governing boards. The large bureaucracy managing the health care system was heavily constrained in the speed and character of its decision making (Okma 1997).

Moreover, while the central government could fix budgets, plan capacity, and issue regulations, it had little ability to shape how money was spent. For instance, the government could cap hospital budgets but because the medical specialists who worked in the hospitals were self-employed, these caps could not fully control costs or shape the way care in the hospital was provided. Even worse, the system gave private and social insurers and providers incentives to maximize, rather than control, budgets (Schut 1995). As one senior official from the Ministry of Health put it: "The problem was an inflexible system that was not able to cope with problems of medical innovation, aging population and so on – it was not a system we would need for the next decades. Budgets gave no incentives for anyone to search for effective solutions" (Interview: Hugo Hurts, Ministry of Health official, 2004).

Given these problems of cost control, inefficiencies and inequities, all the major parties agreed that reform was necessary. These generic concerns about the health care system met with specific concerns in the political parties (Okma 1997, 2004). Through the 1980s, the CDA emerged as the defender of a gentle form of fiscal austerity, looking to appeal to the electorate through its plans to limit, but also sustain, the state. The VVD was much more supportive of cuts, looking to separate income policy from health policy and echoing the concerns of employers over cost control. The PvdA also had long-standing ideological concerns about the system. The fragmentation across the social and private insurance systems created differential access to care. Private insurers usually paid physicians fee-for-service, whereas social insurers paid doctors for registered patients (capitation), leading to concerns that physicians had incentives to cater to the privately insured, who by law were upper income.

In this light, the parties advocated varying solutions. The parties split on conventional Left-Right lines in the area of allocation. On the right, in its 1982 manifesto, the VVD proposed privatizing parts of the social insurance system, limiting public coverage to a residual level, and increasing "individual responsibility" through private financing (Okma 2004: 29, Okma 1997: 72). On the left, the PvdA had long pushed for expanding the publicly funded system and socializing the private insurers (Okma 1997). The center-right CDA maintained an intermediate position, advocating a sizeable public package alongside extra privately financed insurance (Okma 2004: 29–30).

The parties held more complex preferences over how to structure production. The VVD, like the Moderates and British Conservatives, expressed a desire to reduce state intervention and limit the bureaucracy, later promoting for-profit alternatives. The party considered a range of proposals, from expanded choice to selective contracting, and over time pushed for greater purchaser contracting (Blomqvist 2002; Okma 2004: 30). The CDA was more ambivalent about expanding the purchasing role of the insurers, as it had long-standing links to incumbent providers and was cautious about disrupting their position. Finally, the PvdA, while not enthusiastic about competition, was willing to consider limited contracting providing it was sufficiently regulated (Okma 1997: 72).

To account for these differences, the Lubbers II (CDA-VVD) government established an independent committee with representatives of all the major parties charged with developing reforms to promote more integration of health care and long-term care, improve the efficiency and flexibility of health care provision, and move from government regulation to greater market regulation and self-regulation (Ministry of Welfare Health and Cultural Affairs 1988). This remit and the choice of Dekker, the Chairman of Philips Electronics, as committee chair, set the stage for market reforms. The committee's inclusive membership and technocratic approach led it to propose reforms combining the PvdA's overriding preferences for greater integration of the private and public insurance systems with the CDA's and VVD's preferences for more competition in the provision of services and greater cost-sharing.

At first, these proposals met with support – albeit often tepid – from the major political parties and outside actors. The social insurers and health providers saw the creation of a single health care system as leading to more resources and operational autonomy (Harrison 2004). Doctors and patient organizations, while concerned, were not immediately hostile (Okma 1997: 100). In this light, the CDA-VVD governing coalition (1986 to 1989) agreed to take Dekker's plans forward.

The 1989 election produced a new CDA–PvdA governing coalition, changing the tenor of health care reform. The task of introducing Dekker's reforms fell to a new PvdA junior minister, Hans Simons. In introducing the reforms, Simons had to perform a difficult balancing act between his party's preferences for greater uniformity between social and private insurers in the health care system and the CDA's (and the opposition VVD's) desire for competition and private financing. To accomplish this dual shift, Simons proposed integrating the private and social insurers by creating a single care package under the auspices of the already universal insurance for catastrophic care (the AWBZ). Insurers would then compete based on this new package. Given that the AWBZ was already a universal insurance, using it to build the basic package was logical. However, Simons' plan essentially turned the fragmented health care system into a more uniform system *before* introducing market competition, by expanding the AWBZ and proposing that ninety percent of expenditure be covered through it (up from Dekker's proposed eighty-five percent) as a prerequisite for the competitive reforms.

This decision to emphasize greater solidarity over increased competition proved to be incredibly controversial. Much of the parliamentary debate focused on the income effects of this shift, debating the introduction of a flat rate – rather than a tax-financed – premium. Outside of Parliament, health stakeholders focused on other issues. The employers expressed concerns that Simons' plans could increase costs. Employers had to pay fifty percent of health expenditure, and they vociferously opposed a system in which entitlements could increase absent strong cost-control measures. They also joined the unions representing higher-paid professionals in protesting the income effects of the reforms, which they argued would penalize higher-income individuals. The private insurers further rejected the reforms, which they saw as essentially ending the private insurance sector. The unions took a different stance, protesting the new flat rate premium. Physicians and hospitals were also unhappy, seeing not too little but too much competition for resources (Okma 1997: 130, 144).

These external criticisms combined with the preferences of the political parties to galvanize opposition to Simons' changes. The VVD, voicing the employers' objections, argued that competition in this more uniform system could be inflationary, absent a strong logic of contracting (van de Ven and Schut 2000; Okma 1997: 70, 130). In the early 1990s, it withdrew its support from the Dekker reforms, pushing instead for incremental change. At the same time, support from the CDA began to fall apart. While the CDA leadership agreed with the VVD in many respects, in practice, one wing of the party was unwilling to support a dramatic increase in the power of purchasers at the cost of producers. The parliamentary party supported a strike by the association of general practitioners (LHV), who were concerned about both the integration of general practice into the universal package and insurer contracting (van de Ven and Schut 2000; Okma 1997: 144). At the same time, another wing of the CDA, represented primarily in the Senate, sided with the VVD and effectively blocked reform (Okma 1997: 144). P. B. Boorsma, an original member of the Dekker committee and a CDA representative in the Senate, emerged as a vociferous opponent of the Simons plan, claiming Simons had gone "too far" in moving towards greater socialization of benefits (Interview: P. B. Boorsma, 2004).

Although opposition from key stakeholders – and the public – was important in determining the fate of these early reforms, it was the strategic interests of the parties themselves in the Dutch system that determined the outcome. All three parties were willing to consider markets, but they parted on the details. The PvdA would accept greater competition based on a mix of choice and contracting only if the health care system moved to a more uniform benefit structure, erasing the distinctions among insurers and offering a comprehensive package. The VVD was concerned that competition in this uniform system would cause cost inflation without a strong purchasing role for insurers. Finally, the CDA was cautious about introducing stronger contracting because of its constituents among physicians and providers. The PvdA, CDA, and VVD further disagreed over cost-sharing, battling over the size of the nominal premium and the scope of the basic package. Because Dekker's proposals had to be introduced in steps and each step emphasized different aspects of the plan – integrating the private and social insurers, changing the premium structure, and expanding contracting – the generic consensus over the reforms gave way as the details of each step emerged (van de Ven and Schut 2000).

Reform in the 2000s: A second move towards Austerity Markets

When the PvdA-VVD-D'66 governing coalition was elected in 1994, it turned away from systematic reform in health care, maintaining the nascent market structure alongside strong central control over expenditure and planning. Tight budgeting through the 1990s though, led to growing queues and citizen dissatisfaction. Employers too, were dissatisfied. Reforms to the disability system in the 1990s had increased their financial responsibility for illness, giving them an interest in the speed and quality of medical care. In the face of long queues, some employers had begun to purchase care privately for their employees (Brouwer and Hermans 1999).

Thus actors from the Left to the Right faced pressure to reform the system. Both the PvdA and D'66 saw growing public discontent as a threat to solidarity, and supported reducing waiting lists and improving quality in the publicly funded system. By contrast, the VVD, while also supporting waiting list reduction, saw rising demand as insatiable, and advocated more private expenditure and a reduction of the basic package to control health expenditure in the long-run (Okma 2004). Moreover, the electorate was demanding change. In 2002, over half of citizens named health the most important issue, and seventy-seven percent of the population reported problems with the government's waiting list policies (TNS NIPO 2002).

As these demands began to peak, the government "took off the brakes" and removed budgetary caps (Ministry of Health 2002). However, once again, there was consensus across the political parties that simply spending to appease the public was unsustainable in the long run (Interview: Els Borst, D'66, 2004). In response to these pressures, in 2002, the Minister for Health, Els Borst from the centrist D'66 party, reintroduced a proposal to integrate the social and private insurers and introduce greater competition among providers for contracts with the insurers. However, in contrast to the emphasis on cost control in the 1980s, this plan looked to create a greater "demand orientation" by pairing market forces with more spending and uniform benefits. As one of the chief architects of the reforms stated: "In 2000 the economy was booming and so the idea was to put less emphasis on cost containment and more to innovation and client preferences. We saw reintroducing market mechanisms as helping with this" (Interview: former Ministry of Health official, 2004).

As in the 1980s, the details of these reforms ran up against the preferences of the different coalition partners. Partisan conflict emerged over the size of the public package, the extent of cost sharing, and the scope of contracting (Helderman *et al.* 2005). As the parties went into the 2003 election, the PvdA promised to reduce waiting lists through government spending, and to avoid cost sharing, while both the VVD and CDA advocated bringing the insurance system under private law and increasing the size of the nominal premiums (Piersma 2003).

The 2003 elections produced a more ideologically cohesive governing coalition of the CDA–VVD–D'66, both willing and able to take more extensive reform ahead. The combination of the earlier health care reforms and the need to tackle rising costs brought the CDA closer to the position of the VVD. Moreover, the growing secularization of Dutch society and the CDA's weakened relationship with providers made it more willing to change the system (see ch. 3). These shifts in position created a government with more homogenous views on how to introduce markets in an increasingly uniform health care system, allowing it to move towards a more extensive Austerity Market that expanded contracting and direct costs to users.

The 2006 reforms followed a traditional negotiated path, but partisan officials from the Ministry of Health and Ministry of Finance emerged as strong proponents of reform. This time stakeholders' concerns met with less political support. A poll of physicians found that sixty percent did not support the reforms, seeing them as threatening quality and professional control (Putters *et al.* 2006). Instead, the physicians largely supported the existing system, pushing for more spending within it (Putters *et al.* 2006). Yet, the earlier reforms had weakened the position of providers and other actors in the system, creating fewer independent sources of power among doctors and hospitals. Unlike in the early 1990s, the CDA did not support the physicians' protest against the 2006 reforms. Equally, the VVD was committed to a long-term restructuring of the welfare state and although receptive to employers' concerns, it was less tied to them. Indeed, the VVD minister Hans Hoogevorst followed employers' calls for "collective contracts"; but the final reforms did not fully address their concerns about financing half of health expenditure without a strong influence on cost control (Interview: Machel Nuyten, VNO-NCW official 2004; Interview, ZN official 2005). The majority position of the governing coalition combined with a weakening of the stakeholders' position, a partial consequence of the earlier changes, allowed the government to push ahead. The electorate was also hardly supportive of these changes, with over half expressing doubts about the reforms (Putten *et al.* 2006), and more recently, in a poll commissioned by the labor federation, sixty percent expressed doubts about markets in public services (TNS NIPO 2010). However, its discontent over waiting lists, fueled by decades of austerity and long queues, emboldened reformers.

Subsequent elections again produced new governing coalitions in the Netherlands. The fourth Balkenende coalition (2007 to 2010), this time composed of the CDA, PvdA, and the Christian Union party, moved ahead with the reforms, moderating them slightly in the face of some rising costs and concerns about affordability about the uninsured. However, as citizens face higher out-of-pocket payments, as hospitals face greater competition, and insurers begin to act like private companies, the question of whether subsequent governments will be willing to follow through on them is still open.

The story of Dutch health care reform is one of broad consensus among political actors that the system needed reform and that this reform should involve substantially changing the incentives for doctors and hospitals. However, differences in the preferences of key actors over the type of market limited actual reform. The first attempts fell apart as the PvdA emphasized solidarity, the CDA pushed for more limited competition, and the VVD looked for extensive competition and strong levers of cost control. As the health care situation worsened and the pressure on the government grew, consensus over the necessity of reform re-emerged. Once again, the parties battled over the details, however, this time these differences largely divided the government and opposition, not the government itself, allowing more extensive reform to go forward.

4.5 CONCLUSION

The market has been a key motif of reform in European health care systems since 1980, yet once we examine "under the hood" of these reforms, we actually find a great deal of diversity in how they were constructed, who benefited from them, and ultimately why they were chosen. Looking at developments across time and across countries, in fact there have been multiple market-making exercises in European health care over the last two decades. Early market reforms in the UK and Sweden look different from their more recent incarnations, and these differences follow the broad logic of markets outlined in this project. While Dutch markets varied less over time, they, too, look substantially different from the more recent English or Swedish markets. Markets in health care vary dramatically.

When we examine the politics of market reforms, we see that arguments that focus on either functional pressures or business interests do not hold up. In all three countries, while policymakers' desire to control costs and create incentives for efficiency was important, the move to introducing markets and the debates around them did not follow purely from these considerations. The presence of multiple types of markets in a single country, and multiple interpretations of markets across political parties, belie this technocratic approach. An emphasis on business pressure for markets also falls short in explaining these developments. While there was a rising tide of market reforms in the 1980s, the move to the market was not driven exclusively by the force of neo-liberal ideas or by business lobbying. The Left has not only used markets, but it has also used them in ways distinct to the Right. Indeed, the Dutch case demonstrates a peculiar example of left-wing parties advocating markets and right-wing parties resisting them at points. This apparent paradox, as well as market advocacy by the Left in Sweden and the UK, can be resolved by investigating the different kinds of markets preferred by each party. The calculus for the British, Swedish, and Dutch Left, to employ markets as a way of sustaining the welfare state, differed substantially from that of their Right counterparts.

Parties on the Right in each of these three countries considered markets aimed at widely increasing private financing and provision of health, but they introduced markets that looked quite different from these ambitions. Existing institutional structures in health care – which are largely uniform and universal – placed significant constraints on their action. By contrast, the Left could achieve its "first-best" options in health, pursuing its goals for more responsiveness and equity through a greater consumer orientation. These same institutional structures were thus more conducive to the Left's preferences than the Right's. The health care policy terrain remains highly contested, and far from symbolizing convergence or a rising tide of neo-liberalism, we see that markets in health have been constructed differently based on different political interests. The following chapter expands this analysis, turning to the development of education markets.

5

Education markets

The reform of education has provoked some of the fiercest clashes in modern times – among defenders of the Church and the state, hierarchy and a classless society, racial segregation and integration, the center and the periphery. The politics of education has been so divisive in part because of the promise education offers to shape how society changes. The debate over markets in education is no exception, with proposals to introduce everything from school vouchers, to Charter schools, to private companies providing education services, provoking intense political and scholarly conflict. For proponents of markets, competition is "the tide that lifts all boats," promising to improve equity and efficiency in the public sector (Hoxby 2003). Critics have been equally fierce in their opposition to markets, claiming they substitute the private good of a few for the public good of many (Molnar 1996; Apple 2001a).

In contrast to the grandiose claims by proponents and opponents of markets in education about their impact on equity, achievement, and costs, this chapter argues that there is considerable diversity in *how* markets in education work. Early market reforms in England and the Netherlands expanded choice in the publicly funded school system, both strengthening the state and devolving power to parents. The result was increased competition among schools to appeal to parents, while also placing more responsibility on parents (Two Tier market). In both cases, the Right introduced these markets in a fragmented system, targeting the benefits of choice to its constituents, while also making a broader appeal. Conversely, the Left in both countries altered these competitive incentives, with the Dutch Labour party (PvdA) supporting more state regulation, while British Labour supplemented the choice-based market with a less popular but more direct form of contracting (Managed Market). This latter move used markets as an addendum to new state control over low-performing schools and local governments. By contrast, in the uniform

Swedish system, the Right introduced private school choice absent strong national or local control, ceding much power to private schools while also placing some costs on parents (a mild Private Power market). The Left, preferring to maintain public control, kept the choice orientation but enhanced regulation (Consumer-Controlled market).

This chapter first examines broader debates about competition in education and the politics of market reforms, and then analyzes the market outcomes and differing partisan preferences in England, Sweden, and the Netherlands.

5.1: MARKETS IN EDUCATION

Since the 1980s, debates over markets in education have become more pronounced in both political and academic circles. Proponents of markets generally concede a role for the public funding of education to achieve desirable "neighborhood effects," but argue that centralized government control of the education system has both worsened pupil performance and created inefficiencies (Friedman 1955). Competition improves education by not only offering parents new alternatives and incentives for schools to improve, but also by disempowering a dysfunctional public bureaucracy and teachers' unions (see Chubb and Moe 1990; Rinehart and Lee 1991). By contrast, opponents of markets argue that as schools put profits above the people they serve, the education system becomes removed from the goal of educating all pupils (Molnar 1996; Apple 2001b). Markets enhance social inequity in the education system, undermining the public sector in a corrosive way.

The evidence on the outcomes of market reforms does not match this ideological furor. Some markets have delivered performance gains, saved money, or limited inequities, others clearly have not (Belfield and Levin 2005). More fundamentally, the trade-off between the market and the state is more complex than this debate allows for. Many OECD countries have not only expanded market forces but also state and local control over the curriculum, testing, and inspection (Eurydice 2007). In light of this diversity in outcomes, how do we understand markets? Why, given a lack of unambiguous results, have policymakers introduced markets in education? Why have they introduced particular types of markets?

This chapter argues that, as with health, different types of markets have been part of a substantial, ongoing, and multifaceted reorganization of contemporary education. Debates over university fees, school busing, and school selection have reinvigorated long-standing questions about what equitable education means and what responsibility the government has in securing it. At the same time, policymakers debate the proper balance among the state, parents, and teachers. Should schools be liberated from a cumbersome public bureaucracy or should the government maintain strong pedagogical standards? Should the state ensure the diversity and viability of schools, or do parents have the right to choose their school? These questions have emerged in debates over standardized testing, teaching sexual education, decentralization, home-schooling, and, of course, markets (Fuhrman and Lazerson 2006). Even in countries with a long history of parental rights and religious education, such as the Netherlands, concerns about the integration of Muslim minorities have politicized broader questions about who should control the education system (Driessen and Merry 2006).

At the core of these debates are questions about how to distribute resources and power in the education system; who bears the risk in ensuring high-quality and equitable public education, and who calls the shots over it? Policymakers across and within each country have not solved these debates in a single way. Standardized testing has often empowered central and local governments, home-schooling and school choice have empowered parents, and yet other reforms have expanded school and teacher autonomy over resources and pedagogical practices.

The introduction of markets has contributed to this diversity. As in health, there are different ways to structure the allocation dimension of education. Although few market proponents advocate placing extensive costs on pupils at the primary and secondary level, some do advocate allowing schools more scope for private financing through "top-up" fees (West 1991; Friedman 1955) and giving individuals more risk for accessing education by expanding academic selection across or within schools (Cox and Dyson 1971). They argue that these shifts will lead pupils to take their education more seriously, and lead to a more efficient societal allocation of education resources. By contrast, others argue that policymakers should not put any costs on pupils when introducing competition among schools, advocating extra funding for costly pupils and / or limits on selection to reduce the risk of cream-skimming (Viteritti 2003). Market reforms that introduce more individual risk (Austerity Markets, Two Tiered and Private Power) produce different outcomes to those that maintain a collective guarantee (Managed Markets, Consumer-Controlled, and Pork Barrel). The former systems give pupils more incentive to pay attention to the costs of education but risk increasing inequity and segregation among schools, while the latter systems avoid these potential gains and pitfalls.

In practice, more significant reform has targeted the production dimension. The most well-known method of creating competition in schooling involves expanding pupil choice, allowing students to choose a school (either in the public or private sector) and paying schools based on pupil numbers (Chubb and Moe 1990). However, choice is not the only way of introducing competition. Other reforms, such as Charter schools (publicly funded independent schools) and contracting with private firms, create competition for contracts from the government, not for direct pupil choice (Hill *et al.* 1997). How schools actually compete depends on how the government configures control over them. Whether the government maintains control over market entry, pricing, and more controversially, the content of education (i.e., through tests, teacher assessments, graduation rates) will affects how schools behave. Some market proponents advocate a deregulated model that gives schools the freedom to respond to wishes of their constituents without detailed control over market entry or pedagogy (Sexton 1987; Friedman 1955; Friedman 1995), while others argue that markets only deliver social benefits in highly regulated, information-rich environments (Levin 1991).

These debates suggest that the basic typology introduced in previous chapters applies to education markets. Choice-based markets (Consumer-Controlled and Two Tier) promise to deliver more responsiveness to parents but risk focusing on parental preferences to the exclusion of other educational goals. Clearly specified contracting (Managed Markets and Austerity Markets) will create more incentives for schools to be efficient and meet governmental performance goals but dampen schools' incentives to respond to parents and innovate. Finally, markets that give schools much power allow more flexibility and innovation (Pork Barrel or Private Power) but threaten to give schools the space to pursue their own interests without addressing the needs of parents or the government.

The politics of markets

Why do policymakers choose to distribute resources and power differently through market reforms? Much work on the politics of education reform stresses the role of interest groups in promoting or inhibiting change. For proponents of market forces, teachers' unions are an obstacle to change, preventing beneficial reforms and protecting a sub-standard status quo (Friedman 1995). Opponents of markets, by contrast, view the move towards markets as pushed by right-wing ideologues and pro-business lobbies looking to promote their own bottom-line (Apple 2001a; Molnar 1996; Apple 2001b).

By contrast, I argue that partisan politics shapes the logic of market making. Political actors have long battled over education, with the Right spending less on education than the Left in the aggregate and targeting funding to higher education over the primary and secondary levels (Ansell 2010). Moreover, the Right has often supported academic streaming, selection, and "back to basics" education, while the Left has focused on developing common schooling with less emphasis on student differentiation (see Heidenheimer 1974; Chitty 1989; Knight 1990; Lundahl 1990; Galston 2005).

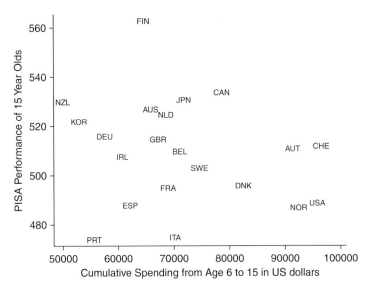

FIGURE 5.1: Resources spent and performance in science
The relationship between cumulative per pupil spending and student performance in PISA science tests.[1]

These traditional cleavages still matter, but over the past three decades both left- and right-wing parties have questioned traditional instruments of education policy. While escalating costs have been less important in education than in health, a growing disjuncture between the rising political and economic importance of education and declining public confidence in existing education practices has produced an equally fundamental re-evaluation. On the one hand, both left- and right-wing parties turned to education reform as part of new "supply side" economic agendas, looking to promote economic growth and oftentimes greater social opportunity (Boix 1998). On the other hand, academic research began to demonstrate a tenuous link between spending and performance (Hanushek 2003).

Figure 5.1 (see above) demonstrates this finding, plotting the average performance of fifteen-year-olds on standardized science tests against the cumulative resources that countries spend educating pupils. This finding politicized questions of education spending, giving parties the incentive to examine pedagogical practices and the structure of schools. Combined with the weakening political power of teachers' unions, this opened up questions over who should control the production of education, leading policymakers to explicitly challenge the educational establishment.

[1] Drawn from OECD 2008a.

As the political importance of education quality and performance grew, the political appeal of the Right's traditional preferences for lower spending and more selective education fell. However, these same pressures, in many cases, opened the door for the Right to frame education as not just a public good but also a private consumer good (Brown 1990). In this climate, market-based thinking on the value of choice and competition in education found an audience in the electorate, allowing the Right to make the first moves towards introducing markets in education, both in the United States and elsewhere (Murphy *et al.* 1998).[2]

As these market logics diffused, the Left took them up. Information on school performance not only led the Left to question education spending, but the structure of the education status quo more generally. Schools reproduced, not eliminated, social inequality. At the same time, parents were demanding change, creating new electoral pressures. Sustaining and promoting public support for an equitable and broad-based education system required reform. While using markets as an instrument of change ostensibly challenged more traditional left-wing notions of education as a tool of solidarity (Ball 1993), the Left saw specific types of markets as offering it a chance to both appeal to voters and tackle problems of equity, performance, and costs.

In general then, the Right has been far more positive than the Left towards market-based reform in education, promoting increased rights for private schools, parental choice, and reduced public funding, while the Left has supported more state control and choice in some contexts. However, parties have also had to respond to their particular national institutional context. Across the OECD, education is a universal service, meaning all children from the ages of five to seven up to sixteen are entitled to publicly funded education. The universality of education thus limits unpopular policies like reduced state funding. Education systems across the OECD vary though, in whether they offer education uniformly across pupils. Some give all pupils a uniform package of education – schools offer a set curriculum that does not vary across public and confessional schools, schools cannot select pupils based on ability, and pupils are not streamed within the school. By contrast, others are fragmented and allow differentiation across schools or pupils, streaming pupils into different

---

[2] Studies of public opinion on vouchers are notoriously unreliable because support rates vary substantially based on question wording. However, the Phi Delta Kappa/Gallup survey of a sample of the US population shows that from the 1970s through the late 1990s, just under half the population supported voucher programs. Through the 1990s, support for policies that allow parents to choose a private school increased from 24% in 1993 to 38% in 2005 (peaking at 46% in 2002), as did support for charter schools (see www.pdkintl.org/kappan/kpollpdf.htm). These data suggest that a sizeable portion of the electorate supports choice and other market policies, but is also favorable to the public system.

schools or programs. Chapter 2 argued that these two features shape the strategic trade-offs for parties. Right-wing parties tend towards choice in more fragmented systems where they can target it to their constituents, while the Left will resist choice in these systems and prefer contracting. The logic is reversed for more uniform systems.

The following section develops these arguments by examining England, Sweden, and the Netherlands, showing that in each case markets in education followed a particular logic, and that partisan preferences were crucial to determining this logic.

5.2: ENGLAND – MORE CHOICE AND CONTRACTING[3]

The 1944 Education Act established the modern structure of English education, creating a system of universal secondary education provided through state and religious schools. Initially, both the Conservative and Labour parties accepted this system, but over time, two of its features became increasingly controversial: the system of academic streaming, and local authority and professional control over schooling.

The 1944 act instituted academic streaming, dividing students across three types of secondary schools based on aptitude – selective grammar schools, and non-selective secondary moderns and technical schools. Through the 1950s and 1960s, Labour reformers argued that this system was divisive and elitist. Instead, the party promoted "comprehensive" schools that would provide high-quality education for pupils of all ability in a single school. The move towards comprehensives gained steam, with the number of pupils being educated in comprehensives growing from forty percent to ninety percent between 1970 and 1980 (Pring and Walford 1997). This trend ignited concerns in the Conservative party, as party leaders supported selective grammar schools and argued that comprehensives reduced educational standards (Lawton 1992).

Debates over academic streaming divided the Left and the Right, but in the 1970s, politicians across the political spectrum began to question the structure of local control. The 1944 act decentralized control to Local Education Authorities (LEAs), giving them responsibility for organizing school admissions, planning, staffing, and allocating funds to schools. The absence of a fixed curriculum or timetable for instruction further gave teachers and school heads wide latitude on a number of pedagogical and organizational issues (Lawton 1992). Through the 1970s, media reports emerged of progressive teaching practices and LEA policies out of touch with parental concerns. For instance, in 1974, newspapers reported on the

---

[3] Most reforms were also introduced in Wales. Scotland and Northern Ireland have separate systems.

William Tyndale school in the left-wing London LEA of Islington, where pupils allegedly had a choice of "whether or not to learn to read" and the headteacher claimed he "did not give a damn about parents" (Lawton 1992: 28; Woodward 2001). In response, both Labour and the Conservative politicians began to question the educational establishment. Parents too, began to question the system, with the percentage of people rating education as "the most important issue" facing Britain doubling from twelve percent of respondents to twenty-four percent between 1974 and 1980 (MORI 2007).

Against this background, both the Conservative and Labour parties turned to market reforms as a way of reorganizing the education system and changing the balance of power among the state, teachers, and schools, and parents and pupils. The Conservatives made the first move in the late 1980s, introducing a Two Tiered market (individual responsibility, consumer choice) within the public sector. Labour extended this market, but it also introduced a Managed Market (collective responsibility, state contracting) built around private contracting for LEA and school management. The former market placed costs on individuals and structured competition around individual choices, while the latter insulated pupils from costs and created competition to respond to the state's preferences. This section argues that in order to understand these two markets we need to look at how the fragmented institutional structure of English education allowed the Conservatives to achieve their preference for more choice and preserving elite schools without major cost inflation, while the same structure limited Labour.

The Conservatives and choice

In 1988, the Conservative government introduced the Education Reform Act (ERA), creating a new privileged set of schools, dramatically expanding the role of the central government, and extending parental choice in the publicly funded system (referred to as "state schools"). Together, these changes created a Two Tiered market (individual responsibility, user choice) that gave parents more "risk" in procuring education and reoriented how schools operated to make them more responsive to parental demands.

First, as with the early NHS reforms, the ERA introduced small changes in the allocation of benefits. The ERA did not explicitly change the financing of education, but tight funding during this period meant education spending as a percentage of GDP fell from 5.57% in 1980 to 4.69% in 1989 (World Bank 2002). The ERA did change the system of access, creating a privileged new class of new "Grant Maintained" (GM) schools independent of local control and funded directly by the central government.[4] The reforms gave GM schools extra funding and more scope for selection. Indeed, seventy-nine percent of GM schools received a real increase in per pupil funding between 1990 and 1991 and 1995 to 1996, compared to only forty-three percent of LEA schools (Levačić and Hardman 1998). Although GM schools were not immediately allowed to change their admissions policy (for example to change from a comprehensive to a grammar), grammars and former grammars were heavily over-represented among GM schools, and they were later given some scope to select pupils.[5] Stephen Ball (1993) further estimates up to thirty percent of GM schools used "covert" methods like admissions interviews to select more able pupils.

State policy then, funneled additional resources to a privileged class of schools. Although there is debate about the impact of choice on school segregation, we do see increased segregation in areas with large concentrations of GM schools (Taylor *et al.* 2005). In London, 34% of LEA pupils were eligible for Free School Meals (a standard measure of deprivation) compared to only 20% of GM school pupils, and 18.1% of LEA pupils were not fluent in English in contrast to 8.2% of GM school pupils (Levačić and Hardman 1999).

More substantially, the 1988 reforms redistributed power in the system, explicitly introducing a logic of competition based on pupil choice. Before the reforms, LEAs had the power to determine admission to schools, and actively redistributed students across local schools. In 1985, sixty-one percent of LEAs used catchment areas to allocate pupils to schools, with only thirty-nine percent allowing some form of parental choice (Forrest 1996). The ERA challenged LEA control, giving parents the right to choose any school, requiring schools to admit pupils up to their maximum physical capacity, and allowing parents to appeal LEA admission decisions. At least eighty percent of school funding now came from a weighted per-pupil payment, making schools dependent on pupil numbers to secure their budget. The reforms further provided parents with new performance indicators, motivating them to select schools based on performance.

Alongside these changes on the "demand" side of the market, the reforms also altered the "supply side," giving schools more autonomy to respond to

---

[4] The reforms also established City Technology Colleges (CTCs), self-managed secondary schools funded partly by private sponsorship, which targeted low-income pupils. In practice, only fifteen of these schools emerged (Chitty 2009).

[5] All schools with a minimum of three hundred pupils could apply for GM status (including religious schools), following a vote by the school governors and approval through a parental ballot. In 1997, seventeen percent of secondary schools and three percent of primary schools were GM and nearly forty percent of schools had some type of special status, as a grammar school, GM school, City Technology College, or a religious school (Fitz *et al.* 1997).

parental preferences. The new principle of Local Management of Schools (LMS) gave the schools (headmasters and governing boards) control over internal management issues, including day-to-day expenditure and staffing. Schools were allowed to dismiss teachers, with the costs covered externally, and to expand in response to demand.

The logic of control accompanying this new market backed up parental choice. The ERA was the Conservatives' longest piece of legislation, giving the Secretary of State for Education 451 new powers, including establishing a national curriculum covering seventy percent of school activities and standardized testing (Chitty 2009). The ERA expanded the role of Her Majesty's Inspectorate (HMI) in monitoring schools, and reforms in 1992 created a new independent body (Ofsted) responsible for inspecting schools and publishing the results. The reforms also directly limited local actors, abolishing the powerful Inner London Education Authority.

The Conservatives, then, pursued a different strategy in education than in health or elderly care, creating a Two Tiered market that placed some risks on parents and primarily structured competition among schools to attract parents in a heavily regulated environment. Actual competition was slow to emerge and geographically variable, but it did start to reshape the way schools produced education. Hardman and Levačić's (1997) study of 276 secondary schools from 1991 to 1994, finds that a hundred schools gained pupils and thirty-one lost pupils (with 145 remaining roughly constant) and that these gains and losses were largely related to differential popularity among schools. A survey of school heads further supports the idea that real competition began to emerge, with eighty-six percent of heads reporting their local market was competitive in 1998, up from only sixteen percent of heads in 1992 (Davies *et al.* 2002).

In contrast to the early NHS market, schools competed to get pupils – not to improve efficiency. In so doing, they emphasized visible "quality" indicators, such as test scores and responsiveness to parents. There is some evidence that objective measures of quality did improve following the introduction of the market, with an across-the-board increase (albeit not dramatic) in test scores (Bradley *et al.* 2000). Schools with good exam results and low rates of truancy experienced growth (Bradley *et al.* 2000). More telling than these aggregate changes, are changes in the behavior of schools themselves. In looking to compete, schools engaged in a range of promotional activities aimed at appealing to parents (Davies *et al.* 2002). In contrast to what many proponents of school choice hoped, this competition often led schools to emphasize similar features, such as past-history (for example, grammars) and non-academic policies (for example, school uniforms) rather than pedagogical diversity (Gorard 1997; Halpin *et al.* 1997).

While activity at the school level increased faster than costs through the 1990s (Levačić 2004), the structure of competition did not necessarily improve efficiency. Stuart Maclure (1992) argues that in moving to open enrolment, parental preferences, not efficiency, became the key criteria for school size. Schools looking to attract pupils often offered the same programs as other schools in their area, creating surplus capacity, particularly at the senior levels, and a mismatch between pupils and places (Audit Commission 1996a).

Despite this lack of competition on costs, the Conservative government's strict budgeting kept overall expenditure under control, and some schools experienced a real decline in resources (Levačić and Hardman 1998). In response to the falling birth rate, the central government and the LEAs eliminated 1.25 million places through the 1980s (Maclure 1992). The combination of "inflationary" market measures and tight spending created problems for the government. In some urban areas, good schools were so heavily oversubscribed that they were able to select pupils, frustrating parents. Challenges to school admissions decisions grew from 4.2% to 8.7% between 1993 and 1998, with a steeper increase in London (Taylor *et al.* 2002).

The changes brought by the Two Tier market substantially redistributed power in the education system. The days when LEAs could restrict choice and schools could disregard parental concerns were over, as parents had new sources of power (Lawton 1992). Unlike competition in the NHS, education markets did not substantially empower the state over financial allocation and management. Finally, the market antagonized the unions and LEAs, but it enabled individual schools and their headmasters to emerge as important actors in the system. These groups increasingly had access to the policy process, and were influential players when Labour entered office in 1997 (Interview: former political advisor to Labour 2004). The emerging playing field, then, reflects the more fragmented power structure of a choice-based market.

Labour's changes

After coming to government in 1997, Labour largely accepted the Two Tiered market. It maintained the more individualized structure of allocation. The party developed more transparent rules for school selection but did not abolish the remaining 164 grammar schools. Instead, it transformed existing GM schools and other specialized schools into a new category of "Foundation Schools" that continue to be independent (albeit less so) from LEA control. Indeed, it actually expanded selection, allowing schools with a specialism to select up to ten percent of pupils based on fit with their profile. Taylor *et al.* (2005) find that Labour's agenda has increased segregation since 1997.

Equally, Labour kept the basic competitive structure in school production, tightening the link between pupil choices and school budgets. Starting in 2000, Labour began to promote specialist schools as a way to expand parental options. Specialist schools, first introduced by the Conservatives, are schools that offer a particular academic profile, like dance or technology. When a school achieves specialist status, it receives an outright grant of £100,000 and an increase of £126 per pupil for four years (Taylor *et al.* 2005). Initial policy restricted specialist status to high-performing schools that could raise funds through outside sponsorship, with Labour loosening these requirements and extending the program to fifty percent of secondary schools (Fitz *et al.* 2006). In emphasizing specialism and diversity, Labour abandoned its advocacy of the old comprehensive model and sharpened competition among schools for pupils.

However, other aspects of Labour policy have moved in different directions. Most prominently, Labour increased education spending by sixty percent in real terms between 1999 and 2007 to 2008, with the bulk of this spending going to primary and secondary schools (Johnson 2004). Part of this increased funding went to specialist schools, but much of the central government's effort looked to combat educational disadvantage. Labour altered the funding system within LEAs to be more sensitive to cost differences among pupils, making low-income pupils and those with special needs more attractive to schools. Alongside spending, Labour dramatically increased state regulation of performance, even establishing centrally directed pedagogical strategies.

As part of this increase in state control, Labour introduced new markets: Managed Markets (collective responsibility, state contracting) that work through a range of centrally or locally directed contracts. Initiatives such as Education Action Zones (EAZs), which used competitive bidding for plans to improve education in "deprived areas," the "Excellence in Cities" program, which supported a range of school-level programs (including specialist schools), and the City Academy program that funds independently managed schools in deprived areas, all used contracts with private and public producers to address the problems of "failing" schools and local governments (Power *et al.* 2004). Labour also expanded private funding for capital investment, signing 239 deals with private actors to build or remodel schools by 2003 alone (Driver and Martell 2006). Furthermore, Labour passed legislation in 1998 giving the Secretary of State for Education the power to force LEAs to outsource their management, and further legislation in 2002 allowing LEAs to voluntarily contract out with the private sector. The government first used this power in 2000 when it outsourced entire local governments perceived to be failing, such as Leeds, Doncaster, Hackney, and Islington, later extending contracting to other LEAs.

These diverse reforms maintained a collective structure of allocation while creating a distinct logic of competition for contracts. Initially, the government had to "create a market," as there were few private providers willing to take over some of the poorest or most troubled schools and LEAs. However, providers did start to enter the market, and most contracts linked their compensation to a range of centrally or locally determined performance measures. Even though many of these reforms occurred in areas of weak governments, such as failing LEAs, the central government and Ofsted maintained control by remaining closely involved in monitoring producers. The skill of LEAs in writing and monitoring contracts also improved in some areas (Power *et al.* 2004). The contracts were not always efficiency oriented, yet they left little question that it was the state – not parents – that schools and management firms should respond to.

Scholars debate the impact of contracting on schools' academic performance and the quality of local governance. In some LEAs, such as Hackney, the private contractors appear to have considerably improved local governance (as assessed by Ofsted); however, in other parts of the country, such as the Northern LEA of Doncaster, there has been less improvement (Ofsted 2003a, 2003b). More broadly, debate exists over the scope of overall improvements in contracting and other initiatives (Confederation of British Industry 2005; Hatcher 2006).

Despite these debates, there is agreement that these evolving markets reshaped the balance of power in the education system. The Managed Market essentially operated as an addendum to strengthening state control over LEAs and low-performing schools. An official at the Department for Education and Skills stated that her department saw contracting as one of the "finest achievements" of early Labour policy, forcing LEAs to raise standards (Interview: Sheena Evans, DfES official). By contrast, the local government response was more hostile and frustrated (Interview: Graham Lane, Labour former chair of the Local Government Association 2005). These markets did advantage new private actors, but ongoing central government control avoided merely delegating power to the private sector. Finally, the market benefited parents in poorly performing schools, but did not provide any direct benefits to parents as a group.

Why these markets?

Why did the Conservatives initially pursue a Two Tier strategy? Why did Labour accept elements of this market and yet also pursue a Managed Market? Answering these questions requires looking at the preferences of both parties over the direction of the education system and the particular constraints – and opportunities – the fragmented education structure offered.

The Conservative party was elected in 1979 against a background of long-standing debates over selection and rising public discontent with the system. The Conservatives' core education reform preferences were for academic streaming and a more differentiated public system. The party opposed Labour's move to comprehensives and questioned prevailing educational standards (Cox and Dyson 1971). Through the 1970s, market-based approaches gained steam within the party. The new cadre of "voucher men" occasionally clashed with those supporting a "back to basics" approach, but both groups were deeply critical of the public sector (Chitty 2009: 31). Keith Joseph, the Secretary of State for education (1981 to 1986), and a key market proponent, stated: "We believed leveling in schools had to stop, that excellence had to return. Our key perception was differentiation" (Knight 1990: 152).

These proposals antagonized many teachers' unions and local authorities. The English educational landscape was highly fragmented, with teachers organized in multiple and often competing unions and the local education authorities (LEAs) acting both independently and collectively. Despite these divisions, these actors had substantial power. Formally, the "Burnham system" involved the unions in national-level negotiation of teacher's pay; informally, they had a strong relationship with the Department of Education (Chitty 2009). LEAs further had much control over the content and structure of local education. Both groups largely embraced the move towards comprehensive education and new pedagogies, complaining of underfunding and opposing proposals (from both Labour and the Conservatives) for more regulation of the curriculum, assessment, and the profession itself (Chitty 1989; Timmins 2001).

This opposition, combined with internal divisions within the Conservative party, initially tempered the Conservative government, leading it to pursue only minor reforms. The first major reform in 1980 introduced the "Assisted Places" scheme, which provided funding to "able" pupils from needy backgrounds to attend fee-charging private schools. While ideologically important, the scheme was limited in scope, and in 1995 it only covered 29,800 pupils at 294 schools (West 1997). The 1980 reforms also appeared to expand parents' choice of school. However, they allowed the LEAs to restrict the number of places in a school by up to twenty percent below its overall capacity, inadvertently increasing their control over school admission policy (Maclure 1992).

When strident voucher proponent Keith Joseph became Secretary of Education in 1981, the stage seemed set for more radical reform (Lawton 1992: 30). However, Joseph faced bureaucratic and political resistance to his voucher proposals, leading him to declare vouchers a "dead issue" before the 1983 election (Lawton 1992; Chitty 2009). Later, Joseph elaborated on this failure, stating it was largely political: "Finances certainly didn't enter into it. No, it was political. In the sense . . . that you would have to have very controversial legislation, which would take two or three years to carry through, with my Party split on the issue and the other Parties all unanimously hostile on the wrong grounds" (quoted in Callaghan 2006: 47).

However, as open conflict between the government and the teachers' unions erupted over pay negotiations, alongside ongoing conflict with Labour-controlled LEAs over spending targets, the Conservative party became more committed to reform which reduced the dominance of education "producers" (Lawton 1992: 35; Maclure 1992). Both these pay disputes and growing concerns about performance led the Conservatives to see the LEAs and teachers as an impediment, in both pedagogical and organizational terms, to better education policy. These concerns partly built on Labour Prime Minister James Callaghan's famous 1976 "Ruskin College" speech, where he questioned whether the educational establishment was adequately responsive to parents and the needs of industry (Chitty 2009). Research in the 1980s further showed that Britain's students were lagging behind those in other European countries (Prais and Wagner 1985). This work further galvanized Conservative critiques of teacher control of pedagogy, and reinvigorated questions of how to pursue "excellence" in education (Knight 1990).

In response, a number of Conservative think tanks and internal government reviews offered reform proposals. These proposals were largely united in advocating market-based change, but they differed in how they envisaged structuring competition and control. Both the Institute for Economic Affairs (IEA) and the Hillgate Group advocated expanding private school funding and pupil choice (Seldon 1986; Sexton 1987). However, the IEA also supported greater deregulation of schools, with the Hillgate Group looking to promote traditional values in education through increased state control over the curriculum. Margaret Thatcher presented a third approach, supporting private ownership and selection through direct government funding of private and grammar schools (Thatcher 1993: 578; Baker 1993). As in the NHS (see ch. 4), the Conservatives had multiple options on the table, but in education the party chose a Two Tier market. In order to understand this choice, we need to look at how the party's preference for a more differentiated system played out in the universal but fragmented education system.

The universality of the system limited movement on both the allocation and production dimension. When Thatcher mentioned that the government had not ruled out the charging of fees, the political furor was instant and fierce, forcing the reformers to rapidly backtrack (Baker 1993; Chitty 2009). Key politicians, including Thatcher herself, pushed to introduce a new category of highly privileged schools, yet these shifts were also more limited than those on the Right of the party had hoped for (Callaghan 2006: 94). Equally, the party rejected proposals for more producer control, turning away from plans allowing public money to go to private schools absent public oversight and proposals to give Grant Maintained schools exemptions from the national curriculum (Chitty 2009; Maclure 1992). The Conservative leadership saw the former moves as too politically risky and subject to parliamentary opposition, while the latter ran up against the more authoritarian impulses in the party as well as bureaucratic resistance (Chitty 2009; Callaghan 2006; Baker 1993). Reforms that would delegate power to schools without clear oversight (i.e., Pork Barrel or Private Power markets) were off the table.

In contrast to the NHS, whose uniform structure meant that choice risked cost inflation without delivering clear benefits, the fragmentation in the education system meant choice promised to deliver targeted benefits to middle-class constituents and extend its differentiated structure. Even though few grammars remained, the reforms, in enhancing choice and introducing GM schools, gave a powerful tool to grammars and other schools dissatisfied with their LEAs. Indeed, both Thatcher (1993) and Kenneth Baker (the Secretary of State who enacted the reforms) expressed the hope that choice would accomplish precisely this outcome. Baker stated "I would have liked to bring back selection but I would have got into such controversy at an early stage that the other reforms would have been lost." When probed on the question of whether parental choice would "kill off the comprehensive," Baker replied: "Oh, yes. That was deliberate. In order to make changes, you have to come from several points" (quoted in Davies 1999). This move combined with the expectation that schools who opted out of LEA control would provide a powerful lobby able to resist further change, preserving the more differentiated structure (Maclure 1992). Moreover, in contrast to the NHS, where demand was increasing, the risks of increased spending in education were attenuated by the smaller size of the post-baby-boom birth cohorts.

The Conservative leadership was the key force behind these changes, reorienting the education system around its own goals. Both the market reforms and the centralizing elements of the reforms antagonized teachers and LEAs. As in the health care system, the Conservatives largely ignored these protests. The party had never been close to these groups, and lost little from their antagonism. It did, by contrast, compromise with the churches (who had close ties to several Conservative peers in the House of Lords) but these concessions did not fundamentally alter the legislative package. The party had a solid majority in Parliament and, by introducing both new national standards and markets, it was able to quell internal party concerns over the reforms (Callaghan 2006). Equally, it waited out the electoral concerns over the reforms. The market was popular in the long-run, but public opinion polls at the time showed low levels of support for it

(Whitty and Menter 1988). However, the public was receptive to aspects of the Conservative critique of teachers and nervous about Labour's links to the unions, which emboldened the Conservatives (Whitty and Menter 1988). In enacting the reforms shortly after its 1987 electoral victory, capitalizing on the power of the British executive, and building on public concerns about teaching practices, the Conservative party was able to work around this opposition.

The Two Tiered market, then, emerged from Conservative elite strategy. It constituted an internal party compromise between those advocating hierarchical control of the system and those advocating markets, combining both state control over the curriculum and greater school competition. While targeting benefits to constituents, this move also recognized that education was a mass good and that the Conservatives could no longer defend grammars and the private sector without dealing with the system as a whole. Nonetheless, the new market moved the education system closer to the party's preferred point, allowing more competition and differentiation among schools, with less differentiation in basic program or pedagogy. As we see below, this strategy worked, changing the options available to Labour in reforming the system.

Labour's changes

Labour's 1997 election campaign slogan "education, education, education" promised to improve education as a way of reviving the economy, promoting equity, and improving public services. However, this promise occurred against the backdrop of the Two Tiered market and the changed political playing field that it created. On the one hand, the market exposed the Conservatives' tight education spending, provoking public discontent, something Labour capitalized on. By 1992, forty-two percent of voters preferred Labour on education, compared to twenty-six percent preferring the Conservatives, up from thirty-one percent and twenty-nine percent respectively in 1987 (MORI 2009). Furthermore, it increased state power vis-à-vis the unions and LEAs, giving Labour stronger instruments of central control. On the other hand, the Two Tier market's emphasis on parental choice limited the appeal of Labour's old rallying cries for comprehensive education. Labour felt under pressure to respond to middle-class parents and develop an "inclusive strategy that would bind the middle class to the system" (Interview: Senior Labour political advisor 2004b), dispelling the perception it was anti-parent, anti-excellence, and overly pro-teacher.

Politically, Labour needed to appeal to the middle classes and their preferences for more differentiated and responsive education (Tomlinson 2001). At the same time, Labour had a long-standing preference for improving the education of lower-income pupils as a way of producing greater social opportunity (Lawton 2005). Indeed, as Labour moderated ideologically through the 1990s, Blair began to promote education (rather than income redistribution) as a means to reduce poverty (Blair 1998). The British school system had one of the highest rates of income inequality in educational performance, one of the largest low-skill populations, and one of the lowest rates of post-sixteen pupil education in Europe (Glennerster 2001; Johnson 2004). Educational disadvantage bred societal disadvantage, and tackling failure in schools was key to addressing social exclusion (Shaw 2008). Blair's (1996) promise to make the "state education system in Britain so good, so attractive, so supported by the overwhelming majority of parents that we can put behind us the educational apartheid, private and public, of the past" required reforms that appealed to the "top" of the income spectrum while addressing the problems at the "bottom" end.

In opposition, Labour looked to balance these dual concerns by shifting the debate away from markets and grammar schools, while also accepting much of the Conservatives' expansion of choice and state control over standards. Shadow Secretary of Education, David Blunkett, argued for attention to "standards" not "structures" as a way of refocusing the education debate towards improving performance. Blunkett told the party's left wing in 1995, "Read my lips, no more selection." Rather than stressing selection, though, he built on the work of former trade unionist and education professor Michael Barber to promote an investment in early-years education and national strategies for teaching math and reading (Barber 1996).

When elected, Labour continued this juggling act, leaving much of the existing educational structure, and to some extent, its ethos, in place. Both Labour's rhetoric and policy emphasized parental power, central authority, and some mistrust of teaching professionals and local government. The Labour leadership chose not to abolish the remaining grammar schools, much to the disappointment of the unions and the party's left wing, and supported the controversial head of Ofsted, Chris Woodhead, a vocal critic of the teaching profession (Chitty 2009). Politically, and also increasingly ideologically, Labour did not want to roll back the Conservatives' market, but equally, the party felt it could not rely on it alone to address the problems it saw in the education system. It targeted elements of the market that it perceived as particularly divisive, for example, abolishing funding for pupils to go to private schools. Moreover, it initially relied on regulation, not markets, focusing on its centrally constructed programs for primary school numeracy and literacy.

The centrally directed strategy was remarkably successful in the short-term, with increasing test scores. These improvements rapidly reached a plateau and, as with the NHS, this outcome led Labour to reorient its strategy. Here too, it chose to dramatically increase spending and consider structural reforms in the education sector (Glennerster 2001; Johnson 2004). This consideration partly stemmed not only from the more intractable nature of improving secondary education but also from a broader questioning of the ability of teachers and LEAs to tackle disadvantage absent strong incentives (Shaw 2008; Tomlinson 2005).

The fragmented education system made it difficult for Labour to achieve its dual goals of appealing to the middle class and tackling inequity with a single approach. The success of the Conservatives' reforms meant that repealing or reducing choice was not an electorally viable strategy (Interview, Senior Labour Politician 2004). Moreover, Blair and his education advisors supported choice as a good in itself. Blair named market-proponent Andrew Adonis as his chief education adviser, later making him life-peer and an education minister. In so doing, Blair threw his weight behind Adonis' proposals for both more choice and the Academies program (which allowed private actors to run state schools). For Adonis, and his supporters, the old comprehensive ideal had failed, perpetuating class inequity (Adonis and Pollard 1997) and particular types of market reforms offered a way of addressing school failure and promoting "excellence" in education.

Yet, for many in the party, including those in leadership positions in education, choice, in itself, was not enough. In the NHS, the uniform structure of the health service meant that Labour's political concerns about middle class opt out were explicitly linked to concerns about equity, as improving the service as a whole promised to appeal to all groups. By contrast, the fragmented structure of the education system, exacerbated by the Two Tier market, meant that choice alone was unlikely to solve the problems of sink schools or failing local authorities. Many in the education bureaucracy were skeptical about whether choice could drive improvement across the whole system (Interview: senior DfES official 2004a). Parts of the Labour leadership echoed these concerns. A senior political advisor – and market proponent – within the Blair government argued that choice in education risked more "segregation and oversubscription" than in health, making it easier to introduce choice in the NHS (Interview: Senior Labour Political Advisor 2004c). A Labour minister further argued that the party aimed to "honor parents' interest in trying to choose ... in a way that does not overestimate the demand side effect" and that "the political reality is that we [Labour] cannot be against it [choice], but the policy debate is more nuanced" (Interview: Senior Labour Politician, 2004). Choice, particularly absent an oversupply of school capacity, was not enough to rapidly address failing schools and low standards. As one Labour advisor, heavily involved in education reform stated: "At first we needed to act for the consumer ... the market [i.e., consumer-driven market in place] was too slow" (Interview: Michael Barber, former senior Labour Political Advisor, 2004).

Yet, even those skeptical about choice saw the need for more incentives for addressing poor performance and failing schools. Labour's solution to this dilemma was to complement the existing Two Tier market structure with a centrally directed Managed Market strategy. Managed Markets enhanced the power of the state, undercutting sources of opposition in LEAs and schools. In contracting out LEAs, for instance, the government saw the market as allowing it to explicitly address the question of failure (Interview, Sheena Evans, DfES official 2004).

The public, although generically supporting better schools, was hardly the driving force behind these changes. Surveys have found that the public favors, by a wide margin, LEA-run schools over private contractors (MORI 2010) and the party's support from the public on the education issue dipped through the mid-2000s as it pushed for expanding market reforms (MORI 2009).

Labour further ran into opposition from both the teachers and local authorities. The unions were at first positive towards Labour's centralizing reforms. Labour's use of targets and standards challenged professional autonomy but Labour also engaged in a significant re-professionalization of teaching – raising wages, investing in further education and training for teachers, and expanding the number of teachers (Martin and Muschamp 2008). However, animosity grew through the 2000s, with the unions rejecting reforms aimed at establishing Academies, school autonomy, and selection, rejecting not only their impact on teachers – professional autonomy, workforce differentiation – but also the emphasis on school differentiation and more private control (Chitty 2009). These concerns combined with unease in the Labour backbenches. As the Labour leadership progressively abandoned the comprehensive ideal, long at the core of its education policy, and emphasized choice and diversity, rebellion mounted. In 2006, the Labour leadership lacked support for reforms expanding school autonomy and private management, and facing the prospect of relying on Conservative support, watered down its proposals (Shaw 2008). Despite this opposition, like the Thatcher government, Labour was largely able to capitalize on its strong position in government to force through reform. Its investment in education – including teachers' salaries– further softened opposition.

Labour, like the Conservatives, approached education as a strategic actor looking to reshape the system around its core preferences. Despite taking up many of the Conservatives' reforms, Labour's strategy hinged on a fundamentally different set of preferences. The party wanted to reshape the system to improve the performance of weak schools and disadvantaged pupils, without losing the support – either electorally or through opt out to the private sector – of the middle classes. This stance meant reshaping central intervention to more directly address failure, while keeping the competitive incentives around choice. Maintaining Two Tiered markets was electorally necessary and attractive to at least some of the party, while Managed Markets became an important addendum for aggressively addressing failure. In using these markets, Labour marked out a distinct stance to the Conservatives, successfully politicizing questions of school failure without returning to the debates over comprehensives that dominated the 1960s and 1970s.

5.3: SWEDEN – EMPOWER SCHOOLS AND PARENTS

Like the British education system, the politics of education in Sweden long revolved around questions of academic selection and the balance of central and local control. Before the 1960s, there were two parallel education systems in Sweden, a compulsory six-year *folkola* serving the vast majority of pupils, and a nine-year program of lower and upper secondary schools (*realskola* and *gymnasium*) that largely catered to higher-income pupils. The Social Democrats (SAP) challenged this system of selection and the resulting class bias in secondary education, and following a period of experimentation, introduced comprehensive schools across Sweden in 1962 (Paulston 1968). The result was the contemporary Swedish education system, where all pupils receive nine years of compulsory education in a common school (*Grundskola*) with no selection across or within schools based on ability and little formal grading of pupils. After completing the compulsory system, most pupils go on to upper secondary education, which, since 1992, offers seventeen vocational and academic programs. Upper secondary education is not compulsory, but it is guaranteed for all pupils up to the age of twenty. Even those who have not successfully completed Swedish, English, and Mathematics at the compulsory level are eligible for an "individual program." Only when demand for a program outstrips supply is a pupil's performance taken into account.

Not only did Sweden move more resolutely towards a comprehensive education system than Britain, it also resolved the tensions between central and local governments by empowering the center. While the municipalities traditionally controlled the provision of Swedish education and remained responsible for its day-to-day operations, through the post-war period the central government assumed responsibility for setting the overall goals, inspecting schools, employing the teachers, and allocating resources – determining everything from class sizes to when the students should study the Vikings (Lundahl 2005; Lane and Murray 1985). Finally, in further contrast to Britain, Sweden devoted substantial resources to education, reaching 8.63% of GDP in the 1980s (World Bank 2002). This public funding was matched by nearly exclusively public provision, with fewer than ninety privately run schools (and fewer than thirty privately financed schools) in all of Sweden in 1989 (Miron 1993).

Today, this basic structure of comprehensive education remains in place, but a series of reforms radically altered the way education is provided. In 1992, the non-Socialist government introduced a school voucher program that slightly increased individual responsibility and allowed private schools to receive public funding absent strong central or local control, creating a mild Private Power market (individual responsibility, producer control). When the SAP returned to national government in 1994, it introduced new regulations, moving towards a Consumer-Controlled model (collective responsibility, pupil choice).

This evolving market has become a model for market proponents, lauded by free-market proponents across the OECD (*The Economist* 2008). In order to understand how Sweden, with its extensive welfare state, became a model for market pioneers, we need to look at how the Moderates' preferences for private entrepreneurship and lower costs and the SAP's preferences for equitable and uniform education played out in the universal and uniform system.

From Private Power to Consumer-Controlled

Two major reforms introduced in the late 1980s and early 1990s transformed the Swedish education system – the first decentralizing responsibility for the education to the municipalities and the second permitting private schools to enter into this decentralized system absent strong oversight and control. Taken together, these reforms produced a mild Private Power market, where private schools had much control over where, when and what to offer. The third set of reforms, beginning in the mid-1990s, modified this market towards its current Consumer-Controlled structure.

In 1989, the SAP introduced legislation that decentralized both organizational and financial responsibility for education to the municipalities and slightly liberalized the education market. Municipalities received autonomy over their education budgets, responsibility for employing teachers, and control over local education governance (OECD 1995). The legislation replaced the powerful National Board of Education with a streamlined National Agency of Education, cutting the national bureaucracy from 1,000 to 250 employees (Johansson 2001). The 1989 legislation also gave parents the option of expressing a preference over their child's school, extended some public funding to private schools with an alternative pedagogy, and allowed parents to enroll their child in school at age six, rather than the age of seven.

On the heels of this decentralization and market liberalization, the new non-Socialist government introduced changes in 1992 that expanded the education market, both placing new risks on parents and allowing private schools to enter the market absent strong oversight. First, in the area of allocation, these reforms allowed new private schools to charge "reasonable fees," without clearly defining what constituted a "reasonable fee." In the first year of the reforms, of the private schools receiving public funds, only thirty-eight percent reported not charging fees, and many schools increased their fees despite the new public funding (Miron 1993). Cutbacks in education spending further gave schools an incentive to raise fees. Central regulation partly offset potential inequities, forbidding schools from selecting pupils and requiring them to educate all students in equivalent terms, but private schools did have some control over admissions if oversubscribed (Miron 1993).

Second, as in England, more significant reforms targeted the production of education. The reforms worked through a logic of competition built on individual choice. They gave pupils the right to attend private schools at the compulsory and upper secondary level, forbade municipalities from restricting this choice, and funded schools through pupil numbers. In contrast to England, the reforms restricted choice to the private sector. Although they supported the principle of public school choice, they did not establish it as a legal right and left the municipalities with control over public school funding and admissions. In this environment, some municipalities expanded competition among their schools, but most did not.

Despite this choice orientation, neither the national nor local governments exerted strong control over the geography or content of schooling, giving the private schools much power. The national government put few restrictions on which schools could enter the market, only requiring that they demonstrate a plan for using the national curriculum and educating pupils in light of democratic values (Miron 1993). The municipalities were not active "payers," and could only express a preference over whether to allow the school and not block entry. Private schools effectively had the right to enter the market and in the first years following the reform no schools were denied entry (Miron 1993). Moreover, the legislation did not obligate private schools to provide all the services offered by municipal schools (for example, home language training, school health programs).

In contrast to the centralization that accompanied competition in England, the Swedish market followed on the earlier decentralizing reforms that had reduced the size of the national bureaucracy and its capacity to monitor the market. The municipalities had little scope to compensate for this situation as they did not have a legal right to monitor private schools' performance or financial status (Miron 1996). Schools could decide where to locate and to some extent what to offer. The combination of more costs for individuals and this weak structure of control meant that this market developed a Private Power character (individual responsibility, producer control), offering private schools new benefits and latitude to pursue their own interests.

However, just as the market began to develop, the SAP returned to power nationally and modified it in three ways. First, the SAP reintroduced a more collective structure of allocation, limiting the scope for independent schools to charge fees and subsequently banning fees outright. The government also increased education spending, aiming to compensate for the cuts in the early 1990s (Björklund *et al.* 2005).

Second, the SAP dulled the direct competitive stimulus among schools. Initially, it reduced the value of the private school "voucher" from eighty-five percent to seventy-five percent of public expenditure, looking to counter a perceived over-funding of private schools. Further reform in 1996 required municipalities to fund private schools based on their needs, rather than to allocate them a fixed sum based on pupil numbers. However, the SAP maintained the emphasis on choice – begun initially in its 1989 reforms – expanding information for parents and giving public schools more ability to develop special profiles (Klitgaard 2007b). Moreover, more parents actually report selecting a public school outside their catchment area than a private school, suggesting that choice has taken hold in parts of the public system (Björklund *et al.* 2005).

Finally, although the market remained quite liberal, the SAP increased central and local control over it (Miron 1996). The central government required all private schools to have at least twenty students, follow the centrally set goals, and provide more services (Lundahl 2002b; Lundahl 2002a, 2005). After 1998, the government required both private and public schools to use certified teaching staff and provide in-house training (Lundahl 2005). The government further expanded national monitoring, and after 1996 conducted inspections based on quality, rather than just meeting basic standards (Helgøy and Homme 2004). The national bureaucracy, slimmed down to 250 employees during the decentralizing reforms of the early 1990s, grew again – by 2004 the National Agency for Education employed 433 people and a newly created National Agency for School Improvement employed a further 144 people (Statistics Sweden 2004b).[6] Equally, at the local level, while municipalities still could not control market entry, they did determine the level of private school payments, giving them more control over their "friendliness" to private schools (Hwang 2003).

What did all these shifts mean? Reduced costs for individuals, less direct competition among schools, and greater central and local control produced a limited Consumer-Controlled market, where some schools compete to

---

[6] The non-socialist government abolished the new agency in 2008 and staffing numbers have declined since then.

attract pupils within a system that shields pupils from costs. However, we see that the early Private Power market nonetheless left a mark.

The early movements on the allocation dimension, combined with Sweden's economic crisis in the early 1990s, created some new inequities. The decentralizing reforms gave the municipalities new financial responsibilities just as their local tax bases deteriorated. As a consequence, municipalities cut spending on instruction by seventeen percent between 1991 and 1994, with even steeper cuts for programs for vulnerable groups, such as home language instruction and special needs education (Miron 1996). Decentralization itself did not produce major divergences in performance across municipalities, but the combination of less money for education, greater municipal control over spending, and weak control over school entry, meant private schools tended to enter more urban and profitable markets like Stockholm, Gothenburg, and Malmö (Björklund *et al.* 2005). These schools catered to highly educated urban parents, and to some extent, immigrants (albeit in different private schools). School segregation, while low overall, increased as the market developed (Hwang 2003; Björklund *et al.* 2005). Some local level reforms enhanced these inequities. Starting in 2000, the non-Socialist government in Stockholm City allowed upper secondary schools to select students based on ability, while other municipalities have flaunted national restrictions on grading pupils and allowed schools to conduct more pupil assessments (Söderström and Uusitalo 2005; Bjerkén 2000). These moves put more risk on pupils in procuring high-quality education. Indeed, in Stockholm, they led to increased segregation across schools, with Stockholm's best upper-secondary schools increasingly catering to more able and middle-class pupils (Söderström and Uusitalo 2005). National level changes, however, pulled the education system in the other direction, and Sweden remained at, or below, the OECD average in terms of the effects of socio-economic status on academic achievement (OECD 2006).

More significantly, the market produced a substantial new private sector. In 2009, there were over 700 private schools at the compulsory level, which educated over ten percent of pupils, up from under ninety schools in the late 1980s (Swedish National Agency for Education 2010). In contrast to many countries with a long history of funding private schools (like the Netherlands), few schools are confessional, and for-profit companies run over thirty percent of private schools (Bergström and Sandström 2002). The for-profit chain, Kunskapsskolan, for instance, operates thirty schools (Swedish National Agency for Education 2007).

In this Consumer-Controlled market, schools compete to attract parents, putting quality and responsiveness at the fore. Scholars debate whether competition has actually improved objective performance indicators such as test scores. Björklund *et al.*'s (2005) comprehensive review of the data concludes that competition from private schools has produced modest gains in performance but that these gains have been concentrated among higher-income pupils. More substantially, the market has pushed a broader responsiveness to parental demands. About one third of private schools have developed special profiles such as Montessori, Steiner, or Waldorf, to attract parents (Björklund *et al.* 2005). Others have responded more directly to parental demands – for instance, by grading younger pupils, despite national regulations against it, or moving in the other direction, with schools catering to immigrant groups engaging in significant grade inflation (Bjerkén 2000; Wikström and Wikström 2005).

While Björklund and his coauthors (2005) argue that private schools have not increased total costs and many private schools operate on smaller budgets, overall, this market has not reduced costs either. Indeed, many local actors believe private schools push up costs, with a study of municipal leaders finding ninety percent of respondents from municipalities with independent schools felt that these schools had contributed to cost increases, and close to half reporting they contributed to overcapacity and / or wasted resources, due to pupil switching (Swedish National Agency for Education 2006; Hwang 2003). More recent work suggests increased competition from private schools has also led to higher wages for teachers, particularly in competitive fields (Hensvik 2010).

The Consumer-Controlled market produced important changes in the power of key players. Even though only a minority of parents actually chooses an alternative school, the expansion of choice has increased political attention to parental preferences in the system. However, in contrast to England, far from challenging the position of producers as a whole, the market established a new group of winners among private providers and some teachers. Private schools are now organized in a small but vocal lobby, aimed at preserving their position (*Friskolornas Riksförbund*). Public schools, by contrast, have received fewer benefits, and in some cases, have lost out as competition has forced their closure (Swedish National Agency for Education 2006). Finally, the early market undercut the power of political actors both nationally and locally. Municipalities still report planning problems, and unlike the early Dutch and British health care markets, or competition in Swedish elderly care, the market has not strengthened their control over local schooling (Swedish National Agency for Education 2006). From the mid-1990s though, the national government has re-asserted control.

Overall, the SAP's initial decentralizing reforms moved Sweden from one of the most centralized to one of the most decentralized countries in the OECD, and the non-Socialists' voucher reforms moved Sweden from one of the most restrictive systems for private schools to one of the most liberal markets in the OECD (Miron 1996; Lindblad *et al.* 2002). A third set of reforms by the SAP banned tuition fees and re-layered control onto this market, reshaping the Swedish education system along the lines of a Consumer-Controlled market. Taken together, these shifts meant that private schools initially emerged as the major winners of reform, with parents later re-emerging as the key players.

Why these markets?

Why did the Moderates pursue a Private Power market? Why did the SAP modify it to a Consumer-Controlled market? In order to understand these shifts, we need to look at the parties' preferences and the strategic situation they faced.

From the early twentieth century, the Social Democrats saw a comprehensive education system as central to promoting economic growth; as both a prerequisite of a more equal society and an expression of it (Rothstein 1996). Initially, this stance led to promoting uniform schools with little parental choice and suspicion of a parallel private school sector (Paulston 1968; Kallós and Nilsson 1995). Other actors took a range of positions. Teachers, for example, had long had an uneasy relationship to the SAP and the comprehensive reforms, supporting a more differentiated system (Rothstein 1996).

In the late 1970s, many in the SAP began to question the structure of the education system. One line of criticism picked up on numerous studies showing that the system tended to reproduce – rather than eradicate – existing class structures (Rothstein 1996; Lindblad *et al.* 2002; Kallós and Nilsson 1995). Another questioned whether Sweden's education spending, which was well above the OECD average, was producing adequate results (Schüllerqvist 1995).

Concerns about budgetary pressures initially won the day – through the 1980s the government capped spending growth, with spending falling from 8.68% of GDP in 1980 to 6.81% in 1989 – a larger fall than under the Conservatives in Britain (albeit from a much higher baseline). However, the government felt spending caps were a crude instrument for achieving improved efficiency and quality in schooling and began to look at structural reforms (Lundahl 2002b). The central education bureaucracy had grown substantially and the SAP saw this system, and the educational specialists who staffed it, as difficult to control and out of touch with the needs of industry, pupils, and local communities (Carlgren and Kallós 1997; Kallós and Nilsson 1995: 182). The position of teachers was of equal concern. The party had long been ambivalent about the teaching profession (Interview: Widar Andersson, Former SAP Member of Parliament, 2004) and through the 1980s, this ambivalence combined with concerns about costs. The SAP's spending cuts had reduced teachers' wages in real terms but spending was still high and the government could not control how labor was used at the school level (Björklund *et al.* 2005).

In light of these concerns, the party began to entertain proposals for greater decentralization to the municipalities. The SAP first proposed decentralization in the 1970s but it was not until it returned to government in 1982 that decentralization appeared forcefully on its agenda. Proponents argued that decentralization would create more flexibility in the education labor market and give municipalities the scope to cater to local populations. It would also shift difficult decisions about spending to the municipalities (Lundahl 2002b). Following on the recommendation of a 1987 Parliamentary Committee, the SAP government gave the education minister (and future Prime Minister) Göran Persson the task of enacting decentralizing reforms. Persson went much further than the Committee recommended, shifting responsibility for spending, staffing, and the organization of the education system to the municipalities.

These changes met with considerable discontent among teachers, particularly the union representing upper secondary school teachers and academics (*Lärarnas Riksförbundet*), who argued that the reforms would lower their professional status. Indeed, nearly two decades later, Lärarnas Riksförbundet continued to point to decentralization as a cause of reduced quality and poor conditions for teachers (Fjelkner 2008). The Moderates and other non-Socialist parties supported these protests, opposing local control. The SAP largely circumvented this opposition, working with the Left party to force the legislation through the Riksdag. In the area of industrial relations, where the government had less control, the unions did exact more concessions.[7]

The SAP's reforms introduced substantial change, but they did not aim to fundamentally alter the principles of the system. Instead, as Kallós and Nilsson (1995) argue, they looked to achieve centrally determined goals through new means. The SAP moved away from an understanding of equality that hinged on a fully uniform educational offer, yet it upheld the basic logic of the education system (Englund 2005). The reforms maintained a system of universal comprehensive schooling and central government infrastructure to ensure high quality (i.e., testing and curriculum). The SAP also resisted the Moderates' calls to introduce more differentiation among students, and did not introduce grading, standardized testing, and academic selection (Lundahl 1990). The government further

---

[7] Initially, the system of wage bargaining remained highly centralized. In 1995, the unions agreed to a decentralization of bargaining on pay and conditions, following considerable concessions from the municipalities (for example, a minimum guaranteed salary for new entrants, increases in pay). However, the issue remains contentious and conflict over pay decentralization flared up again in 2000 (Strath 2004).

shied away from fully opening up market entry, rejecting calls from the Moderates to provide public funding to all private schools, leaving significant control over private schools in the hands of the central and local governments (Schüllerqvist 1995: 71). The reforms then, represented an attempt to sharpen incentives for cost control and more user power within the universal and uniform system. In so doing, the SAP made the first steps towards more choice, including private school choice, but it remained cautious about extending substantial autonomy to the private sector or extending competition among public schools (Schüllerqvist 1995: 80).

The Moderates took a different stance. Through the 1980s, the Moderates began to advance serious proposals for market reform. The Moderates' stance on education policy, like that of the British Conservatives, had long revolved around issues of grading, academic selection, and traditional pedagogy, rather than privatizing the public system (Paulston 1968; Lundahl 1990). However, in the 1970s and early 1980s, complaints from the Swedish Employers Confederation (SAF) that pupils lacked adequate skills for the needs of industry galvanized a more radical critique of the system within the party (Lundahl 1990; Lundahl 2002b). This renewed interest in reforming education involved a broad critique of public sector education. Indeed, the Moderates listed education – along with tax cuts and market liberalization – as one of its top three reform priorities within the Swedish welfare state (Lundahl 1990).

This stance led the party to consider market-based proposals. The first such proposals emerged in the party's youth wing in the early 1980s and drew on American academic work on school vouchers (Nilsson 2003; Bergström and Sandström 2002). These ideas did not initially gain widespread currency in the general population, yet as in health care, they did gain a growing constituency on the political right (Lundahl 1990; Lundahl 2002b; Schüllerqvist 1995). Through the 1980s, Moderate politicians heavily pushed market-based reform proposals in the Riksdag and in local governments (Schüllerqvist 1995). This advocacy cast markets as a means and as an end: a way of creating more efficient and high-quality education while also challenging the public sector's education monopoly. Indeed, Beatrice Ask, the Moderate minister who introduced the market stated these goals: "The reform to increase freedom of choice within the school system aims to dismantle the existing state monopoly in order to produce increased variation" with the further aim of improving quality (quoted in Kallós and Nilsson 1995: 182). The Moderates' core goal was thus to create an alternative to the public sector, not just to expand choice. In this light, the Private Power market was ideologically appealing, offering a direct way to support the private sector.

The existing uniform education system constrained how far the Moderates could push these markets. When the non-Socialist government was elected in 1991, the Moderate party was well-positioned to achieve its preferences. Although part of a coalition with the Liberal Party, the Christian Democrats, and the Centre Party, it was the leading coalition partner and assumed both education portfolios. However, radically reforming the uniform and universal education system was both politically risky and administratively difficult. The party considered more dramatic reforms expanding competition in the public system, but admitted it could not enforce this feature beyond what the municipalities would allow (Miron 1993: 66–8). Even with a number of options on the table, from reforming the public system to the more limited changes favored by its coalition partners (who Schüllerqvist (1995) argues took position closer to the SAP in the 1980s), it chose a restricted, but ideologically preferred, Private Power market.

Because the actual legislation did not create new private schools or change the status of any existing schools – it just allowed market entry – the non-Socialists' changes were less electorally threatening (Interview: Mikael Sandström, Moderate party advisor 2004). The public was initially skeptical about more private schools, but gradually expressed more support for them (although this support dipped in the late 2000s) (Nilsson 2009: 273). Although initially one of the teachers' unions expressed concerns about the Moderates' reforms, these teachers gradually saw private schools as offering them greater professional autonomy and also saw advantages to having multiple employers (Interview: teacher's union official, 2004). Some local authorities, particularly those run by the SAP, did protest the move – especially the requirement that they fund private schools at eighty-five percent of local schools irrespective of need – but they held little sway over the Moderates. The limited nature of the reforms also allowed the party to broker a compromise with its coalition partners, who were less enthusiastic about school choice and private schooling.[8] The Moderates dropped proposals for more substantial school fees as part of this compromise (Dagens Nyheter 1992).

Once again, we see a specific partisan response to a constrained environment. Unable to dramatically change the whole Swedish education system, the Moderates traded "depth" for "breadth": a small but ideologically preferred step towards privatization over the mass expansion of choice. As one Moderate party education strategist stated, "the reforms were mainly undertaken for ideological reasons ... we did not envision an explosion of independent schools" (Interview: Mikael

---

[8] More recent policy from the non-Socialist government (2006 to 2010), with a Liberal party education minister, has focused less on markets than on expanding grading for younger pupils, moving away from the simple four-grade system to a more fine-grained scheme, and creating advanced classes in upper secondary education.

Sandström, Moderate party advisor 2004). Instead, the goal was to create a stable market: "This is a question for a political scientist, how do you create a vested interest in school organization that is very powerful, so that you cannot make reforms against independent schools" (Interview: Mikael Sandström, Moderate party advisor, 2004).

The SAP had resisted the Moderates' calls for extensive markets when in government; however, once the non-Socialists had expanded choice and private actors, the SAP was forced to respond. The non-Socialists introduced the education reforms at the beginning of their term and a number of new schools had already entered the market by the time the SAP returned to office. Moreover, the reforms were popular with parents, with sixty percent of citizens supporting greater choice (Carnoy 1998). As one SAP Member of Parliament in a senior education position argued: "even if we wanted harder legislation we could not [introduce it]" because of electoral constraints. Moreover, despite ongoing debate "in every party group there was support for independent schools" (Interview: SAP Member of Parliament, 2004). The SAP's minority status in Parliament furthered these limitations, as it relied on support from the Greens, who supported private school choice, limiting dramatic change (Interview: Widar Andersson, former SAP Member of Parliament, 2004).

Moreover, it was not competition around choice in itself that the SAP rejected (although some members did), but the Private Power market. Indeed, the SAP began considering education markets in the 1980s, expanding choice with its 1989 reforms. The party argued "Freedom of choice should widen when it comes to school, health care and day care" (quoted in Schüllerqvist 1995: 68). Choice was a way of appealing to middle class voters, particularly those the party was trying to win back after its defeat in 1991.

In reacting to the reforms then, the SAP chose to extend choice into the universal and uniform structure of education, modifying the market to a Consumer-Controlled structure that best fit with its preferences. In opposition, the SAP expressed concerns that the voucher system over-funded private schools, giving them too few responsibilities, and that the market risked creating inequities by allowing private schools much control over admissions and fees. Alongside these concerns, the SAP expressed philosophical concerns that a "voucher," in placing a price tag on pupils, did not take account of their differing needs (see Miron 1993: 78–87 for a discussion of this critique). In other words, the SAP saw the move to fragmenting benefits across citizens and allowing private schools more control as threatening. As in health care, the party reacted to both the movement along the allocation dimension and a greater producer orientation in the market.[9]

---

[9] The SAP followed a similar strategy in Stockholm city, where pupils have much choice within the public sector. While not rejecting choice, the SAP, and its coalition partners,

But the uniform structure of the service meant that the party could deploy choice through a Consumer-Controlled market to improve support for the system, and thus once it modified the market to reduce the divisive elements, the SAP saw choice as attractive.

The Dutch school system had long given parents much choice and schools much autonomy, without operating as a competitive market. The roots of Dutch school choice emerge from the nineteenth-century conflict between the Liberal party, as representatives of the state, and the various churches over control of schooling. The "pacification" of 1917 solved the "schools question" by enshrining the legal right of non-state schools to secure public funding and guaranteeing the freedom of organization and conviction within schools (de Kwaasteniet 1985). This guarantee initially fit with the "pillarization" of Dutch society, where different confessional and secular groups participated in parallel civil society organizations (Lijphart 1977). However, the principle of choice and religious schooling outlasted these sharp social divisions, with non-public (primarily confessional) schools enrolling a stable seventy percent of pupils even as the number of citizens belonging to a church fell sharply (Dijkstra *et al.* 2001).

This diverse structure of provision rested on a fragmented educational curriculum. Reforms in 1963 consolidated post-primary education into four academic streams, leading to university (VWO), general higher education (HAVO), and vocational training (MAVO and VBO, now VMBO). Reformers jettisoned plans for an "American-style" high school with no academic streaming, and further attempts at introducing a comprehensive school system also floundered (Stellwag 1967). In contrast to the Swedish system where conflict between a public comprehensive model and a more differentiated structure was decided in favor of a uniform system, and the English system where this issue was continually debated, in the Netherlands there was widespread consensus over a universal but fragmented system with a large private component.

Despite this seeming market orientation in the Dutch system, through much of the twentieth-century, the dominant Christian Democrats insulated schools and universities from actual competition. The question of

supported more pupil weighting for schools with different costs, in order to ensure schools with large immigrant or low-income populations had adequate resources. The Moderates rejected this move, supporting a flatter per-pupil component, and more school-level discretion (and responsibility) over spending (Jällhage 2002).

whether and how to introduce market competition then, while not as hotly debated as in Sweden and England, was nonetheless contentious. The following section shows that the CDA–VVD coalition introduced competition within the existing system, extending its fragmentation and giving it a Two Tiered character (individual responsibility, pupil choice). The PvdA reacted to this movement by dampening competition and increasing uniformity.

The path to a Two Tiered market

Until the mid-1980s, rigid pillarization and centralized rules, not competition, largely drove resource allocation in education. The constitutional guarantee of parity in school funding meant that schools were funded equally on the basis of costs, not according to need or student numbers, giving them few incentives for efficiency, competition for pupils, or school level discretion over funding (Karsten and Meijer 1999). One senior education expert repeated a common anecdote that the guarantee of parity meant: "If a window broke at a municipal school, we had to compensate the Catholic one" (Interview: Education Specialist 2004).

Between 1985 and 1988 the Lubbers government (CDA–VVD) began a series of reforms, rolled out in the following decades, which changed the system of school financing to make schools more responsive to student numbers and bear more financial responsibility. These reforms were not as dramatic as in either England or Sweden, but they slowly began to transform the Dutch system into a Two Tier market where schools increasingly competed for pupils and parents faced more responsibility for procuring high-quality education. However, the development of the Two Tier market was not seamless, with the move towards more responsibility offset by reforms socializing responsibility, and with reforms extending choice-based competition challenged by those enhancing state and local control. The following paragraphs outline the logic of the market reforms, the countermovement, and the resulting market structure.

First, in the area of allocation, growing competition among schools has enhanced the risks that individuals have long faced in the Dutch system. Pupils do face some small financial risks – private schools are allowed to charge voluntary fees for additional activities and all schools may charge fees for pupils over sixteen – but these costs are relatively limited. More importantly, the system of regulation on access gives schools some scope to select better pupils. Technically, schools must accept all pupils (with exceptions for religious criteria), yet they can choose which secondary education programs they offer, allowing them to cater to elite groups of pupils.

Second, a series of reforms expanded competition based on pupil choice, reshaping the production of education. Changes in the 1990s tightened the link between school funding and pupil numbers, turning the historical principle of pupil choice into a competitive principle. Reforms formally introduced in 1996 gave upper secondary schools a "lump sum" budget based largely on pupil numbers as well as some government set-performance criteria (for example, completion) (Karsten and Meijer 1999; Teelken 1998). These changes sharpened the competitive stimulus in the system, with Sjoerd Karsten and Joost Meijer (1999: 422) arguing that "the production of education is, as it were, outsourced to independently operating schools." Initially, the government exempted primary and lower secondary schools from the move towards lump-sum funding, giving them a budget linked to pupil numbers, but earmarked for particular purposes. However, in the late 1990s, the government extended lump-sum funding to all secondary schools and in 2006 to primary schools. Alongside lump-sum funding, the government gave schools more budgetary autonomy (for example, to spend on teachers, or capital expenditures) and control over timetables and management, even giving upper secondary schools the freedom to raise funds from selling educational services to companies (Karsten 1999).

The logic of control supported this competition for pupil choices. The Dutch government has long set national standards as a way of steering the curriculum. In the mid-1990s, it enhanced the role of the inspectorate in monitoring performance, requiring schools to submit an annual report of their performance and activities. The government further provided parents with information on school performance and, from 1997, it required schools to publish brochures describing their goals (Teelken 1998). These shifts all pushed towards a Two Tiered market, where individuals face some costs and schools compete for pupils.

However, other reforms moved in a different direction. First, in the area of allocation, several changes actually reduced individual risks. Reforms in the 1980s altered the school funding formula to compensate for the higher costs of pupils from disadvantaged backgrounds. For instance, today a pupil from a non-Dutch background brings almost double the per-head funding to a school than a pupil living with native Dutch parents who do not have a low-income background (Eurydice 2003). Moreover, changes in the early 1990s raised the age for academic streaming, creating a new "basic" curriculum (*basisvorming*) for the first three years of secondary education. This program provided all students with a common introductory education, making it easier to transfer across streams. Further reforms in 2001 looked to counter the perceived low quality of the pre-vocational tracks by merging the two vocationally oriented streams (MAVO and VBO) into a newer higher-quality program (VMBO) (Bronneman-Helmers *et al.* 2002). Taken together, these reforms reduced, but did not eliminate, the incentives for schools to cream-skim pupils, gave pupils new opportunities to switch streams, and aimed to improve the quality of the pre-vocational stream.

Second, the Purple coalition promoted school consolidation, dampening competitive incentives around choice. The move towards "upscaling" schools reduced the number of secondary schools from over 1,400 to slightly over 600 between 1992 and 1996. The government also increased the minimum number of anticipated pupils for a new school to qualify for state funding (from 200 to 333 in cities, and 80 to 200 in rural areas) leading the number of new schools entering the market to decline through the 1990s (Walford 2001). These restrictions limited schools wishing to enter the market. However, market entry remains relatively liberal, and prospective schools (or those faced with closure) can often successfully protest limitations on funding through the courts and Parliament (Interview: Ministry of Education official 2004).

What did this uneven movement towards a Two Tier market mean for the Dutch education system? In the area of allocation, at an aggregate level, upscaling led to less segregation among schools over time, with the number of students in schools offering all four academic streams increasing from 9.1% in 1992 to 59.8% in 1996 (Teelken 1998). However, this trend hid problems of urban segregation. Much of the consolidation in schools occurred through mergers of management rather than physical changes in location. In practice, many urban schools continued to physically house different streams in separate buildings or campuses, effectively segregating pupils (Bronneman-Helmers *et al.* 2002). In Amsterdam, Utrecht, Rotterdam, and the Hague, a growing divide emerged between "White" and "Black" schools, with much larger racial segregation among schools than socio-economic segregation (Karsten *et al.* 2006). This level of segregation was more than predicted by neighborhood segregation or the rise of Islamic/Hindu schools alone. Indeed, Karsten *et al.* (2006) argue that it often resulted from explicit choices by the schools themselves. In order to attract increasingly choosy upper-income parents, schools emphasized their pre-university stream – sometimes even dropping the other streams – effectively excluding the largely poorer and immigrant students who attend the pre-vocational stream. Even some of the urban schools that did offer mixed track programs, such as Montessori and Jena schools, tended not to be ethnically mixed because they drew pupils from feeder primary schools that targeted upper-income native Dutch pupils (Karsten *et al.* 2006). Moreover, a high-profile government-sponsored commission, the Dijsselbloem commission, found that the basic curriculum and other reforms had little impact on stemming inequality (Commissie parlementair onderzoek Onderwijsvernieuwingen, 2008). Thus parents and pupils, particularly in urban centers, faced risks.

Schools, too, faced a new environment. On the one hand, the reforms layering more central and local control in the system continued with the long-standing bureaucratization of Dutch education (see Commissie parlementair onderzoek Onderwijsvernieuwingen 2008, for a critique of excessive bureaucratization). On the other hand, schools increasingly had to compete to attract "choosy" parents interested in quality (Dijkstra *et al.* 2001). Parents moved away from their traditional allegiances to local religious schools and began to more actively choose schools (Janssens and Leeuw 2001). Parents used a number of heuristics to select schools, including pupil composition (even racial composition) to assess quality as well as school performance. When the Dutch newspaper *Trouw* first published exam results by schools in the mid-1990s, it sold out in under two hours (Patrinos 2002). These shifts meant that schools, particularly religious schools, could no longer take their base of pupils for granted. In response, they began to change their behavior and emphasize academic results. Dijkstra *et al.* (2001) argue that the resilience of confessional schools in an increasingly secular Dutch society largely followed from both their real and perceived effectiveness in educating pupils.

There is much debate as to whether competition on quality actually improved quality. There is some evidence that performance improved (Dijkstra, Dronkers, and Karsten 2001). Competition, though, also pushed schools to market themselves as effective, not to cut costs. Schools in a favorable financial position spent their extra resources to reduce class size and make services more attractive to students, rather than reduce expenditure (Karsten and Meijer 1999). Private schools did tend to be less expensive than public schools, but this advantage largely stemmed from their lower burden of responsibilities and control over staffing and other inputs (Dijkstra, Dronkers, and Karsten 2001).

As in England, we see that the Two Tier market reshaped the relative power of schools, parents, and the state. Individuals were increasingly in the driver's seat. Market proponent Hans Wansink (2001) argues that government policy and informal changes in the market (such as *Trouw* newspaper's publication of test results) shifted power from the government and workers to parents and pupils – genuinely putting parents as consumers in a prominent position. However, the uneven system of allocation meant that some parents, particularly middle-class urban parents who have access to high-quality schools eager to respond to their needs, were more powerful than others. Parental preferences played an important role in the political environment more generally. For instance, the government responded to the popularity of *Trouw*'s publication of test results by publishing its own results, and repeatedly promising to spare education from serious cuts.

Schools also gained autonomy. In order to respond to competition, "managers" were increasingly important players within schools, and individual schools became progressively more influential in the policy process (Karsten and Meijer 1999; Interview: official from the Association of School Managers, 2004). Both moves changed the role of the state, reducing its control over a number of day-to-day issues but empowering it in other ways.[10] Traditionally, decision-making relied on multiple rounds of negotiation with many corporatist partners (the churches, unions and other groups). In order to manage the market, the state now played a more central role in directly setting financial incentives and steering performance through decisions over the curriculum and testing, weakening (albeit certainly not eliminating) the traditional system. A more complex set of relationships among parents, individual schools, and a more independent central government replaced the relationship between the state and its corporatist partners.

This Two Tier market then, looked much like its English counterpart. Schools were competing for pupils, while some were also creaming off the more attractive pupils. Parents became increasingly choosy, and this choice had broader political ramifications. The central government, as arbiter of this competitive system, had a new role in managing the system and ensuring schools actually did compete for pupils.

Why these markets?

What explains this movement towards the Two Tier market? What explains the countermovement towards more state and local control? The path to the Two Tier market unfolded across four different governing coalitions with ministers from three different political parties, and these actors built the market differently.

The Dutch education market has long been described as one of the most liberal in the world, but in practice, by the 1980s it had grown highly centralized and regulated. Beginning in the 1960s and accelerating in the 1970s, the central government began to play an active role in steering the system through detailed regulation. This role was concentrated in the Ministry of Education, and spanned across a range of societal organizations. By 1985, 3,000 officials were employed in the education bureaucracy, with the number of support services for education growing from fifteen to sixty-one between 1970 and 1980 (Karsten 1999). Representatives of the confessional organizations and local government participated in both central decision-making and the day-to-day management of the system. The education playing field was crowded, and political parties often deferred to

---

[10] Although the lump-sum funding to schools largely followed pupil numbers, the state did attach some performance pay to the lump sum. Moreover, local governments contracted out school management as a way of regaining control over failed and poorly performing schools (Karsten 2001). These moves are more akin to some of Labour's reforms in England.

state and local bureaucrats, confessional groups and schools themselves in managing the system.

By the early 1980s, this crowded educational field, far from continuing to broker support for the Dutch system, was increasingly the source of tension. The critique of corporatism, particularly from the CDA, was far less thoroughgoing in education than in other sectors, but nonetheless parties across the political spectrum began to question its logic. Although spending in the Netherlands was in line with the OECD average in the mid-1980s, a tighter fiscal climate prompted the government to examine education. At the same time, growing secularization, combined with new concerns about the inclusion of immigrants, raised the specter of rising inequality among schools. Traditionally, pupils chose a school based on religious grounds, and although schools were segregated by religion or belief there was less socio-economic segregation (de Kwaasteniet 1985). This situation began to change, as Dutch society became more secular (Dijkstra *et al.* 2001). By the 1980s, policymakers also began to acknowledge that the immigration of the 1960s and 1970s was permanent, and that educating immigrants posed new challenges to the system (Driessen 2000).

Concerns over both equity and efficiency created a broad political constituency for change, but through the 1980s, the major political actors emphasized different solutions. The CDA had long defended the autonomy and viability of confessional schools and school boards, looking to protect their interests. The party was heavily vested in the status quo, and it had little interest in moving away from autonomous private schools and high levels of parental choice. But, it could no longer rely solely on support from confessional voters. To make a broader appeal it began to emphasize choice in education as a way of courting middle-class voters. This appeal built on its long-standing preferences. The CDA advocated giving providers more autonomy and space, arguing that government regulation was not only inefficient but limiting civil society (Karsten 2001: 38; CDA 1989). In so doing, the CDA put choice and diversity first, turning away somewhat from the system of corporatist control that it had long supported.

This move met with support from the VVD. The VVD had long promoted more differentiation and fragmentation in education, opposing comprehensive education and supporting school autonomy, reduced public bureaucracy, and differentiated academic programs (Karsten 2001: 38; VVD 1989). Unlike the CDA, it lacked close ties to provider groups, largely supporting abstract principles of pupil choice rather than the particular system of corporatist control that had grown up around it. The VVD did not emphasize schooling as an electoral issue to the same extent as did the CDA, but as the space opened for more change, it supported extending the existing structure and enhancing private alternatives and individual responsibility.

The PvdA, by contrast, had far less vested in the status quo from an ideological perspective and it faced a more difficult balancing act between its ideological preferences and electoral imperatives. The party had long supported more equity in the Dutch system, promoting comprehensive schools and secular municipal schools. However, given public support for choice and private schooling, the PvdA was cautious about advocating this agenda. Through the 1980s, it toned down support for radical change, focusing instead on reducing differentiation in the system, reaffirming support for municipal control, a more unified common educational program at the secondary level, and limited de-bureaucratization (PvdA 1989).[11] Some within the party did question the disjuncture between education specialists in the central government and teachers on the ground, wishing to target the internal organization of the system, albeit to different ends than those from the CDA and VVD.

Players outside of government, despite complaining of inadequate funding and excessive regulations, tended to support the status quo. Organizations of confessional schools lobbied the government hard to maintain their position in the system, as did individual schools. This involvement grew more pronounced through the 1970s and early 1980s, leading to the paradoxical situation where confessional organizations repeatedly lobbied for more school autonomy and a limited state, while playing an integral role in expanding the size and scope of the state through participation in advisory bodies (de Kwaasteniet 1985).

In light of these concerns, the first and second Lubbers governments (CDA–VVD) began a discussion of structural reform to all levels (from primary to higher). The government argued that the system of bureaucratic control created a slow and inefficient system, with CDA Education minister Wim Deetman (1982 to 1989) promoting enhanced choice and school autonomy as a way of sharpening incentives in the system. Between 1985 and 1988, the Lubbers government published a series of papers on education, advocating first deregulation and decentralization in higher education and later applying these goals to primary and secondary schools (Ministerie van Onderwijs Cultuur en Wetenschappen 1985, 1988). In both cases, the government's aim was to "steer at a distance" by setting objectives and allowing the individual schools autonomy and flexibility to determine their actions (Karsten 2001). The government explicitly promoted choice-based market competition in the Dutch system.

---

[11] The parties also clashed on higher education, debating university autonomy and competition, student fees, and the expansion of higher education to a broader group of pupils.

However, following the 1989 election of a CDA–PvdA government, the education portfolios went to PvdA ministers, Jo Ritzen and Jacques Wallage. The PvdA largely took up Deetman's reform plans to tighten the link between funding and pupil numbers and grant schools more autonomy, modifying them to ensure that all schools had the capacity to provide high-quality education. Unlike the emphasis on choice, the PvdA took more limited and low-visibility steps to increase state and local control over the emerging market. First, it looked to reduce the fragmentation in the education system and make it more uniform, pushing for a comprehensive program for the first years of secondary education (*basisvorming*). Second, it promoted the process of "upscaling" (Karsten 1999). Despite costs being average by international standards, small schools were often more expensive and were seen as a source of cost inefficiency (Dijkstra *et al.* 2001; Patrinos 2002). Additionally, the PvdA was concerned that greater school competition would be inequitable if schools lacked the capacity to compete, and saw larger schools as a solution. The PvdA matched the move to expanding school-level capacity with attention to the central level. It promoted government control over the curriculum, supporting an independent inspectorate in 1993, and requiring schools to report quality plans annually to the central government – something the VVD and CDA expressed concerns about (Teelken 1998; ANP 1993). Third, it advocated greater educational decentralization to the municipalities. Between 1993 and 1994, there was a series of administrative meetings (Scheveningen talks), where Ministry officials and the corporatist players negotiated on reform. These talks extended the plans for greater school autonomy and clarified the responsibility and accountability of schools to the government, and within this forum, the PvdA involved the municipalities, opening the door for more decentralization (Teelken 1998). Actual changes, of course, required cross-party support, yet the PvdA heavily supported these policies.

When the Purple coalition was elected in 1994, it largely took up the earlier policies enhancing school autonomy and quality. However, the exclusion of the CDA from the governing coalition changed the parameters of the education debate. Confessional schools had long been involved in providing school support services targeted at overcoming educational disadvantage. The CDA, as long-time defenders of both the corporatist system of education administration and local school autonomy, resisted reforms that reduced the power of the churches and other groups in these services. The Purple coalition introduced a bill that both decentralized responsibility for support services to the municipalities, and allowed them to contract with private for-profit providers. This bill constituted a classic compromise between the VVD and the PvdA, bearing both the PvdA's preference for decentralization with the VVD's preference for more private actors. Yet it also bore the mark of the CDA's exclusion, challenging the dominance of the corporatist partners in delivering services.

This bill, though, was an uneasy compromise, with PvdA and VVD parliamentarians expressing displeasure at the emphasis on marketization and decentralization respectively (Voogt *et al.* 1997). Stakeholders too, raised concerns. Both the Catholic (NKSR) and the Protestant School Organization (NPCS) argued that the government's decision to remove school-support services from the "lump-sum" grants to schools, giving municipalities more power, eroded school autonomy and the rights established in 1917 regarding educational freedom more generally (*Trouw* 1994; *Volkskrant* 1997). The CDA expressed similar opposition (ANP 1995). The Purple coalition pushed ahead, but in comparison to reforms in other sectors, these were relatively minor.

When a second senior education minister, Loek Hermans from the VVD, arrived in 1998, he put markets prominently on the agenda. The government requested that the Onderwijsraad, an educational advisory committee, examine the question of markets in education, and Hermans floated ideas from allowing private for-profit providers to student fees (Onderwijsraad 2001). Hermans was limited in enacting actual change. The junior minister responsible for schools was from the PvdA and the PvdA resisted these moves. Moreover, the coalition had to focus on immediate problems, such as growing discontent from teachers (including a strike), recruiting problems, and public calls for more education spending (Wansink 2001).

The CDA–VVD–D'66 coalition (2003 to 2006) reinvigorated the idea of markets. This coalition did not enact as much change in the education sector as in health or long-term care (see chs. 4 and 6), but it did move away from decentralization and back towards issues of school autonomy and market incentives. The Balkenende governments, prompted by the interests of the CDA, removed school support services from the municipalities and returned control to the schools, and completed the extension of lump-sum financing to the boards of primary schools. This move was set in motion by the previous government, but it became controversial because primary schools have small budgets, meaning the loss of a single teacher to illness could pose serious budgetary problems to the school (Interview: Ministry of Education official 2004). Both changes placed more responsibility on school boards and gave them more scope and incentives to compete, by sharpening competition in the system.

Taken together, we see education reform in the Netherlands has not been as overtly political as elsewhere, but nonetheless, different partisan actors have been central to putting different types of markets on – and off – the agenda. The overall thrust of the past twenty years of educational policy demonstrates two competing tendencies: on the one hand the CDA and

VVD pushing for more autonomy for schools and sharpening the choice-based competitive incentives in the system while also allowing some risks for parents, and on the other hand the PvdA, and to a lesser extent the CDA, building up state control at the central and local level through increased curricular control, monitoring, and equity-oriented policies.

In contrast to the health care system where the CDA and VVD supported reforms aimed at increasing the control of purchasers (for example, insurers and the state) over costs, both parties have resisted reforms that would hurt small schools and consolidate power in local government, favoring those that sharpen incentives for schools and increase their autonomy. Traditionally, the CDA was reticent about competition, seeing it as potentially harmful to religious schools. However, as the party began to consider the need for clearer incentives in the system, reforms that worked with the grain of the existing structure – providing more choice and school autonomy – promised to benefit schools (especially religious schools) and parents and the CDA itself (CDA 2006). The VVD was a natural ally in this reform process, supporting more competitive incentives (VVD 2002). Both parties cautioned against aspects of the PvdA's reforms, looking to preserve the more differentiated structure and autonomous schools. Choice in the fragmented education system offered a way to make a popular appeal through markets without the risks of radical cost inflation or a dramatic increase in state control.

Most stakeholders supported these moves expanding school autonomy, with religious organizations, in particular, mobilizing to protect and expand it in the face of more regulations. From an electoral perspective, these reforms occurred largely under the public radar (Karsten 2001). The long-standing tradition of choice meant that questions of markets in education were not as heavily politicized in the Netherlands as elsewhere, and the reforms themselves were incremental and more technical.

By contrast, neither the move towards competition nor the deregulation of the education sector fit with the PvdA's traditional preferences. Through the 1990s, the PvdA began to accept greater school autonomy and competition around choice, but it also attempted to reduce unevenness in the system of allocation and increase state and municipal control over the curriculum and the market. Like British Labour, this approach demonstrates the PvdA's reticence about the effects of competition through choice on social equity, with a preference for more direct forms of steering (for example, upscaling, central and local regulation) to offset the risks accompanying choice in a fragmented system.

The Dutch case shows that even in a historically market-oriented system embedded in consensual policy space, differing points of view among the major political parties have shaped the development of the market. As all actors faced pressure to reform education, they challenged the logic of the consensual corporatist system. However, as their interests in doing so varied, so too did the market instruments they used. Early CDA–VVD policy set the overall thrust towards a Two Tier market in motion, whereas the dominance of the PvdA in education through much of the 1990s slowed this movement and weakened the choice orientation and the risks placed on parents. The outcome is a Two Tier market embedded in a strong system of state and local control.

5.5: CONCLUSION

The picture that emerges from market-oriented education reform over the past two decades in England, Sweden, and the Netherlands, is less varied than in health or elderly care. Nonetheless, far from being uniformly good or bad, market reforms in these countries have worked differently. The increase in central power accompanying the English, Dutch, and more recently, Swedish markets, challenges claims that markets work to uniformly undermine state power. Equally, the outcomes have hardly been as beneficial or as dire as market proponents and opponents claim. While choice-based markets have emphasized performance and created some new inequities, these markets have often been far more important for distributing power than raising test scores.

These changes have been highly political. In many countries, including those surveyed here, the Right had long supported more selection and differentiation in the education system and a more limited public offer, while the Left challenged school selection and looked to increase state or municipal control over the education system. The 1980s brought growing concerns about performance and rising parental demands, limiting the Right's ability to pursue traditionally hierarchical education policies and the Left's ability to spend to solve problems in education.

In response to these concerns, political parties began to turn to structural reform of the education system. Right-wing parties in the Netherlands, Sweden, and England all put markets on the agenda, looking at strategies to support private schools or selective publicly funded schools and expand choice. However, how each party turned its interest in markets into an actual market depended on the logic of the existing system. In Britain and the Netherlands, the popularity of the education system limited more radical producer-based reforms. Parties on the Right though, saw the existing fragmentation in the system as attractive, and were able to pursue their core preferences by layering more choice and individual responsibility onto the existing system, rather than changing it. The result was Two Tier markets, where schools competed for pupils, money followed the pupil, and there was less attention to costs than responsiveness to parental demands.

In Sweden, by contrast, the education system had a more uniform structure. The Swedish Right, facing heavy constraints in reforming the public sector, left it largely intact and targeted its efforts on more ideologically preferred reforms outside the public sector. The early voucher reforms allowed private schools to receive public funding, without extensive regulation on their location, pedagogical or organizational approach, creating a Private Power market.

Rather than reversing these reforms, left-wing parties have looked to manage them, layering more control onto the system and challenging perceived inequities. In England and the Netherlands, Labour and the PvdA were in a weak position – they saw fragmentation in the existing system as problematic, but unlike in health, lacked tools to address this through a popular political appeal. The public supported choice, but expanding competition through choice alone threatened to fragment, rather than bridge, lower- and upper-income citizens. In this inhospitable environment, both parties cobbled together a mix of approaches, maintaining the core principle of choice as a way of maintaining middle-class support but increasing oversight, compensatory mechanisms, and targeting policies at vulnerable groups. While Labour has been vocally supportive of choice, its actions tell a more complex story, as it moved towards a Managed Market and directly targeted failing schools. The more uniform Swedish system, by contrast, offered the SAP more opportunities. While the party outrightly rejected a producer orientation in education, it saw highly regulated choice through a Consumer-Controlled market as acceptable and even desirable.

6

Markets in elderly care

While all human societies have had to broach the challenge of caring for the elderly, public funding and provision of high-quality care services are a recent and often uncertain development. Across the OECD, there is no single model for care services, with countries varying widely in how much they spend, how many services they offer, and what mix of institutional, home, and family care they encourage (OECD 2005). While this diversity in cross-national experience is striking in itself, different national models are not fixed, with some countries (most prominently Germany and Japan) recently introducing or expanding long-term care benefits. Indeed, markets and public responsibility for care are growing in tandem. Most countries lack a halcyon past of public-sector dominance, or a fully private market against which they are either privatizing or expanding the public sector. Instead they are developing care services for the first time in an era of markets, and often through markets.

However, countries have done so in sharply differently ways. In England, the Conservatives introduced early reforms in the care sector allowing more private provision in a weakly regulated environment, with the emerging Pork Barrel market insulating users from heavy costs while putting producers in a position to earn extra revenue from the state. As the costs of this market exploded, these same policymakers cut funding but kept the orientation towards producers, moving to a Private Power market. By contrast, while Swedish local governments in the early 1990s also cut benefits and contracted with the private sector, they faced less pressure to do so. As a consequence, they largely (but not exclusively) introduced Austerity markets, which paired increased costs for users with competition that enhanced, rather than undercut, political and managerial control. Finally, in the Netherlands, after nearly a decade of resisting markets, the Left–Right coalition of the late 1990s introduced a limited Consumer-Controlled market, expanding individual choice without increasing costs.

Before this consumer-driven market could develop, however, the more conservative government moved towards an Austerity Market built around state contracting and individual cost sharing. While market making in care has often been less controversial than in either health or education, once again, we see different partisan strategies across institutional contexts.

6.1: MARKETS IN ELDERLY CARE

Questions about different market structures in care are deeply linked to a range of fundamental issues about care itself: what responsibility do individuals and families have for financing their own care? Should state policy look to enhance users' autonomy? To what extent should the state patrol the market? Scholars and policy advocates have answered these questions in strikingly different ways, advocating varied types of market (and non-market) organization in the care sector.

On the allocation dimension, debate rages over the proper scope of public responsibility for financing and regulating care. One group of scholars builds on both moral and economic reasoning to argue in favor of greater private responsibility. These scholars argue that the need for care services is difficult to define and a fully subsidized system will both lead to an over-consumption of unnecessary services and distort incentives for individuals to plan for old age carefully (Pauly and Zweifel 1996). Critics of this approach argue that because the costs of care are steep and difficult to plan for and because the costs of informal care fall disproportionately on women, public funding and valuing of care of the elderly is a moral duty (see Royal Commission on Long Term Care (1999) for a policy perspective; Sevenhuijsen (2000) for a theoretical perspective). Those supportive of greater public funding argue that individual cost-sharing creates perverse incentives for elderly citizens, requiring them to "spend-down" their capital in order to qualify for public funding (Wiener *et al.* 1994). The debate over regulation to ensure access follows similar lines, with some arguing that providers should be allowed to select patients following market demand, while others argue that the state should force providers to accept all patients and compensate them for high-needs users in order to ensure universal access (see Latimer (1997) and Walshe (2001) on this debate).

Both debates rest on questions of who should bear the costs for care, and what the consequences are of public-private mixes. Ultimately, varied market structures answer these questions differently. Markets allowing more cost-sharing or fewer regulations on access (Austerity Markets, Private Power, Two Tier markets) tilt the balance towards greater individual responsibility. Markets introducing competition within a publicly funded and regulated sector socialize the costs of care and its future growth

(Managed Markets, Consumer-Controlled, Pork Barrel markets). These latter markets reduce the burden on individuals and may promote greater equity in consumption but they may also reduce citizens' incentives to plan and use care carefully.

On the production dimension there are equally fierce debates. Scholars and policy advocates struggle with questions such as: should the government promote care in the home rather than nursing homes? Should it support care by unlicensed family or friends, or solely from professionals? Should care providers compete? While rarely cast in the language of this project, at the heart of this debate is the question of whether care providers should respond to the preferences of the users or the buyers of services. A strong disability rights movement in the United States politicized this question in the 1970s, explicitly arguing that people with disabilities should have the right to choose their service providers (Benjamin 2001). While these activists advocated a policy of direct cash budgets for users, other commentators looked to policies that expand choice through vouchers or to policies that pay caregivers based on client numbers (OECD 2005). These proposals generally do not focus on costs, but rather, on creating a system that responds to the needs of users.

By contrast, others argue that elderly users lack the capacity to act as effective "consumers" of care, and these authors support either regulatory reforms or government purchasing that gives the state control over the sector. While not all of these proposals involve markets, proponents of contracting often agree with those advocating public production that the government should determine how and how much care should be provided. Unlike proponents of public production, they argue that competition among providers will improve efficiency, making the sector as a whole more cost-effective (Almqvist 2001).

Finally, a third group argues that a more deregulated marketplace best meets the needs of users and taxpayers, allowing producers to innovate and respond to demand. This position is controversial, with proponents of strong state oversight arguing that care services have too many quality components for vulnerable recipients to assess, and that a deregulated marketplace may allow producers to waste money or lower quality without innovating or improving care (Walshe 2001).

These debates point to the choices politicians face in structuring markets. Whether policymakers introduce competition through contracts set by strong government or insurer purchasing (Managed Markets or Austerity Markets), through increased consumer choice of producer where money follows the elderly person's wishes (Consumer-Controlled or Two Tier markets), or through less regulated competition that gives producers of services much scope to follow their own preferences (Pork Barrel or Private Power markets) will shape how, and for whom, the services are produced.

In sifting through these varying options, politicians face a complicated set of trade-offs. The politics of elderly care involves an amalgam of issues, organized interests, and political concerns. While many of the issues surrounding care are new – from the use of technology to enable homecare, to addressing the quality concerns of the baby-boom generation – the playing field is far from empty. Organizations that developed to defend the interests of the elderly with regard to pensions or health care have increasingly used their considerable organizational power to address care issues. Although the care workforce (in the public and private sector) often draws on low-skilled, immigrant, and part-time labor, and is less organized than doctors and teachers, it too has made demands. Moreover, as the number of both the elderly and of working-age adults (often women) facing the dual pressures of child and elder care grows, so too does the electoral prominence of access to care.

Despite these pressures, parties on the Left and the Right have often been hesitant about how far to extend care services. Historically, the Left focused its efforts on securing the welfare of the elderly through extensive pension systems, not care. The success of mature pensions systems in alleviating elderly poverty created a dilemma for the Left. Restricted care funding threatened to ghettoize poor recipients in low-quality services, while extensive care funding might effectively underwrite middle-class inheritances rather than improve equity. In the area of production there were also trade-offs, as eschewing private or informal care might leave the state with a heavy bill or low capacity to deal with citizens' needs. As a result, the Left has tended to support strong state regulation of the care market and generous funding for those in need, but was also open to market reforms in both financing and producing care services.

By contrast, both the Christian Democratic and economically liberal right-wing parties viewed the role of the state in rather narrow terms, supporting both more individual responsibility for care and more room for private entrepreneurship. However, elderly voters and their middle-aged children matter electorally to the Right and it was the Right that introduced the most extensive new benefits for the elderly in recent years (from prescription drugs in the United States to care insurance in Japan and Germany).

What does this partisan ambivalence mean for markets in care? In general, the logic presented in previous chapters holds, with parties on the Right more likely to support less regulation, greater private entrepreneurship and cost-sharing, while those on the Left support a more robust public guarantee in terms of both regulation and financing. As in other sectors, where services are provided universally, the Right faces heavy electoral constraints on cutting funding or delegating power to the private sector, leading it to support broad electoral appeals through choice where it can target benefits and more regulated contracting where it cannot. Equally, for the Left there are clearer ideological and electoral gains to making broad, popular, choice-based appeals for services that are already universal and uniform, while ensuring basic performance through contracting is more attractive for residual or fragmented services. However, for both parties, these basic patterns are also met with a greater caution than in health and education, as care is a less prominent service, with uncertain future growth, and fewer ideological gains.

6.2: MARKETS IN ENGLAND

In England the public commitment to providing care for older people developed more slowly and less extensively than it did for health. The roots of public care for the elderly lay in the punitive nineteenth-century poor laws. Through the early to mid-twentieth century, the government began to transform this system, delegating responsibility for extensive care to long-stay NHS hospitals while giving the local authorities (LAs) responsibility for low-intensity services.[1] However, these services remained limited, standing in stark contrast to the universal and uniform health service.

Reforms by the Conservatives in 1980 transformed the system, introducing a Pork Barrel market that extended profitable contracts to producers without accompanying regulation. In response, a flurry of small producers entered the market, and costs exploded. In 1993, the Conservatives modified the market, moving to a Private Power market, limiting spending while continuing to contract with providers without extensive regulation. Despite Labour's attempts to re-regulate this market, it continues to support a large private sector of uncertain quality, inequities in access, and an emphasis on cost-cutting. In order to understand the evolution of this market, we need to look at how the residual nature of the care sector allowed the Conservatives to introduce privatization, and at the same time limited Labour's incentives to change it.

Producer-driven markets in care

The first move to the market in the British care sector emerged as part of an extensive reform of the social security system in 1980. Since 1948, the social security system had allowed funding for individuals in care homes, but local offices had much discretion in determining eligibility. Reforms in 1980 gave all individuals with low incomes and fewer than £3,000 in assets

---

[1] The local government body responsible for personal social services varies across England.

the right to apply for benefits from the social security system to cover the costs of private residential care (Bauld *et al.* 2000). These changes produced a classic Pork Barrel market, insulating individuals from costs while funneling money directly to private firms.

In the area of allocation, the 1980 reforms changed the system of financing to provide new funding. Although the presence of means-testing meant that individuals did face some direct costs, the regulations on access were permissive, with few gatekeepers restricting care. Older individuals with limited incomes, even those with little need, could enter into care homes with a state subsidy. Indeed, inequality in access to care fell through the 1980s (Bartlett and Phillips 1996).

The reforms reoriented production around the interests of the producers themselves. Although this move ostensibly created competition for individual choices, it was introduced absent strong regulatory control. The government allowed homes to choose whether, where, and when to enter the market. Homes could determine their fees. Local average costs, rather than fixed rates, determined the initial reimbursement level, giving homes an incentive to raise rates and push up the local average (Glennerster and Lewis 1996). Alongside this weak control over market entry and pricing, the government did not closely monitor the actual care the homes provided. In 1984, it introduced the Registered Homes Act, which required private homes to meet basic quality standards and gave the LAs and health authorities responsibility for inspecting homes for compliance with the Act. However, both the regulations and the LAs' role as inspectors were unclear, producing wide local variation (Gibbs and Bradshaw 1990). Moreover, the LAs were restricted in examining whether the fees a home charged were in line with its quality (Arai 1993).

Predictably, this Pork Barrel market, in offering private firms public funding absent strong regulations or contracts specifying what they were to produce, where, or how, led to both a rapid privatization of care and a surge in spending. Places in the private for-profit residential care sector grew 255% through the 1980s, compared to a fall of 13% in the public sector, reaching 49% of places by 1990 (Hudson 2000). These new private homes entered profitable markets, converting dilapidated hotels along the coasts of Devon and Cornwall into care homes (Means *et al.* 2002; Andrews and Phillips 2002). Because this geographically skewed concentration of homes did not necessarily track the needs of the elderly population, homes responded by creating their own demand, with over twenty-seven percent more claimants emerging through this period than demographic and need variables would predict (Hardy and Wistow 2000). Fees also rose, often with little relation to improvements in the quality or the intensity of service provision (Bradshaw and Gibbs 1988; Forder *et al.* 1996). The combination of new claimants and rising fees led total spending on supplementary benefits to increase dramatically, with social security spending as a percentage of total spending on institutional care growing from 0.8% before the reforms to 25.9% by 1986, and absolute spending skyrocketing from £6 million in the late 1970s to £2.4 billion in 1991 (Bauld *et al.* 2000; Klein and Day 1987). The data on the quality of care are fragmented but homes catering to publicly funded patients often provided few high-level amenities, suggesting that the escalating spending was not supporting improved quality (Laing and Buisson 1985).

In reshaping the care system around a dedicated funding stream funneled exclusively to private homes absent strong regulation, this market created new winners among private producers at a cost to individuals and the state. Lower-income individuals did benefit from generous care funding, but the market encouraged them to enter institutions, rather than receive care at home, with few guarantees of quality. Equally, the market allowed the LAs to off-load costly care for the elderly onto the social security system, leaving the public sector as a whole to pay for expensive services of uncertain quality, uncertain use, and often with little relation to needs.

In response to the Pork Barrel market, the Conservative government introduced legislation in 1990 (implemented in 1993) aimed at cutting costs and reshaping the market. These reforms claimed to promote greater care management, enhance co-ordination between the NHS and the care sector, give individuals more choice over what type of care they received, and move care from institutions into the community (Department of Health 1989). However, the core thrust was to limit funding, decentralize financial responsibility for care to the LAs, and require them to contract out much of this care from the private sector. In conjunction, these shifts created strong incentives for the LAs to pass cost-cutting onto providers without regulating how they did so, creating a Private Power market that maintained private control and shifted costs onto users.

Unlike the early reforms, the 1990 reforms moved towards a more individualized allocation of benefits. The reforms targeted care financing, replacing the system of open-ended spending with a fixed transfer to the LAs. At first glance, the new care-funding system appeared quite generous, transferring £1.5 billion over a three-year transition period to the LAs, increasing their budgets by a third (Glennerster and Lewis 1996). This additional funding, though, was meant to cover the entire care sector, including new recipients in private homes previously funded out of the social security budget.[2] This move combined with ongoing efforts to shift people from NHS beds into the means-tested, cash-limited, care system

---

[2] The social security system continued to pay for the "preserved rights" of those already in care homes.

(Blackman 1998). Moreover, after a three-year transition period, the government would no longer ring-fence funding for care, giving the LAs freedom to allocate funds among their different tasks. These shifts meant that the LAs had considerable incentives to reduce the growth of spending, by limiting access or charging fees. The government further instructed the LAs to both asset- and income-test institutional care, and income-test home care; and despite requirements to assess the needs of all citizens, the LAs could define needs locally. As a result, substantial variation emerged in what the LAs covered, the quality of care, and the charges users faced (Challis *et al.* 2001).

While Means *et al.* (2002) argue that it is important not to romanticize pre-1993 service provision, the Private Power market did lead cash-strapped LAs to limit coverage (Clark *et al.* 1998). Between 1993 and 1997, the number of households receiving help fell by seven percent, even though cuts in NHS care increased need (Bauld *et al.* 2000). These problems dovetailed with informal changes in the sector, with care homes charging higher fees, even to those with public funding (Walsh and Bennett 2000). Indeed, as recently as 2005, a government study found illegal fee-charging continued to constitute a significant barrier to access (Office of Fair Trading 2005).

The structure of production continued to delegate control to the private sector. Ostensibly, the reforms required the LAs to offer individuals choice. However, in practice, they introduced a logic of competition for both home and residential care that built on contracting. The LAs, not individuals, determined the flow of funding to providers, and had wide latitude to negotiate with whom to contract, as well as the duration, type of contract and price (Means and Smith 1998). A majority of users reported receiving no choice about whether to enter a home or receive domiciliary care, and many had little choice of provider (Knapp *et al.* 2001). Indeed, the only real restriction on LA purchasing was that they had to spend eighty-five percent of the new funding on non-public providers.

The combination of the LAs' inexperience in contracting and a weakly developed regulatory environment created a logic of control that delegated much power to producers. On paper, the reforms required the LAs to inspect and monitor private facilities, and gave the Audit Commission and Social Services Inspectorate (SSI) oversight of the LAs and providers. However, the LAs faced strong pressure to cut costs, and many chose to construct contracts that passed on incentives for cost cutting without specifying or monitoring of quality or responsiveness to users (Hardy and Wistow 2000). Many LAs did not gather basic information on what clients needed, giving them few tools to scrutinize the performance of care providers (Kerrison and Pollock 2001; Warburton and McCracken 1999). In the lead-up to the reforms, a survey by the *Independent* newspaper in 1994 found that as many as half of LAs failed to meet their statutory obligations to inspect homes every two years (Kelsey 1994). These problems persisted over time. A study seven years after the reforms were introduced found that only twenty-one percent of LAs differentiated among private providers based on quality and only eleven percent used this information to calculate differential fees (Continuing Care Conference 2000). Unlike in the NHS, central regulation did not counteract these weaknesses in contracting, ensuring little more than the "fitness" of the proprietor. Indeed, the government rejected calls to regulate the quality of employees in the domiciliary care sector, common registration standards across the country, and a national inspectorate (Fry 1992; Laing 1994; Laing and Buisson 1994).

The result was a Private Power market that expanded the power of new private home care providers. In 1992, local authorities provided 98% of home care, purchasing only 2% from the private sector. By 1997, 56% was public, with 39% purchased from the private sector and 5% from the non-profit sector (Hudson 2000).[3] Through the 1990s, the LAs controlled costs by keeping payment increases to providers below the rate of inflation (Laing and Saper 1999). This strategy, when combined with weak contractual specification on quality, rewarded the new private providers for cutting costs rather than improving quality or efficiency (Knapp *et al.* 2001). Indeed, a study in 2001, found that fifty percent of care homes failed to meet basic standards, and a more recent study found instances of poor quality, and even abuse, continue to abound (Netten *et al.* 2005; Joint Committee on Human Rights 2007). Laing and Saper (1999) argue that LA purchasing did lead to some quality improvements through the 1990s (for example, the number of homes providing single rooms), but that to ensure adequate quality, public funding of care homes would need to increase substantially.

Although not as beneficial to them as the heyday of the Pork Barrel market, the basic logic of the Private Power market maintained the interests of private providers. Even Laing and Saper (1999), who echo providers' frustration with LA fees, admit that the reforms stimulated the private home care sector far beyond what private demand alone would have. Most users, by contrast, lost out, as the market developed a trifurcated character. Wealthy users could buy high-quality care at high prices from

---

[3] Even though the 1989 reforms explicitly looked to support home care, the LAs had a number of financial incentives to continue to fund residential care. In determining eligibility for public funding, the LAs could consider individuals' assets for residential-care funding, but not home-care funding, and thus could recoup more of the spending for residential care (Laing 1994). The LAs also looked to the residential-care sector to meet their requirement to spend in the private sector, as few private home-care providers initially existed, and to provide continuity for patients already in the residential-care sector.

exclusive private providers, low-income users received public funding for low-quality care, while middle-income users were stuck paying high fees while receiving the same low-quality care as the publicly funded users. Finally, the state only won in crude terms: the market controlled costs, but it also exacerbated the state's already weak control over the production of services.

Labour – changes around the edges

Upon entering office in 1997, Labour modified the Private Power market towards an Austerity Market (individual responsibility, state contracting). On the allocation dimension, this effort partly looked to combat inequity in access – between 2001 and 2008 Labour increased spending on adult social care by over fifty percent (King's Fund 2010). Labour also extended NHS funding to the nursing care provided in residential homes and raised the level of assets individuals could keep while receiving public funding. However, Labour did not follow through a proposal from the Royal Commission on long-term care to offer all elderly people free personal care (non-medical care provided in institutions). The Scottish Parliament did choose to introduce free personal care for the elderly and Labour floated plans to move towards free personal care for high-needs citizens but, when it left office in 2010, it had not done so.

In the area of production, Labour maintained the basic structure of contracting and the mixed economy of care provision, but pursued a substantial reorganization of control. Its primary push was for LAs to contract, particularly "block contract" for care (Interview: manager of a Northern LA, 2005; Interview: senior official in Care Inspectorate, 2005a). Labour no longer required the LAs to contract with the private sector, but put more financial responsibility on LAs to act quickly to move patients out of hospitals (avoiding so-called "bed blocking") and encouraged them to use the existing private sector to do so. Labour expanded choice around the edges of the system through the "Direct Payments" program. The Conservatives first introduced this program in 1996, allowing people eligible for LA-funded care to opt for a cash budget to purchase care on their own terms. From 2004, Labour committed itself to expanding direct payments and user choice (Department of Health 2005) and later pledged further funds for pilot programs devolving budgets to users (Brindle 2007). In practice, though, few elderly people received direct payments and the bulk of care was provided through the LAs.

However, Labour did dramatically expand central regulatory control and oversight of providers, changing the nature of this contracting. In 2000, it enacted the Care Standards Act, introducing a National Minimum Standard in care homes, that more extensively regulated aspects of quality (for example, on room size) and required care employees to have a minimum level of vocational training. Alongside this changed regulation, Labour first expanded the role of the SSI and then established the independent Commission for Social Care Inspection (CSCI) to inspect providers. "Bottom up" changes in the LAs accompanied these shifts, but slowly, with the government largely emphasizing regulation rather than improved contracting skills (Interview: Senior Official at Care Inspectorate, 2005b). Taken together, these shifts started to move towards an Austerity Market, with more regulated contracting and individual cost-sharing. However, problems in the care sector, such as uneven access, high costs, and poor quality remained (Robinson and Banks 2005).

Why these markets?

Why did the Conservatives introduce a Pork Barrel and then a Private Power market? Why did Labour modify, but not radically alter, this market? Like the education and health sectors, we see that the Conservatives had strong preferences for more private entrepreneurship and a streamlined role for the state. Unlike these sectors though, the party faced far fewer electoral constraints in reforming care, permitting producer-based markets. For Labour, the calculus differed, as it faced few benefits to radically reforming the residual sector, but also saw the status quo as problematic.

Through the 1970s, politicians, bureaucrats, and advocates for the elderly alike began to question whether the existing care system was appropriate for a growing elderly population with new needs and demands, and many began to advocate expanding care for the elderly in their own homes. When the Conservative party was elected to office in 1979, it claimed to support these ideas, continuing the previous government's rhetoric of promoting community care (home care rather than institutional care), presenting this approach as key to limiting a looming cost explosion (Means and Smith 1998).

The first set of reforms, though, did precisely the opposite, supporting private nursing homes through a Pork Barrel market. Despite the Conservatives' attraction to funding private facilities, claimants' groups and bureaucrats largely drove these particular changes, without extensive political scrutiny (Klein and Day 1987; Glennerster and Lewis 2000). In contrast to the major reforms in health and education, the Conservatives stumbled into these first reforms of the elderly care system.

The party's attention to the sector grew as costs exploded. Initially, the government tried to cap expenditure growth through a series of incremental changes to the supplementary benefit system. However, there was a growing consensus within the government that it needed to enact more fundamental reform. In 1986, an Audit Commission (1986) report argued that while social workers and health economists alike pointed to the efficiency and humanity of providing care in the home, public policy was promoting the opposite. Increasingly, the Conservatives saw the Pork Barrel market care as having perverse effects (Klein 2006: 127).

In response, the Conservatives began to consider various reform options, including multiple types of market reforms. Many proposals looked to decentralize responsibility for elderly care to the LAs but others, such as the government-sponsored Wagner report and the right-wing Adam Smith Institute, suggested expanding choice through a national voucher-like system of elderly care payments (Brindle 1988; Hencke 1989; Means and Smith 1998). These varying proposals further split on the level of regulation, for instance, the Wagner report called for introducing stricter standards for care providers and more inspection (Brindle 1988).

In sifting through these plans, the Conservatives were initially ambivalent, if not hostile, to proposals for decentralization, expressing concern that the LAs could use their new powers to undercut the private market (Glennerster and Lewis 2000; Means and Smith 1998; Timmins 2001: 474). A solution emerged in 1988, following a review of the system by Sir Roy Griffiths, who had earlier chaired a review of the NHS. Griffiths proposed giving the LAs responsibility for promoting community care, but requiring them to purchase, rather than provide, this care. The Conservatives had already experimented with mandatory LA contracting for services like refuse collection, and Griffiths' proposals, although not entirely equivalent, built on this experience. Despite continuing reticence towards decentralization, the Conservatives proceeded with a modified version of Griffiths' plan (Timmins 2001).

Why did the government make this particular choice? The Conservative party's core preferences in the elderly care sector were for more private entrepreneurship and lower spending. In the documents introducing the reforms, the government explicitly outlined its desire to support private entrepreneurship, arguing that it was necessary to force the LAs to contract in order to give them "every incentive to make use of the independent sector" and to avoid local authority "empire building" (Department of Health 1989; junior minister, Tim Yeo, Hansard, 3/23/1993). Moreover, the government touted light regulation in the face of criticism from the Royal College of Nursing and others, later stating: "If the industry feels there is a problem, or administrative difficulties come up, we will think again. We are very keen that the private sector should grow and that the Government should not bind them up with red tape" (Ogden 1993; Clay 1989). The government was equally clear on its desire to limit spending. It refused to specify the level of resources that it would devote to care (despite criticism from the Audit Commission and Griffiths on this point), and rejected calls from the LAs to increase spending (Smith 1990; Souster 1989; Audit Commission 1992). Actors across the political spectrum supported a cash-limited local budget for care, yet the Conservatives broke with Griffiths, the House of Commons Social Services Select Committee, and Labour, in initially refusing to provide a dedicated care budget. Although the government later agreed to temporarily "ring-fence" care spending, this delay suggests that the government preferred to allow care to jockey with other local spending priorities.

The Private Power market, then, in cutting spending, limiting state regulation, and supporting the private sector, fit with the party's core goals. Unlike in the NHS, the Conservative party was able to introduce this market because it faced fewer electoral constraints in reforming the residual care sector. For instance, despite being delayed for three years, in 1993 fewer than four out of ten people reported knowing about the reforms and only two out of ten reported any knowledge of their content (Papworth 1993). When the reforms were finally implemented in 1993, the press declared it a "low key affair," with government making little effort to publicize its changes (Waterhouse 1993). The delay in the implementation of the reforms largely occurred because the government faced electoral pressure in the area of local government taxation. The Conservatives' attempt to introduce a fixed per-person local government tax (the so-called "poll tax") was bitterly unpopular. Concerns among policymakers that the decentralization of care would increase the size of the poll tax led the government to delay the changes (Glennerster and Lewis 1996). However, when the political heat around the poll tax passed, the government pushed ahead with the reforms with only minor revisions, demonstrating again the low salience of the care sector.

The government also faced few concentrated interests resisting reform. The professionals in the care sector supported the move to community care (Interview: Department of Health official, 2005). The LAs were eager to gain new responsibilities and, although they saw the reform as potentially a "poisoned chalice," they accepted its basic thrust (Interview: Department of Health official, 2005). The government did face stark opposition from current pensioners and private-care providers, concerned that the reforms would jeopardize their existing benefits. In light of this pressure, it grandfathered the policy provisions; ensuring existing recipients would maintain their benefits and private homes would experience a "soft landing" (Laing 1994). Because so many major players were dissatisfied with the fragmented and limited nature of care services, and the Conservative government compensated those that were happy with the existing system, it was able to forge ahead.

The existing logic of the care system meant that despite being introduced in the same bill as the NHS reforms, the Conservative party was better able to cut spending and expand the private sector without building up local or central control in care. The Private Power market reshaped the care system around the Conservatives' core preference, limiting spending and encouraging private production.

Labour's calculations

Where the residual structure of the care sector enabled the Conservatives to follow their core preferences, it limited Labour's ability to make a broad appeal through reform. In opposition, Labour's attention to care was relatively modest but it increased as public dissatisfaction grew through the 1990s. Rising property prices meant more elderly citizens were failing the means-test, and unable to secure publicly funded services (Means *et al.* 2002). These concerns combined with problems of poor quality, instability, and regional variation in care provision, making it a more salient issue. In the lead up to the 1997 election, Labour promised to address these concerns by defining a long-term care plan, introducing more independent care inspection, and establishing a Royal Commission to examine care financing (Means *et al.* 2002).

Although Labour's support for elderly care was hardly as robust as its support for the NHS, the party was concerned with ensuring the system continued to provide care for the weakest in society without harming the middle classes. Tony Blair, in 1997, stated that "I don't want them [children] brought up in a country where the only way pensioners can get long-term care is by selling their home" (Blair 1997). Yet, in contrast to health and education, the party did not have a clear strategic vision in the sector. It was not vested in the status quo but it was also politically unwilling to extend the public system.

The more residual structure meant that dramatically expanding public funding threatened to create state subsidization of middle-class (and Tory voters') inheritances, rather than enhancing equity (Interview: Official in Care Inspectorate, 2005b). In response to the Royal Commission's suggestions for greater public funding of personal care, parts of the Labour party, particularly in the Treasury, expressed concerns that this move would only substitute public for private funding without increasing overall spending in the sector, and that as the population aged, needs changed, and informal care arrangements wilted, care spending would become insatiable (Interview: official in Care Inspectorate, 2005b; Means *et al.* 2002). A commitment to a greater collective guarantee threatened to increase expenditure without delivering clear electoral or ideological gains.

However, failing to address the care system was not an option. The government was skeptical about the power of private producers (Interview: Department of Health Official, 2005b). It was not as ideologically committed to promoting private entrepreneurship as the Conservatives and it was much more willing to layer more control over the market in order to address concerns of abuse and low quality in both the public and private sector. As former health minister Stephen Ladyman stated: "Those of us who want to improve care of older people and drive out abuse from the care system have to become as vociferous and as loud as the care providers are in defending their own interests" (Ladyman 2004). Yet, moving away from private provision was not a viable option, as capacity in the care system was integrally linked to the NHS. LAs often left elderly patients in hospitals because they could not find adequate care, and this "bed blocking" was hampering the NHS' ability to cut waiting lists. Although Labour wanted to avoid the excesses of the producer-driven market, it could not risk reducing existing private sector capacity. John Denham, a former health minister, stated it would be "daft" not to use private capacity (Rumbelow 2000).

The urgency of building capacity in this sector grew through the early 2000s, as more care homes closed because the LAs continued to hold down payments while costs rose (partly due to Labour's regulations in the care sector, a new minimum wage, and higher payments to NHS staff pushing up nursing wages in care). In response, Labour saw supporting the existing private sector as central to stopping further reductions in capacity. The challenge for the party was to increase regulation to ensure more quality and equity, without further hampering the supply of services.

The move to an Austerity Market presented a solution. This market kept much private funding but dulled its edges by increasing state spending, and increased regulation over private and public providers. Thus the care sector, which offered the Conservatives the opportunity to pursue their ideologically preferred policies, offered far less politically to Labour, leading the party to manage the sector rather than fundamentally change it. This market was hardly ideal for Labour, yet it moved the care system, to a limited degree, towards its preferences for a more equitable system with adequate quality.

6.3: SWEDEN: CHANGES FROM BELOW

In the nineteenth and early twentieth centuries, poor houses provided the bulk of public care for the elderly in Sweden, offering indigent elderly people extremely limited and low-quality assistance. The SAP made improving the financial situation of the elderly a key plank of the post-war welfare state. Historically, it put pensions, not care, at the forefront, but beginning in the 1930s and accelerating in the 1950s, the SAP also supported the expansion of higher quality dedicated care facilities for elderly citizens (Trydegård 2000). In the 1970s, it began to expand care for the elderly in their own homes, with the municipalities building on a reserve army of low-paid local women to deliver these services (Korpi 1995). As the care sector grew in size, the percentage of people who reported receiving care from their families or friends fell from seventy-seven percent in 1954 to only thirty-nine percent in 1975 (Johansson *et al.* 2003). By the 1980s, Sweden had developed an extensive public system of long-term care for the elderly.

Sweden now spends close to three percent of GDP on care, the top of the OECD, and public providers remain dominant (OECD 2005). Since the early 1990s, however, locally driven markets have transformed care. These markets vary: with different levels of cost-sharing, mixes of choice and contracting, and degrees of regulation. The overriding trend has been towards Austerity Markets that combine individual cost-sharing with regulated contracting. The following section examines these markets, and the political dynamics behind them.

Markets in Sweden

There is no single Swedish elderly care market. The story of markets in Swedish elderly care is, rather, largely a story of local political choices to introduce markets. These local initiatives have roots in several national policy decisions that expanded municipal control over the care sector. In the late-1980s, the Swedish care system was fragmented across the counties, who were responsible for hospital care, and the municipalities, who provided home care and special housing.[4] The "Ädel Reform," introduced by the SAP and implemented in 1992, unified responsibility for care in the municipalities, providing them with some extra funding and giving them strong financial incentives to avoid leaving elderly patients in hospitals. The SAP's 1991 Local Government Act paired this increased local responsibility with greater local autonomy. These changes gave the municipalities more autonomy over their own internal organization, including contracting with the private sector. Further legislation introduced by the non-Socialists expanded municipal discretion over both spending and contracting.

Many local politicians seized on this new autonomy, dramatically reforming elderly care, often along market lines. By the end of the 1990s, half of the municipalities had introduced a purchaser-provider split, separating the responsibility for "buying" care services from providing them (Trydegård and Thorslund 2001). A number of these new purchasers

---

[4] Sweden has 289 municipalities (*Kommuner*) and 21 counties (*Landsting*). Counties are responsible for health care, while the municipalities are responsible for education, child and elderly care, local welfare policy, and culture and recreation.

turned to the private sector, with the number of private producers growing from 1% to 8% of all providers through the 1990s, and with the number of private care employees increasing from 2.5% to 13% of the care workforce (Swedish Welfare Commission *et al.* 2003; Suzuki 2001). These numbers have remained relatively stable, increasing slightly through the first part of the 2000s (Socialstyrelsen 2004b).

This general movement towards the market though, rests on substantial local variation. At the simplest level, local actors have made different choices over whether to introduce markets. In 2004, 200 of 289 municipalities reported no private care in residential facilities, with only a slightly larger number reporting private care in home help (Statistics Sweden 2004a). Indeed, even in the most market-friendly part of Sweden, the county of Stockholm, there is wide variation, with the municipality of Solna contracting privately for close to eighty percent of care services, whereas thirteen of the twenty-six municipalities used no private care (Statistics Sweden 2004a). Furthermore, local politicians have chosen to structure markets differently, raising fees to differing extents, and introducing different logics of competition, through strong purchasing (Managed Markets/Austerity Markets), consumer choice (Consumer-Controlled/Two Tiered), or less regulated contracting that gave care providers much power (Pork Barrel/Private Power). Despite this local variation, where local actors have introduced markets, they have largely (albeit not exclusively) fallen into two camps: combining higher fees with either clearly specified contracting (Austerity Markets) or user choice (Two Tier markets).

The 1990s witnessed many municipalities using their new autonomy to raise fees, creating significant movement on the allocation dimension (Bergmark 2000). The Ädel reforms put the entire care sector under the 1982 Social Services Act, requiring the municipalities to allocate services based on individual needs. However, unlike the health sector, the structure of regulation on access allowed municipalities much scope to define needs locally and to consider other sources of care (for instance, the availability of care by relatives) in determining access to the public system. Some municipalities both limited access to care and raised fees, placing direct costs and risks on individuals.

These moves reduced equity in the care sector. In absolute numbers, Sweden still offers one of the most extensive care packages in the OECD; however, from the 1980s the number of care recipients has declined. During the economic crisis of the early 1990s, nearly 100,000 fewer citizens over sixty-five received home help care (Sipilä *et al.* 1997). As the number of recipients fell, municipalities targeted care to the most frail and highest-need elderly citizens (Szebehely 1998). This combination of higher fees and municipal control over defining needs reduced some individuals' access to care. In the 1990s, one in six people over seventy-five reported foregoing care because of fees (Trydegård 2003). Fees hit married couples particularly hard: when one spouse entered a nursing home it often left the other spouse with only a subsistence living (Bergmark 2000). Moreover, the benefits individuals received varied substantially. Thorslund and Trydegård (2001) find that some municipalities offered services to as few as five percent of citizens over eighty, while others offered services to over half of this group. Government policy in the early 2000s limited fees, but municipalities facing tight budgets still restricted access to care, hence some citizens still faced barriers accessing the publicly funded system (Interview: official at the Swedish Association of Local Authorities, 2005; Swedish Welfare Commission *et al.* 2003).

The municipalities were more split on how to structure competition on the production dimension. Most chose to introduce markets through contracting, allowing private and public providers to compete for contracts from municipal purchasers. From the users' perspective, these markets are often invisible and analyses of market reforms have found little sustained expansion of choice for clients (Svensson and Edebalk 2001). However, around a dozen municipalities did introduce competition through client choice, rather than contracting. These municipalities allowed users to choose among multiple accredited providers, and funded providers based on these choices (Edebalk and Svensson 2005). The municipality of Nacka pioneered this approach, giving clients a voucher to visit private providers, with public providers financed through grants, and later extending choice to the public sector and funding all providers on a weighted per-case basis (Kastberg 2001). This model remained limited and was more prevalent in home care than institutional care, but Stockholm introduced choice in the late 1990s and several other municipalities, such as Linköping, introduced a flat voucher available to all citizens regardless of need. Within these choice systems, not all clients were actively choosing, but up to forty percent of users did opt for private alternatives in Stockholm and Nacka (Socialstyrelsen 2004a), enough to create real competition for clients.

Most municipalities paired contracting and choice with a logic of control that limited provider power. Initially, the structure of control was similar to that in England, with a 1995 study of municipal contracting finding that over half of municipalities had no clear follow-up or oversight mechanisms relating to contracts (Socialstyrelsen 1995). There was little national infrastructure for monitoring the providers or the municipalities to compensate for these weaknesses. In this environment, a number of highly publicized scandals emerged.[5]

---

[5] For instance, in the municipality of Solna, a nurse at the home run by the Danish multinational ISS Care, exposed it for leaving elderly residents unattended for hours and lacking basic amenities (Jällhage 1996).

However, municipalities retained control over market entry. Even municipalities using choice, like Nacka, accredited providers and largely did not give them a positive right to enter the market. Moreover, the municipality, not the provider, determined user fees, with no difference between what private and public producers could charge users. This control over entry and pricing stands in contrast to early reforms in the Swedish education and health sectors (see chs. 4 and 5), where legislation gave private providers a positive right to enter the market absent municipal control.

Case studies of municipalities demonstrate substantial variation in contract structures, with some municipal purchasing involving the certification of external providers, inspection, and ongoing review of their services, while other municipalities engaged in little inspection or review (Trenneborg 1999). Two factors mitigated against an overall loss in municipal control. First, in contrast to England, the municipalities faced far fewer pressures to outsource, they did not have to contract with the private sector, and where they did encounter problems, they had the scope to improve. For instance, the municipality of Solna, which experienced a highly publicized scandal exposing the poor quality of a private nursing home, was able to rapidly intervene and bring the home back under municipal control, later reforming its purchasing practices (Trennborg 1999; Interview: care sector official, Solna 2005). Second, the national government played a more active role in regulating the production of care than in England. National procurement laws limited cost cutting by providers, requiring contracted private companies to accept existing employees at the same rate of pay and abide by collective bargaining agreements. More recently, the National Board of Health and Welfare set quality guidelines, and the national government enacted legislation requiring workers in the sector to report problems that they witness (the *Lex Sarah* requirements). Some local markets looked much like those in England, but on the whole, municipalities faced less pressure to privatize and retained more control of private providers than did their English counterparts.

The dominant trend in Swedish care markets was towards Austerity Markets, with a subsidiary trend towards Two Tier markets. Initially, given the paucity of private care provision, both contracting and choice reforms encouraged a number of small care providers (often former public employees) to enter the market. However, in areas of strong contracting, providers increasingly faced pressures to rationalize and appeal to municipalities' preferences for cost control, leading to a consolidation on the provider side. In 1999, four major private firms accounted for half of the total contracted care in the sector in Sweden (Swedish Welfare Commission *et al.* 2003).

These Austerity Markets encouraged providers to focus on costs. There is evidence that the new contract-based providers were less costly at a given level of quality (Suzuki 2001). The cost advantage though, was not necessarily permanent, with a "bottom" in terms of price emerging, particularly as municipal providers also start to reduce costs to compete (Suzuki 2001) (Interview: official, National Board of Health and Welfare, 2005). As in the early Austerity Market in the NHS (ch. 4) administrative costs increased in some areas, driving up expenditure by as much as 2.5% (Kissam 2004). Overall, the effect of contracting on costs is unclear (Socialstyrelsen 2004b). However, competition fundamentally changed the way public and private care providers operated, disseminating commercial management and accounting models through the care sector (Suzuki 2001; Almqvist 2001; Svensson and Edebalk 2001).

These changes privileged cost containment over improved quality, but unlike in England, they did not encourage massive cuts in quality. Cuts in funding may have somewhat reduced quality, but there is little systematic evidence of quality differences between public and private providers, or competitive and non-competitive services (Gustafsson and Szebehely 2001; Suzuki 2001). There is equally little evidence that markets have improved quality (Suzuki 2001). Competition focused on costs but there was not uncontrolled cost cutting, and municipalities avoided contracts threatening quality (Interview: official at the Swedish Association of Local Authorities, 2005). There have been few comprehensive studies of the Two Tier markets but there is some suggestive evidence of differences. Choice markets tended to have a greater number of smaller providers, less direct political control, and a greater emphasis on user satisfaction than in the past (Kastberg 2001).

Both sets of markets altered the playing field around care. The introduction of Austerity Markets, by splitting purchasing from provision and expanding contracting, often gave municipal managers a more distinct, though demanding, role (Trydegård 2000). One official heavily involved in the care sector argued that the threat of contracting created new pressures on providers, strengthening managers' control (Interview: former official, National Board of Health and Welfare, 2005). These municipal managers, in gaining control over the system of needs assessment and the cost structure, were new "winners" in this market. Municipalities though, "lost" in other ways, namely in facing a higher duty of care with more limited resources.

While the introduction of markets benefited new private producers, particularly a few large private firms, this move was less advantageous than in England. Professionals in the care sector also suffered from fiscal austerity. These trends developed outside of the Austerity Market but worked with it to put producers in a defensive position vis-à-vis purchasers (Interview: Rolf Andersson, official at Kommunal, 2005). Individuals "lost" in this market as well, primarily through cuts in service availability. The Swedish elderly care market then, was one primarily built around a pragmatic attempt to reduce costs through contracting and cost-shifting onto individuals, but unlike England, this cost-cutting did not come from a dramatic reduction in quality or a loss of state and local control to producers.

Why these markets?

The Swedish pattern of elderly care markets offers several puzzles. Why did national level politicians partially liberalize local municipal activity, but engage in little actual market making in this sector? Why did most municipalities move towards Austerity Markets? Why did some municipalities follow a different path towards Two Tier markets? As in Britain, we see partisan preferences, particularly the goals of the Right, were crucial in determining this pattern, however, unlike in Britain, the Right faced far more constraints because of the universal and more uniform care system.

The care sector was historically less politicized than either health or education. However, as in these other sectors, both political parties and key actors did maintain distinct preferences. Traditionally, the SAP supported a more extensive public sector and generous public funding and the Moderates supported a more limited state. While care providers never enjoyed the same professional control as either doctors or teachers (Trydegård 2001) these workers are heavily unionized and represented by the union of municipal employees who historically supported the public sector. Other actors, such as the pensioners' lobby (PRO), also supported a generous public system.

Despite this support for extending the existing Swedish system, policymakers across the political spectrum began discussing substantial reforms to the care sector in the 1980s. Through the 1980s, demand for care services grew in line with Sweden's aging population. Rising demand combined with a worsening economy, putting the municipalities and counties in a difficult financial position. The pressure for reform did not just stem from demographic shifts. Policymakers across the political spectrum increasingly saw the division of responsibility between the municipalities (for care) and the counties (for health) as creating perverse incentives. Cash-strapped municipalities were tempted to leave elderly patients in expensive hospital settings, shifting the costs onto the counties (so called "bed blocking").

These incentives for "bed blocking" were not only a cost, but also a quality, concern. Through the 1970s, social workers led a movement to provide care in the home, rather than institutions, and by the 1980s the social work community began to promote home care (Interview: official National Board of Health and Welfare, 2005). Care officials further questioned the quality of institutional care, as many providers offered relatively basic accommodations and services (Interview: official at the Swedish Association of Local Authorities, 2005).

The non-Socialists first raised concerns about "bed blocking" in 1979 and established a commission to study the problem. The Commission did not report until 1987, and offered few reform proposals (Bäck 1999). In 1988, the governing SAP established a second commission to examine problems in the care sector, restricting membership to the minister of social affairs and municipal representatives, in order to rapidly reach reform plans (the government later added representatives of municipal non-Socialists) (Bäck 1999). This Commission advocated decentralizing full financial responsibility to the municipalities, forcing them to "de-medicalize" care and move it out of hospital settings (Trydegård 2003).

These proposals fell on fertile ears. The SAP was increasingly worried about the viability of the system. Substantial decentralization, combined with liberalization of local government activities, promised to address rising costs by both unifying financial responsibility in the municipalities and shifting some of the burden of decision-making over access to care downwards. Thus, the SAP introduced both the decentralizing Ädel reforms and the 1991 Local Government Act, which expanded the scope for local market making. However, it was market making within limits – the party maintained strong national regulations on care, ring-fenced care funding, and did not force municipalities to tender out their activities despite calls from the opposition to do so.[6]

When the non-Socialists came to office in 1991, they had a rather different care agenda. Through the 1980s, the leading coalition partner, the Moderate party, had advocated more choice and contracting, private provision, and private financing in care. The party critiqued the public monopoly in elderly care as both inefficient and weakening family bonds (Moderata samlingspartiet 1990) and promoted more choice and private options in all social services (Moderata samlingspartiet 1984). However, the Moderates did not put care reform at the top of their agenda. Instead, the party focused on child care (see ch. 3), where employers had long allied with parents eager to experiment with non-public alternatives, and education (see ch. 5). Moreover, the other coalition partners, although open to reform, were less enthusiastic about competition than the Moderates. The Liberal minister responsible for care, Bengt Westerberg, expressed strong support for the underlying principles of the Swedish welfare state, including public regulation and financing (Westerberg 1994) and personally

---

[6] The government-sponsored Competition Committee considered, but did not recommend, forced contracting (SOU 1991). Within this Committee the SAP member expressed reservations about forced contracting, with the Liberal party member much more positive towards it.

pushed through reforms providing more public services and infrastructure for people with disabilities (including the elderly) (Dahlström 2005). As a result, when it came to care reform, the government lumped care together with changes to local governance, ending ring-fencing of care expenditure, giving municipalities more scope to raise fees, and expanding their rights to contract with for-profit providers (Bryntse and Greve 2002). Despite complaints from employers, the government shelved several plans requiring municipalities to outsource to the private sector (Lemmel 1993; Westerberg 1992). Introducing either substantial private provision or funding in the universal and uniform system was politically difficult, and given the lower importance of care to the national Moderate party, it was not willing to fight that battle.

The municipalities though, faced a different calculus. The decentralization of responsibility for care and the broader deregulation of municipal activity coincided with two major shifts: the election of non-Socialist governments in 212 of 285 municipalities in 1991 and a severe economic decline in the early 1990s (Montin and Elander 1995). These pressures created incentives on both the "demand" and "supply" sides for municipalities to introduce market forces. On the "demand" side, municipalities faced pressure to address the care sector. For instance, Moderate and SAP voters in Stockholm in 2000 split on their top priorities in the local election (Moderate voters named education and SAP voters housing), but both listed care as the second most important (Tenfält 2002). Yet the Ädel reforms asked municipalities to do more with less. The reforms gave the municipalities additional funds, but many had shrinking local tax bases that more than offset this increase. The national government further limited local tax increases in light of Sweden's crumbling economy. In response, many municipalities looked to cut costs across the board, including the elderly care sector (Swedish Welfare Commission *et al.* 2003). On the "supply" side, both the decentralization and deregulation under the SAP and the non-Socialists' support for markets gave the municipalities new market "tools."

In this environment, local actors on both the Left and the Right turned to markets. Indeed, at first glance, partisan preferences explain little of the move to markets. In the area of financing, Thorsland and Trydegård's (2001) find no relation between political majority and the level of service provided. When we turn to private production, studies show that municipalities with a higher number of Moderate voters used more private providers, but it is difficult to disentangle the impact of the governing majority from the demographic composition of the voters (Suzuki 2001; Trydegård 2003). Case studies further show it was not only the Right that introduced or sustained market forces. Henry Bäck's (2003) analysis of Västerås, a municipality close to Stockholm, shows that the SAP introduced an early purchaser-provider split in 1991. Although the example of Västerås is unusual in the degree of innovation, the use of market forces by the SAP is not. In some cases the local SAP introduced market reforms, in other cases, frequent partisan rotation meant that the SAP inherited contracts from previous governments.

However, when we move beyond the question of whether a market exists, to look at how markets are constructed, a different picture emerges. Local politics in Sweden is not as party-driven as national politics; nonetheless, in some municipalities, we see local non-Socialists responded to new municipal autonomy to galvanize the issue of markets on the care agenda.

Overall, as in other sectors, the Swedish population has a negative net support for private actors in care, but it is positive among Moderate party voters (Nilsson 2009: 276). Local Moderate politicians in highly favorable circumstances (i.e., homogenous, supportive populations) built on this limited support to introduce markets that targeted choice to their constituents. In the right-wing-controlled Stockholm suburb of Nacka, this promise involved a radical program of "choice." Nacka first introduced client vouchers for foot-care services for the elderly, later extending choice to child care, schools, and elderly care, explicitly linking choice to non-public providers (Kastberg 2001). Initially, few other municipal governments adopted the Nacka model; however, in the late 1990s, as the economy improved and local actors faced fewer immediate budgetary constraints, a number of prominent Right-controlled governments did introduce choice. Most prominently, Stockholm City, led by Moderate politician Carl Cederschiöld, expanded client choice in care and allowed care recipients to purchase "top-up" care services from private (but not public) providers. Cederschiöld was able to increase care spending as part of these reforms, without raising taxes, by using windfall profits from privatization and the higher revenue emerging from Stockholm's growing economy.

However, given the universal and uniform care system, most non-Socialists encountered a less hospitable environment, where it was more difficult to expand choice without severe budgetary consequences. Politicians facing tighter budgets and a more volatile electorate, such as Stockholm City in the early 1990s (before turning to choice in the late 1990s) took a different tack. These governments introduced programs of forced local contracting that required municipal administrators to open up local activities to outside bids. This move elevated contracting with private actors to a pre-eminent position, in some cases above cost savings, with studies finding higher costs among private providers in right-wing municipalities (Suzuki 2001). Here, the goal was to limit the public system by allowing some private provision, rather than making a broad, and potentially costly, appeal to users.

Both the unions and pensioners' organizations initially resisted these shifts. Indeed, in many cases, local politicians pushed reforms through over the heads of these organizations. However, beginning in the late 1980s and through the 1990s, cuts in the sector began to lead to a "casualization" of care workers and deterioration in their working conditions (Gustaffson and Szebehely 2001). The unions saw municipal employers as uneasy allies and they began to accept some limited market reforms. The union *Kommunal*, which traditionally opposed market-oriented reforms, began to support some contracting, hoping it would reward high-productivity units (ultimately raising wages) and that having multiple employers would improve the working conditions for employees (Interview: Rolf Andersson, official at Kommunal, 2005).

Despite this tepid support for limited markets, the unions, among others, lobbied the national government for more elderly care funding and quality regulation. The SAP had close links to elderly voters and the pensioners' lobby, which expressed concerns about the cuts in the early 1990s (Feltenius 2007). This lobbying, combined with the SAP's longstanding support for the care sector, led it to take a different path at the national and the local level. In opposition (1991 to 1994), the national SAP began to develop a more critical approach to markets. Party leaders accepted limited market reform as a way to improve efficiency and sustain the sector over the long run, but they were increasingly critical of markets that threatened to support private actors absent strong oversight.[7] As a result, when the SAP returned to power nationally in 1994, it prioritized addressing the problems that cuts, and some markets, had brought to the elderly care sector. The new minister for social affairs, Margot Walström, announced that improving care for the elderly was a key political priority, later introducing a National Action Plan that reaffirmed the government's commitment to publicly funded elderly care based on need (Gould 2001).

The SAP provided resources to match this commitment, targeting so-called "Persson money" to improving local services, particularly elderly care. From 1993 to 1999, it increased expenditure by twenty percent and staff by thirteen percent, despite an increase of people above eighty of only ten percent (Swedish Welfare Commission *et al.* 2003). After increasing funding, the government turned to limiting fees, introducing maximum fees (*maxtax*) in the care sector, increasing the number of people exempt from fees to thirty-four percent (up from fourteen percent), and decreasing regional variation (Trydegård 2003). The SAP also expanded national quality regulation, for instance, by providing a stronger legal basis for the national government to investigate public safety.

---

[7] See for instance the parliamentary debate on local contracting (Swedish Riksdag, 1992).

Thus, through the 1990s and 2000s the SAP neither rhetorically nor in practice promoted markets in care, but neither did it fully reverse them. The rate of increase in the number of private providers was the highest in the last year of the 1990s, when the SAP was in national government (Swedish Welfare Commission *et al.* 2003). The SAP's policy allowed the presence of private and competitive care, but capped fees, expanded funding, and enhanced central regulation, limiting moves on the allocation dimension and supporting a state presence in the sector.

Locally, SAP politicians followed a similar strategy, parting with their non-Socialist counterparts on questions of funding and regulation. While local SAP politicians in Västerås and elsewhere introduced markets, through the 1990s many moved towards managing the existing markets, rather than either expanding or limiting them. In municipalities like Nacka the SAP has little power, but in Stockholm, where there is frequent partisan rotation, the SAP governed from 1994 to 1998 and 2002 to 2006. Here, it moved to raise taxes, expand care funding, and regulate the sector. However, while decrying the excesses of the non-Socialists, key local SAP politicians did express support for the principle of private alternatives (Nyberg *et al.* 1995) and did not limit private contracts.

In contrast to the Moderates, the SAP clearly focused on sustaining the public care sector and ensuring overall access to services, rather than supporting the private sector. However, like New Labour, the SAP's approach to care also differed from that in health and education, where it articulated a more explicit vision of the development and direction of markets. In contrast to the introduction of a "stop-law" banning for-profit hospitals (see ch. 4), the SAP accepted private for-profit providers in the care sector. Equally, despite its general support for the sector and its uniform nature, it did not expand choice or look to claim credit through markets. This mixed stance follows from a more geographically fragmented system facing potentially inexhaustible growth in the future, making the party more open to reforms that promised to save costs while less certain about promoting greater choice and potentially inflationary market measures.

Taken together, we see that some non-Socialist governments in favorable circumstances have pushed Two Tiered markets as a way to promote private alternatives and appeal to wealthier constituents. However, most, facing less hospitable environments, where fiscal difficulties or incentives provided by the uniform and universal care system limited the appeal of choice-based reforms, turned to contracting. The SAP's actions at the local and national level, further regulated this contracting as well as fees. The large number of Austerity Markets then, largely resulted from this trend.

6.4: THE NETHERLANDS: TO MARKET AND BACK, AND THERE AGAIN

Before the late 1960s, informal caregivers or voluntary providers at the local level provided most care for the elderly in the Netherlands. In 1968, the government created a new system of population-wide catastrophic insurance through the Exceptional Medical Expenses Act (AWBZ). Since its inception, politicians have looked to claim credit by expanding the AWBZ, extending it to cover long-term care, mental health, rehabilitation, and medical aids (den Exter *et al.* 2004). This expansion came at a high cost, with AWBZ contribution rates reaching 13.25% of the first 30,000 Euros of income in 2004 (OECD 2005). The AWBZ, despite being funded through social insurance and private contributions, had a system of entitlements that was in some respects more similar to Sweden than other social insurance systems – it ensured all Dutch residents some funding for long-term care. Unlike the Swedish system, however, the non-profit sector provided most care, with little direct public provision.

Initial market reform in the late 1990s began to introduce competition around individual choice without increasing cost-sharing (Consumer-Controlled market). However, no sooner was this market introduced, than the CDA–VVD–D'66 coalition (2003 to 2006) enacted reforms extending greater contracting and cost-sharing (Austerity Market). To understand this dual move towards competition in the Netherlands, we need to look at how varying political interests emerged in this universal and largely uniform care system.

Markets in care

The first proposals for market reforms to the AWBZ emerged in the 1980s as part of a broader package of health care reforms (see ch. 4). Policymakers failed to implement these proposals though, putting market reform on hold until the mid-1990s. In 1995, a VVD junior minister from the Purple coalition (PvdA–VVD–D'66) introduced plans to expand choice in the care sector through a voucher allowing home care recipients to opt for a cash budget to purchase care from public, private, or informal caregivers. This move involved a limited "person-related budget" (*persoonsgebonden budgetten* – PGB), with further reforms in the early 2000s expanding choice in the care system as a whole, paying providers based on demand, and lifting a moratorium on for-profit home care firms. These changes started to restructure the AWBZ, moving towards a Consumer-Controlled market built around largely collective funding and user choice.

These first changes left the basic structure of allocation in place. The Dutch system does demand extensive individual cost-sharing, but all citizens are guaranteed some benefits and the changes in the early 2000s increased public financing.[8] They also maintained strict rules regulating individual access. From the early 1990s, regional care assessment offices (Regional Indicatie Organization – RIOs) determined both what care a user was entitled to and the cost. All individuals had a right to receive care based on need, with income-related cost sharing.

The Purple coalition made more dramatic changes on the production dimension, moving towards competition through user choice. The government first looked to increase the supply of care services, removing spending production limits and permitting new for-profit providers into the home care sector. In 2003, it altered the way it paid providers to make them more responsive to demand. Instead of funding providers based on historical costs or supply characteristics (for example, size, or staff), funding would partly follow patient demand, using reimbursement levels based on seven functional needs. Both the PGB and the move towards "function"-oriented entitlements looked to create competition around choice, and unlike in Sweden and England, policymakers paired these shifts with increased spending and investment in capacity.

The logic of control supported choice. In the early 1990s, the government briefly allowed commercial providers into the market without supporting infrastructure for monitoring the market. This move produced a flood of new commercial providers, and claims of cream-skimming and disorganization in the sector, leading the government to temporarily ban for-profit provision (Schut and van Doorslaer 1999; Knijn 1998). When reintroducing commercial providers in the 2000s, the Purple Coalition responded to these early problems by asking the Dutch market regulator (NMa) to examine the sector, and establishing a health care market regulator (NZa) to patrol market competition. This move was combined with supervision of providers by the health care inspectorate (IGZ).

This first step towards a Consumer-Controlled market moved away from fixed budgeting and towards expanding choice and paying providers based on what they actually produced. While this early market was only partially implemented, there is some evidence that it did have an impact. Extra spending combined with structural reforms increased production. New producers began to enter the market, with one study estimating that in 2001 there were fifty commercial home care providers in receipt of public funds, and 150 more that were seeking public funds following the regulatory changes (de Klerk 2001). As a result, waiting lists fell (Ministry of Health Welfare and Sport, 2005). Predictably, this move came at a cost.

---

[8] In 2004, cost-sharing was income-dependent and could reach 1,631 EUR per month for institutional care (den Exter *et al.* 2004). This cost-sharing is more extensive than in Sweden but less than in England.

Not only did planned investment increase through the early 2000s but costs also shot up in other areas. A study by the CVZ (the tariff-setting body) found that although later reforms held down costs in large parts of the care sector, they were still exploding in the area of the PGB, which maintained a strong choice orientation (Kiers 2006).

However, no sooner did the Consumer-Controlled market begin to develop, than a new CDA–VVD–D'66 (Balkenende II) government introduced reforms aimed at moving to an Austerity Market (individual responsibility, state contracting). The Balkenende II government continued the move towards paying services based on functions and allowing more for-profit provision, but it also introduced new charges, reintroduced production caps, and began to decentralize responsibility for some services to the municipalities, while also requiring the municipalities to contract out for providing care.

These shifts explicitly looked to increase individual responsibility on the allocation dimension, expanding both individual financing and risk in accessing services. The key thrust of these recent reforms was to reduce the size of the AWBZ, moving some services into the competitive health care sector and removing others from the AWBZ package. The Social Support Act (WMO), introduced in January 2007, integrated the social welfare services and disability act (WVG) as well as a range of AWBZ services under municipal control. In so doing, it transformed some formerly AWBZ services into discretionary municipal services, giving the municipalities the option to limit access and charge higher fees. Indeed, an explicit goal of these shifts was to increase individual incentives, with the Balkenende II government stating: "Our freedom of choice is embraced with open arms, but at the same time we are doing too little to encourage people to take responsibility for themselves," with the object of reform being to correct this imbalance (Ministry of Health 2004b).

These reforms also aimed to reshape service production. The Balkenende II government maintained the PGB and the new function-oriented payment system, but it also moved to stimulate competition through contracting. The government introduced legislation allowing health insurers to selectively contract in the home care sector for AWBZ services and required the municipalities to contract out care services where possible. The reforms also permitted the municipalities to use companies providing more basic services (for example, cleaning companies) to provide some care services. In promoting contracting, while maintaining the structure of control developed in the late 1990s and 2000s, these reforms moved towards an Austerity Market.

The fourth Balkenende IV government (CDA–PvdA–ChristienUnie) suspended health insurer contracting for AWBZ services, and increased regulation on municipalities contracting for WMO services. Nonetheless, the logic of the Austerity Market remained on the agenda. Despite the Balkenende governments' publicly declared intention to preserve the AWBZ, in practice these moves looked to hollow out much of its structure by shifting services to the municipalities or to the health system.

Equally, they targeted the traditional providers of services, encouraging purchasers to clamp down on costs. It even allowed municipalities to move away from care professionals altogether by contracting with lower-skilled workers or new for-profit firms. Thus, choices by municipalities, not users, became increasingly central to determining the flow of resources. Indeed, in the reform's first year, municipalities did move to lower-cost (and less trained) providers. Firms competed on price, reducing their bids by an average of twelve percent following the changes (van Staveren 2010). To do so, many firms fired or reclassified workers, giving them lower levels of employment protection and lower wages. In response, in 2007 the government issued some new protections for existing workers, but the major thrust of the market remained: it promised to benefit some new providers but hurt incumbents and, in the long run, strengthen the role of the municipalities and insurers in purchasing – potentially leaving the patient out.

Why these markets?

Why did markets emerge and then fall from the agenda in the late 1980s? Why did they re-emerge first as a Consumer-Controlled market and second as an Austerity Market in the 2000s? Why did a different pattern emerge in the Netherlands than in Sweden or England? Once again, to understand this movement we need to examine both the parties' prefer-ences over care and the way these played out in the universal and more uniform AWBZ.

Over the last two decades, a broad elite consensus developed in Dutch politics that something "needed to be done" in the care sector due to rising costs, concerns about quality, and lack of control over either. However, political parties came to the care sector with different overriding prefer-ences over the structure of care and the structure of markets. As in the health and education sectors, the CDA traditionally maintained close ties to the non-profit care sector and resisted competition, but through the late 1980s and 1990s it began to distance itself from providers and to support more competition, albeit within limits. The VVD, on the other hand, had long supported more individual cost-sharing and private provision. While enthusiastic about both contracting and choice in the abstract, its over-riding preference for fiscal austerity led it to reject markets that risked cost inflation. Finally, the PvdA historically opposed all types of market reforms, supporting public funding and provision and enhancing municipal control. Like the CDA, in the 1990s it too began to accept some market reforms, largely aiming to improve quality. However, it rejected proposals to empower the private sector and radically enhance contracting based on cost, and was ambivalent about combining markets with decentralization.

The political parties were embedded in a system with strong non-state actors. Not only did private actors provide most care services, but they also were involved in central decision-making. The Ministry of Health traditionally widely consulted on changes to the AWBZ, involving insurers, providers, employers, and unions in national decision-making. As elsewhere, the broad playing field that had long limited reforms began to motivate them in the 1980s. Through this decade, concerns about the costs of the care sector grew. Alarm over growing short-term costs in the sector initially led the Lubbers I and II governments (CDA–VVD) to consider cutbacks in service entitlement (van den Heuvel 1997). However, these cuts ran into electoral limits, forcing the government to back off. These experiences, combined with deeper concerns about the long-run cost trajectory of care spending, pushed policymakers towards a broader analysis of the central government bureaucracy and corporatist system in the sector.

The central government regulated prices, quality, and overall spending, yet the autonomy of the insurers and providers meant it had few tools to promote efficiency in how providers used the funds (Okma 1997). Moreover, the Dutch system long had one of the highest rates in Europe of elderly citizens in expensive residential and hospital care (Nies 2002). Many policymakers attributed this trend to structural features of the care system. Providers had few incentives to move elderly citizens out of more expensive care (such as hospitals) and into the home and the varying rules across the health and long-term care sectors further discouraged "substituting" home care for institutional care (van den Heuvel 1997). In the 1980s, the AWBZ did not cover all care services; some services had separate financing systems, distorting the incentives for care substitution. As the government looked to address these problems by moving people to home care, it did so through yet more regulation, raising further questions about the efficacy of this approach. In examining these problems, policymakers began to question the infrastructure of state decision-making as well as incentives for providers at the delivery level.

Against this background the Lubbers II government convened a special committee, the Dekker Committee, to suggest reforms enhancing the overall efficiency of the health and care sectors and promote more cost-effective substitution of care from institutions and into the home. Chapter 4 provides a fuller discussion of the Dekker Committee and its recommendations; however, it is important to note that these recommendations targeted the AWBZ as much as they did the curative care sector.

The core of Dekker's recommendations involved abolishing divisions between both social and private insurance and health and long-term care, creating a single insurance package financed by a mix of payroll taxes and flat-rate premiums. Providers would then compete for contracts with insurers, and Dekker recommended allowing for-profit home care providers in the market (Ministry of Welfare Health and Cultural Affairs 1988).

Although Dekker aimed to bridge different partisan stances towards the AWBZ, the parties' interests in reform still split on the question of how large the AWBZ should be, to what extent it should be financed through income-related premiums, and the extent of marketization in the sector. The CDA, although supporting more integration of health and care and income-related premiums, also promoted some individual responsibility and the role of health stakeholders (CDA 1989). The PvdA looked to expand the sector more extensively, integrating it with the health care system through largely income-based premiums and maintaining a large government presence (PvdA 1989). The VVD rejected the PvdA's proposals, advocating a slimmer income-dependent high-risk package, with a more marketized health care sector (VVD 1989).

When a third Lubbers government was elected in 1989, this time in coalition with the PvdA, responsibility for taking Dekker's plans forward fell to the PvdA junior minister Hans Simons. Simons looked to use the AWBZ as a "carrier" for integrating public and private health insurance, expanding the size of the AWBZ to bring all care and long-term care under its mostly universal and uniform umbrella. Put differently, he aimed to introduce Dekker's competitive plans into a system that integrated long-term care and health care and provided a strong collective guarantee on access.

This idea spurred vociferous political debate. Chapter 4 reviews in more depth the resistance from stakeholders. The employers mounted the most vigorous opposition, seeing too few levers for cost control in the AWBZ. Non-profit providers also rejected more commercial providers in the sector. These concerns put pressure on the government.

The bulk of the political debate ostensibly centered on what the AWBZ should cover and the scope for user fees (Verhagen 2005). Behind this overt polarization around the costs individuals faced, the parties also disagreed over how to restructure production. Both the CDA and VVD initially supported Dekker's proposals. However, echoing the employers, they began to express concerns that because the AWBZ covered catastrophic risks, the insurers had few tools to control costs and competition could increase expenditure (see ch. 4). In the lead up to the 1994 election, the VVD actually argued that the government should restrict competition to the curative care sector and exempt the AWBZ from market forces. At the same time, the CDA's parliamentary party backed the VVD, while the PvdA also broke with Simons and advocated decentralization rather than market forces (Okma 1997: 136–44). The initial reformers could not reconcile the CDA's reticence to protect providers from competition, the VVD's concerns about cost control, and the PvdA's desire to ensure a collective guarantee on access. As support for market forces fell apart, the government made a small move towards allowing commercial providers into the home care sector, but put more fundamental reforms on hold. Even this move towards commercial providers was limited; as evidence of problems in this sector emerged, the Purple coalition suspended competition in 1997.

Following the 1994 election, the Purple coalition announced a moratorium on systematic health reform, explicitly stating that market reforms were inappropriate for the AWBZ as a catastrophic insurance system (Trappenburg and de Groot 2001). During the early to mid-1990s, the Purple coalition experimented with regulatory and participatory reforms, focusing its efforts on improving quality and keeping people at home (van den Heuvel 1997). Moreover, the government further consolidated care funding through the AWBZ, extending benefits for nursing homes, eschewing not only market forces on the provider side but also benefit cutbacks.

Seemingly then, by the late 1990s, the political pendulum had swung quite resolutely against markets in the care sector. The insurers played a passive role: they neither conducted the needs assessment (this task fell to regional needs assessors) nor determined prices. From 1998, a care office (*Zorgkantor*), run by the largest insurer in a region, was responsible for contracting and distributing funds to the local care providers. The national tariff setting body (CTG), not the care offices, determined market entry and reimbursement. The limited supply of care providers further meant that there was little implicit competition for contracts. The insurers, then, had few incentives to either restrict access or cut costs through contracting.

This system left few major players satisfied. Public concern over waiting lists had grown through the 1990s. Initially, the government addressed the waiting list problem by increasing spending, allowing the budget for health care to rise 2.3% in 1998 (rather than the planned 1.3%) and by 3% in the elderly care sector (ter Meulen and van der Made 2000). Waiting lists continued to increase, and in 2000 a government study found over 100,000 people waiting for AWBZ care services (Ministry of Health 2004a).

These pressures pushed for more spending, at the same time as the costs of the AWBZ were skyrocketing. In 1990, the AWBZ cost employees 5.4% of wages, increasing to 13.25% in 2004, with the government projecting that premiums could rise to 20.7% to 25.1% of wages in 2020 (Ministry of

Health 2004b). Given that the AWBZ was financed through a payroll tax on employees, these increases threatened to place a large burden on the working population (Ministry of Health 2004b). However, restricting demand for services in the AWBZ was not an option – a national court decision in 1999 reinforced the right of citizens to AWBZ services and the duty of the state to ensure these services were available.

The combination of growing public demands for waiting-list reduction and concerns about spending led policymakers to once again question the efficacy of both the state and corporatist partners in managing the system. The major parties admitted that simply spending money to appeal to public concerns was only a short-term solution and supported structural reforms (for example, ANP 2000). However, as in the 1980s, this structural critique emerged for different reasons across the political parties, shaping ensuing reform dynamics. The PvdA largely accepted the principle of tax-financed care insurance, but saw the division between health care and the organization of the system as problematic, leading to unclear responsibilities and little attention to patients. It advocated combining all care and medical insurance into a single system with an income-related premium, decentralizing responsibility to the municipalities (PvdA 1998, 2002). It further supported market competition in provision, but within limits, seeing it largely as a way to promote patient-oriented care *not* to reduce costs (PvdA 2002). By contrast, the VVD, although accepting some catastrophic insurance as necessary, saw the AWBZ as too extensive, with inadequate incentives for individuals. It asked whether patients could pay more (VVD 1998) and supported a broader move away from linking income and health policy. The CDA took an intermediary position, supporting the AWBZ but also questioning whether it should include certain benefits (CDA 2002).

The Purple coalition made the first move towards the market with the PGB. This program built on lobbying from the Dutch Council of Handicapped People (*Gehandicaptenraad*) and other groups representing disabled people (Kremer 2006). The VVD was drawn to calls for a PGB, because it promised to reduce professional control, increase personal autonomy, introduce more competition, and open up the system to more change (Kremer 2006). The PvdA (the leading coalition partner) was initially more reticent than its right-wing partners. However, it felt under further pressure to act – there was growing public discontent and concerns about the quality, and long waiting lists (Interview: PvdA Member of Parliament, 2005a). As result, this reticence towards the PGB gave way as it proved popular and promised to address these concerns (Interview: PvdA Member of Parliament, 2005a).

The PvdA's willingness to consider further market reforms combined with both the VVD's longstanding goal to expand competition, and the exclusion of the CDA, the defenders of the non-profit sector, to put further competitive reform on the agenda. However, the move to the market exacerbated partisan fault lines. The PvdA and D'66's unwillingness to cut entitlements alongside the VVD's concerns about inflationary potential of removing production caps and expanding choice made for an uneasy coalition. The task of reform fell to a PvdA junior minister Margot Vliegenhart, who built on the Consumer-Controlled orientation of the PGB, putting quality and productivity above cost control in the reform process. Even before the government introduced these reforms expanding choice, the VVD suggested alternatives aimed at reducing the size of the AWBZ, and expanded local level contracting. The VVD's parliamentary fraction expressed reticence over extra spending on the AWBZ and Vliegenhart's reforms, proposing a more general review of its structure (for instance, the parliamentary debate on AWBZ reform, Tweede Kamer der Staten-Generaal 2000). Allowing spending to follow demand, absent such changes, threatened further cost inflation. Although favoring the idea of choice and the PGB, the VVD's health working group advocated it alongside a more limited package, new private providers, and more scope for citizens to purchase privately and "top-up" AWBZ care (VVD 2000). The PvdA though, bristled at the VVD's proposals for cuts in the sector. The consensus over the desirability of competition around client choice was very fragile.

The 2002 election produced a center-Right governing coalition less positive about the inflationary implications of the earlier reforms. The first Balkenende governments remained overtly supportive of the PGB and function-oriented financing, but were cautious about guaranteeing its expansion (Het Financieele Dagblad 2002; Bassant 2004). The second Balkenende government placed the VVD's interests for cost control in a central position, as the VVD assumed control of the health and finance ministries. Increasingly, the CDA agreed with the VVD that cuts were desirable. Although supporting the Purple coalition's modernization of the AWBZ, the CDA saw problems with its emphasis on reducing queues, questioning the structure of the AWBZ. The CDA broke with its traditional reticence about hurting non-profit providers, working with the VVD on promoting contracting. However, CDA members rejected the VVD's (and the PvdA's) hopes for more extensive decentralization, arguing the state needed to guarantee certain core areas (Gibbels 2006). The CDA and VVD agreed on moving towards an Austerity Market, with continuing state control and greater contracting, introducing markets in the universal and uniform system without the risks of dramatic cost increases.

In opposition, the PvdA was critical of proposed cuts to the AWBZ and the new system of contracting, arguing that it could reduce quality for users and existing care workers, by allowing less qualified workers to provide care

(Interview: PvdA Member of Parliament, 2005b). However, the PvdA's long-standing support for decentralization tempered this opposition, and the party voted for the WMO, and when it re-entered government in 2007, it pushed to moderate, but not fully reverse, these reforms.

Equally, many stakeholders supported the changes, including the insurers, municipalities, and even many providers. These groups (including providers) were positive towards a smaller AWBZ, reducing their burden as employers, albeit some expressed reservations about funding (Interview: official from Arcares, provider organization, 2005) while others saw government policy as giving too few levers to insurers (Interview: official from ZN, insurers' organization, 2005). More recently, providers have expressed concerns about the effects of the WMO on choice, quality, and the workforce (for example, see Actiz 2009). Equally, the public has been cautious about the reforms, with more than half of the public rejecting any cuts to the AWBZ (TNS NIPO 2009).

These positions put pressure on the government, but did not stop the reforms. Instead, the experience of the last decade shows the importance of partisan strategies. First, the Left–Right Purple coalition was able to put a Consumer-Controlled Market on the agenda because the PvdA's desire to improve services and the VVD's desire to introduce markets, alongside a growing economy, temporarily glossed over differences between them. In the universal and uniform AWBZ system, the PvdA was willing to accept some choice as a way of making a broader appeal, while the VVD was willing to compromise in order to introduce markets. Second, the CDA, facing growing concerns about costs and the viability of the sector, began to move towards the VVD on issues of cost sharing and contracting, creating more scope for change toward an Austerity Market under the CDA–VVD coalitions. This stance combined with historical overlap between the parties in promoting more change on the allocation dimension, to produce a coalition willing to introduce more cuts and contracting in the sector.

6.5: CONCLUSION

Markets have been a key motif of reform in the elderly care sector over the past two decades in England, Sweden, and the Netherlands, with much variation over time and place. While parties have not always responded in strong terms to the care sector – with the exception of the British Conservatives – even their weaker and less-defined preferences have been central in shaping the sector. Beginning in the 1980s, concerns about the costs of an aging population brought issues of long-term care spending on the agenda. At the same time, academics and advocates began promoting more home care and individual autonomy in the sector. In response to these concerns, political parties began to turn to structural reform of the care system. Both the Left and the Right put markets on the agenda – but pursued different strategies. In England, the Conservatives were able to introduce quite radical producer-oriented market forces, because the residual structure of the service meant they faced few electoral constraints. By contrast, in Sweden, the left-wing government opened up the room for more market forces, but it was the local governments, responding to a variety of forces that shaped their development. However, the universal system of care meant that the more radical reform seen in England was off the table politically and local actors have constructed a broad range of responses. In the Netherlands, there was both an early ideological and pragmatic push towards markets in the 1980s, but the differing understanding of market forces across the patchwork Dutch coalitions stifled progress. It was only recently, in a booming economy, that the Left and the Right agreed to choice-oriented reforms, and as the economy deteriorated and an ideologically right-wing coalition emerged, these were replaced by contracting reforms and greater individual responsibility that best met the Right's goals in the universal and uniform system.

The resulting markets and their consequences show great variation. In England, private producers gained clear benefits, but at a cost to the elderly. While the rapid rate of expenditure in the 1980s was brought under control, the Private Power character of this market meant that users often faced high costs and low-quality care. In Sweden, the Austerity Market maintained basic quality but did not necessarily improve it, emphasizing cost-efficiency and greater local control. Finally, in the Netherlands, more recent reforms brought the system closer to the Swedish model, but this occurred after the brief emergence of a Consumer-Controlled market emphasizing choice, that started to reorient care around users albeit at a heavy cost to the public purse.

7

Conclusion

This book has laid out, both theoretically and empirically, the way markets in public services operate and the political dynamics behind them. These claims both contribute to our substantive understanding of markets and engage in broader debates about emerging political dynamics in advanced industrial countries. The first section of this concluding chapter looks at these broader contributions. The second section turns to the question of their generalizability, examining the politics of market reforms in health care across the OECD. The concluding section argues that these claims can inform our thinking about markets in an era of credit crises and newly assertive government.

7.1: THE MAIN CONTRIBUTIONS OF THE BOOK

The following sections outline three major contributions of this book: its attention to markets in the public sector, the theorization of market variation, and the discussion of the partisan politics of market reforms.

Markets in public services matter

Markets in public services have dramatically reshaped the lives of citizens, producers, and the state. In the early 1980s, despite variation in health care, education, and care systems across the OECD, they shared a number of common features. Central governments often played a strong role in setting budgets and basic regulations but the lack of information technology, detailed measurement of outcomes, or professional management, limited their power to monitor what actually happened on the ground. Despite the boasting of politicians in France and elsewhere that they only needed to look at the clock to know what pupils were studying, in fact, producers had much autonomy. Equally, while pupils and patients faced substantially different amounts of choice, they, too, often lacked real information to make meaningful choices.

Since this time, markets have transformed public services, often in profound ways. To take an example, likely familiar to the audience of this book, new financial incentives have substantially changed the work of college professors in recent years. Tightening public budgets have pushed many universities to rely more on tuition and grants as core revenue sources. These shifts, combined with the diffusion of budget models giving individual departments more financial responsibility, have changed the work environment. Many departments have cut tenured positions, relying increasingly on adjunct lecturers and graduate students to teach courses. This move creates anxiety for graduate students over their future job prospects. At the same time, tuition-dependent departments, facing rising pressure to fill seats, have pushed even relatively secure tenured professors to market courses differently, changing their content or grading. Students, in turn, face higher fees, but also universities that cater to them with new facilities and, sometimes, more responsive educators. Reliance on external grants or new government funding sources for "super universities" can push in another direction, away from students and towards a research focus. Of course, such incentives are not entirely new, and universities have resisted markets more successfully than many other domains, but more financial incentives have nonetheless changed the way that education professionals, as well as students and administrators, operate.

This book is not a treatise on the lived experience of markets; nonetheless, it shows that markets have substantially altered the lives of those who work in, use, and manage services. Behind the abstract language of contracting and control, are real people – doctors, teachers, patients, pupils, and civil servants – who relate to the public service complex differently in the era of markets.

In bringing these shifts to the fore, this study points to two under-examined changes in contemporary life: distributional changes within the public sector and a broader politicization of the structure of the state itself. The following sections take these points up in detail, but more generally, they speak to a long-standing interest in markets in comparative political science.

Much recent scholarship has focused on how developments in private markets have changed the distribution of income and wealth across the OECD (Bartels 2008; Pontusson 2005; Kenworthy and Pontusson 2005). This research agenda asks, at a broad level, what are the distributional, normative, and political implications of these changes? Yet, markets in public services, although not unnoticed by the scholarly literature, have not figured prominently in the study of advanced welfare states or political economies. This research has largely focused on changes in transfer programs, such as pensions and unemployment insurance and the subsequent trajectory of labor market security and income distribution (Häusermann 2010; Korpi and Palme 2003; Pierson 2001; Allan and Scruggs 2004; Pontusson and Kenworthy 2005).

These developments are undoubtedly of central political and social importance, yet they are not necessarily equivalent to those occurring within the state. This book shows that markets have distributive implications beyond changing what citizens receive from the state, affecting also the relative power of the professionals, users, and the state. These changes have a social and a material dimension: markets change both how people work in, use, and manage public services and the amount and distribution of benefits. In examining both aspects of markets, this book brings the political economy literature, which has long looked at how markets are deeply intertwined with political life, to the study of the public sector, showing that it too is a place of distributional conflict and change.

Markets vary in profound and important ways

The second major contribution of this book is its theorization of markets themselves. Much of the discussion of markets, from newspaper op-ed pages through to academic studies, has a strong normative tone. Markets are either a savior to the problems of modern governance or its death knell. Despite long arguing that there is substantial diversity in market and state structures, the scholarly literature on the welfare state also presents market reforms in relatively simple terms. The welfare state, whether a mechanism to compensate against market risks or a vehicle for left-wing parties to redistribute resources, is a buffer against markets. Markets in the public sector, then, are either equivalent to retrenchment (Clayton and Pontusson 1998) or they amount to incremental "recalibration" of existing structures (Pierson 2001).

In contrast to both sets of claims, this book shows that markets are both important and diverse. This diversity is not a matter of chance, but rather, follows from the nature of services themselves. Many public services are beset by a range of market "failures," as complex goods with multiple principals (the public sector as a buyer and individuals as users). These features give policymakers the scope to build markets in distinct ways.

These distinctions cluster on two dimensions – the allocation and the production of services. First, markets in public services can, but do not necessarily, retrench benefits to individuals. Managed Markets, Consumer-Controlled markets, and Pork Barrel markets all introduce competition in production without introducing greater price signals or risks for individuals. However, Austerity Markets, Two Tier markets, and Private Power markets do increase cost-sharing or put new risks on users, creating divisions among them.

Second, there is substantial variation in how markets structure competition among the producers of services. One type of market introduces competition among hospitals, schools, and care providers for regulated contracts from government bodies or insurers. These Managed Markets and Austerity Markets are not a diluted approximation of a "real market"; rather, in allowing purchasers to specify, measure, and monitor providers' activity, the competitive mechanism actually increases their control. These markets push providers to follow purchasers' preferences for cost-efficiency or performance improvement, challenging professional power and offering little to users.

By contrast, the competitive mechanism at the heart of Consumer-Controlled and Two Tiered markets works differently. These markets expand the scope for pupils, patients, and care recipients to choose a provider, with money following these choices. Providers, in these markets, are competing for quality-conscious users, not cost-conscious buyers. The resulting competition emphasizes responsiveness, benefiting users but costing the state in terms of budgetary control.

Finally, Pork Barrel and Private Power markets constitute a third type of competition, which empowers neither the state nor users but new providers of services. The complexity of public service "products" means that introducing competition among providers without clear contractual specification, regulation, or oversight, can give them much autonomy. While encouraging innovation and the rapid growth of the private sector, these markets limit state and user control over delivery, potentially allowing providers to inflate costs, or cut benefits.

The empirical chapters of this book support these larger theoretical claims. Markets operate differently, and these differences have profound implications. All good or all bad things do not go together. Instead, markets produce varying outcomes and winners and losers, depending on their design.

In so doing, this book speaks to questions about how advanced welfare states are changing and what the implications of change (or lack thereof) are. Scholars of the welfare state have faced what Christoffer Green-Pedersen (2004) calls the "dependent variable" problem – difficulties in defining what constitutes state retrenchment (Clayton and Pontusson 1998; Pierson 1996, 2001; Allan and Scruggs 2004; Korpi and Palme 2003). Even as the bulk of current research on the welfare state suggests substantial change is occurring, there remains a dearth of conceptual tools to discuss the distributional stakes of this change, particularly in services. The current literature still relies on terms such as "recasting" or "recalibration," without specifying their distributional and political consequences (Pierson 2001).

This book not only casts doubt on the relatively simple normative claims many pundits make about markets, but also provides a clear framework to move beyond them. In specifying the nature of market variation in ways that transcend the state-market dichotomy, it offers a vocabulary to understand their distributional implications and relationship to existing welfare structures.

Partisan politics are central to explaining and shaping markets

The third contribution of this book lies in its analysis of partisanship. Building on the previous two claims – that markets profoundly change services but in varying ways – the book traces how parties have used market reform as a new terrain for distributive policy. This book asks: what are parties fighting about? Why? In so doing, it argues that contemporary political parties often battle over the "micro" structure of the welfare state and that debates over markets represent a new form of partisan politics.

This argument speaks to debates about the relevance of parties in the contemporary era and theorizes how they behave under the intense pressures of modern governance. It argues that partisan strategies do not remain invariant in the face of electoral, economic, or institutional constraints, but nor do these constraints erase differences among parties. Instead, parties are constantly battling to reform services in ways that achieve their broader aims, while also responding to the existing context.

Over the last two decades, political scientists have fiercely debated the ongoing relevance of political parties for policy outcomes. Scholars have put forth a number of different – and sometimes conflicting – mechanisms suggesting that partisanship is declining in significance. Changes in the electorate (Dalton *et al.* 1984), rising economic interdependence (Strange 1995), and new institutional constraints (Pierson 2001; Huber and Stephens 2001) all limit the scope for parties, or governments more generally, to act.

This book firmly disputes these claims, arguing throughout that parties remain central to determining policy outcomes. It shows repeatedly that parties have the capacity to act, that they are the key actors who introduce markets, and that they select different markets. Across the empirical chapters, we see that the Left has aimed to sustain the public sector's legitimacy in financing and regulating services, whereas the Right has looked to promote lower taxes and private alternatives. Each has used markets to accomplish these aims. The Left has turned to markets to uphold the long-run viability of the welfare state by improving its efficiency and limiting middle-class opt out into the private sector. By contrast, the Right has used markets to slim the size and role of the state itself. The resulting market structures vary profoundly in terms of their implications for users, producers, and the state itself.

This defense of the ongoing relevance of parties rests on a broader theoretical response to critics of political parties, showing how parties adjust to new (a) electoral, (b) economic, and (c) institutional constraints. The following paragraphs argue that parties have turned to reforming the structure of the state itself as a way of navigating these constraints, bringing distributive policy to a new terrain.

Research on electoral dynamics notes two major changes in contemporary electorates: changing class structures and rising electoral volatility. Both changes complicate traditional partisan approaches. The Left, in particular, no longer has a secure working-class constituency and in appealing to new groups it often must navigate a demographic environment with substantially changed class structures (Kitschelt 1999). Scholars debate the effects of such shifts. Some argue that the nature of partisan competition is central to determining policy outcomes: sometimes encouraging parties to pursue retrenchment (Kitschelt 2001) and other times pushing them to emphasize non-economic issues (Kitschelt 1999). Others argue that parties maintain distinct positions across competitive contexts, but that these follow largely from constituent preferences, sometimes to the detriment of electoral success (for example, Rueda 2005). In both cases, changing electoral dynamics create sharp trade-offs that limit parties' ability to combine electoral and distributive aims.

By contrast, this book emphasizes partisan agency in responding to changing demographic and electoral trends. Parties, of course, maintain links to distinct social groups, and these are important to determining their overall distributive preferences, but they also act strategically to create new bases of social support. Policy choices are not purely derivative of existing constituents or the competitive dynamics of party systems. Instead, the claim here is that parties respond to social and economic changes offensively, using new distributive policies to tie a broad group of citizens to their core goals. This activity is not new: the relative success of left- and right-wing parties through the so-called "golden age" of the welfare state depended on how they made cross-class appeals. What is new is that this argument specifies a novel way parties make such appeals in the contemporary era. In reforming public services, a major public consumption item, parties can appeal to citizens in ways that transcend their attitudes towards retrenchment or position in the labor market. Here, parties are not tied to the interests of labor market "insiders" or employers, but can appeal broadly to voters as service users. Markets in public services, in tying citizens together, or pulling them apart, give the Left and the Right strategic tools to achieve both electoral and distributive aims.

This understanding of the partisan politics of markets also sheds light on how parties navigate contemporary economic constraints. Through the 1980s and early 1990s, policymakers faced heavy fiscal constraints on macro-economic policy and welfare spending. These constraints eased slightly through the late 1990s and 2000s with rising prosperity, but policymakers, particularly in the area of macroeconomic policy, still faced many limits to their action (Scharpf, 1991). As traditional instruments of partisan policy become more constrained, many questioned precisely what could differentiate parties. Indeed, for some, the rise of market reforms signaled (for better or worse) the dominance of a single neoliberal agenda (Leys 2003).

This book addresses these claims, arguing that markets, far from symbolizing the end of distinct partisan policy, are actually instruments of it. In an era of fiscal constraints, rather than trading off state and market interventions, parties use different markets to achieve their varying long-run economic and distributive goals. Market reforms to the public sector remain squarely under political control, with important "micro" level distributive implications for how citizens consume and producers deliver services. Parties build on these differences. Just as recent literature argues that the supposed enemies of the welfare state, employers, and business associations, actually supported its development (Mares 2003), this book shows how the alleged "enemies" of markets, the Left, often use them to achieve their aims.

Finally, this research also shows how parties respond to institutional constraints. Much of the partisanship literature argues that parties pursue similar policies across time and place. Parties may be more or less able to achieve these goals in certain political systems, but stronger Left control should lead to a different set of outcomes over time than stronger Right control. Yet, as Pierson (1996) and others argue, reforming welfare states that spend upwards of thirty percent of GDP and have created new systems of social support is not the same as building them.

Accepting the importance of institutions, however, does not mean accepting their determinacy. This book argues that existing welfare state institutions pre-structure political battles but do not preclude them. Contra the depoliticizing thrust of early institutional analysis, it shows institutional constraints shape, not eliminate, partisan strategies. Existing institutions create either electoral or ideological costs to particular types of change, systematically advantaging different parties.

In general, the closer a party's preference is to the status quo, the more leeway it has in reform. This claim is not just rehashing those about programmatic path-dependence. Support for the basic principles of the status quo does not mean opposition to change: instead, it implies a support for the distributive logic underpinning the existing structure. Where parties are closer to this existing structure, they face fewer ideological or electoral costs to substantially reforming it, but where they are farther away from it, costs mount, leading to less preferred (but not necessarily incremental) reform strategies. In looking at how institutions condition actors' strategies without eliminating distributive conflict, this book speaks to an emerging research agenda looking to theorize change while also taking institutionalist insights seriously (Streeck and Thelen 2005; Thelen and Mahoney 2010).

Taken together, this understanding of parties goes beyond showing that they matter. It argues that (a) parties maintain distinct distributive preferences, (b) different types of markets give parties the opportunity to pursue these preferences and work around electoral, economic, and institutional constraints that limit other policy instruments, but (c) parties also must respond to their particular institutional environment in building markets.

7.2 DO THE FINDINGS TRAVEL?

Where would we look for additional support for the claims made in this work? The following section turns to one sector that has experienced a slew of market reforms – health care – to examine how the claims of the book fit with this broader experience (Ranade 1998). As chapter 4 argued, the outcomes of such market reforms have been more varied than the polarized debate around them would suggest. Thus, the health care sector offers a good test case for the claims developed in this book: it has undergone many changes drawing on markets and yet there is little popular or academic consensus about what the causes or effects of these changes are. The following section focuses on a range of OECD countries well-known for market reforms and argues that underneath the seemingly uniform movement towards markets in health we see structured variation in outcomes and partisan strategies.

Health care reform

Much work on health care politics downplays both systematic diversity in markets and partisanship. When it comes to questions of markets, the voluminous literature on health policy tends to fall into two camps. A first strand, outlined in chapter 4, sees markets in ideological terms, promoting them as either a uniformly positive or negative development. A second literature avoids these normative claims, emphasizing the highly specific features of markets (for example, Saltman *et al.* 2002). Neither approach sees a role for strategic partisan interests in structuring markets, presenting them as a replacement for politics or a technocratic tool for improvement.

Although many single country studies of health reform do emphasize partisan dynamics (for example, Oberlander 2003), much comparative analysis of health politics focuses on broad trends outside of partisan politics. Cross-national time-series studies of health care spending find few partisan effects on overall spending (Jensen 2008). Indeed, two major trends of the past decades, expanding access for citizens, and introducing measures aimed at improving efficiency, appear to cut across party control, with differences in these trends following national patterns (for example, see Freeman 2000) or institutional or interest configurations (Immergut 1992; Hacker 2004; Tuohy 1999) rather than partisan strategic calculations.

Yet, health care issues are at the heart of much of what political parties care about: income redistribution, growth, and the shape of the public and private sectors. Health care systems have important distributive effects (Wagstaff and van Doorslaer 2000), as do health markets (Evans 1997). Rising costs amplify these effects. In the US, for instance, real wages have stagnated as health costs skyrocketed, shifting wealth from workers to the health care industry. At the same time, health care is a major economic sector, crucially linked to labor markets and economic growth (Moran 1999).

I argue that parties have indeed taken different approaches to health care reform. The Right, seeing rising costs as a major distributive issue, has looked to separate income policy and health policy by supporting private financing and individual risks. These moves often run into electoral limits, yet the Right has waged important ideological battles to introduce change on the allocation dimension. In production, the Right has pushed to limit public sector growth and promote private alternatives that reshape the long-run trajectory of state effort in health.

The Left, by contrast, has looked to enhance or sustain redistribution through the health care system, limiting changes on the allocation system that enhance individual risk or turn medical risks into income risks. Some left-wing parties have defended public production, but many have also introduced markets in production as a way of maintaining the state's legitimacy and capacity to regulate the sector.

I show these trends in an abbreviated, but telling, way in the following pages, demonstrating that parties approached markets differently and that these differences reshaped health care systems in important ways. I first examine the strategies employed by right-wing parties and then those by left-wing parties, noting how these strategies differed across uniform or fragmented systems.

Health care reform by the Right

In most countries, the Right made the first moves towards introducing markets in the health care sector. Rising costs and growing public concerns about quality gave the Right a political opening to introduce more substantial reform. Yet, the Right often faced institutional constraints on introducing changes directly building on its preferences for limiting the state and supporting private actors. In response, right-wing parties proposed a wide range of reforms – from co-payments to privatization to expanding choice – coalescing on two major strategies depending on whether they faced (a) uniform or (b) fragmented systems.

In the more uniform health care systems of the Nordic countries, the UK, Canada, the Antipodean countries, and to a lesser extent Southern Europe, right-wing parties have introduced Austerity Markets that aim to manage costs and set the stage for further reform without antagonizing the public. Although often strongly critical of uniform systems, their popularity and benefit structure heavily constrain the Right both electorally and ideologically. In response, right-wing parties have challenged the existing uniformity by introducing some – but not dramatic – change on the allocation dimension, largely through targeted support for individuals or firms to purchase private insurance. At the same time, they have used competition in production to increase state control over costs and to support non-state actors. The Right has refrained from opening up the entire public sector to competition through choice, which threatens cost increases, or dramatic contracting with the private sector, but at times has experimented with these approaches in limited ways. We saw this strategy in the UK, where the Thatcher government made some small, but ideologically important, steps towards private financing (for example, giving elderly citizens tax breaks for purchasing private insurance) while introducing more substantial competition in production through contracts that expanded state control.

A similar pattern emerged in New Zealand. New Zealand was one of the earliest market innovators in the public sector, but it was not until the National government was elected in 1990 that markets entered the health care agenda. The National government faced a health sector that was – as in England – relatively uniform and the public was skeptical about market-based change (Laugesen 2005). This structure shaped its strategies. On the allocation dimension, it moved to introduce more individual charges, later reversing these fees in the face of public protests. In production, despite promising choice, in 1993 it introduced a competitive structure similar to that in the UK under Thatcher. These reforms gave funding to new purchasers (both groups of GPs and regional purchasers) who had heavy incentives to show financial results. Purchasers could buy from either public or private hospitals, and public hospitals became independent "Crown Health Enterprises" which could make a profit. In the language of this work, this market was an Austerity Market, with providers competing for contracts and individuals facing new costs. After 1996, New Zealand's National party moved away from this model, largely due to pressure from its new coalition partner, and weaknesses in the model itself. Nonetheless, the reforms did begin to change providers' behavior, pushing them to consider costs in making treatment decisions and changing their relation to purchasers (Ashton *et al.* 2004).

In Australia, nationally, Right politicians have supported the private insurance sector, while subnationally they expanded contracting. Australia has elements of a uniform public health care system (managed by the states) next to a sizeable privately provided and funded sector. Conservative politicians rejected Australian Labour's moves to build the public system in the 1970s and 1980s and advocated more change on the allocation dimension. When elected in 1996, the Liberal-National coalition left the public system intact and toned down more dramatic privatization proposals in order to win electoral support (Palmer and Short 2000). However, in 1999 this coalition introduced legislation supporting the private insurance sector, providing individuals rebates for the purchase of private insurance and charging penalties to higher-income citizens without insurance. The result was a dramatic expansion of private insurance, with the percentage of the population with private insurance growing from thirty percent to forty-five percent in the first three years (Healy *et al.* 2006). At the state level, the Right engaged in market reforms to production, moving towards contracting and managerial reforms. For instance, in Victoria, the Conservative government in 1992 initially moved towards expanding health care funding based on patient flows (Duckett 2000). However, as costs shot up, this government introduced a more managerial stance, supporting stronger purchasing and partnerships with the private sector. These moves, like those in the UK and New Zealand, prioritized managerial power in production over waiting-list reduction.

We saw a slightly different strategy in Sweden, where the non-Socialist government both nationally and locally explicitly promoted private actors in production (see ch. 4). These reforms were important but often less systematic than changes in production using highly regulated contracting. The Danish non-Socialist government also targeted both health allocation and production to promote private actors. In 2002, it introduced important changes in allocation through legislation providing tax relief to companies purchasing private insurance for their employees. This move, combined with a generous waiting-list guarantee, dramatically expanded private insurance. In 2007, 13.5% of the population had private supplementary health insurance, a tenfold increase from 2001, with upper-income citizens, whose employers are much more likely to offer insurance, benefiting the most (Vrangbæk 2008a). The reforms introduced some competition around choice in health production. However, the reforms limited choice in the system as a whole, linking it largely to private providers, substantially expanding private care underwritten by public funds. Indeed, private provision grew 71.7% following the 2007 reforms (Vrangbæk 2008b). In Norway, there has been less actual reform, but the right-wing Conservative

and Progressive parties have also advocated limited choice of private providers in production – something the Labor party has been more reticent
about. In all three Scandinavian cases, the Right has supported inroads into
public financing, and support for private actors in the public system,
reshaping the system in small but politically important ways.

In Italy the move towards markets in medicine initially followed a less
partisan path. Through the 1980s problems in Italy's newly created
national health service emerged: the structural separation of financing
and provision led to inefficiencies and skyrocketing costs and the system
of local control allowed partisan actors to use it for patronage, rather than
programmatic, aims. The corruption scandals of the early 1990s led to a
series of short-lived technocratic governments, who built on aspects of
both the British and Swedish reforms to target these problems (France
and Taroni 2005). Reforms in 1992 expanded the power of managers in
production – explicitly removing political control – but they also maintained patient choice and expanded payment based on patient volume. As
such, these non-partisan reforms lacked a clear model (France and Taroni
2005), with competing and often incoherent tendencies.

Partisan politics did, however, emerge around the margins. Through the
reform negotiations, the Right (first the Northern League and later the
newly established Forza Italia) pushed for changes in allocation that would
allow citizens to opt out of the public system and support private financing
(Ferrera 1995). This advocacy met with temporary success. In 2004, the
right-wing Berlusconi government again pursued this strategy in allocation, reversing legislation that banned doctors from combining public and
private activities (and thus limited the private sector) and returned substantial control to them. Locally, in Lombardy (Italy's biggest and richest
region), right-wing parties targeted health production, introducing a strict
purchaser-provider split and making hospitals independent. Contra the
above arguments, the Right has promoted "choice" for patients, often
limiting the role of the purchasers, but like the Swedish and Danish
Right, it linked choice to the private sector. To combat the cost-increases
following from choice, it expanded macro-budgets and managerial control
within the public sector: combining managerialism with targeted support
for private actors. The result was the expansion of the private sector
(Anessi-Pessina *et al.* 2004).

In other uniform systems, right-wing parties have had less reform
success but have nonetheless promoted markets. Spain developed universal
health care relatively late (1986 to 1989). No sooner had it expanded
benefits than both the national Socialist government and the governments
of some regions (namely Catalonia) began to consider reforms aimed at
improving efficiency. In 1996, the Conservative party (PP) was elected,
promising more extensive reforms, including changes in allocation that

would support private insurance (which has a special status for some high-income citizens) and more private hospital production (Cabiedes and Guillén 2001). It had to back off of these plans due to widespread opposition but it did introduce managerial autonomy in hospitals (allowing them to operate as independent foundations) and more contracting and managerial formulas in the public (INSALUD) sector (Petmesidou and Guillén 2008). As in Italy, the PP ostensibly supports choice, but this is largely targeted to the private sector.

In the more fragmented health care systems of Continental Europe and the United States, we see right-wing parties equally keen to place more risk on individuals for health allocation by expanding private funding and charges. Yet in the area of production, right-wing parties, particularly the Christian Democrats, have tended to support existing non-public provision. Moreover, these parties have seen few electoral gains from reforms rescinding patient choice, which is often extensive. Thus, despite worries about rising costs, the Right has been more hesitant about introducing Austerity Markets in fragmented systems. Instead it has promoted more limited market reforms that work with the grain of the existing structure, ostensibly expanding the autonomy of insurers over purchasing but in practice maintaining largely Two Tier-based markets.

The Dutch case demonstrates a dramatic example of such changes in allocation, with the CDA-VVD-D'66 government substantially expanding individual cost-sharing in 2006. These parties did introduce more contracting in production, but in response to a move towards a more uniform structure as a precursor to reform (see ch. 4).

In Germany, we see a similar strategy. German governments have introduced a series of market-inspired reforms, most prominently the Christian Democratic-Liberal (CDU-FDP) Kohl government in 1993 and 1997 and Merkel's grand coalition (CDU-SPD) in 2006. Through the 1980s and 1990s, the Kohl government made a number of incremental reforms to allocation, expanding cost sharing. In its 1993 and 1997 reforms, it further targeted care production. Traditionally, German patients had much choice of doctors and doctors had autonomy over what and how much to provide. The market reforms expanded citizens' choice of social insurer, ostensibly to create more competition among insurers that would encourage them to act as stronger "payers" in the system – potentially limiting patient choice and physician autonomy. However, the CDU, and even more the FDP, did not want to harm the position of private providers, or reduce the choices of patients, and thus rejected selective contracting tools (Jochem 2007).

Markets remained on the health reform agenda and emerged as a major electoral issue in 2005. Initially, questions of allocation dominated the debate. Both the CDU and FDP advocated a flat-rate health insurance model, which would allow insurers to set variable group-rated premiums and then provide some ex-post redistribution to individuals. This plan looked to move away from funding health through wage-related premiums, explicitly changing the allocation dimension to reduce the link between redistributive income policy and health policy. Following the election, the CDU compromised with the Social Democrats (who advocated more income redistribution), introducing a system where all individuals pay 14.9% of wages into a central fund that redistributes this revenue to individual insurers based on their risk profile. If costs exceed revenues, the insurers can charge a flat premium to the insured. This move followed the SPD's push to pool resources more extensively with the CDU preferences for some non-income-dependent premiums and maintaining wage- (not income-) based premiums. However, these shifts also targeted the production of services. Here, the CDU again pushed to maintain the independent private sector. The reforms expanded state control and insurer contracting, but not dramatically. Thus, the new system continues to fragment risks across different categories of citizens, place some costs on individuals, and maintain substantial patient choice and (albeit lessened) autonomy for providers.

For other well-known European market reforms, partisan influence has been less pronounced, with the resulting markets often containing competing tendencies. Switzerland introduced reforms in 1994 that both expanded compulsory health insurance and encouraged more "managed competition." Since all the major parties co-govern in Switzerland, health policy is less political. Nonetheless, within the government, different partisan emphases did shape the character of reform. Indeed, the fact that the government did not require health insurance until 1994, speaks not only to the conservative bias of Swiss political institutions (Immergut 1992) but also to the strength of Right (Liberal) parties in Switzerland (Armingeon 2001). In the area of allocation, the 1994 reforms did expand benefits but also maintained a private regulated (largely non-profit) insurance sector that puts direct costs on individuals. In the area of production, the reforms moved away from strong cantonal administration towards more competition among insurers. Although they encouraged insurers to offer managed care programs and to clamp down on costs, they also required them to maintain free-choice options – which most citizens select (Reinhardt 2004). The result is competition that mostly preserves patient choice. In Belgium, there was also a move towards limited market reforms in the early 1990s that followed a negotiated cross-party path. The result was new financial incentives for insurers (Schut and van Doorslaer 1999) but few tools to really limit costs.

In the United States, health politics also involves multiple actors and arenas. Nonetheless, we see party politics playing a major role in shaping the overall configuration of the system and market reforms in the public system. The Republican party has long defended private provision and insurance. In the area of allocation, it has supported both limits on public programs and more individual risk-bearing within them. Republicans have generally been less favorable to Medicare and Medicaid than Democrats (Marmor 2000). The party clearly broke with this preference to dramatically extend new Medicare prescription drug benefits in 2003, but it linked these benefits to support for the private insurance and pharmaceuticals sectors. In 2010, all Congressional Republicans voted against the health care reforms expanding benefits to the uninsured. On top of supporting limits to the scope of the public system, Republicans have also pushed to expand differentiation within it. For the major federal health care program, Medicare, the Republicans responded to electoral pressure and largely backed off proposals to means-test Medicare, but moved towards reshaping it as a "defined contribution" program, where individuals receive a fixed sum with which to purchase private insurance rather than unlimited Medicare benefits. Reforms to Medicare in 1997 made a small step towards this goal, allowing recipients to opt for private managed care within Medicare. The Medicare Modernization Act (MMA) of 2003 extended this approach. The MMA forced recipients to choose a private plan for prescription drug coverage and gave them the option to choose private "Medicare Advantage" (MA) plans for Medicare services. The reforms increased payments to MAs by fifteen percent over traditional Medicare and allowed plans to charge recipients extra fees (Oberlander 2007). This move gave many individuals an incentive to use private plans, increasing the number of private insurers in the Medicare market (Gold 2005). In changing aspects of Medicare's allocation, creating new benefits, and stimulating support for private insurance within Medicare, many analysts argue that the Republicans were looking to fragment long-run political support for traditional Medicare (Hacker 2002; Marmor 2000; Oberlander 2003).

In the area of production, the Republicans largely supported reforms maintaining patient choice within Medicare, while, as argued above, encouraging recipients to opt out into private plans (that can restrict choice through managed care). Medicare long has had a Two Tier structure, allowing recipients to select their physicians, and paying physicians (to varying extents) on a fee-for-service basis without limiting the volume of treatment. Despite co-operating on regulatory reforms aimed at cost control in the 1980s and mid-1990s, in more recent years the Republicans saw little to gain by challenging Medicare beneficiaries or extending state power over costs. In adding prescription drug benefits in 2003, it gave the pharmaceutical sector substantial autonomy – choosing not to build up the government's purchasing power (Oberlander 2007). Moreover, although MA plans could limit choice, the party supported extra funding for these plans, giving them incentives to compete by expanding – not cutting – benefits (Gold 2005). In the existing fragmented system, the Republicans supported existing private alternatives and the overall distributional thrust of the system, pushing to bring these elements into Medicare, even above issues of cost control.

Taken together, we see that right-wing parties have pursued consistent approaches to markets in healthcare, dependent on their institutional environment. Across all systems, right-wing parties have reformed the allocation dimension to expand more differentiated benefits and private financing. In uniform systems, the Right pursued a seemingly paradoxical approach – supporting reforms to allocation that limited state responsibility and sometimes providing private actors with new power, while also expanding managerialism and state power in the public sector. This support for Austerity Markets makes sense when we examine the strategic position of the Right in these systems. These systems have often experienced the most intense waiting-list pressures, providing an audience for the Right's proposals; yet, the public in Scandinavia, Britain, and elsewhere is also resistant to privatization. Moreover, while addressing waiting lists by expanding patient choice is likely to be popular, it encourages more public activity and expenditure with few benefits for the Right. In response, the Right has used reforms that expand state control over the cost-structure, relegating support for choice to the margins of the system. In fragmented systems, the Right has been more positive towards the initial structure, and thus to extending its framework. While not always introducing full-blown Two Tier markets, the Right worked within the logic of choice and supported greater differentiation, often above cost-control measures. These markets have had profound effects. Both the support for private insurance and the diffusion (or lack thereof) of managerial incentives have pushed health care systems in new directions.

Health care reform by the Left

The Left has behaved differently. In both uniform and fragmented systems, it has resisted the Right's attempts to target funds to the private insurance sector, looking to preserve or extend a more uniform allocation of benefits. Yet, the Left has not avoided markets in production, using competition in production to respond to new pressures.

In uniform systems, the Left has limited reforms promoting private insurance and creating differentiation on the allocation dimension. Chapter 4 reviewed the actions of the Swedish and British Left, with the former using regulation to limit the Right's support of the private sector and the latter dramatically expanding public funding. However, facing growing waiting lists and concerns about "middle class opt-out" to the private sector, left-wing parties have been much more willing to introduce market-based change in production. These reforms have tended to expand patient choice, through Consumer-Controlled markets, and state control of quality.

This move started in Sweden in the 1980s, where the Left expanded the Right's first cautious moves towards patient choice (see ch. 4). In Denmark, the Social Democratic opposition has criticized the Right's support for private insurance and provision, and the corresponding changes in allocation. However, the Social Democrats worked with the non-Socialist parties to introduce more choice for patients waiting for long periods, expanding financial incentives following this choice. In Norway, a cross-party compromise led to both the nationalization and marketization of public hospitals in 2001 – removing county control while expanding financial incentives and patient choice. Much analysis of these reforms focuses on their centralizing elements, but it is important to note that they also created incentives for hospitals to increase activity (and reduce waiting lists) to appeal to patients. The Norwegian Labor party introduced these changes in production, expanding choice and national control over quality, which non-Socialist politicians later picked up (Byrkjeflot 2005). In both cases, the Left resisted changes in allocation, while promoting choice-based reforms in production.

In Spain, through the 1980s, the Spanish Socialists (PSOE) pushed to develop the public system, expanding coverage and moving away from social insurance to general taxation financing. These changes directly moved towards more uniform allocation of benefits. As costs grew, the PSOE began to consider alternatives in the area of production, including changes similar to those in the British NHS. However, in the face of both external pressure and unease within the party, it introduced weaker reforms, creating new managerial formularies but giving them few teeth (Cabiedes and Guillén 2001; Petmesidou and Guillén 2008). The party did follow through, however, on more popular reforms expanding patient choice of both GPs and specialists. Like the Left elsewhere, it took a strong line against both privatizing acute care hospitals and targeted support for private insurance – changes in production and allocation that could potentially fragment support for the public system.

In New Zealand, through the 1980s, the Labour party engaged in dramatic market-oriented reforms of the economy. Despite this pro-market stance, it was more cautious in the health care sector, considering, but not implementing, a range of marketizing reforms. Following the National government's dramatic changes in 1993, Labour began to move away from markets. In the late 1990s, it campaigned on a non-competitive model of reform. When it entered office, it followed this up: expanding subsidies to reduce co-payments (limiting risk in allocation) and reorganizing the system to promote primary care and more integration across types of care (restructuring the production of services). However, the government maintained the mixed economy of care, some choice of provider, and created new democratic accountability mechanisms in primary care (Ashton 2005). These shifts largely eschewed markets, focusing on improving quality and reducing costs through organizational reforms.

In Australia, the Labor party pushed for the development of a universal health system through the 1970s and 1980s. In 1984, it introduced Medicare, a public health insurance system funding all citizens. This system allowed substantial private insurance and provision alongside the public system, and unlike in other countries, Labor has supported this sector (Palmer and Short 2000). Nonetheless, Labor did push for uniform allocation in the development of Medicare, and reacted to the extra funds the Liberal-National government gave the private insurance sector. The Rudd government (2007 to 2010) reduced support for private insurance, raising the income cap from over which Australians are fined if they do not purchase it. At the state level, some Labor governments supported early managerial reforms in production, for instance, laying the groundwork for changes in Victoria. Although not supporting choice in the same way the Left elsewhere has, Labor did take a distinct strategy, supporting the public sector, a more detached position from the private insurance industry, and only cautiously pursuing markets in production.

As argued above, partisan politics has been less important, in a programmatic sense, in Italy, but it has had an impact at the margin of the system. The Italian Left also protested reforms fragmenting the allocation dimension. It heavily criticized policy introduced by the technocratic Amato government that allowed citizens to opt out of the national health service into the private insurance sector. In the late 1990s, the center–Left government directly reduced the incentives for physicians to funnel patients privately, limiting their ability to combine public and private work (France and Taroni 2005). In the area of production, the Left took a more mixed stance. Unlike its Scandinavian and British counterparts, it has not emphasized choice. The reforms of the late 1990s largely looked to establish both national clinical guidelines and elements of local political control (possibly for patronage purposes) in the system (Mattei 2006; France and Taroni 2005). Nonetheless, the Left did target perceived quality problems and waiting lists, taking a distinct stance to the Right.

In fragmented systems, we see that the Left has often taken more aggressive steps than the Right in challenging the status quo, turning to Managed Markets as a way to overcome cost and equity problems by building up state control. The Left, long critical of differentiation in these systems, has promoted changes in allocation to allow more state control of the redistributive mechanisms in health financing. These moves look to create more homogeneity in risk groupings based on medical status or income. In the area of production we also see the Left take a reformist position. The Continental and US health care systems have often experienced high costs, leading to concerns about the long-run sustainability of public financing. Left-wing parties, with less vested in protecting existing non-state providers (physicians, insurers and so on) have proposed reforms aimed at enhancing state control – through purchasing or regulatory measures – over costs.

Chapter 4 showed the Dutch PvdA taking this approach, promoting reforms leveling the distinctions between the social and private insurers as a precondition for marketizing reforms. Recent German health care reforms demonstrate a similar strategy from the Social Democrats (SPD). In considering systematic health care reform, the SPD–Green governing coalition (1998 to 2005) initially pushed for major changes in allocation, promoting a model of "Citizen's Insurance" that would erase the divisions between the private and social insurers and fund health care through a proportional income-based tax. These moves would have substantially reduced differences in benefits across citizens. As part of the grand CDU–SPD coalition government, the SPD compromised, adopting a new financing model that maintains the division between social and private insurers, but reintroduces constant wage-related premiums. In the area of production, the SPD, like the PvdA, was willing to introduce competition in the system as part of a strategy of expanding state control. The SPD's early proposals envisioned more state control over both the social insurers (limiting variation among them) and the social partners in structuring reimbursement and controlling the system. The SPD further supported a variety of payment reforms that enhanced the state as a purchaser of hospital services and pharmaceuticals. In compromising with the CDU, the SPD brought these centralizing elements into the competitive system, with the creation of the national new health fund and more state regulation. In other countries, such as Belgium and Switzerland, there are fewer partisan tendencies, although we see the Left here has at times pushed for more redistribution and state control over competition.

In the US, recent reforms by the Democrats have attempted to navigate the constraints of the fragmented American health care system through reforms expanding citizens' access to insurance and levers for fiscal control. Democrats have often supported Managed Markets to do so, looking to reduce fragmentation in benefits and expand state and insurer purchasing to enhance the fiscal viability of the overall system. In the area of allocation, the Democrats long pushed to expand public benefits and limit fragmentation within them. The party supported universal health care legislation at multiple points in the post-war period, most recently (and successfully) in 2010, as well as more incremental expansion of other public programs such as Medicaid (Marmor 2000; Oberlander 2003). These moves largely looked to maintain a competitive private insurance market but also reduce individual risks. For instance, the 2010 reforms regulate risk-related premiums for private individual insurance and extend public subsidies to lower-income citizens. Within Medicare, the Democrats have also resisted fragmentation in benefits. Most Democrats opposed the 1997 and 2003 Medicare reforms, particularly proposals to turn Medicare into a "defined contribution" system that would limit benefits and allow private plans to manage the entire system.

In the area of production, Democrats have proposed a number of different market logics, but have tended (cautiously) towards using markets that expand state and insurer control through contracting. This strategy first emerged with President Clinton's failed health plan, which looked to introduce managed competition and budgeting alongside universalized insurance coverage – breaking with the traditional system of employment-based insurance and open-ended expenditure (Tuohy 1999). Here, the Democrats looked to build on the existing private infrastructure but extend incentives for stronger purchasing. The health care reforms of 2010 furthered this strategy, albeit in a much weaker form. Facing electoral pressure to avoid a reduction in patient choice for the already insured, the Democrats did not push for heavy cost control through contracting and dropped plans to create a strong public purchaser. The legislation did make some small steps in this direction: reforming Medicare payments, cutting back on the extra funding for Medicare Advantage plans, taxing expensive plans, and introducing more oversight of pricing. Although the Democrats' interest in cost control was weaker than expanding coverage, the ultimate shape of the new market will depend on what this emerging regulatory structure looks like. However, in enacting this legislation, the Democrats advanced a distinct vision of markets in health care. Markets were not a replacement for the state, but something that could be co-opted as part of a larger government strategy to expand access to health care and, potentially, control costs.

Taken together, these markets differ substantially from those introduced by the Right, with the Left looking to sustain public funding and enhance the responsiveness or cost-effectiveness of existing systems. The Left aimed to preserve the basic logic of uniform systems, reacting against proposals that would increase risk on the allocation dimension while taking more active steps to reorient production around choice to address quality or timeliness concerns. Here, the Left supported Consumer-Controlled markets as a way to sustain a system that it saw as attractive. In fragmented systems, the Left also looked to enhance equity, but it saw that doing so required both expanding benefits and addressing cost control in order to build a constituency for reform across those receiving different benefits.

Where these parties turned to markets, they aimed for Managed Markets that reduce individual price signals and maintain the fiscal viability of the public system through enhanced state or insurer purchasing. These varying strategies have had real effects. The expansion of health insurance in the United States demonstrates the stakes in changing allocation. Equally, in production, chapter 4 shows that the move towards more choice across more uniform systems has reduced waiting lists and shored up public support for the system.

7.3: RETHINKING MARKETS AFTER THE CREDIT CRISIS

Starting in 2007 and accelerating in 2008, the world economy entered a severe crisis. As stock markets across the globe plummeted, governments stepped in, aiming to prevent an escalation of the crisis. In the United States, the investment banking sector disappeared and governments in Europe, who had spent the last decades cautiously deregulating markets and privatizing the state sector, suddenly had to rapidly issue new regulations and reassume an ownership role in the financial sector. In a matter of months, the unfolding crisis appeared to overturn the dominant wisdom about markets and the state. Scholars, policymakers, and journalists either decried or celebrated the end of neo-liberalism, pronouncing a "crisis in capitalism."

In the wake of this crisis, the stage seemed set for a new stance towards markets. In his inaugural address to the nation, President Barack Obama promised "The question we ask today is not whether our government is too big or too small, but whether it works ... Nor is the question before us whether the market is a force for good or ill. Its power to generate wealth and expand freedom is unmatched, but this crisis has reminded us that without a watchful eye, the market can spin out of control" (Obama 2009). The findings of this book, while not directly examining the financial sector, speak to these larger questions about the role and evolution of markets and the state.

Commentators examining the growing political interventions, planned stimulus packages, and the willingness of government to regulate (or re-regulate) financial markets and corporate governance, argued that the center of political gravity had shifted towards state intervention. Big states are back in vogue, for better or worse. At one level, these claims are true. The American government passed a multi-trillion dollar stimulus package in 2009, which promised to dramatically expand state spending in the economy.

Yet, in flipping the polarity between states and markets, with market promotion giving way to more state control, these analyses continue to miss the point. Not only have American governments always interfered in markets (including financial markets), with both extensive spending and regulation, but they have also long built different types of markets in the financial sector and elsewhere. In focusing on the dichotomy of states and markets, this work fails to acknowledge either this past diversity or the future options for policymakers in structuring markets.

Indeed, much of the difficulty that commentators have in diagnosing the failures of the current market structure stems from disagreements about how markets work. Most agree that the proximate cause of the crisis lay in proliferation of risky mortgages in the United States, and their subsequent repackaging by the highly leveraged financial sector. The analyses of the structural causes of the crisis though, have been far more varied. Some blame individuals: greedy bankers, poorly trained realtors. Others blame the government, pointing to programs that distorted the market by encouraging homebuyers to purchase houses beyond their means (Rajan, 2010). Yet others blame the structure of American capitalism, with its emphasis on highly leveraged financial institutions and executive compensation that rewarded short-term increases in shareholder value, as encouraging risky behavior (Roubini and Mihm, 2010). Others look to inadequate regulation or captured regulation (Johnson, 2009). And finally, old Marxist tropes of fundamental structural flaws in the capitalist system reemerged.

Because there is little agreement over precisely how these markets worked, the debate over these ensuing policy proposals has been equally opaque. Those that blame idiosyncratic features of the system (a few bad bankers) or the government itself, call for a restoration of financial markets and caution against interference in executive compensation or corporate governance. If the government oversteps, it will frustrate, not save the market (Zingales, 2009). By contrast, others advocate an extensive role for the state, including a dramatic rethinking of the financial sector (Johnson, 2009). Centrist positions have largely tried to split the difference, a large government stimulus but continued private management.

This book suggests that the question of whether these solutions will work depends on three issues: how financial markets work, how we want them to work, and for whom should they be made to work? Careful attention to the specific features of these markets, rather than promoting the market or the state, is crucial to constructing policy. While Obama's remarks, in mapping out a pragmatic stance, would seem to accept this multiplicity, centrism in and of itself does not. If states and markets do not vary on one dimension, but on multiple dimensions, then "splitting the difference" is not an option. Instead, policymakers need to make tough trade-offs among different options, privileging some outcomes over others and empowering some actors rather than others. Promising to make the state or the market "work," does not articulate whom it works for. Although the concepts of the allocation and production dimensions do not translate seamlessly from social services to financial markets, they suggest that financial regulations and reforms might create different types of market rather than simply replace a "free" market with brute state intervention.

Given that the stakes of building different types of markets are tremendous, partisan actors have understandably taken different positions. Within countries battles over markets are ongoing, both between government and opposition, and within governing coalitions. The precise shape of ensuing markets depends on who wins the battles. As we debate the future of the markets this book reminds us that the structure of markets, in the welfare state and in other sectors, is very much in the hands of voters and their elected representatives. How politicians choose to answer the question of who markets work for will have a long-lasting legacy.

Interviews

Over 165 individuals were interviewed for this project, most in high-ranking or senior positions in their field (civil service, political parties, outside organizations, producer groups). Only selected interviews have been cited in the text, and these cited interviews are listed below. In order to comply with the institutional review process, these interviews are noted by the individual's position and the date, unless the individual explicitly consented to having their name used. Further information is available on request.

UNITED KINGDOM

Michael Barber: Former senior Labour political advisor, 2004
Stephen Thornton: Former DHA Manager, 2004
Sheena Evans, Department for Education and Skills official, 2004
Sheila Scales, Department for Education and Skills official, 2004
Graham Lane, Labour former chair of the Local Government Association, 2005
Senior Labour political advisor (health), 2004a
Senior Labour political advisor (education), 2004b
Senior Labour political advisor (health), 2004c
Former political advisor to Labour (education), 2004
Former Labour political advisor (health), 2005
Senior Labour politician (education), 2004
Department of Health official (health policy), 2004
Senior Department for Education and Skills official, 2004
Department of Health official (care policy), 2005
Senior official in Care Inspectorate, 2005a
Senior official in Care Inspectorate, 2005b
Manager of a Northern Local Authority, 2005

SWEDEN

Stig Nyman, Christian Democrat, head of Stockholm County Health
   Committee, 2004
Widar Andersson, Former SAP Member of Parliament, 2004
Rolf Andersson, official at Kommunal, 2005
Mikael Sandström, Moderate party advisor, 2004
SAP politician Stockholm County, 2006
Former SAP advisor (health), 2006
Senior SAP advisor (health), 2005
SAP Member of Parliament, 2004
Former official, National Board of Health and Welfare, 2005
Official, National Board of Health and Welfare, 2005
Official at the Swedish Association of Local Authorities, 2005
Former Stockholm County official, 2005a
Former Stockholm County official, 2005b
Senior Representative Vårdförbundet (Nurses' union), 2004
Teacher's union official, 2004
Care sector official, Solna, 2005

NETHERLANDS

P. B. Boorsma, former CDA senator and member of the Dekker committee,
   2004
Els Borst, former Minister of the Health D'66, 2004
Ton Sonneveldt, senior official at Health Care Inspectorate, 2004
Hugo Hurts, Ministry of Health official, 2004
Machel Nuyten, official, VNO-NCW (employers' organization), 2004
PvdA Member of Parliament, 2005a
PvdA Member of Parliament, 2005b
Ministry of Health official, 2004
Former Ministry of Health official, 2004
Ministry of Education official, 2004
Education Specialist, 2004
Official at Arcares (care providers' association), 2005
Hospital manager, 2004
Official at ZN (Insurers' association), 2005

Works cited

Actiz (2009). www.actiz.nl/website/onderwerpen/wmo

Adema, Willem, and Maxime Ladaique, (2009). "How expensive is the welfare state?: Gross and net indicators in the OECD Social Expenditure Database (SOCX)" *OECD Social, Employment and Migration Working Papers*. No. 92. Paris: OECD.

Adonis, Andrew, and Stephen Pollard, (1997). *A class act: The myth of Britain's classless society*. London: Penguin.

Alberti, George, (2007). "Emergency care ten years on: reforming emergency care," London: Department of Health. HMSO.

Allan, James P. and Lyle Scruggs, (2004). "Political partisanship and welfare state reform in advanced industrial societies," *American Journal of Political Science* 48 (3): 496–512.

Almqvist, Roland, (2001). "'Management by contract': a study of programmatic and technological aspects," *Public Administration* 79 (3): 689–706.

Alt, James, (1985). "Political parties, world demand, and unemployment: domestic and international sources of economic activity," *American Political Science Review* 79 (4): 1016–1040.

Alvarez-Rosete, Arturo, Gwyn Bevan, Nicholas Mays, and Jennifer Dixon, (2005). "Effect of diverging policy across the NHS," *British Medical Journal* 331: 946–50.

Andeweg, Rudy B., (1988). "Less than nothing? Hidden privatisation of the pseudo-private sector: the Dutch case," *West European Politics* 11: 117–28.

Andeweg, Rudy B., and Galen A. Irwin, (2002). *Governance and politics of the Netherlands*. New York: Palgrave MacMillan.

Andrews, Gavin, and David R. Phillips, (2002). "Changing local geographies of private residential care for older people 1983–1999: lessons for social policy in England and Wales," *Social Science and Medicine* 55 (1): 63–78.

Anell, Anders, (1996). "The monopolistic and integrated model and health care reform: the Swedish experience," *Health Policy* 37 (1): 19–33.

Anell, Anders, Per Rosen, and Catharina Hjortsberg, (1997). "Choice and participation in health services: a survey of preferences among Swedish residents," *Health Policy* 40 (2): 157–68.

Anessi-Pessina, Eugenio, Elena Cantù and Claudio Jommi, (2004). "Phasing out market mechanisms in the Italian National Health Service," *Public Money and Management* 24(5): 309–316.

Algemeen Nederlands Persbureau (ANP), (1993). "Wallage en CDA-fractie verwijten elkaar 'onfatsoen,'" March 10, 1993.
  (1995). "Dijkstal blijft bij twijfel aan artikel 23," December 5, 1995.
  (2000). "Kamer geirriteerd over suggestie aanpak wachtlijsten te frustreren," December 5, 2000.

Ansell, Benjamin, (2010). *From the ballot to the blackboard.* New York: Cambridge University Press.

Ansell, Christopher, and Jane Gingrich, (2003). "Trends in decentralization," in Bruce Cain, Russell Dalton and Susan Scarrow (eds.), *Democracy transformed? Expanding political opportunities in advanced industrial democracies.* Oxford: Oxford University Press.

Apple, Michael W., (2001a). "Comparing Neo-liberal projects and inequality in education," *Comparative Education* 37 (4): 409–23.
  (2001b). *Educating the "Right" way: markets, standards, God, and inequality.* New York: Routledge Falmer.

Appleby, John, Paula Smith, Wendy Ranade, Val Little, and Ray Robinson, (1994). "Monitoring managed competition," in Julian Le Grand and Ray Robinson (eds.) *Evaluating the NHS reforms.* London: King's Fund Institute.

Arai, Yumiko, (1993). "Quality of care in private nursing homes: improving inspection," *International Journal of Health Care Quality Assurance* 6 (3): 13–16.

Armingeon, Klaus, (2001). "Institutionalising the Swiss welfare state," *West European Politics* 24(2): 145–68.

Arrow, Kenneth, (1963). "Uncertainty and the welfare economics of medical care," *American Economic Review* 53 (5): 941–73.

Ashton, Toni, (2005). "Recent developments in the funding and organisation of the New Zealand health system," *Australia and New Zealand Health Policy* 2 (9).

Ashton, Toni, Jacqueline Cummings and Janet McClean, (2004). "Contracting for health services in a public health system: the New Zealand experience," *Health Policy* 69: 21–31.

Audit Commission, (1986). *Making a reality of community care.* London: HMSO.
  (1992). *The community revolution: personal social services and community care.* London: HMSO.
  (1996a). *Trading places: the supply and allocation of school places.* London: HMSO.
  (1996b). *What the doctor ordered: a study of GP fundholders in England and Wales.* London: HMSO.

Australian Bureau of Statistics, (1994). *Private hospitals Australia 1992–1993.* Canberra: Australian Bureau of Statistics.
  (2007). *Private hospitals 2005–2006.* Canberra: Australian Bureau of Statistics.

Bäck, Henry, (1999). "Local politics, markets and parties." Paper read at ECPR Joint Session of Workshops Mannheim, March.
  (2003). "Party politics and the common good in Swedish local government," *Scandinavian Political Studies* 26 (2): 93–123.

Baggott, Rob, (1997). "Evaluating health care reform: the case of the NHS internal market," *Public Administration* 75 (2): 283–306.

Biais, Bruno, and Enrico Perotti, (2002). "Machiavellian privatization," *American Economic Review* 92 (1): 240–258.

Baker, Kenneth, (1993). *The turbulent years: My life in politics*. London: Faber and Faber.

Ball, Stephen J., (1993). "Education markets, choice and social class: the market as a class strategy in the UK and USA," *Journal of Sociology of Education* 14 (1): 3–18.

Barber, Michael, (1996). *The learning game*. London: Gollancz.

Barnes, Hilary, (2001). "Local authorities come under attack" London: *Financial Times*. December 12, 2001.

Barr, Nicholas, (2004). *The economics of the welfare state* 4th ed. Oxford University Press.

Bartels, Larry M., (2008). *Unequal democracy: the political economy of the new gilded age*. Princeton University Press.

Bartlett, Helen P., and David R. Phillips, (1996). "Policy issues in the private health sector: examples from long-term care in the U.K.," *Social Science and Medicine* 43 (5): 731–7.

Bassant, Eric, (2004). "Persoonsgebonden budget onder vuur," *Het Financieele Dagblad*, November 13, 2004.

Bauld, Linda, John Chasterman, Bleddyn Davies, Ken Judge, and Roshni Mangalore, (2000). *Caring for older people: an assessment of community care in the 1990s*. Aldershot: Ashgate.

Beer, Samuel H., (1965). *Modern British politics*. London: Faber and Faber.

Belfield, Clive, and Henry M. Levin, (2005). "Vouchers and public policy: when ideology trumps evidence," *American Journal of Education* 111 (4): 548–67.

Benjamin, A. E., (2001). "Consumer-directed services at home: a new model for persons with disabilities," *Health Affairs* 20 (6): 80–95.

Benner, Mats, and Torben Bundgaard Vad, (2000). "Sweden and Denmark: defending the welfare state," in Fritz W. Scharpf and Vivian A. Schmidt (eds.), *Welfare and work in the open economy: Volume 2: Diverse responses to common challenges*. New York: Oxford University Press.

Bergman, Sven-Erik, (1998). "Swedish models of health care reform: review and assessment," *International Journal Health Planning Management* 13 (2): 91–106.

Bergmark, Åke, M. Thorslund, and E. Lindberg, (2000). "Beyond benevolence – solidarity and welfare state transition in Sweden," *International Journal of Social Welfare* 9 (4): 238–49.

Bergmark, Åke, (2000). "Solidarity in Swedish welfare – standing the test of time?" *Health Care Analysis* 8 (4): 395–411.

Bergström, Fredrik, and Mikael F. Sandström, (2002). *School choice works! The case of Sweden*. Indianapolis: Milton & Rose D. Friedman Foundation

Bergström, Hans, (1991). "Sweden's politics and party system at the crossroads," *West European Politics* 14 (3): 8–30.

Berliner, David C., and Bruce J. Biddle, (1995). *The manufactured crisis: myths, fraud, and the attack on America's public schools*. Redding MA: Addison-Wesley Publishing Company.

Bjerkén, Torsten, (2000). "Country report: Sweden controversy about marks," *European Journal of Education Law and Policy* 4 (2): 171–2.

Björklund, Anders, Melissa A. Clark, Per-Anders Edin, Peter Fredriksson, and Alan Krueger, (2005). *The market comes to education in Sweden: an evaluation of Sweden's surprising school reforms*. New York: Russell Sage Foundation.

Blackman, Tim, (1998). "Facing up to underfunding: equity and retrenchment in community care," *Social Policy and Administration* 32 (2): 182–95.

Blair, Anthony, (1996). "Speech to Labour Party Conference." Blackpool.
   (1997). "Speech to the Labour Party Conference." Brighton.
   (1998). *The third way: new politics for the new century*. London: Fabian Society.
   (2006). Speech 21st Century Public Services – Putting People First Conference. London.

Blendon, Robert, and Karen Donelan, (1989). "British public opinion on National Health Service reform," *Health Affairs* 8 (4): 63–6.

Blomqvist, Paula, (2002). *Ideas and policy convergence: health care reforms in the Netherlands and Sweden in the 1990s*. Ph.D. Thesis in Political Science. New York: Columbia University.
   (2004). "The choice revolution: privatization of Swedish welfare services in the 1990s," *Social Policy and Administration* 38 (2): 139–55.

Blyth, Mark, (2001). "The transformation of the Swedish model: economic ideas, distributional conflict, and institutional change," *World Politics* 54 (1): 1–26.

Böe, Sigrid, and Ewa Stenberg, (1996). "Privatvården blev en dyr affär," Stockholm: *Dagens Nyheter*. June 17, 1996.

Boix, Carles, (1998). *Political parties, growth and equality: Conservative and Social Democratic economic strategies in the world economy*. New York: Cambridge University Press.

Box, Richard C., Gary S. Marshall, B. J. Reed, and Christine M. Reed, (2001). "New public management and substantive democracy," *Public Administration Review* 61 (5): 608–19.

Bradley, Steve, Robert Crouchley, Jim Millington, and Jim Taylor, (2000). "Testing for quasi-market forces in secondary education," *Oxford Bulletin of Economics and Statistics* 62 (3): 357–90.

Bradshaw, J., and I. Gibbs, (1988). "Public support for private residential care," *Social Indicators Research* 23 (3).

Brazier, Margaret, Jill Lovecy, Michael Moran, and Margaret Potton, (1993)."Falling from a tightrope: doctors and lawyers between the market and the state," *Political Studies* 41 (2): 197–213.

Brindle, David, (1988). "Elderly need 'more right to choose,'" London: *The Guardian*, March 9, 1988.
   (2007). "Disabled to get cash to choose care options," London: *The Guardian*, December 10, 2007.

Bronneman-Helmers, H.M., L.J. Herweijer, and H.M.G. Vogels, (2002). *Secondary education in the 1990s*. The Hague: Social and Cultural Planning Bureau.

Brooks, Clem and Manza, Jeff, (2007). *Why welfare states persist: The importance of public opinion in democracies*. University of Chicago Press.

Brouwer, Werner B., and Herbert E. Hermans, (1999). "Private clinics for employees as a Dutch solution for waiting lists: economic and legal arguments," *Health Policy* 47 (1): 1–17.

Brown, Gordon, (2008). "Speech on the future of the NHS." London. January 7, 2008.

Brown, Phillip, (1990). "The 'Third Wave': education and the ideology of parentocracy," *British Journal of Sociology of Education* 11 (1): 65–85.

Browne, Anthony, (2001). "Health: one in eight go private," London: *The Guardian*, December 2, 2001.

Bryntse, Karin, and Carsten Greve, (2002). "Competitive contracting for public services: a comparison of policies and implementation in Denmark and Sweden," *International Public Management Review* 3 (1): 1–21.

Buchanan, James, and Gordon Tullock, (1962). *Calculus of consent: logical foundations of constitutional democracy*. Ann Arbor: University of Michigan Press.

Budge, Ian, Hans-Dieter Klingemann, Andrea Volkens, Judith Bara, and Eric Tanenbaum, (2001). *Mapping policy preferences: estimates for parties, electors, and governments, 1945–1998*. Oxford University Press.

Butler, Eamonn, Madsen Pirie, and Peter Young, (1985). *The omega file*. London Adam Smith Institute.

Butler, Eamonn, and Madsen Pirie. *The health of nations*. London: Adam Smith Institute.

Byrkjeflot, Haldor, (2005). "The rise of a healthcare state? Recent healthcare reforms in Norway." Stein Rokkan Center for Social Studies. Working Paper 15.

Cabiedes, Laura, and Ana Guillén, (2001). "Adopting and adapting managed competition: health care reform in Southern Europe," *Social Science and Medicine* 52 (8): 1205–1217.

Callaghan, Daniel, (2006). *Conservative Party education policies 1976–1997*. Brighton: Sussex Academic Press.

Campbell, Colin, and Graham Wilson, (1995). *The end of Whitehall: death of a paradigm?* London: Blackwell.

Carlgren, Ingrid, and Daniel Kallós, (1997). "Lessons from a comprehensive school system for curriculum theory and research: Sweden revisited after twenty years," *Journal of Curriculum Studies* 29 (4): 407–30.

Carnoy, Martin, (1998). "National voucher plans in Chile and Sweden: did privatization reforms make for better education?" *Comparative Education Review* 42 (3): 309–37.

Challis, David, Kate Weiner, Robin Darton, Brian Hughes, and Karen Stewart, (2001). "Emerging patterns of care management: arrangements for older people in England," *Social Policy and Administration* 35 (6): 672–87.

Chitty, Clyde, (1989). *Towards a new educational system: the victory of the new right?* Sussex: Falmer Press.

(2009). *Education policy in Britain*. Second edition. Houndmills: Palgrave Macmillan.

Christen Democratisch Appèl (CDA), (1989). "Verantwoord voortbouwen," *Tweede-Kamerverkiezingen*.

(1994). "Samen leven doe je niet alleen," *Tweede-Kamerverkiezingen*.

(2002). "Betrokken samenleving, betrouwbare overheid," *Tweede-Kamerverkiezingen*.

(2006). "Vertrouwen in Nederland, vertrouwen in elkaar," *Tweede-Kamerverkiezingen*.

Chubb, John E., and Terry M. Moe, (1990). *Politics, markets and America's schools*. Washington, DC: Brookings Institution.

Cioffi, John, and Martin Hopner, (2006), "The political paradox of finance capital-ism: Interests, preferences, and center-left party politics in corporate gover-nance reform," *Politics and Society*, 34 (4): 463–502.

Clark, Heather, Sue Dyer, and Jo Horwood, (1998). *That bit of help: the high value of low level preventative services for older people*. Bristol: Policy Press/Joseph Rowntree Foundation.

Clarke, Kenneth, (1990). "NHS review. Kenneth Clarke: hatchet man or remoulder. Interview by John Roberts," *British Medical Journal* 301 (6765): 1383–6.

Clay, Trevor, (1989). "The threat to community care." London: *The Guardian*. July 24, 1989.

Clayton, Richard, and Jonas Pontusson, (1998). "Welfare state retrenchment revis-ited: entitlement cuts, public sector restructuring and inegalitarian trends in advanced capitalist societies," *World Politics* 51 (1): 67–98.

Commissie parlementair onderzoek Onderwijsvernieuwingen, (2008). *Eindrapport Tijd voor Onderwijs*. Tweede Kamer, vergaderjaar 2007–2008, 31 007, nr. 6.

Commonwealth Fund, (2007). *International health policy survey in seven countries*. New York: Commonwealth Fund.

Confederation of British Industry, (2005). *The business of education improvement: raising LEA performance through competition*. London: CBI.

Continuing Care Conference, (2000). "Local authority contracting policies for residential and nursing home care. A report of independent research prepared for the consumer issues group of the continuing care conference." London: Continuing Care Conference.

Cox, C. B., and A. E. Dyson, (1971). *The black papers on education*. London: Davis-Poynter.

Cox, Robert Henry, (1993). *The development of the Dutch welfare state: from workers' insurance to universal entitlement*. University of Pittsburgh Press.

Daalder, Hans, and Ruud Koole, (1988). "Liberal parties in the Netherlands," in Emil J. Kirchner (ed.), *Liberal parties in Western Europe*. Cambridge University Press.

Dagens Medicin, (1999). "Engqvist vill hejda privatiseringarna," *Dagens Medicin*. August 6, 1999.

Dagens Nyheter, (1992). "Begränsad rätt till skolavgifter," Stockholm: *Dagens Nyheter*. March 28, 1992.

(1994). "Allt färre litar på privat vård," Stockholm: *Dagens Nyheter*. April 2, 1994.

Dahlström, Carl, (2005). "Big cuts – little time welfare state retrenchment in Sweden," *Center for European Studies Working Paper*. Cambridge MA; Harvard University.

Dalton, Russell J., Scott C. Flanagan, Paul A. Beck, and James E. Alt, (1984). *Electoral change in advanced industrial democracies: realignment or dealignment?* Princeton University Press.

Davies, Nick, (1999). "Political coup bred educational disaster," London: *The Guardian* September 16, 1999.

Davies, Peter, Nick Adnett, and Jean Mangan, (2002). "The diversity and dynamics of competition: evidence from two local schooling markets," *Oxford Review of Education* 28 (1): 91–107.

de Klerk, M. M. Y. (ed), (2001). *Report on the elderly 2001: changes in living situation.* The Hague: Social and Cultural Planning Office of the Netherlands.

de Kwaasteniet, Marjanne, (1985). "Denominational education and contemporary education policy in the Netherlands," *European Journal of Education* 20 (4): 371–83.

de Vries, Jouke, and Kutsal Yesilkagit, (1999). "Core executives, party politics, and privatisation in the Netherlands," *West European Politics* 22 (1): 115–37.

den Exter, André, Herbert Hermans, Milena Dosljak, and Reinhard Busse, (2004). *Health care systems in transition: the Netherlands.* Copenhagen: European Observatory of Health Care Systems, World Health Organization.

Department for Education and Skills, (2004). *Five year strategy for children and learners.* London: HMSO.

Department of Health, (1989). *Caring for people: community care in the next decade and beyond.* London: HMSO.

(1989). *Working for patients.* London: HMSO

(1997). *The new NHS modern and dependable.* London: HMSO.

(2000). *The NHS Plan: a plan for investment, a plan for reform.* London: HMSO.

(2004). *The NHS improvement plan: putting people at the heart of public services.* London: HMSO.

(2005). "Independence, well-being and choice: our vision for the future of social care for adults in England." Social Care Green Paper. HMSO. London.

(2007). *Tackling health inequalities: 2004–06 data and policy update for the 2010 National Target.* London: HMSO.

Department of Health and Social Security, (1983). *NHS management inquiry report (Griffiths Report).* London: HMSO.

Derthick, Martha, and Paul J. Quirk, (1985). *The politics of deregulation.* Washington DC: Brookings Institution Press.

Diderichsen, Finn, (1995). "Market reforms in health care and sustainability of the welfare state: lessons from Sweden," *Health Policy* 32 (1–3): 141–53.

Dijkstra, AnneBert, Japp Dronkers, and Sjoerd Karsten, (2001). "Private schools as public provision for education: school choice and marketization in the Netherlands and elsewhere in Europe." *Occasional Paper Number* 20. National Center for the Study of Privatization in Education. New York: Columbia University.

Docteur, Elizabeth, and Howard Oxley, (2003). "Health-care systems: lessons from the reform experience." *OECD Health Working Papers Number* 9. Paris: OECD.

Downs, Anthony, (1957). *An economic theory of democracy.* New York: Harper & Row.

Driessen, Geert, (2000). "The limits of educational policy and practice? The case of ethnic minorities in the Netherlands," *Comparative Education* 36(1): 55–72.

Driessen, Geert, and Michael Merry, (2006). "Islamic Schools in the Netherlands: Expansion or marginalization?" *Interchange* 37 (3): 201–23.

Driver, Stephen, (2009). "Work to be done? Welfare reform from Blair to Brown," *Policy Studies* 30 (1): 69–84.

Driver, Stephen and Martell, Luke, (2006). *New Labour*. Second Edition. Cambridge, Polity.

Duckett, Stephen, (2000). "The evolution of the purchaser role for acute in-patient services in Australia," in Abby Bloom (ed.) *Health reform in Australia and New Zealand*. Oxford University Press.

Economist, (2008). "The Swedish model." London: *The Economist*. June 12, 2008.

Edebalk, Per Gunnar, and Marianne Svensson, (2005). *Kundval för äldre och funktionshindrade i Norden: konsumentperspektivet*. Lund: Nordisk Ministerråd.

Eggleston, Karen, and Richard Zeckhauser, (2002). "Government contracting for health care," In J. D. Donahue, and J. Nye Jr. (eds.) *Market-based governance: supply side, demand side, upside, and downside*. Washington D.C.: Brookings Institution Press.

Ellis, Randall, and Thomas G. McGuire, (1993). "Supply-side and demand-side cost sharing in health care," *The Journal of Economic Perspectives* 7 (4): 135–51.

Elmbrant, B., (1993). *Så föll den svenska modellen*. Stockholm: T. Fischer.

Englund, Tomas, (2005). "The discourse on equivalence in Swedish education policy," *Journal of Education Policy* 20 (1): 39–57.

Enthoven, Alain C., (1978). "Consumer-Choice health plan (second of two parts): A national health-insurance proposal based on regulated competition in the private sector," *New England Journal of Medicine* 298 (13): 709–20.

Esping-Andersen, Gøsta, (1990). *The three worlds of welfare capitalism*. Princeton University Press.

(1996). "Welfare states without work: The impasse of labour shedding and familialism in continental European social policy," in Gøsta Esping-Andersen (ed.) *Welfare states in transition: national adaptations in global economies*. London: Sage.

Esping-Andersen, Gøsta and Korpi, Walter, (1984). "Social policy as class politics in post-war capitalism," in J. Goldthorpe (ed.) *Order and conflict in contemporary capitalism*. Oxford University Press.

Eurydice (2003). "The education system in the Netherlands." *Eurybase*. Brussels: Eurydice European Unit.

(2007). *School autonomy in Europe: Policies and measures*. Brussels: Eurydice European Unit.

(2009). *National testing of pupils in Europe: Objectives, organisation and use of results*. Brussels: Eurydice European Unit.

Evans, Eric, (2004). *Thatcher and Thatcherism*. London: Routledge.

Evans, Geoffrey, Anthony Heath, and Clive Payne, (1999). "Class: Labour as a catch-all party," in Geoffrey Evans, and Pippa Norris (eds.) *Critical elections. British parties and voters in long-term perspective*. London: Sage.

Evans, Robert G., (1997). "Going for the gold: the redistributive agenda behind market-based health care reform," *Journal of Health Politics, Policy and Law* 22 (2): 427–465.

Federation of County Councils, (1991). *Crossroads: Future options for Swedish health care*. Stockholm: Federation of County Councils

Feigenbaum, Harvey, Jeffrey Henig, and Chris Hamnett, (1998). *Shrinking the state: the political underpinnings of privatization*. New York: Cambridge University Press.

Feltenius, David, (2007). "Client organizations in a corporatist country: pensioners' organizations and pension policy in Sweden," *Journal of European Social Policy* 17 (2): 139.

Ferlie, Ewan, Andrew Pettigrew, Lynn Ashburner, and Louise Fitzgerald, (1996). *The new public management in action*. New York: Oxford University Press.

Ferrera, Maurizio, (1995). "The rise and fall of democratic universalism: Healthcare Reform in Italy, 1978–1994," *Journal of Health Policy, Politics and the Law* 20 (20): 275–302.

Ferris, James, and Elizabeth Graddy, (1986). "Contracting out: for what? With whom?" *Public Administration Review* July/August: 322–43.

Figueras, Josep, Ray Robinson, and Elke Jakubowski, (2005). *Purchasing to improve health systems performance*. Buckingham: Open University Press.

Fitz, John, Brian Davies, and John Evans, (2006). *Educational policy and social reproduction: class inscription and symbolic control*. London: Routledge Falmer.

Fitz, John, David Halpin, and Sally Power, (1997). "'Between a rock and a hard place': diversity, institutional identity, and grant-maintained schools," *Oxford Review of Education* 23 (1): 17–30.

Fjelkner, Metta, (2008). "Göran Persson sänkte medvetet lärarnas status," Stockholm: *Dagens Nyheter*. May 13, 2008.

Forder, Julian, Martin Knapp, and Gerald Wistow, (1996). "Competition in the mixed economy of care," *Journal of Social Policy* 25 (2): 201–21.

Forrest, Keith, (1996). "Catchment 22," *Education*. March 8.

France, George, and Francesco Taroni, (2005). "The evolution of health-policy making in Italy," *Journal of Health Policy, Politics and the Law* 30 (1–2): 169–88.

Franzese, Robert, (2002). "Electoral and partisan cycles in economic policies and outcomes," *Annual Review of Political Science* Vol. V: 369–421.

Freeman, Richard, (1998). "Competition in context: the politics of health care reform in Europe," *International Journal for Quality in Health Care* 10 (5): 395–401.

(2000). *The politics of health in Europe*. Manchester University Press.

Freeman, Richard, and Michael Moran, (2000). "Reforming health care in Europe," *West European Politics* 23 (2): 35–58.

French, Sian, Andrew Old, and Judith Healy, (2001). *Health care systems in transition: New Zealand*. Copenhagen: European Observatory of Health Care Systems, World Health Organization.

Frieden, Jeffry, (2006). *Global capitalism: its fall and rise in the Twentieth Century*. New York: Norton.

Friedman, Milton, (1955). "The role of government in education," in R. Solow, (ed.) *Economics and the public interest*. New Brunswick: Rutgers University Press.

(1995). *Public schools: make them private*. Washington DC: Cato Institute.

Friedson, Elliot, (1986). *Professional powers*. University of Chicago Press.

Fry, Anne, (1992). "An open door to abuse," London: *The Guardian*. December 2, 1992.

Fuhrman, Susan, and Marvin Lazerson, (2006). "Introduction," in Susan Fuhrman, and Marvin Lazerson (eds.) *The institutions of American democracy: the public schools*. New York: Oxford University Press.

Galston, William A., (2005). "The politics of polarization: education debates in the United States," in Susan Fuhrman, and Marvin Lazerson (eds.) *The institutions of American democracy: the public schools*. New York: Oxford University Press.

Gamble, Andrew, (1988). "Privatization, Thatcherism, and the British state," *Journal of Law and Society* 16 (1): 1–20.

Garpenby, Peter, (1994). "The role of national quality registers in the Swedish health service," *Health Policy* 29: 183–95.

(1997). "Implementing quality programs in three Swedish county councils: the views of politicians, managers and doctors," *Health Policy* 39: 195–206.

Garrett, Geoffrey, (1998). *Partisan politics in the global economy*. New York: Cambridge University Press.

Ghodse, Barbara, (1996). "Extracontractual referrals: safety valve or administrative paper chase?" *British Medical Journal* 310: 1573–6.

Giaimo, Susan, (2002). *Markets and medicine: the politics of health care reform in Britain, Germany, and the United States*. Ann Arbor: University of Michigan.

Gibbels, Mario, (2006). "Het einde van de AWBZ?: 'De AWBZ moet blijven,'" *Zorgvisie* January 6, 2006.

Gibbs, Ian, and Ian Bradshaw, (1990). "Quality of life and charges in private old people's homes in Great Britain," *Social Indicators Research* 23: 269–282.

Giddens, Anthony, (1998). *The third way: the renewal of social democracy*. Cambridge: Polity.

Gilardi, Fabrizio, Katharina Füglister, and Stéphane Luyet, (2009). "Learning from others: The diffusion of hospital financing reforms in OECD countries," *Comparative Political Studies* 42 (4): 549–73.

Glennerster, Howard, (2001). "United Kingdom Education 1997–2001." *CASE Paper 50*. London: Center for the Analysis of Social Exclusion, London School of Economics.

Glennerster, Howard and Jane Lewis, (1996). *Implementing the new community care*. Buckingham: Open University Press.

(2000). "Why change policy? Community Care in the 1990s," in C. Davies, L. Finlay and A. Bullman (eds.) *Changing practices in health and social care*. London: Sage.

Glyn, Andrew, (2001). *Social Democracy in neoliberal times: the Left and economic policy since 1980*. Oxford University Press.

Glyn, Andrew, Alan Hughes, Alain Lipietz, and Ajit Singh, (1990). "The rise and fall of the golden age," in S. A. Marglin and J. Schor, *The golden age of capitalism: reinterpreting the postwar experience*. Oxford University Press.

Glyn, Andrew, and Stewart Wood, (2001). "Economic policy under New Labour: how Social Democratic is the Blair government?" *Political Quarterly* 72 (1): 50–66.

Gold, Marsha, (2005). "Private plans in Medicare: another look," *Health Affairs* 24 (5): 1302–10.

Goodman, John C., Gerald L Musgrave, and Devon M. Herrick, (2004). *Lives at risk: single-payer national health insurance around the world.* Lanham MD: Rowman & Littlefield.

Gorard, Stephen, (1997). "Market forces, choice and diversity in education: the early impact," *Sociological Research Online* 2 (3).

Gould, Arthur, (2001). *Development in Swedish social policy: resisting Dionysus.* New York: Palgrave.

Gourevitch, Peter, and James Shinn, (2007). *Political power and corporate control. The new global politics of corporate governance.* Princeton University Press.

Gratzer, David, (1999). *Code Blue: reviving Canada's health care system.* Toronto, Ontario: ECW Press.

Green-Pedersen, Christoffer, (2001a). "Puzzle of Dutch welfare state retrenchment," *West European Politics* 24 (3): 135.

(2001b). "Welfare-State retrenchment in Denmark and the Netherlands, 1982–1998: the role of party competition and party consensus," *Comparative Political Studies* 34 (9): 963–85.

(2004). "The dependent variable problem within the study of welfare state retrenchment: defining the problem and looking for solutions," *Journal of Comparative Policy Analysis* 6 (1): 3–14.

Greer, Scott, (2004). *Territorial politics and health policy.* Manchester University Press.

Greß, Stefan, Kieke G. H. Okma, and Jürgen Wasem, (2002). "Private health insurance in social health insurance countries: market outcomes and policy implications." Copenhagen: European Observatory on Health Systems.

Gustaffson, Lenart, (1987). "Renewal of the public sector in Sweden," *Public Administration* 65: 179–191.

Gustafsson, Rolf, and Marta Szebehely, (2001). "Women's health and changes in care for the elderly," in P. Ostlin, M. Danielsson, F. Diderichsen, A. Harenstam and G. Lindberg (eds.) *Gender inequalities in health: a Swedish perspective.* Cambridge MA: Harvard University Press.

Hacker, Jacob, (2002). *The divided welfare state: the battle over public and private social benefits in the United States.* Cambridge University Press.

(2004). "Review article: dismantling the health care state? Political Institutions, Public Policies and the Comparative Politics of Health Reform," *British Journal of Political Science* 34 (4): 693–724.

Hajighasemi, Ali, (2004). *The transformation of the Swedish welfare system: fact or fiction?: Globalisation, institutions and welfare state change in a social democratic regime.* Stockholm: Sodertorns Hogskola.

Hakansson, Stefan, Eric Paulson, and Kaj Kogeus, (1988). "Prospects for using DRGs in Swedish hospitals," *Health Policy* 9 (2): 177–92.

Hall, Peter, (1993). "Policy paradigms, social learning, and the state: the case of economic policymaking in Britain," *Comparative Politics* 25 (3): 275–96.

Hall, Peter, and David Soskice, (2001). *Varieties of capitalism: the institutional foundations of comparative advantage.* New York: Oxford University Press.

Halpin, David, Sally Power, and John Fitz, (1997). "Opting into the past? Grant-maintained schools and the reinvention of tradition," in Ron Glatter, Philip A. Woods, and Carl Bagley (eds.) *Choice and diversity in schooling*. London: Routledge.

Ham, Christopher, (2000). *The politics of NHS reform, 1988–97: Metaphor or reality?* London: Kings Fund.
　(2004). *Health policy in Britain: the politics and organisation of the National Health Service. Fifth Edition*. New York: Palgrave.

Hancock, M. Donald, (1998). "Sweden's nonsocialist parties: what difference do they make?" in Frank L. Wilson, (ed.) *The European center-Right at the end of the twentieth century*. New York: St. Martin's Press.

Hanning, Marianne, (1996). "Maximum waiting-time guarantee – an attempt to reduce waiting lists in Sweden," *Health Policy* 36 (1): 17–35.

Hanushek, Eric, (2003). "The failure of input-based schooling policies," *Economic Journal* 113 (485): 64–98.

Hardman, Jason, and Rosalind Levačić, (1997). "The impact of competition on secondary schools," in Ron Glatter, Philip A. Woods, and Carl Bagley (eds.) *Choice and diversity in schooling*. London: Routledge.

Hardy, Brian, and Gerald Wistow, (2000). "Changes in the private sector," in Bod Hudson, (ed.) *The changing role of social care*. London: Jessica Kingsley Publishers.

Harrison, Michael, (2004). *Implementing change in health systems: market reforms in the United Kingdom, Sweden, and the Netherlands*. London: Sage.

Harrison, Michael and Johan Calltorp, (2000). "The reorientation of market-oriented reforms in Swedish health-care," *Health Policy* 50 (3): 219–40.

Harrison, Stephen, and Waqar I. U. Ahmad, (2005). "Medical autonomy and the UK state 1975 to 2025," *Sociology* 34 (1): 129–46.

Hart, Oliver, Andrei Shleifer, and Robert Vishny, (1997). "The proper scope of government: theory and application to prisons," *Quarterly Journal of Economics*. 112 (4): 1127–62.

Hatcher, Richard, 2006, "Privatization and sponsorship: the re-agenting of the school system in England," *Journal of Education Policy* 21 (5): 599–619.

Häusermann, Silja, (2010). *The politics of welfare state reform in Continental Europe: Modernization in hard times*. New York: Cambridge University Press.

Healy, Judith, Evelyn Sharman, and Buddhima Lokuge, (2006). *Health care systems in transition: Australia*. Copenhagen: European Observatory of Health Care Systems, World Health Organization.

Heclo, Hugh, and Henrik Madsen, (1987). *Policy and politics in Sweden: principled pragmatism*. Philadelphia: Temple University Press.

Heidenheimer, Arnold, (1974). "The politics of educational reform: explaining different outcomes of school comprehensivization attempts in Sweden and West Germany," *Comparative Education Review* 18 (3): 388–410.

Helderman, Jan-Kees, Frederik T. Schut, Tom E. D. van der Grinten, and Wynand P. M. M. van de Ven, (2005). "Market-oriented health care reforms and policy learning in the Netherlands," *Journal of Health Politics, Policy and Law* 30 (1–2): 189–210.

Helgøy, Ingrid, and Anne Homme, (2004). "Governance in primary and lower secondary education: comparing Norway, Sweden and England," Stein Rokkan Centre for Social Studies.

Hencke, David, (1989)."Ministers clash over hiving off community care for the elderly," London: *The Guardian.* May 23, 1989.

Hendriks, Frank, (2001). "Polder politics in the Netherlands: the 'Viscous State' revisited," in Frank Hendriks, and Theo Toonen (eds.) *Polder politics: The re-invention of consensus democracy in the Netherlands.* Aldershot: Ashgate.

Henrekson, Magnus, (2001). "The entrepreneur and the Swedish model," in M. Henrekson, M. Larsson, and H. Sjögren (eds.) *Entrepreneurship in business and research. Essays in honour of Håkan Lindgren.* Stockholm: Förlag and Institute for Research in Economic History.

Hensvik, Lena, (2010). "Competition, wages and teacher sorting: four lessons learned from a voucher reform," Stockholm: IFAU report.

Her Majesty's Treasury, (2009). *Public expenditure statistical analyses.* London: HMSO.

Het Financieele Dagblad, (2002). "Kabinet vertraagt modernisering AWBZ," *Het Financieele Dagblad.* October 30, 2002.

Hibbs, Douglas A., (1977) "Political parties and macroeconomic policy," *American Political Science Review* 71 (4):1467–87.

Hicks, Alexander, and Duane Swank, (1992). "Politics, institutions, and welfare spending in industrialized democracies, 1960–82," *American Political Science Review* 86 (3): 658–74.

Hill, Paul T., Lawrence C. Pierce, and James W. Guthrie, (1997). *Reinventing public education: how contracting can transform America's schools.* Chicago: University of Chicago Press.

Hirsch, Donald, (1994). *Schools: a matter of choice.* Paris: OECD.

Hirschman, Albert O., (1970). *Exit, voice and loyalty: response to decline in firms, organizations and states.* Cambridge MA: Harvard University Press.

Hjertqvist, Johan, (2004). "The end of the beginning: the healthcare revolution in Stockholm, part II," in *Timbro Health Policy Unit.* Stockholm: Timbro.

Hjortsberg, Catharina, and Ola Ghatnekar, (2001). *Health care systems in transition: Sweden.* Copenhagen: European Observatory of Health Care Systems, World Health Organization.

Hood, Christopher, (1990). "De-Sir Humphreyfying the Westminster model of bureaucracy: a new style of governance?" *Governance: An International Journal of Policy and Administration* 3 (2): 205–14.

 (1991). "A public management for all seasons," *Public Administration* 69: 3–19.

Hoogervorst, Hans, (2004). "Speech Minister Hans Hoogervorst (Health, Welfare and Sport) The Netherlands, OECD Health Ministerial Meeting." Paris.

Hoxby, Caroline M., (2003). "School choice and school productivity (or could school choice be a tide that lifts all boats?" in Caroline M. Hoxby (ed.) *The economics of school choice.* University of Chicago Press.

Huber, Evelyn, and Stephens, John, (2001). *Development and crisis of the welfare states: parties and politics in global markets.* University of Chicago Press.

Hudson, Bob, (2000). *The changing role of social care*. Philadelphia: Jessica Kingsley publishers.

Hwang, Sun-Joon, (2003). *School choice and its effects in Sweden*. Stockholm: The Swedish National Agency for Education.

Immergut, Ellen, (1992). *Health politics: interests and institutions in Western Europe*. New York: Cambridge University Press.

Irwin, G. A., and J. J. M. van Holsteyn, (1989). "Decline of the structured model of electoral competition," *West European Politics* 12 (1): 21–41.

Irwin, Galen A., (1998). "Ups and Downs on the Right VVD and CDA," in Frank L. Wilson, (ed.) *The European center-right at the end of the twentieth century*. New York: St. Martin's Press.

Iversen, Torben, (2001). "The dynamics of welfare state expansion: Trade openness, de-industrialization, and partisan politics," in Paul Pierson (ed.) *New Politics of the Welfare State*. Oxford University Press.

Jällhage, Lenita, (1996). "Äldreomsorg: timmar av väntan i sängen," Stockholm: *Dagens Nyheter*. October 11, 1996.

    (2002). "Skolpengen skiljer partierna åt," Stockholm: *Dagens Nyheter*, December 9, 2002.

Janssens Frans J. G., and Frans L. Leeuw, (2001). "Schools make a difference, but each difference is different. On Dutch schools and educational equality: trends and challenges," *Peabody Journal of Education* 76 (3 & 4): 41–56.

Jensen, Carsten, (2008). "Worlds of welfare services and transfers," *Journal of European Social Policy* 18 (2): 151–62.

Jochem, Sven, (2007). "Germany: The public-private dichotomy in a Bismarckian welfare regime," in Daniel Beland and Brian Gran (eds.) *Comparative Social Policy: The Public-Private Dichotomy*. Houndmills: Palgrave MacMillan.

Johansson, Astrid, (1993). "S vill ompröva husläkarlag." Stockholm: *Dagens Nyheter*. December 30, 1993.

Johansson, Lennarth, Gerdt Sundström, and Linda B. Hassing, (2003). "State provision down, offspring's up: the reverse substitution of old-age care in Sweden," *Ageing and Society* 23 (3): 269–80.

Johansson, Olof, (2001). "School leadership training in Sweden: perspectives for tomorrow," *Journal of In-service Education* 27 (2): 185–202.

Johnson, Paul, (2004). "Education policy in England," *Oxford Review of Economic Policy* 20 (2):173–97.

Johnson, Simon, (2009). "The quiet coup," *Atlantic Monthly*, May.

Joint Committee on Human Rights, (2007). *Human rights of older people in healthcare*. London: House of Commons.

Jones, Tudor, (1996). *Remaking the Labour Party: from Gaitskell to Blair*. London: Routledge.

Jonsson, Ralf, (2002). *Fortsatt avtalsuppföljning, S:t Görans sjukhus*. Stockholm Revisionkontoret.

Jowell, Roger, and C. Airey, (1984). *British social attitudes survey, 1984*. London: Ashgate.

Kallós, Daniel, and Ingrid Nilsson, (1995). "Defining and re-defining the teacher in the Swedish comprehensive school," *Educational Review* 47 (2): 173–88.

Kalyvas, Stathis, and Kees van Kersbergen, (2010). "Christian Democracy," *Annual Review of Political Science* 13: 183–209.

Karlsson, Börje, (1992). "Inblick: Massivt motstånd mot husläkaren," Stockholm: *Dagens Nyheter*. August 23, 1992.

Karsten, Sjoerd, (1999). "Neoliberal education reform in the Netherlands," *Comparative Education* 35 (3): 303–17.

(2001). "Vadertje staat naar een verpleegtehuis' enkele historische beschouwingen over het marktprincipe in het onderwijs," in *Onderwijs in de markt*, A. M. L. van Wieringen (ed.) Den Haag: Onderwijsraad.

Karsten, Sjoerd, Charles Felix, Guuske Ledoux, *et al.* (2006). "Choosing segregation or integration?: The extent and effects of ethnic segregation in Dutch cities," *Education and Urban Society* 38 (2): 228–247.

Karsten, Sjoerd, and Joost Meijer, (1999). "School-based management in the Netherlands: the educational consequences of lump-sum funding," *Educational Policy* 13 (3): 421.

Kastberg, G, (2001). "A tool for influence: the effects of introducing a voucher system into in-home elderly care." Goteberg: Goteberg University.

Kelsey, Tim, (1994). "Councils failing in duty to inspect homes," London: *The Independent*. October 17, 1994.

Kenworthy, Lane, and Jonas Pontusson, (2005)."Rising inequality and the politics of redistribution in affluent countries," *Perspectives on Politics* 3 (3): 449–71.

Kerrison, Susan H., and Allyson M. Pollock, (2001). "Regulating nursing homes: caring for older people in the private sector in England," *BMJ* 323: 566–69.

Kettl, Donald, (1993). *Sharing power: public governance and private markets*. Washington DC: Brookings Institution Press.

Kiers, Bart, (2006). "'70 miljoen extra voor PGB," *Zorgvisie*. September 8, 2006.

Kimberly, John, and Gerard de Pouvourville, (1993). *The migration of managerial innovation. Diagnosis-related groups and health care administration in Western Europe*. San Francisco: Jossey Bass.

King's Fund, (2010). "Social care – what has been achieved?" www.kingsfund.org.uk

Kircheimer, Otto, (1966). "The transformation of the Western European party system," in Joseph La Palombra and Myron Weiner (eds.) *Political Parties and Development*. Princeton University Press.

Kissam, Stephanie, (2004). "The impact of privatization on the social welfare state," *Michigan Journal of Public Affairs* 1.

Kitschelt, Herbert, (1999). "European social democracy between political economy and electoral competition," in Herbert Kitschelt, Peter Lange, Gary Marks, John D. Stephens (eds.) *Continuity and change in contemporary capitalism*. Cambridge University Press.

(2001). "Partisan competition and retrenchment," in Paul Pierson (ed.) *New politics of the welfare state*. Oxford University Press.

Klein, Rudolf, (2006). *The new politics of the National Health Service*. Sixth edition. London: Longman.

Klein, Rudolf, and Patricia Day, (1987). "Residential care for the elderly: a billion pound experiment in policy making," *Public Money* March 19–24.

Klingemann, Hans D. and Andreas A. Volkens (2006). *Mapping policy preferences II: estimates for parties, electors, and governments in Eastern Europe, European Union, and OECD 1990–2003*. Oxford University Press.

Klitgaard, Michael B., (2007a). "Do welfare state regimes determine public sector reforms? Choice reforms in American, Swedish and German schools," *Scandinavian Political Studies* 3 (4): 444–68.

(2007b). "Why are they doing it? Social democracy and market-oriented welfare state reforms," *West European Politics* 30 (1): 172–94.

Knapp, Martin, Brian Hardy, and Julien Forder, (2001). "Commissioning for quality: ten years of social care markets in England," *Journal of Social Policy* 30 (2): 283–306.

Knight, Christopher, (1990). *The making of Tory education policy in post-war Britain, 1950–1986*. Lewes: Falmer Press.

Knijn, Trudie, (1998). "Social care in the Netherlands," in J. Lewis. (ed.) *Gender, social care, and welfare state restructuring in Europe*. Hants, England: Ashgate Publishing.

Korpi, Walter, (1995). "The position of the elderly in the welfare state: comparative perspectives on old-age care in Sweden," *Social Services Review*: 69 (2): 242–73.

Korpi, Walter, and Joakim Palme, (2003). "New politics and class politics in the context of austerity and globalization: welfare state regress in 18 countries, 1975–95," *American Political Science Review* 97 (3): 425–46.

Kremer, Monique, (2006). "Consumers in charge of care: the Dutch personal budget and its impact on the market, professionals and the family," *European Societies* 8 (3): 385–481.

Kumlin, Staffan, (2004). *The personal and the political: how personal welfare state experiences affect political trust and ideology*. New York: Palgrave Macmillan.

Ladyman, Stephen, (2004). "Speech to the Action on Elder Abuse Conference." March 22, 2004.

Laing and Buisson, (1985). *Care of elderly people: the market for residential and nursing homes in Britain*. London: Laing and Buisson.

(1994). *Care of elderly people: Market survey 7th Edition*. London: Laing and Buisson.

Laing, William. 1994. *Laing's Review of Private Health Care*. London: Laing and Buisson.

Laing, William, and Paul Saper. (1999). "Promoting the development of a flourishing independent sector alongside good quality public services," in *With respect to old age: long term care – rights and responsibilities*. London: Royal Commission on Long Term Care.

Lane, Jan-Erik, (1994). "Sweden: privatization and deregulation," in Vincent Wright, (ed.) *Privatization in Western Europe*. London: Pinter.

Lane, Jan-Erik, and Mac Murray, (1985). "The significance of decentralisation in Swedish education," *European Journal of Education* 20 (2/3): 163–70.

Latimer, Joani, (1997). "The essential role of regulation to assure quality in long-term care," *Generations: Journal of the American Society on Aging* 21: 10–14.

Laugesen, Miriam, (2005). "Why some market reforms lack legitimacy in health care," *Journal of Health Politics, Policy and the Law* 30 (6): 1065–1100.

Lawson, Nigel, (1992). *The view from no. 11: Britain's longest-serving cabinet member recalls the triumphs and disappointments of the Thatcher era.* New York: Doubleday.

Lawton, Denis, (1992). *Education and politics in the 1990s: conflict or consensus?* London: Routledge.

(2005). *Education and Labour Party ideologies 1900–2001 and beyond.* Abingdon, Oxon: Routledge.

Le Grand, Julian, and Will Bartlett, (1993). *Quasi-markets and social policy.* London: Macmillan.

Le Grand, Julian, Nicholas Mays, and Jo-Ann Mulligan, (1999). *Learning from the NHS internal market: a review of the evidence.* London: King's Fund.

Lemmel, Magnus, (1993). "All offentlig produktion bör konkurrensutsättas," Stockholm: *Dagens Nyheter.* June 29, 1993.

Levačić, Rosalind, (2004). "Competition and the performance of English secondary schools: further evidence," *Education Economics* 12 (2): 177–93.

Levačić, Rosalind, and Jason Hardman, (1998). "Competing for resources: the impact of social disadvantage and other factors on English secondary schools' financial performance," *Oxford Review of Education* 24 (3): 303–28.

(1999). "The performance of grant maintained schools in England: an experiment in autonomy," *Journal of Education Policy* 14 (2): 185–212.

Levin, Henry M., (1991). "The economics of educational choice," *Economics of Education Review* 10 (2): 137–58.

Levy, Jonah, (1999). "Vice into virtue? Progressive politics and welfare reform in continental Europe," *Politics and Society* 27 (2): 239–273.

Leys, Colin, (2003). *Market-driven politics: neoliberal democracy and the public interest.* London: Verso.

Lieverdink, Harm, (2001). "The marginal success of regulated competition policy in the Netherlands," *Social Science and Medicine* 52 (8): 1183–94.

Lijphart, Arend, (1968). *The politics of accommodation: pluralism and democracy in the Netherlands.* Berkeley: University of California Press.

(1977). *Democracy in plural societies.* New Haven: Yale University Press.

Lindbeck, Assar, and Dennis J. Snower, (2001). "Insiders versus outsiders," *The Journal of Economic Perspectives* 15 (1): 165–88.

Lindblad, Sverker, Lisbeth Lundahl, Joakim Lindgren, and Gunilla Zackari, (2002). "Educating for the new Sweden?" *Scandinavian Journal of Educational Research* 46 (3): 283–303.

Lipset, Seymour Martin, and Stein Rokkan, (1967). *Party systems and voter alignments: cross-national perspectives.* New York: Free Press.

Lofgren, Ragnar, (2002). "The Swedish health care system: recent reforms, problems, and opportunities." *Fraser Institute Occasional Paper 59.* Vancouver: Fraser Institute.

Lowery, David, (1998). "Consumer sovereignty and quasi-market failure," *Journal of Public Administration Research and Theory* 8 (2): 137–73.

(1999). "Answering the public choice challenge: a neoprogressive research agenda," *Governance: An International Journal of Policy and Administration* 12 (1): 29–55.

Lucardie, Paul, (2004). "Christian democracy in the Netherlands: paradise lost, paradise regained?" in S. van Hecke and E. Gerard, *Christian democratic parties in Europe since the end of the Cold War*. Leuven University Press.

Lucardie, Paul, and Hans-Martien ten Napel, (1994). "Between confessionalism and Liberal Conservatism: The Christian Democratic parties of Belgium and the Netherlands," in David Hanley, (ed.) *Christian Democracy in Europe: a comparative perspective*. New York: Pinter Publishers.

Lundahl, Lisbeth, (1990). "New variations on old themes: the Swedish Conservative party and the battle over comprehensive education 1900–1985," *Journal of Education Policy* 5 (2): 157–66.

2002a. "From centralisation to decentralisation: governance of education in Sweden," *European Education Research Journal* 1 (4): 625–36.

2002b. "Sweden: decentralization, deregulation, quasi-markets – and then what?" *Journal of Education Policy* 17 (6): 687–97.

2005. "A matter of self-governance and control. The reconstruction of Swedish education policy: 1980–2003," *European Education* 37 (1): 10–25.

Lundsgaard, Jens, (2002). *Competition and efficiency in publicly funded services*. Paris: OECD.

Maclure, Stuart, (1992). *Education reformed: a guide to the education reform act*. Third edition. London: Hodder and Stoughton.

Madeley, John, (1999). "The 1998 Riksdag election: Hobson's choice and Sweden's voice," *West European Politics* 22 (1): 187–95.

Mahon, Rianne, (2005). "Rescaling social reproduction: childcare in Toronto/Canada and Stockholm/Sweden," *International Journal of Urban and Regional Research* 29 (2): 341.

Majone, Giandomenico, (1994). "The rise of the regulatory state in Europe," *West European Politics* 17 (3): 77–101.

Mares, Isabela, (2003). *The politics of social risk: business and welfare state development*. New York: Cambridge.

Market and Opinion Research International (MORI), (2004). Attitudes to public services reform. London: Ipsos MORI.

(2006). "Choice? What choice?" Say Patients. London: Ipsos MORI.

(2007). "The most important issues facing Britain today," in *Political Monitor: Long Term Trends*. London: Ipsos MORI.

(2009). "Best party on key issues." London: Ipsos MORI.

(2010). "Ipsos MORI survey of the general public for NASUWT and Unison." London: Ipsos MORI.

Marmor, Theodore, (2000). *The politics of Medicare*. New York: Aldine De Gruyter.

Martin, Susan, and Yolande Muschamp, (2008). "Education: from comprehensive to the individual," in Martin Powell, (ed.) *Modernising the welfare state: the Blair legacy*. Bristol: Polity.

Mattei, Paola, (2006). "The enterprise formula, new public management and the Italian health care system: remedy or contagion?" *Public Administration* 84 (4): 1007–1027.

Maynard, Allan, and Street, Andrew, (2006). "Seven years of feast, seven years of famine: boom to bust in the NHS?" *BMJ* 332 (7546): 906–908.

Means, Robin, Hazel Morbey, and Randall Smith, (2002). *From community care to market care?: The development of welfare services for older people.* Bristol: Policy Press.

Means, Robin, and Randall Smith, (1998). *From Poor Law to community care: the development of welfare services for elderly people 1939–1971.* Bristol: Policy Press.

Megginson, William, and Jeffrey N. Netter, (2001). "From state to market: a survey of empirical studies on privatization," *Journal of Economic Literature* 39: 321–89.

Milburn, Alan, (2003). "Parliamentary Debates, House of Commons." May 7, 2003. London: Hansard.

Ministerie van Onderwijs Cultuur en Wetenschappen, (1985). *Hoger onderwijs: autonomie en kwaliteit.* Den Haag: Ministerie van Onderwijs Cultuur en Wetenschappen.

Ministerie van Onderwijs en Wetenschappen, (1988). *De school op weg naar 2000, een besturingsflosofie voor de negentiger jaren.* Den Haag: Ministrie van Onderwijs en Wetenschappen.

Ministry of Health, Welfare, and Sport (VWS), (2002). *A question of demand.* The Hague.

  (2004a). *Care sector report 2000–2003.* The Hague.

  (2004b). *En route to a sustainable system of long-term care and social support.* The Hague.

  (2005). *New foundations for health care with a solid future.* The Hague.

Ministry of Welfare, Health, and Cultural Affairs, (1988). *Changing health care in the Netherlands.* The Hague.

Miron, Gary, (1993). *Choice and the use of market forces in schooling: Swedish education reforms for the 1990s.* Stockholm: Institute of International Education, Stockholm University.

  (1996). "Choice and the quasi-market in Swedish education," *Oxford Studies in Comparative Education* 6 (1): 33–47.

Moderata samlingspartiet, (1984). *Partiprogram.* Stockholm.

  (1990). *Idéer för vår framtid.* Stockholm.

Molnar, A. (1996). *Giving kids the business: the commercialization of America's schools.* Dunmore, PA: Westview Press.

Montin, Stig, and Ingemar Elander, (1995). "Citizenship, consumerism and local government in Sweden," *Scandinavian Political Studies* 18 (1): 25–51.

Moore, John, (1992). "British privatization – taking capitalism to the people," *Harvard Business Review* 70 (1): 115–24.

Moore, Stephen, (2009). "Missing Milton: who will speak for free markets?" *Wall Street Journal* May 29, 2009.

Moran, Michael, (1999). *Governing the health care state: A comparative study of the United Kingdom, United States, and Germany.* Manchester University Press.

Moses, Jonathan, (1994). "Abdication from national policy autonomy: what's left to leave?" *Politics and Society* 22 (2): 125–148.

Murphy, Joseph, Scott W. Gilmer, Richard Weise, and Ann Page, (1998). *Pathways to privatization in education.* Greenwich CT: Ablex Publishing Corporation.

National Institute for Health and Welfare, (2007). *Facts about social welfare and health care in Finland 2007*. Helsinki National Institute for Health and Welfare.

Netten, Ann, Robin Darton, Vanessa Davey, Jeremy Kendall, Martin Knapp, Jacquetta Williams, José-Luis Fernández, and Julien Forder, (2005), *Understanding public service and care markets*. London: King's Fund.

Nies, Henk, (2002), "Current and new policies on care for older people," in E. Van Rooij, L. D. Kodner, T. Rijsemus, G. Schrijvers, and G. Maarsen (eds.) *Health and health care in the Netherlands: a critical self-assessment of Dutch experts in medical and health sciences*. Elsevier Gezondheidszorg.

Nilsson, Lennart, (2009) "Välfärdsopinion och krishantering," in S. Holmberg and L. Weibull (eds.) *Svensk höst. Trettiofyra kapitel om politik, medier och samhälle*. Goteborg: SOM-Institutet, 2009. 267–280.

Nilsson, Torbjorn, (2003). *Moderaterna, marknaden och makten – svensk höger-politik under avregleringens tid, 1976–1991*. Stockholm: Sodertorns Hogskola.

Nyberg, Lena, Tjia Torpe, and Annika Billström, (1995). "Våga främja privatalter-nativ," Stockholm: *Dagens Nyheter*, October 7, 1995.

Nyman, John A., (2003). *The theory of demand for health insurance*. Palo Alto: Stanford University Press.

Obama, Barack, (2009). "Obama's inaugural speech." Washington DC.

Oberlander, Jonathan, (2003). *The political life of Medicare*. University of Chicago Press.

(2007). "Through the looking-glass: the politics of the Medicare Prescription Drug, Improvement and Modernization Act," *Journal of Health Politics Policy and Law* 32 (2): 187–219.

OECD, (1992). "The reform of health care: a comparative analysis of seven OECD countries," in *Health Policy Studies Number 2*. Paris: OECD.

(1994). *Economic survey of the United Kingdom*. Paris: OECD.

(1995). *Reviews of national policies for education: Sweden*. Paris: OECD.

(2005). *Long-term care for older people*. Paris: OECD.

(2006). *PISA 2006: science competencies for tomorrow's world*. Volume I. OECD, Paris.

(2008a). *Education at a glance*. Paris: OECD.

(2008b). OECD Health Data 2008. OECD.

(2010). "Health systems institutional characteristics: a survey of 29 OECD countries." *OECD Health Working Papers No. 59*. OECD, Paris.

Office of Fair Trading, (2005). *Care homes for older people in the UK: a market study*. London: OFT.

Ofsted, (2003a). *Inspection report: Doncaster Local Education Authority*. London: Office for Standards in Education.

(2003b). *Inspection report: Hackney Local Education Authority*. London: Office for Standards in Education.

Ogden, Joy, (1993). "When help runs out," London: *The Guardian*. November 17, 1993.

Öhrlings PricewaterhouseCoopers AB, (2005). "Granskning av vårdupphandling samt de nya avtalen avseende S:t Görans sjukhus AB." Stockholm.

Okma, Kieke G. H., (1997). *Studies on Dutch health politics, policies and law*. Utrecht: University of Utrecht.

(2001). "The Netherlands," in W. W. Wieners (ed.) *A comprehensive guide to regions, trends, and opportunities shaping the international health arena*. San Francisco: Jossey-Bass.

(2004). *De beleidsagenda voor de gezondheidszorg in de komende decennia*. Amsterdam: Ministry of Health, Sport, and Welfare.

Okma, Kieke G. H., and James W. Björkman, (1997). "Restructuring health care systems in the Netherlands: the institutional heritage of Dutch health policy reforms," in Christa Altenstetter and James Björkman (eds.) *Health policy, national schemes and globalization*. London: MacMillan.

Olausson, Anna, (1999). "Engqvist vill stoppa börsnoterade sjukhus," Stockholm: *Dagens Nyheter*. September 3, 1999.

Olsson, Sven E. (Hort), (1993). *Social policy and welfare state in Sweden*. 2nd edn. Lund: Arkiv.

Onderwijsraad, (2001). *Onderwijs in de market*. Den Haag: Onderwijsraad.

Osborne, David, and Ted Gaebler, (1992). *Reinventing government: how the entrepreneurial spirit is transforming the public sector*. Reading, MA: Addison Wesley Publishing Company.

Palmer, George, and Stephanie Short, (2000). *Health care policy and politics in Australia*. Third edition. Australia: Macmillan.

Papworth, Jill, (1993). "Ignorance no bliss when care act comes into effect," London: *The Guardian*. March 27, 1993.

Partij van de Arbeid (PvdA) (1989). "Kiezen voor kwaliteit," *Tweede-Kamerverkiezingen*.

(1998). "Een wereld te winnen," *Tweede-Kamerverkiezingen*.

(2002). "Samen voor de toekomst" *Tweede-Kamerverkiezingen*.

(2005). "Manifesto of the Dutch Labour Party."

Patrinos, Harry Anthony, (2002). "Private education provision and public finance: the Netherlands as a possible model," *Occasional Paper Number 59*. National Center for the Study of Privatization in Education. New York: Columbia University.

Paulston, Rolland G., (1968). *Educational change in Sweden: planning and accepting the comprehensive school reforms*. New York: Teachers College Press.

Pauly, Mark V., (1974). "Overinsurance and public provision of insurance: the roles of moral hazard and adverse selection," *The Quarterly Journal of Economics* 88 (1): 44–62.

Pauly, Mark V., and Peter Zweifel, (1996). *Financing long-term care*. Washington, DC: AEI Press.

Petmesidou, Maria and Ana Guillén, (2008). "'Southern-style' national health services? Recent reforms and trends in Spain and Greece," *Social Policy and Administration* 42 (2): 106–24.

Pettersson, Lars Olaf, (2001). *Från rivstart till stopplag: privatiseringsvägen i välfärden 1979–2001*. Stockholm: Agora.

Pierre, Jon, (1993). "Legitimacy, institutional change, and the politics of public administration in Sweden," *International Political Science Review* 14 (4): 387–401.

Piersma, Jeroen, (2003). "Hervorming zorgverzekering bijna weer terug bij af," *Het Financieele Dagblad*, January 18, 2003.

Pierson, Paul, (1996). "The new politics of the welfare state," *World Politics* 48 (2): 143–79.

   (2000). "Increasing returns, path dependence, and the study of politics," *American Political Science Review* Volume 94 (2): 251–67.

   2001. *The new politics of the welfare state*. Paul Pierson (ed.) Oxford University Press.

Pollitt, Christopher, and Geert Bouckaert, (2004). *Public management reform: A comparative analysis*. Oxford University Press.

Pollock, Allyson, (2004). *NHS plc: the privatisation of our health care*. London: Verso.

Pontusson, Jonas, (2005). *Inequality and prosperity: social Europe vs. liberal America*. Ithaca: Cornell University Press.

Pontusson, Jonas, and Sarosh Kuruvilla, (1992). "Swedish wage-earner funds: an experiment in economic democracy," *Industrial and Labor Relations Review* 45 (4): 779–91.

Powell, Martin, (1997). *Evaluating the National Health Service*. Buckingham: Open University Press.

   (1999). "New Labour and the Third Way in the British National Health Service," *International Journal of Health Services* 29 (2): 353–70.

Power, Sally, Geoff Whitty, Sharon Gewirtz, David Halpin, and Marny Dickson, (2004). "Paving a 'third way'? A policy trajectory analysis of education action zones," *Research Papers in Education* 19 (453–475).

Prais, Sig, and Karin Wagner, (1985). *Schooling standards in Britain and Germany*. London: NIESR.

Prasad, Monica, (2006). *The politics of free markets: the rise of neo-liberal economic policies in Britain, France, Germany and the United States*. University of Chicago Press.

Premfors, Rune, (1991). "The 'Swedish Model' and public sector reform," *West European Politics* 14 (3): 83–95.

   (1998). "Reshaping the democratic state: the Swedish experience in a comparative perspective," *Public Administration* 76: 141–59.

Pring, Richard, and Geoffrey Walford, (1997). *Affirming the comprehensive ideal*. Vol. XXXXVI. Washington DC: Falmer Press.

Propper, Carol, Bronwyn Croxson, and Arran Shearer, (2002). "Waiting times for hospital admissions: the impact of GP Fundholding," *Journal of Health Economics* 21: 227–52.

Propper, Carol, and Neil Söderlund, (1998). "Competition in the NHS internal market: an overview of its effects on hospital prices and costs," *Health Economics* 7 (3): 187–97.

Przeworski, Adam, and John Sprague, (1986). *Paper stones: a history of electoral Socialism*. University of Chicago Press.

Przeworski, Adam, and Michael Wallerstein, (1984). "Democratic capitalism at the crossroads," in Thomas Ferguson, and Joel Rogers (eds.) *The political economy: readings in the politics and economics of American public policy*. New York: ME Sharpe Inc.

Putters, K., P. H. A. Frissen, and H. Foekema, (2006). *Zorg om vernieuwing.* Universiteit van Tilburg/TNS NIPO.

Rajan, Raghuram, (2010). *Fault lines: How hidden fractures still threaten the world economy.* Princeton University Press.

Ranade, Wendy, (1997). *A future for the NHS? Health care for the millennium.* London: Longman.

(1998). *Markets and health care: A comparative analysis.* Harlow, Essex: Addison Wesley Longman.

Reagan, Ronald, (1982). "Remarks to the Reagan administration executive forum," in John T. Woolley and Gerhard Peters, The American Presidency Project. Santa Barbara, CA: University of California.

Reinhardt, Uwe E. (2004). "The Swiss health system: regulated competition without managed care," *Journal of the American Medical Association* 292 (10): 1227–1231.

Richardson, Jeremy, (1994). "Doing less by doing more: British government 1979–1993," *West European Politics* 17 (3): 178–98.

Rinehart, James R., and Jackson F. Lee, (1991). *American education and the dynamics of choice.* New York: Praeger.

Rivett, Geoffrey, (1998). *From cradle to grave: fifty years of the NHS.* London: King's Fund.

Robinson, Janice, and Penny Banks, (2005). "The business of caring: the King's Fund inquiry into care services for older people in London." London: King's Fund.

Robinson, Ray, and Anna Dixon, (1999). *Health care systems in transition: United Kingdom.* Copenhagen: European Observatory of Health Care Systems, World Health Organization.

Rosenthal, Marilynn, (1986). "Beyond equity: Swedish health policy and the private sector," *Milbank Quarterly* 64 (4): 592–621.

(1992). "Growth of private medicine in Sweden: the new diversity and the new challenge," *Health Policy* 21 (2): 155–66.

Rothstein, Bo, (1996). *The Social Democratic state: the Swedish model and the bureaucratic problem of social reforms.* University of Pittsburgh Press.

(1998). *Just institutions matter: the moral and political logic of the universal welfare state.* Cambridge University Press.

Roubini, Nouriel, and Stephen Mihm, (2010). *Crisis economics.* New York: Penguin Press.

Royal Commission on Long Term Care (1999). *With respect to old age: long term care – rights and responsibilities.* London: HMSO.

Rueda, David, (2005). "Insider–outsider politics in industrialized democracies: the challenge to social democratic parties," *American Political Science Review* 99 (1): 61–74.

Rumbelow, Helen, (2000). "NHS may use private care homes for elderly," London: *The Times.* May 2, 2000.

Sahlin, Mona, and Ylva Johansson, (2006). "*Fredrik Reinfeldt begår löftesbrott.*" Sweden: SAP.

Sainsbury, Diane, (1993). "The Swedish Social Democrats and the legacy of continuous reform: asset or dilemma?" *West European Politics* 16 (1): 39–61.

Saltman, Richard B., and Josep Figueras, (1997). *European health care reform: analysis of current strategies*. Copenhagen: World Health Organization, Regional Office for Europe.

Saltman, Richard B., and Casten von Otter, (1987). "Re-vitalizing public health care systems: a proposal for public competition in Sweden," *Health Policy* 7 (1): 21–40.

(1989). "Public competition versus mixed markets: an analytic comparison," *Health Policy* 11 (1): 43–55.

(1992). *Planned markets and public competition: strategic reform in Northern European health systems*. Buckingham: Open University Press.

Saltman, Richard B., Reinhard Busse, and Elios Mossialos, (2002). *Regulating entrepreneurial behaviour in European health care systems*. Buckingham: Open University Press.

Sveriges Socialdemokratiska Arbetarepartis (SAP), (1990). "Partiprogram." Stockholm.

Savas, Emmanuel, (2000). *Privatization and public-private partnerships*. New York: Chatham House.

Schäfer, Willemijn, Madelon Kroneman, Wienke Boerma, *et al.*, (2010). *Health care system in transition: Netherlands*. Copenhagen: European Observatory of Health Care Systems, World Health Organization.

Scharpf, Fritz W., (1991). *Crisis and choice in European social democracy*. Ithaca, NY: Cornell University Press.

Schüllerqvist, Ulf, (1995). "Förskjutningen av svensk skolpolitisk debatt under det senaste decenniet," in T. Englund, (ed.), *Utbildningspolitiskt systemskifte*. Stockholm: HLS Förlag.

Schut, Frederik, (1995). "Health care reform in the Netherlands: balancing corporatism, etatism, and market mechanisms," *Journal of Health Politics, Policy and Law* 20 (3): 615–52.

Schut, Frederik, and Eddy K. A. van Doorslaer, (1999). "Towards a reinforced agency role of health insurers in Belgium and the Netherlands," *Health Policy* 48 (1): 47–67.

Seeleib-Kaiser, M., S. van Dyk, and M. Roggenkamp, (2005). "What do parties want? An analysis of programmatic social policy aims in Austria, Germany, and the Netherlands," *European Journal of Social Security* 7 (2): 115.

Seldon, Anthony, (1986). *The riddle of the voucher: an inquiry into the obstacles to introducing choice and competition in state schools*. London: Institute of Economic Affairs.

Sevenhuijsen, Selma, (2000). "Caring in the third way: the relation between obligation, responsibility and Third Way discourse," *Critical Social Policy* 20 (5): 5–37.

Sexton, Stuart, (1987). *Our schools: a radical policy*. Warlingham: IEA Education Unit.

Shaw, Eric, (2008). *Losing Labour's soul? New Labour and the Blair government 1997–2007*. New York: Routledge.

Sherman, Jill, (1999). "Labour fails over waiting lists." London: *The Times*. June 4, 1999.

Shleifer, Andrei, and Robert W. Vishny, (1998). *The grabbing hand: government pathologies and their cures*. Cambridge MA: Harvard University Press.

Siciliani, Luigi, and Jeremy Hurst, (2004). "Explaining waiting-time variations for elective surgery across OECD countries." Paris: OECD.

Sipilä, J., M. Andersson, S.E. Hammarqvist, L. Nordlander, P.L. Rauhala, K. Thomsen, and H. Warming Nielsen, (1997). "A multitude of universal, public services – how and why did four Scandinavian countries get their social care service model," in Jorma Sipilä (ed.) *Social care services: the key to the Scandinavian welfare model*. Avebury: Aldershot.

Smit, Marieke, and Philip Mokveld, (2006). "Verzekerdenmobiliteit & keuzegedrag 2006: de feiten." Zeist: Vektis.

Smith, Alison, (1990). "Government looks for way to reverse legislative setback," London: *Financial Times*. June 27, 1990.

Socialstyrelsen, (1995). *Alternativa styr- och driftsformer i äldreomsorgen: Uppföljning, utvädering och avtal*. Stockholm: Socialstyrelsen.

(2004a). *Konkurrensutsättning och entreprenader inom äldreomsorgen Utvecklingsläget 2003*. Stockholm: Socialstyrelsen.

(2004b). *Konkurrensutsättningen inom äldreomsorgen*. Stockholm: Socialstyrelsen,.

Söderström, Martin, and Roope Uusitalo, (2005). "School choice and segregation: evidence from an admission reform." Uppsala, Sweden: Institute for Labour Market Policy Evaluation.

Sörbring, Gunnar, (1998). "M vill privatisera alla sjukhus. Landstinget. S:t Göran och Södertälje sjukhus kan säljas ut först vid en borgerlig valseger," Stockholm: *Dagens Nyheter*. September 12, 1998.

(1999). "Vården lovas miljard. Ingen skattehöjning. Landstingsbudgeten inte trovärdig, anser oppositionen," Stockholm: *Dagens Nyheter*. May 19, 1999.

(2001). "Landstinget. Personal nöjd med privatisering," Stockholm: *Dagens Nyheter*. October 14, 2001.

SOU (1991). *Konkurrensen inom den kommunala sektorn. 1991:104. Delbetänkande av konkurresnkommittén*. Stockholm.

Souster, Mark, (1989). "Agencies seek funding assurances; Community Care," London: *The Times*, July 13, 1989.

Statistics Sweden, (2004a). *Äldre – vård och omsorg. Kommunala insatser enligt social-tjänstlagen samt hälso- och sjukvårdslagen*. Stockholm: Socialstyrelsen.

2004b. *Wage and salary structures and employment in the central government sector*. Stockholm: Statistics Sweden.

Stellwag, Helena W.F., (1967). "On reform of the educational system in the Netherlands," *Comparative Education Review* 11 (3): 360–5.

Stevens, Simon, (2004). "Reform strategies for the English NHS," *Health Affairs* 23 (3): 37–44.

Strange, Susan, (1995). "The limits of politics," *Government and Opposition* 30 (3): 291–311.

Strath, Annelie, (2004). *Teacher policy reforms in Sweden: the case of individualized pay*. Stockholm: Swedish Ministry of Education and Science.

Streeck, Wolfgang, and Kathleen Thelen, (2005). *Beyond continuity: institutional change in advanced political economies*. New York: Oxford University Press.

Suleiman, Ezra, (2003). *Dismantling democratic states*. Princeton University Press.

Suzuki, Kenji, (2001). "Marketization of elderly care in Sweden." Stockholm: EIJS Working Paper Series.

Svallfors, Stefan, (1991). "The politics of welfare policy in Sweden: structural determinants and attitudinal cleavages," *The British Journal of Sociology* 42 (4): 609–34.

Svensson, Marjanne, and Per Gunnar Edebalk. (2001). "90-talets anbudskonkurrens i äldreomsorgen : några utvecklingstendenser." *IHE Working Paper*. Lund: IHE.

Sveriges Regering, (1990). *Regeringens proposition 1990/91:100 med förslag till statsbudget för budgetåret 1991/92*. Stockholm.

Swedish National Agency for Education, (2006). *Schools like any other? Independent schools as part of the system 1991–2004*. Stockholm: Swedish National Agency for Education.

(2007). *Fakta om fristående skolor*. Stockholm: Swedish National Agency for Education.

(2010). *Facts and Figures 2010: Pre-school activities, school-age childcare, schools and adult education in Sweden*. Summary of Report 349. Stockholm, Swedish National Agency for Education.

Swedish Welfare Commission, Joakim Palme, Åke Bergmark, Olof Bäckman, *et al.* (2003). "A welfare balance sheet for the 1990s," *Scandinavian Journal of Public Health* Supplement 60.

Szebehely, Marta, (1998). "Changing divisions of care-work: caring for children and frail elderly people in Sweden," in Jane Lewis, (ed.) *Gender, social care, and welfare state restructuring in Europe*. Hants: Ashgate.

Taylor, Chris, Stephen Gorard, and John Fitz, (2002). "Market frustration?: Admission appeals in the UK education market," *Educational Management Administration & Leadership* 30 (3): 243–60.

Taylor, Chris, John Fitz, and Stephen Gorard, (2005). "Diversity specialisation and equity in education," *Oxford Review of Education* 31 (1): 47–69.

Teelken, Christine, (1998). *Market mechanisms in education: a comparative study of school choice in the Netherlands, England, and Scotland*. Amsterdam: University of Amsterdam.

Tenfält, Torbjörn, (2002). "Skola och bostäder viktigast," Stockholm: *Dagens Nyheter*, May 20, 2002.

ter Meulen, R., and Jan van der Made, (2000). "The extent and limits of solidarity in Dutch health care," *International Journal of Social Welfare* 9: 250–60.

Thatcher, Margaret, (1993). *The Downing Street years*. New York: Harper Collins.

Thelen, Kathleen, and James Mahoney, (2010). *Explaining institutional change: ambiguity, agency, and power*. Cambridge University Press.

Thorbly, Ruth, and Jo Mabin, (2010). *A high performing NHS? A review of progress 1997–2010*. London: King's Fund.

Timmermans, Arco I, (2003). *High politics in the low countries: an empirical study of coalition agreements in Belgium and the Netherlands*. London: Ashgate Publishing.

Timmins, Nicholas, (2001). *The five giants: a biography of the welfare state*. 2nd edn. London: Harper Collins.

(2002). "A time for change in the British NHS: an interview with Alan Milburn," *Health Affairs* 21 (3): 129–35.

(2004). "Under the knife: why investment in the NHS means radical surgery for the private healthcare sector," London: *Financial Times*. June 12, 2004.

(2006). "Time is running out to save a crisis-torn health service." London: *The Financial Times*. April 3, 2006.

Tirole, Jean, (1999). "Incomplete contracts: where do we stand?" *Econometrica* 67 (4): 741.

Tomlinson, Sally, (2001). "Education Policy, 1997–2000: the effects on top, bottom and middle England," *International Studies in Sociology of Education* 11 (3): 261–78.

(2005). *Education in a post-welfare society*. 2nd edn. Berkshire: Open University Press.

TNS NIPO, (2002). "Verkiezingen 2002: zorg belangrijkste thema; kabinetsbeleid wachtlijsten volgens 77% van de Nederlanders slecht." Amsterdam: TNS-NIPO/ 2 Vandaag.

(2009). "AOW-taboe brokkelt af." Amsterdam: TNS-NIPO/ RTL- Nieuws.

(2010). "Kiezers kritisch over marktwerking in publieke sector." Amsterdam: TNS-NIPO/FNV.

Trappenburg, Margo, and Mariska de Groot, (2001). "Controlling medical specialists in the Netherlands. Delegating the dirty work," in Mark Bovens, Paul t'Hart and B. Guy Peters (eds.). *Success and failure in public governance: a comparative analysis*. London: Edward Elgar.

Trenneborg, Michael, (1999). Municipal control of external providers within the elderly care – an example of public sector outsourcing. Masters Thesis Graduate Business School of Economics and Commercial Law. Göteborg: Göteborg University.

Trydegård, Gun-Britt, (2000). "From poorhouse overseer to production manager: one hundred years of old-age care in Sweden reflected in the development of an occupation," *Ageing and Society* 20 (5): 571–97.

(2003). "Swedish care reforms in the 1990s. A first evaluation of their consequences for the elderly people," *Revue française des affaires sociales* (4): 443–460.

Trydegård, Gun-Britt, and Mats Thorslund, (2001). "Inequality in the welfare state? Local variation in care of the elderly – the case of Sweden," *International Journal of Social Welfare* 10: 174–84.

Tullock, Gordon, Anthony Seldon, and Gordon Brady, (2002). *Government failure: a primer in public choice*. Washington DC: Cato Institute.

Tuohy, Carolyn, (1999). *Accidental logics: The dynamics of change in the health care arena in the United States, Britain, and Canada*. New York: Oxford University Press.

Tweede Kamer der Staten-Generaal, (2000). "Modernisering AWBZ." Den Haag.

Van Damme, Eric, (2004). "Pragmatic privatisation: the Netherlands 1982–2002," *Tilburg TILEC Discussion Paper No. 2004–007*.

van de Ven, Wynand P. M. M., and Frederik Schut, (2000). "The first decade of market oriented health care reforms in the Netherlands." Rotterdam: Institute of Care Policy and Management, Erasmus University.

van de Ven, Wynand P. M. M., Rene C. J. A. van Vliet, Erik M. van Barneveld, and Leida M. Lamers, (1994). "Risk-adjusted capitation: recent experiences in the Netherlands," *Health Affairs* 13 (5): 120–36.

van den Heuvel, W., (1997). "Policy towards the elderly: twenty-five years of Dutch experience," *Journal of Aging Studies* 11 (3): 251–8.

van Hatem, Margaret, (1983). "Thatcher orders inquiry into Cabinet leak," London: *Financial Times*. February 18, 1983.

van Kersbergen, Kees, (1995). *Social capitalism: a study of Christian Democracy and the welfare state*. London: Routledge.

(2008). "The Christian Democratic phoenix and modern unsecular politics," *Party Politics* 14: 259.

van Praag Jr., Philip, (1994). "The Dutch Labour Party," in E. Shaw and B. David. *Conflict and cohesion and European Social Democracy*. London: Pinter.

van Staveren, Irene, (2010) "Home care reform in the Netherlands: impacts on unpaid care in Rotterdam," *Forum for Social Economics* 39 (1): 13–21.

Verhagen, Stijn, (2005). *Zorglogica's uit balans*. Utrecht: Utrecht University.

Visser, J., and A. Hemerijck, (1997). *A Dutch "miracle": job growth, welfare reform and corporatism in the Netherlands*. Amsterdam University Press.

Viteritti, Joseph, (2003). "Defining equity: politics, markets and public policy," in A. Wolfe (ed.) *School choice: the moral debate*. Princeton University Press.

Vogel, Steven, (1998). *Freer markets, more rules: Regulatory reform in advanced industrial countries*. Ithaca: Cornell University Press.

Volkskrant, (1997). "Katholieke scholen: kabinet knabbelt aan vrijheid van onderwijs," Amsterdam: *De Volkskrant*. March 8, 1997.

(2010). "Marktwerking. en de duivel," Amsterdam: *De Volkskrant*. May 15, 2010.

Voogt, Janna, Karen Seashore Louis, and A. M. L. van Wieringen, (1997). "Decentralization and deregulation in the Netherlands: the case of the educational support services system." Paper presented at the Annual Meeting of the American Educational Research Association, Chicago, IL, May 24–26, 1997.

Vrangbæk, Karsten, (2008a). "Privatization via PHI and waiting time guarantee," *Health Policy Monitor*, April 2008.

(2008b). "Rapid growth in private health care," *Health Policy Monitor*, October 2008.

Volkspartij voor Vrijheid en Democratie (VVD), (1989). "Verkiezingsprogramma," *Tweede-Kamerverkiezingen*.

(1998). "Investeren in uw toekomst," *Tweede-Kamerverkiezingen*.

(2000). "Kiezen voor keuze: Discussienota het stelsel van ziektekostenverzekeringen en de sturing in de gezondheidszorg," Werkgroep stelsel ziektekostenverzekeringen. Den Haag.

(2002). "Ruimte, respect en vooruitgang; verkiezingprogramma," *Tweede-Kamerverkiezingen*.

(2006). "Election manifesto of the People's Party for Freedom and Democracy 2002–2006," *Tweede-Kamerverkiezingen*.

Wagstaff, Adam and Eddy van Doorslaer, (2000). "Equity in health care finance and delivery," in Anthony J. Culyer, and Joseph P. Newhouse (ed.) *Handbook of Health Economics Volume 1, Part 2*. Amsterdam: Elsevier.

Walford, Geoffrey, (2001). "Evangelical Christian schools in England and the Netherlands," *Oxford Review of Education* 27 (4): 529–41.

Wallin, Gunnar, (1991). "Towards the integrated and fragmented state: the mixed role of local government," *West European Politics* 14: 96–121.

Walsh, K., and G. Bennett, (2000). "Financial abuse of older people," *Journal of Adult Protection* 2 (1): 21–9.

Walshe, Kieran, (2001). "Regulating US nursing homes: are we learning from experience?" *Health Affairs*, 13 (5): 120–36.

Wansink, Hans, (2001). "Marktwerking tegen wil en dank," in *Onderwijs in de markt*. Den Haag: Onderwijsraad.

Warburton, R., and J. McCracken, (1999). "An evidence-based perspective from the Department of Health on the impact of the 1993 reforms on the care of frail, elderly people," in Royal Commission on Long Term Care, *With respect to old age: long term care-rights and responsibilities*. London: HMSO.

Waterhouse, Rosie, (1993). "Community care launched with modest expectations." London: *The Independent*. March 29, 1993.

Webster, Charles, (1998). *The National Health Service: A political history*. Oxford University Press.

Weinberger, Daniel, (1988). "Primarvården byggs ut," *Landstigvärlden*. August 1988.

West, Edwin G., (1991). "Public schools and excess burden," *Economics of Education Review* 10 (2): 159–69.

(1997). "Education vouchers in principle and practice: a survey," *The World Bank Research Observer* 12 (1): 83.

Westerberg, Bengt, (1994). "Acceptera inte ett B-lag," *Dagens Nyheter*, Stockholm: February 17, 1994.

Westerberg, Per, (1992). "Inget avsteg från privatiseringsvägen." *Dagens Nyheter*, Stockholm: May 10, 1992.

Whitehead, Margaret, Rolf A, Gustafsson, and Finn Diderichsen, (1997). "Why is Sweden rethinking its NHS style reforms?" *British Medical Journal* 315 (7113): 935.

Whitty, Geoff, and Ian Menter, (1988) "Lessons of Thatcherism: education policy in England and Wales 1979–1988," *Journal of Law and Society* 16 (1): 42–64.

Widegren, Cecilia, Eva Eriksson, Monica Selin, *et al.* (1999). "'Regeringen vill skrämmas med lögner." Landstingsråd i protest: Vi godtar inte intrång i det kommuna la självstyret för regeringens ålderdomliga sjukvård.: Stockholm' *Dagens Nyheter*, June 24, 1999.

Wiener, Joshua, Laurel Illston, and Raymond Hanley, (1994). *Sharing the burden: strategies for public and private long-term care insurance*. Washington DC: Brookings Institution Press.

Wikström, Christina, and Magnus Wikström, (2005). "Grade inflation and school competition: an empirical analysis based on the Swedish upper secondary schools," *Economics of Education Review* 24 (3): 309–322.

Willetts, David, and Michael Goldsmith, (1988). "A mixed economy for health care: more spending, same taxes." London: Centre for Policy Studies.

Wismar, Matthias, Martin McKee, Kelly Ernst, Divya Srivastava, and Reinhard Busse, (2008). *Health targets in Europe: learning from experience*. Copenhagen: European Observatory on Welfare Systems.

Wolf, Charles Jr., (1979). "A theory of nonmarket failure: framework for implementation analysis," *Journal of Law and Economics* 22 (1): 107–39.

Wolinetz, Steven, (1993). "Restructuring Dutch Social Democracy," *West European Politics* 16 (1): 97–111.

Woodward, Will, (2001). "What's new?" London: *The Guardian*, October 16, 2001.

World Bank, (2002). "World development indicators." Washington DC: World Bank.

Zingales, Luigi, (2009). "Capitalism after the crisis," *National Affairs*. Fall.

ZN Weekly, (2006a). "More people entitled to Zorgtoeslag than claimed," *Zorgverzekeraars Nederland Weekly* April 5, 2006.

  (2006b). "Patients call for health consumers act," *Zorgverzekeraars Nederland Weekly* April 10, 2006.

Zysman, John, (1983). *Governments, markets, and growth: financial systems and the politics of industrial change*. Ithaca: Cornell University Press.

Index

Other Books in the Series

Margarita Estevez-Abe, *Welfare and Capitalism in Postwar Japan: Party, Bureaucracy, and Business*

Henry Farrell, *The Political Economy of Trust: Institutions, Interests, and Inter-Firm Cooperation in Italy and Germany*

Karen E. Ferree, *Framing the Race in South Africa: The Political Origins of Racial Census Elections*

M. Steven Fish, *Democracy Derailed in Russia: The Failure of Open Politics*

Robert F. Franzese, *Macroeconomic Policies of Developed Democracies*

Roberto Franzosi, *The Puzzle of Strikes: Class and State Strategies in Postwar Italy*

Timothy Frye, *Building States and Markets After Communism: The Perils of Polarized Democracy*

Geoffrey Garrett, *Partisan Politics in the Global Economy*

Scott Gehlbach, *Representation through Taxation: Revenue, Politics, and Development in Postcommunist States*

Miriam Golden, *Heroic Defeats: The Politics of Job Loss*

Jeff Goodwin, *No Other Way Out: States and Revolutionary Movements*

Merilee Serrill Grindle, *Changing the State*

Anna Grzymala-Busse, *Rebuilding Leviathan: Party Competition and State Exploitation in Post-Communist Democracies*

Anna Grzymala-Busse, *Redeeming the Communist Past: The Regeneration of Communist Parties in East Central Europe*

Frances Hagopian, *Traditional Politics and Regime Change in Brazil*

Mark Hallerberg, Rolf Ranier Strauch, Jürgen von Hagen, *Fiscal Governance in Europe*

Henry E. Hale, *The Foundations of Ethnic Politics: Separatism of States and Nations in Eurasia and the World*

Stephen E. Hanson, *Post-Imperial Democracies: Ideology and Party Formation in Third Republic France, Weimar Germany, and Post-Soviet Russia*

Gretchen Helmke, *Courts Under Constraints: Judges, Generals, and Presidents in Argentina*

Yoshiko Herrera, *Imagined Economies: The Sources of Russian Regionalism*

J. Rogers Hollingsworth and Robert Boyer, eds., *Contemporary Capitalism: The Embeddedness of Institutions*

John D. Huber and Charles R. Shipan, *Deliberate Discretion? The Institutional Foundations of Bureaucratic Autonomy*

Ellen Immergut, *Health Politics: Interests and Institutions in Western Europe*

Torben Iversen, *Capitalism, Democracy, and Welfare*

Torben Iversen, *Contested Economic Institutions*

Torben Iversen, Jonas Pontussen, and David Soskice, eds., *Union, Employers, and Central Banks: Macroeconomic Coordination and Institutional Change in Social Market Economics*

Thomas Janoski and Alexander M. Hicks, eds., *The Comparative Political Economy of the Welfare State*

Joseph Jupille, *Procedural Politics: Issues, Influence, and Institutional Choice in the European Union*

Stathis Kalyvas, *The Logic of Violence in Civil War*

David C. Kang, *Crony Capitalism: Corruption and Capitalism in South Korea and the Philippines*

Junko Kato, *Regressive Taxation and the Welfare State*

Orit Kedar, *Voting for Policy, Not Parties: How Voters Compensate for Power Sharing*

Robert O. Keohane and Helen B. Milner, eds., *Internationalization and Domestic Politics*

Herbert Kitschelt, *The Transformation of European Social Democracy*

Herbert Kitschelt, Kirk A. Hawkins, Juan Pablo Luna, Guillermo Rosas, and Elizabeth J. Zechmeister, *Latin American Party Systems*

Herbert Kitschelt, Peter Lange, Gary Marks, and John D. Stephens, eds., *Continuity and Change in Contemporary Capitalism*

Herbert Kitschelt, Zdenka Mansfeldova, Radek Markowski, and Gabor Toka, *Post-Communist Party Systems*

David Knoke, Franz Urban Pappi, Jeffrey Broadbent, and Yutaka Tsujinaka, eds., *Comparing Policy Networks*

Allan Kornberg and Harold D. Clarke, *Citizens and Community: Political Support in a Representative Democracy*

Amie Kreppel, *The European Parliament and the Supranational Party System*

David D. Laitin, *Language Repertoires and State Construction in Africa*

Fabrice E. Lehoucq and Ivan Molina, *Stuffing the Ballot Box: Fraud, Electoral Reform, and Democratization in Costa Rica*

Mark Irving Lichbach and Alan S. Zuckerman, eds., *Comparative Politics: Rationality, Culture, and Structure, 2nd edition*

Evan Lieberman, *Race and Regionalism in the Politics of Taxation in Brazil and South Africa*

Julia Lynch, *Age in the Welfare State: The Origins of Social Spending on Pensioners, Workers and Children*

Pauline Jones Luong, *Institutional Change and Political Continuity in Post-Soviet Central Asia*

Pauline Jones Luong and Erika Weinthal, *Oil is Not a Curse: Ownership Structure and Institutions in Soviet Successor States*

Doug McAdam, John McCarthy, and Mayer Zald, eds., *Comparative Perspectives on Social Movements*

Lauren M. MacLean, *Informal Institutions and Citizenship in Rural Africa: Risk and Reciprocity in Ghana and Côte d'Ivoire*

Beatriz Magaloni, *Voting for Autocracy: Hegemonic Party Survival and its Demise in Mexico*

James Mahoney, *Colonialism and Postcolonial Development: Spanish America in Comparative Perspective*

James Mahoney and Dietrich Rueschemeyer, eds., *Historical Analysis and the Social Sciences*

Scott Mainwaring and Matthew Soberg Shugart, eds., *Presidentialism and Democracy in Latin America*

Isabela Mares, *The Politics of Social Risk: Business and Welfare State Development*

Isabela Mares, *Taxation, Wage Bargaining, and Unemployment*